FIRST EDITION

THE HIDDEN WORLD OF THE SEX OFFENDER

READINGS ON SEX CRIMES AND THE CRIMINAL JUSTICE SYSTEM

Edited by Stephen T. Holmes and Ronald M. Holmes

cognella® | ACADEMIC PUBLISHING

Bassim Hamadeh, CEO and Publisher
Michael Simpson, Vice President of Acquisitions
Jamie Giganti, Senior Managing Editor
Miguel Macias, Senior Graphic Designer
John Remington, Acquisitions Editor
Monika Dziamka, Project Editor
Brian Fahey, Licensing Specialist
Berenice Quirino, Associate Production Editor
Joyce Luc, Interior Designer

Cover image copyright © 2014 by iStockphoto LP/alptraum.

Printed in the United States of America

ISBN: 978-1-5165-0747-4 (pbk) / 978-1-5165-0748-1(br)

CONTENTS

CHAPTER FIVE

SEX OFFENDER CHARACTERISTICS   47

BY Ruda Flora and Michael L. Keohane

CHAPTER EIGHT

THE ROAD AHEAD: THE IDENTIFICATION AND ENFORCEMENT OF THE LAW FOR SEX OFFENDERS IN THE INTERNET AGE 87

By Stephen T. Holmes and Bryan M. Holmes

CHAPTER NINE
ABERRANT FORMS OF SEXUAL BEHAVIOR   97

By Thomas S. Weinberg

CHAPTER TEN

INVESTIGATING SEXUAL DREAM IMAGERY IN RELATION TO DAYTIME SEXUAL BEHAVIOURS AND FANTASIES AMONG CANADIAN UNIVERSITY STUDENTS   107

By David B. King, Teresa L. DeCicco, and Terry P. Humphreys

CHAPTER NINETEEN

SEXUAL ADDICTION   225

By Ruda Flora and Michael L. Keohane

CHAPTER TWENTY

CHILDREN AND ADOLESCENTS WHO DISPLAY SEXUAL MISCONDUCT BEHAVIOR   239

By Ruda Flora and Michael L. Keohane

CHAPTER TWENTY ONE
SEX OFFENDERS   255

PROLOGUE

Sex is an integral part of any society. It is also a necessary part of a society, if for no other reason than for the propagation of the species. But "appropriate" sexual practices will vary from one group to another and from one time to another.

To gain some appreciation for sexual behaviors, it is important to examine such behaviors from a historical perspective. Such is the view of Chapter 1 where sex activities are examined from a historical perspective. Chapter 3 discusses the influence that geography may have on sexual acts. If one looks again at the early Christian family and how the influence of religion prejudiced the sexual acts of its members, sex was viewed only as a practice for procreation; when procreation was not a possibility, sex was not permitted (Holmes and Holmes, 2009). Really sex was seen as base and crude even until the early 1920s in America society (ibid.).

In addition to looking at sexual practices from a historical and geographical perspective, this text will also discuss various types of sex offenders, including so-called dangerous sex criminals as well as "nuisance" sex offenders (ibid.). Also, the readings will include a section that deals with female sex offenders. Academic presentations rarely discuss this topic, but it occupies a special place in this volume. The role of fantasy will also be examined: How does fantasy play a role in "aberrant forms of sexual behavior"? Do ritualism and symbolism also play an integral role in the practice of sex (ibid.)?

In the readings in Chapter 7 we will examine various paraphilias, including voyeurism and exhibitionism. We will also read of aberrant forms of sexual behavior including necrophilia and further examples of weird, strange or "perverted" sexual practices.

This book carefully examines the extent and practice of dangerous sexual aberrance directed toward children by adults. The basic etiology of the pedophile, the extent of the practice of pedophilia, and the emerging role of the computer world in the solicitation of children resulting in their own predation is carefully examined and presented to the reader.

Chapters 14 through 16 launch the reader into a far different world of sex practices, examining the common forms of sex trafficking and then further examining the extent and practice of female prostitution. We also take a turn that few other publications do in assessing the forms, extent, victimology and the future of male prostitution in the United States. Few other notable publications examine male prostitution in such a light.

Chapter 17 questions the role of pornography in the commission of sex crimes. How influential is pornography in the basic causation of sex crimes, regardless of the age of the victim? The readings also examine the emerging role of the Internet in making pornography available to the viewers, both from an academic, research perspective and from the sex offender.. Exactly what role does pornography play in the world of the sexual abuser? Can pornography satisfy sexual urges in a socially positive manner?

Chapter 20 examines the issues surrounding identification of children who display behavior at an early age indicating that there may be problems ahead. This is one of the most frequent issues that students of criminal justice want to know—how can we determine the early warning signs that an individual has the propensity to engage in future criminal behavior and, in this case, potential sexual offenses. The second reading examines the foundation of rehabilitation for these offenders—therein lies our hope for success.

The final chapter will look at the road ahead. It suggests that, in the future, law enforcement and the justice system must take a leading role in the investigation and prosecution of those offenders that prey on our most vulnerable populations. In this case, the authors examine how greater emphasis and more resources need to be dedicated to such crimes as the sexual molestation of children and human sexual trafficking. Each of these crimes present special problems in investigations, especially when dealing with multijurisdictional victims and offenders.

This book will help the reader gain insight into the world of the sex offender as well as the "normal" person. There is nothing normal about some acts, such as pedophilia, rape, incest and many other forms of "deviant" sexual behavior directed toward others. The authors recognize that some acts such as these were permitted and even encouraged in some societies and in some eras. This is the focus of this book of readings. We appreciate the insights and the research of the contributing authors. We hope the readers will also.

Stephen T. Holmes, Ph.D.
Associate Professor
University of Central Florida

Ronald M. Holmes, Ed.D.
Professor Emeritus
University of Louisville

CHAPTER 1

SEXUAL BEHAVIOR AND DEVIANCY: A HISTORICAL PERSPECTIVE

LISA WILLIAMS-TAYLOR

American society has decided that there is no greater villain than the sex offender. Terrorists, drug dealers, murderers, kidnappers, mobsters, gangsters, drunk drivers, and white collar criminals do not elicit the emotions and evoke the political response that sex offenders do (Wright, 2008, p. 17).

Definitions of sexual crimes and views of perpetrators have changed throughout history. Society and the court system have defined sex offenders and their crimes differently depending on the mind-set and attitudes of the time. As values and norms change, so does society's tolerance of sexual behavior. Behavior that at some points in time was considered criminal may no longer be thought of in the same way. Also changing has been the amount of attention these crimes receive. This evolution in focus and level of interest has become known as moral or sex crime panics. Crimes involving women and children have had a long history of causing moral panics. These cases often involve violence against our most vulnerable, which outrages society and causes people to advocate for stricter regulation of sex offenders and continued research to aid in understanding why people offend and how to prevent future offenses.

CHANGING VIEWS OF SEXUAL BEHAVIOR

The late ninetieth and early twentieth centuries have become known as the Progressive Era, a time of reform after a long period of societal unrest, disorganization, unemployment, poverty, and crime due to the vast growth within industrialized cities. It was during this period that the social hygiene movement began, "a campaign to change American attitudes toward sex" (Burnham, 1973, p. 885). During the Progressive Era, women and children were given additional rights—women entered the workforce in jobs other than servant work and the justice system explored the abuse and neglect of children (e.g., labor laws were passed). Stricter crime prevention and control tactics were also major efforts of the Progressive Era and "the courts began to regularly monitor sexual behavior," including prostitution and child sexual abuse (Terry, 2006, p. 23). According to Terry (2006), "It was this change in social structure that instigated the modification of "age of consent" laws for sexual behavior. . ." (p. 23). Age of consent has changed dramatically throughout history. At one point, there was no specific legal age of consent for sexual conduct. Then, throughout the eighteenth century, the consenting age was only ten-years-old and now in most jurisdictions it is between 16 and 18 years of age.

Another example of how views of behavior have changed throughout history is incest. In the late 19th century, incest began to be discussed more openly and agencies started taking an active stance against it. For example, in 1878, the Massachusetts Society for the Prevention of Cruelty to Children, an interest group who focused on intrafamilial sexual abuse, heightened the interest on this topic through advocacy and by educating the public (Gordon, 1988). However, at other points in time, the focus was more on "stranger danger" (i.e. the pervert who jumps out from behind a bush to attack his victim), resulting in a decrease in interest and willingness to discuss incest. In fact, during the mid-1900s, incest was rarely discussed because it was believed to be an uncommon event. According to Gordon (1988), academic experts reported that incest was an "extremely rare, one-in-a million occurrence" (p. 60). Thus, as can be surmised from these examples, interest levels fluctuated greatly depending on social influences at the time.

Along with changing views are cycles of legislation regarding the criminalization of sexual behaviors. Classified at one point in time as criminal, now some acts are considered "normal" or tolerated types of behavior. At various points in history, homosexuality, excessive masturbation, and adultery were classified as criminal acts requiring fines, imprisonment, and even death (Jenkins, 1998, p. 22). Although each at different times was highly prosecuted, today, many of the laws regarding these types of crimes are currently not enforced or have been taken completely off the books.

How the legal system defines severity of sexual crimes has also varied by era and by region. For example, during the mid-twentieth century, New York reduced its punishment for homosexual relations from a felony offense with a 12-year sentence to a misdemeanor with a maximum penalty of 90 days in jail. At the same time, California was increasing the sentence for this same crime from ten to 20 years (Guttmacher & Weihofen, 1952, p. 155). These changes in sentencing within states were occurring during a heightened time of unrest. The 1960s and 1970s marked both social and sexual revolutions. There were significant changes in people's perceptions and attitudes towards social injustice and sexual behavior. Traditional roles and beliefs were tested, civil rights were at the forefront, and sex became an open topic. The 1960s also marked the start of the homophile or gay liberation movement, which fought for anti-discrimination in the workforce and in the criminal justice system. As time went on, homosexuality became increasingly tolerated and accepted among mainstream society and in 1973, the American Psychiatric Association no longer categorized homosexuality as a mental disorder (Freedman, 1987, p. 103).

In addition, there were important advances in science and medicine, including the development of oral contraceptives—first introduced in the 1960s. These allowed for a more reliable form of birth control. Pornography was also viewed more openly and the Presidential Commission on Obscenity rejected the assertion that pornography caused harm to those that possessed it (Jenkins, 1998, p. 109). The civil rights movement was also at the forefront during this time and the women's revolution of the 1960s, also known as the second wave of feminism, stressed women's rights and empowerment. It was during this movement that women fought against sexual violence and their revictimization in the court system. While the feminist movement had impacts on many fronts, advocacy for what is now termed rape shield laws was one of the major accomplishments in relation to the criminal justice system and sexual crimes. Until this point, it was common practice in rape trials to blame the victim and question the truthfulness of her accusations. These laws, first enacted in 1970, minimized the type of victim information allowed into trial—prohibiting the defendant's attorney from unwarranted intrusions into the private life of the alleged victim (Call, Nice, & Talarico, 1991; Flowe, Ebbesen, & Putcha-Bhagavatula, 2007). The attorney could no longer attack the victim's morality in an attempt to portray her as unchaste or otherwise 'having asked for it' (Byrnes, 1998; Klein, 2008). All states now have rape shield laws in effect (Flowe et al., 2007). This advancement, among the others discussed, are prime examples of how society has changed its views of sexuality and deviancy throughout time.

SEXUAL DEVIANCY AND WAVES OF PANIC

Definitions of sexual deviancy have evolved in response to educational influences and social morality (Jenkins, 1998). According to researchers, the definition of sex offenders, sexual crimes, and sexual deviancy are socially constructed realities, based on research, case law, and the church (Jenkins 1998; Sutherland, 1950; Terry, 2006). Thus, the concept of sexual deviancy changed significantly between the late nineteenth century and the early twenty-first century with the emergence of the sexual psychopath, sexual murderer, and various periods of sexual panic.

The Sexual Psychopath

Throughout the 1880s into the 1900s, there was a heightened interest in sex offenders, sexual deviancy, and in particular the sexual psychopath. In 1801, Phillip Pinel, recognized as defining the term psychopathy, found that some of his patients engaged in uncontrollable violence towards others. He found that while they knew that what they were doing was irrational, they were unable to stop themselves (Arrigo & Shipley, 2001, p. 327). By the early 1900s, "most discussions of the psychopath included at least a section on sexual types, such as overt homosexuals, exhibitionists, sadists, masochists, and voyeurs. Some authors explicitly linked such deviants to the commission of sexual crimes" (Freedman, 1987, p. 91). Freedman (1987) reports that the concept of a sexual psychopath derived from a combination of factors and people including psychiatrists, social change, sexuality, and the public's perception of "uncontrolled desires" and deviancy (p. 87).

This interest in the sexual psychopath was greatly influenced by the work of Richard von Krafft-Ebing, a German physician and neurologist who in 1886 wrote *Psychopathia Sexualis*, a novel on deviant sexual behavior using a series of case studies. Krafft-Ebing is credited with coining the terms sadism and masochism and asserted that all humans have an "innate desire to humiliate or hurt" and that "sexual emotion, if hyperesthetic, might degenerate into a craving to inflict pain" (quoted in Arrigo & Shipley, 2001, p. 333). Although Krafft-Ebing did note that some individuals might engage in sexual violence, his primary focus was on various sexual disorders and paraphilias. When he used the term *psychopathia sexualis*, he "implied no more than mental disease or disturbance" (Jenkins, 1998, p. 38–39), such as those suffering from pedophilia or homosexuality.

In this work, Krafft-Ebing described the act of pedophilia as the result of a mental weakness due to "senile dementia, chronic alcoholism, paralysis, mental disability due to epilepsy, injuries to the head, apoplexy and syphilis" (Jenkins, 1998, p. 100). In other words, he believed that people "were not wicked, immoral creatures, but merely sick" (Kennedy, 2001, p. 167). He discussed homosexuality in much the same way (Terry, 2006, p. 24). He noted that homosexuality, a perversion, might be inborn (Money, 2003), and that it, like many other sexual acts and perversions, is the result of uncontrollable sexual desires. He believed that perversions occur because of psychological abnormalities and degeneracy. Moreover, according to Bauer (2003), Krafft-Ebing emphasized that perversions were not criminal in nature and he later participated in a petition to abolish paragraph 175 of German law, which criminalized homosexuality (p. 24).

As emphasized by Kraff-Ebing, psychopathic behavior is not necessarily criminal behavior. The diagnosis of psychopathy has changed throughout history, referring to insanity at some points and more currently to describe a person having a personality disorder and displaying antisocial behavior (Andrade, 2008). However, during the 1930s, sexual psychopathy became a legal construct describing individuals that could not control their sexual desires leading to criminal behavior. Sexual psychopath statutes were passed as a means of treating these individuals and allowing for their indefinite incapacitation deeming them at risk to harm themselves or others.

The Sexual Murderer

Another highly discussed topic during the late 1880s and early 1900s was sexual murder. While there have always been incidents of sexual killings, it was not until the late 1800s that these murders became commonly recorded and discussed among the public (Jenkins, 1998). Although research has led to an increase in knowledge regarding deviant sexual interests and behaviors and has shown that violent sexual crimes are rare events in history, the perception that they are pervasive has continued - most speculate this is a direct result of media coverage of high profile cases (Jenkins, 1998). For example, although there were violent sexually motivated crimes occurring in America, none appears to have received as much media attention as the case of Jack the Ripper, a classic example of a sexual predator, psychopath, and murderer. Cases like this one in the 1880s incited the public's interest in understanding this type of behavior— the actions of a mentally unstable sexual murderer. Researchers strived to gain knowledge regarding individuals that were unable to control their sexual desires and behavior and were therefore, driven to kill.

The First Sex Crime Panic: The Early 1900s

Although the case of Jack the Ripper caused a great deal of panic in England, it was not until the early 1900s that the first documented panic occurred in America. This phenomenon of panic was first formulated in the 1970s by British sociologists Stanley Cohen and Stuart Hall. They coined the term, *moral panic*, and described how the media and single cases can promote intense and irrational fear. Their definition is as follows:

> Societies appear to be subject, every now and then, to periods of moral panic. A condition, episode, person or group of persons emerges to become defined as a threat to societal values and interests; its nature is presented in a stylized and stereotypical fashion by the mass media … Sometimes the object of the panic is quite novel and at other times it is something which has been in existence long enough, but suddenly appears in the limelight. Sometimes the panic passes over and is forgotten, except in folklore and collective memory; at other times it has more serious and long-lasting repercussions and might produce such changes as those in legal and social policy or even in the way society conceives itself (Cohen, 1972, p. 9).

These panics can be targeted towards any group believed to be deviant and threatening to society—in regards to the discussion here, the panic is focused on sexual offenders. The crux of the first sex crime panic resulted from, like other panics later, an increase in reported sexual murders of women and children, many of which were covered in the media. For example, the *New York Times* reported 17 serial murder cases between 1911 and 1915 and in Atlanta, between 1910 and 1912, 40 women were found murdered (Jenkins, 1998). In 1912, Frank Hickey was accused of sexually killing boys in New York City. This case was sensationalized in the newspapers. Then in 1913, Leo Frank was accused of the sexual killing of 13-year-old Mary Phagan in Atlanta. Frank was sentenced to death, but before his sentence could be carried out, there was a lynching in 1915 and he was hung by the citizens of the city. This same year marked the sexual murder of two other small children in New York City. According to Jenkins (1998), this heightened media attention caused people to walk the streets looking for sexual perverts. People who were thought to be sexual criminals were attacked in the streets during this time of panic.

The Second Wave of Panic: 1930s through the 1950s

Much like the first sex crime panic, the attention during the 1930s through the 1950s focused on stranger crimes. In fact, this focused attention has been referred to as "stranger danger" or the belief that "dirty old men," sexual perverts or sex fiends were the primary victimizers of children (Gordon, 1988). This period marked a time of heightened fear that sexual deviants were lurking around waiting for just the right time to attack the most vulnerable. This was also a time of fear regarding the sexually motivated murder of children. As Sutherland (1950) claimed, the murder of children is very effective in creating hysteria. He quotes author Austin MacCormick, who published an article in *Mental Hygiene* titled "New York's Present Problem," as stating,

> For a while it was utterly unsafe to speak to a child on the street unless one was well-dressed and well-known in the neighborhood. To try to help a lost child, with tears streaming down its face, to find its way home would in some neighborhoods cause a mob to form and violence to be threatened (p. 143).

Also instigating this fear was the infamous case of Albert Fish, a 65-year-old sexual predator and child murderer. In New York on June 23, 1928, Fish arrived at the Budd household as a potential employer for 18-year-old Paul Budd who had placed an ad in the Sunday edition of a newspaper asking for work. After offering farm work to Paul, he asked whether he could take Paul's younger sister to a party at his own sister's house. Grace was allowed to go and never returned home. Many years later Fish wrote a letter to the Budd's describing the killing. Police were able to trace the letter and Fish was arrested and sentenced to death. Executed in January 1936, Fish is believed to have assaulted many other young people and to have murdered at least three others.

By the mid 1930s, there were many more examples that a sex crime panic was in effect. For example, editors of the *New York Times* created a new column in their newspaper titled "Sex Crimes" due to the vast number of articles that were being published that year (Freedman, 1987, p. 83). Furthermore, J. Edgar Hoover declared a "war on the sex criminal," stating that "the sex fiend, most loathsome of all the vast army of crime, has become a sinister threat to the safety of American childhood and womanhood" and that "should wild beasts break out of circus cages, a whole city would be mobilized instantly. But depraved human beings more savage than beasts, are permitted to rove America almost at will" (quoted in Freedman, 1987).

Because of this war against the sexual predator and highly publicized cases of sexual murderers like Albert Fish, anti-crime legislation dedicated specifically to sexual offenders was drafted. These laws mimicked the "social security" laws found in Europe which aimed to protect the public (Sutherland, 1950). The first "sexual psychopath" statute was passed in 1937 in Michigan and although this groundbreaking act was held unconstitutional, the following year Illinois enacted its first law without incident. These sexual psychopath laws allowed for the civil commitment of a person indefinitely or until he could prove that he was no longer a danger to himself or others. Interestingly, in 1938, a year after the first psychopath law was enacted, at a national conference on "The Challenge of Sex Offenders," numerous psychiatrists pleaded for the halt of any additional castration or long-term sentencing legislation because there was no evidence of an increase in sexual crimes—just an increase in media coverage (Freedman, 1987, p. 95). This plea from psychiatrists did little to prevent further legislation. Rather, California, Massachusetts, Minnesota, Ohio, and Wisconsin implemented sexual psychopathy legislation shortly thereafter.

Interestingly, in the early 1940s, there was a short break in the sex crime panic, as seen by the halt in states passing sex offender legislation (Vermont was the only state to pass a law during this time) and marked decrease in newspaper and magazine articles covering sexual violence (Freedman, 1987, p. 96). One researcher asserts that this was primarily due to World War II and the legitimization of male violence focusing on the external enemy (Freedman, 1987, p. 96). This decline in attention eventually stopped post-war and the pendulum began swinging the other way once again. Between 1947 and 1949, eight states passed sexual psychopath laws (Jenkins, 1998, p. 82) and by the mid-1950s, 13 additional states, as well as the District of Columbia had sexual psychopath statutes in effect (Freedman, 1987, p. 97). In 1950, New York passed its version of a sexual psychopath law, but was innovative in that it required that there was a criminal proceeding for all cases and once found guilty of the sexual crime, then and only then would the offenders' mental capacity be examined to determine psychopathy. In addition, according to Guttmacher and Weihofen (1952), New York was the first state to allow for indeterminate sentencing of criminals, including sexual offenders.

Through the late 1950s, medicalizing crime (meaning focusing on medical causes and interventions) continued, but there was also a focus on social issues at this time. More specifically, most psychiatrists believed that statutory rape, sexual abuse, and incest were the result of social circumstances and mental abnormality. Many believed that these sexual crimes primarily occurred among "groups with low cultural standards" and in overcrowded neighborhoods (Guttmacher & Weihofen, 1952, p. 159). These criminals continued to be labeled degenerates, perverts or psychopaths and the use of civil commitment continuously increased during this time. According to Terry (2006), some psychopathy statutes included peeping, lewdness, and impaired morals as acts that could result in being designated as a psychopath. Terry (2006) also notes that the severity and level of violence used during the commission of the sexual crime was less of an issue than it is now because both misdemeanors and felonies could result in commitment (p. 30). Besides the increase in number of commitments, there was also a distinct racial difference in the type of sentencing. According to Freedman (1987), while white men were mostly found guilty of minor offenses and those involving children, black men were overrepresented in the number found guilty of rape. Whites were more likely to be hospitalized and blacks were more often executed or imprisoned for their crimes (p. 97).

The Third Wave of Panic: 1980s and 1990s

Over time there has been a marked change in how society has labeled sexual offenders—starting with "feebleminded" or as being inflicted with a biological abnormality, to then calling them "perverts" and "psychopathic sex fiends" and finally during the 1980s, the media portrayed most offenders as probable members of pedophile rings or satanic cults (Gordon, 1988; Jenkins, 1998). Much like the previous panics, child sexual abuse was seen as occurring outside of the home.

During this period, the perpetrators were believed to be those that cared for children, such as teachers and child care providers. For example, in 1983 the media covered the McMartin preschool case. The McMartins, who owned and operated a child care center in California, were accused and charged with numerous acts of child sexual abuse. The trial proceeded for over six years and resulted in no convictions. However, this case caused a substantial increase in attention regarding child sexual abuse, as well as increased fear. Newspapers and television channels covered stories about the suspected sexual abuse by caretakers creating public panic causing many families to question the safety of their children while in the care of others (Jenkins, 1998).

Also during this time, the misperception that kidnappers were lurking around every corner expanded. While the media focused attention on kidnappers as strangers taking children, the truth was that non-custodial parents were the most likely offenders. While research has shown that family and other trusted adults, such as acquaintances and friends, commit the vast majority of sex offenses, media coverage has distorted the public's perception. For example, Jenkins (1998) reported that the coverage of pedophilia in the Catholic Church had greatly impacted mainstream society's belief that this crime was quite prevalent, which was a distortion of reality. Another influencer on this panic was the media attention on children murdered during the commission of sexual crimes. In fact, most of the laws passed during this time can be directly linked to a child's death. One example was Megan's Law, which was passed after a young child was kidnapped, sexually assaulted and murdered by a neighbor. Cases like this caused people to question whether their children were safe in their own communities. This anxiety over the safety of the most vulnerable members of our society has caused panic resulting in hurried legislation with various shortcomings (i.e. they are poorly conceptualized, poorly drafted, overly broad in scope, and promote unfortunate consequences).

CHAPTER 2

SEX OFFENDING

SHARON HAYES
BELINDA CARPENTER
ANGELA DWYER

INTRODUCTION

On 26 June 2006, an eight-year-old girl by the name of Sofia Rodriguez-Urrutia Shu visited a public toilet in a Canning Vale shopping centre in Perth, Western Australia, and failed to return to her guardian. She was abducted by a twenty-two-year-old male, Dante Wyndham Arthurs, who strangled her, removed her clothing, digitally penetrated her, and propped her naked body against the cubicle wall. Police collected evidence in Arthurs's home suggesting he had meticulously planned the attack, including "a bag in a wardrobe containing latex gloves, handcuffs and rope along with a collection of pictures of young girls and their addresses".[1] Arthurs pleaded guilty to wilful murder, deprivation of liberty and sexual penetration, and was sentenced to life in prison with a non-parole period of thirteen years. The non-parole period was recently revoked by the Western Australian Attorney-General Christian Porter, and Arthurs's case has been marked "never to be released", one of only three cases in Western Australia.

This case received extensive coverage in the national and international media and sparked overwhelming public outrage. This was further fuelled by allegations that Arthurs had previously been accused of indecently dealing with children, and that it was only because of flaws in the nature of police questioning that this prior case was dismissed. In the murder case, however, Chief Justice Wayne Martin ruled a trial by judge alone was necessary due to the pre-trial case publicity being categorized as "extensive, continuous and in some respects extraordinary".[2] Part of this publicity included the publication by a Perth radio programme of details of Arthurs's address, which resulted in a vigilante attack on his house. He was also the subject of extensive online vitriolic commentary, including calls for the death penalty. The family of the young female victim called for a public register of sex offenders in Australia. Interestingly, such a register would not have prevented a crime like this from occurring, as Arthurs had not previously been convicted of a sex offence. Nonetheless, in the wake of this horrific crime, the public continued to insist upon the implementation of a sex offender register, and this response is typical in relation to similar crimes. The perception of danger in this case created a fear for the public safety of all children, which was regarded as seriously undermined.

In a world in which children are regarded as highly vulnerable, this incident became the paradigm of every parent's worst fear. However, this level of fear, of both sex offenders and public space, is a recent phenomenon, most evident in public discourse since the 1990s.[3] In fact, the significant shift from the 1970s, when sex offenders were perceived as pathetic men in raincoats, to the mass hysteria in the twenty-first century, where sex offenders are perceived of as manipulative, dangerous and predatory, is "a remarkable one".[4] Within this public discourse of fear, those who offend against children are subject to the most extreme hostility, "considered too abominable to even associate with murderers and other criminals".[5]

In such a context, this chapter addresses the ways in which we think about sex offenders as morally dangerous people requiring especial regulation in public space, and the two central influences on which this way of thinking is founded. The first is a traditional religious understanding of sexual immorality as a desire inherent in all of us, contrasted with, and yet related to, the nineteenth-century rise of medical understandings of dangerousness and immutability. More specifically, the emergence of the psychiatric category of "sexual psychopath" amalgamated religious assumptions about a lack of moral worth with medical assessments of dangerous predators. Insisting that sex offenders lack moral worth and are inherently dangerous appeased religious communities by demanding government protection of the private spaces of the nuclear family and the sanctity of marriage, while also satisfying the psychological need for controlling these offenders in public spaces. The latter part of this chapter reflects on how heavily we now restrict the movements, lives and residency of sex offenders because of their presumed inherently perverted and predatory, immoral and immutable characters, even though research suggests these forms of management are not very successful. Finally, the chapter challenges the taken-for-granted notion that sex offenders should be subject to ever-increasing punitive controls implemented to surveil their movements in public, often to the neglect of private spaces.

PUBLIC AND PRIVATE SEX

The argument that sexual perversion as we currently know and understand it has always existed is based on Judaeo-Christian discourses linking sexual sinfulness and humanity's fall from grace.[6] Here it is argued that feelings of desire were increasingly regarded as problematic from the fifteenth century because the body "was possessed by evil forces, the presence of which was felt through the irresistible desires for sexual gratification".[7] From this perspective, sex was rigorously controlled and only permitted in the form of "Godly" procreative, vaginal sex between a monogamously married man and wife: "Sex, except within marriage and then normally in the missionary position, was undesirable (at best) and illegal (at worst)."[8] Sexual acts other than those supporting procreation, according to this simplistic way of thinking about sexual perversion, were targeted by religious and later criminal justice authorities as pleasure-inducing, non-procreative and therefore unnatural and sinful because they breached "a basic divine commandment".[9] Engaging in such forms of non-procreative sexual behaviour identified one as a sinner in need of punishment.

However, a re-reading of history, influenced by the work of Michel Foucault, offers a different story about sex and sexuality. It has been argued that "the West inherited an amorphous set of sexual categories which, although making sharp distinctions between the characteristics associated with men and women, assumed that sexual desire could be directed toward a range of objects".[10] Moreover, many acts were sinful—sodomy, pride, gluttony, masturbation—and while they may have been admonished in different ways, "all sin was part of a continuum of transgressions of which each individual man and woman necessarily partook".[11] Questions asked by priests at confession "covered such diverse elements" as slaying of men, lying, use of magic, and misuse of animals—sins concerned with a range of sinful behaviour and not focused solely on sex.[12] It was only with the decline of humoral understandings of medicine and body functionality, between 1670 and 1820 (see chapter 4), that the idea of a natural sexual differentiation between men and women was conceived. In fact, it was only from the late eighteenth century that it was considered normal for men and women to find each other "naturally attractive".[13] With this way of thinking about the sexes came different discourses about sex and sexuality.

More specifically, sex became equated for the first time with genital contact. This is in contrast to previous understandings of sex, most prominent at the end of the seventeenth century, where sex began with the kiss. According to Hitchcock,[14] sexual activity was characterized by "mutual masturbation, much kissing and fondling and long hours spent in mutual touching, but very little penile/vaginal penetration—at least before marriage". As we noted in chapter 4, sexual activity becomes more and more about the penis during the eighteenth and nineteenth centuries, with all other activities associated with sex relegated to "foreplay". This also supports the ways in which sexual regulation shifted over this time, with increased policing of heterosexual sex and concerns over loss of virginity and unwanted pregnancies for women.[15]

This is even more interesting if we consider the very different issues of prostitution and rape. At the beginning of the eighteenth century, to be called a whore "brought into question one's honesty, probity and personal ability as much as one's sexual behaviour".[16] As discussed in more detail in chapter 9, attempts to regulate this morally inappropriate sexual behaviour was a task fraught with danger. In the tenth century, for example, those to be banished for their crimes included "wizards, sorcerers, perjurers, conspirators to murder and horewenan, which included whores, fornicators and adulterers".[17] Nine hundred years later, the Vagrancy (England) Act of 1822 often classified vagrants, professional beggars, cheats and thieves as well as "any woman who yields to her passions and loses her virtue" as prostitutes.[18] The difficulty of accurately identifying whores was partly due to the way in which such behaviour was understood as an "individual moral failure". As we discussed in chapter 4, women were believed to be more lustful and physically desirous of sex than men, from whom they gained the hot and dry essence of male semen. "It was not their participation in illegal sex which put them beyond the pale of normal society but that their circumstances proved their own lack of moral worth."[19] Thus they could be confused with beggars, thieves and adulterers, whose sinful actions also indicated a lack of moral worth.

However, over the course of the eighteenth century, the idea of the prostitute was re-created from one of individual moral failure to that of a victim of seduction. Due in large part to the different understandings of male and female sexuality that emerged during this time, specifically, that women's capacity to conceive was not linked to their sexual pleasure, men were given the active part, naturally speaking, in sex. "The stereotype of seduction placed new onus on male activity and female passivity."[20] In the space of a century, women went from being lustful and full of barely controlled desire, to being sexually numb and passive. In contrast, men, who had begun the century thinking that they could easily control their sexual desires, "due to their greater rationality and mental strength", and that they had a duty to do so, "ended the period being told that their sexual desires were largely beyond their control".[21]

In such a context, the sin of rape can also be re-imagined. In the eighteenth century, rape went from being seen as equivalent to other forms of violent crime, to a uniquely horrible event. The events that led to this change are similar, and related, to the shift in understanding of prostitution. As Hitchcock notes, sexually explicit accounts of rape and sodomy in the Old Bailey Sessions Papers, for example, formed a prominent site for the discussion of sex in eighteenth-century public culture. Moreover, the vast majority of men and women would have felt it appropriate to read this material, with the brutal details which it inevitably included considered to be the "common coin of everyday conversation for both sexes".[22] However, by the end of the eighteenth century, by arguing that women in public were potential victims of rape, due in part to the new understanding that male sexuality was "out of control", women were encouraged to be fearful of rape "and it was justified to keep women off the streets in order to protect them".[23] This shift occurred despite there being no evidence that the number or brutality of rapes had increased, and is accompanied by the suggestion that women were more in fear of straight violence than sexual attack or rape at this time.[24]

Thus the context of sex and sexuality prior to the nineteenth century offers very different ways of thinking about appropriate sexual behaviour. The relation between privacy and sex is a case in point. As we saw in chapter 3, where we now take for granted the house as a space enclosing a single family unit, most previous historical periods saw many people sharing the private space of the home as an economic necessity. Hawkes[25] also notes that it was not until the late seventeenth century that bedrooms came to be defined as private spaces, and only then in the more elite homes of the wealthy. Before this time, bedrooms were "a public space, rather like a sitting room in modern households". Moreover, sharing a bed was not confined to sexual partners. A seventeenth-century rape trial details this point, among others, very nicely.

According to Naphy,[26] in 1613, Georgeo Aricogue claimed that she had been raped by Guillaume Clemencat. The facts of the case are as follows: one evening a man, later identified as Clemencat, came to the bed of Georgeo and they had sex without a word. The man then left the room and did not return. When Georgeo asked her husband the next morning if he had a break from guard duty the previous night and he had not, she became alarmed. Initially she thought that her brother-in-law had accidentally got into the wrong bed, but careful questioning at a family meeting showed this was not the case. When the same man tried the ruse the next night, she recognized him by his clothes and cried out. He fled, but not before he was recognized.

At the trial, it was discovered that Clemencat had indeed entered the bed of Georgeo, knowing full well that her husband was on guard duty. However, it was also revealed during the trial by Susanne le Maistre, a friend of Georgeo, that the following day, Georgeo had admitted to her that she had sex three times the previous evening with a mystery man. Moreover, she had realized that it was not her husband because this man's penis was much larger and was in fact bigger than anyone else she knew. Despite this, the court accepted Georgeo's version of events and Clemencat was banished.

What can we infer from this case of rape in the seventeenth century? Conjugal sex was often silent and almost fully clothed, for one thing, but perhaps more importantly, the fact that her brother-in-law may have accidentally wandered into the wrong bed during the night and had sex with the wrong woman did not appear to surprise anyone. The subsequent shift towards thinking about the bedroom as a private space culminated in new ways of thinking about and regulating sexual activity in the nineteenth century—recall the increased concern over incest discussed in chapter 3, especially within the overcrowded dwellings of the newly urbanized working class. However, the main outcome of positioning a sexual crime as an individual moral failing was that it was not possible to do anything other than punish the indiscretion once it was brought to light. If immoral sexual desire was inherent in all of us, how did one identify the dangerous individual and prevent them from reoffending?

DANGEROUSNESS AND INCAPACITATION

In 1650 in Massachusetts, a young man by the name of Samuel Terry distressed his neighbours by masturbating in public. He received several lashes on the back to dissuade him from repeating the spectacle, but in 1661 endured another punishment—a fine of four pounds—for indulging in pre-marital intercourse. Finally, in 1673, the court fined Terry and eight other men for performing an "immodest and beastly" play. However, despite this history of sexual offences, a sinner such as Samuel Terry still commanded respect amongst his peers. He served as town constable, and was entrusted by the Court with the custody of another man's infant son. It seemed that "as long as he accepted punishment for his transgressions, he remained a citizen of good standing".[27]

What this example demonstrates is that, while the criminal justice system processed many sex crimes during this time,[28] "there was no sense of the sex criminal as a distinct or especially menacing category of malefactor".[29] The momentous shift which reconceptualized those who committed a prohibited sexual act to a new category of person—someone who had an inner compulsion to violate the innate laws of sex—began with the publication of *Psychopathia Sexualis* by Richard von Krafft-Ebing in 1886.[30] This move by medicine and science into the sexual arena defined and located the boundaries of normal sexual behaviour through the discovery of perversion, for without the identification of perversion, there could be no normality.[31] For the first time, a person who committed a sexually perverse act was perceived of as pathologically driven to do so because of biological and psychological propensities. No longer was an immoral desire inherent in all of us; instead, the sex offender was "essentially supernaturally dangerous and contaminating to the idealized social body".[32]

This did not mean, however, that religious ideas about a "lack of moral worth" shifted out of focus. Rather, the immorality of certain sexual acts was superimposed on legal codes,[33] and governing authorities continued to exercise "wide latitude in penalizing individuals guilty not of serious crime but of moral or sexual unorthodoxy".[34] According to Morrison, such legislation in the nineteenth century "prohibited a few truly dangerous and incurable offenders from acting, but under the same 'sex offense' category, it also outlawed homosexuality, public displays of nudity, obscenity (including pornography), and risqué sexual proposals".[35]

By forging the old discourse of immorality with the new one of uncontrollability, the concept of the sexual psychopath emerged as a form of criminal identity. Scientific understandings of sex offending as being triggered by an internal psychological imbalance married well with the long-standing assumptions that sexual transgressions were the result of a lack of moral worth. These shifts in understanding came about within an increasing raft of psychological and medical discourses which conceptualized the sex offender as a specific type of person whose "deviant acts were symptoms indicating underlying medical or biological flaws … conditions that demanded treatment or incapacitation".[36]

Legislation following this line of reasoning saw the first sexual psychopath laws being adopted in the late 1930s in the United States. This legislation made it possible to civilly commit identified sexual psychopaths for indeterminate periods in psychiatric institutions, based on the decision of a panel of psychological experts. As the most severe type of sex offender, sexual psychopaths were positioned as predisposed to commit further sexual crimes due to their abnormal state of being.[37] Freedman notes how the wording of this legislation was vital in enabling this process: "the sexual psychopath was someone whose 'utter lack of power to control his sexual impulses' made him 'likely to attack … the objects of his uncontrolled and uncontrollable desires'".[38] As a consequence, the term "dangerous" shifted from being an adjective to working as a noun—"dangerousness"—that described and defined the parameters of a "dangerous person".[39] Just as Foucault observed about the homosexual in the nineteenth century, so the dangerous sex offender also became "a personage, a past, a case history, and a childhood, in addition to being a type of life, a life form, and a morphology, with an indiscreet anatomy and possibly a mysterious physiology".[40]

However, this identification of the dangerous sex offender, their incapacitation in psychiatric hospitals and their psychological treatment was limited to those who had already committed dangerous sexual acts. "In assessing dangerousness, the past of an individual is of interest primarily for the purpose of predicting and controlling his future behaviour."[41] By treating dangerousness as an internal quality, it limited any possibility of establishing and maintaining an effective policy of prevention in the larger society. After all, "one could only hope to prevent violent acts committed by those whom one had already diagnosed as dangerous … and such diagnoses … can only be carried out on individual patients one by one".[42] Psychiatrists could not diagnose accurately, and effectively neutralize, dangerousness in every single case—short of confining massive numbers of people on the smallest suspicion of danger. Moreover, "harmless today, they may be dangerous tomorrow".[43]

Once the focus of the criminal justice system moved from the crime to the criminal, the task was to reveal the impetus for dangerousness in the body of the individual. With the increasing medicalization of criminal danger, it was only a matter of time before "any criminal could be treated as potentially pathological, any minor infraction as suspect, any variation an antecedent".[44]

RISK AND PUBLIC SAFETY

The popularity of the idea of risk in criminal justice is precisely due to its capacity for prediction, and such prediction is possible only because risk is associated with a given population, not an individual. Rather than a clinical diagnosis, the analysis of risk offers a statistical probability. Since risk becomes calculable only when spread over a population, it has meaning only when located within a population about which a significant amount of knowledge has been gained. Moreover, the implication of managing populations "at risk" is much more significant than simply relabelling those previously defined as dangerousness. Although dangerousness may be operationalized through risk, what appears as a small semantic change actually signals an important expansion in the possibilities of governmental regulation.[45] Consider the following two examples as a case in point.

In 2003, the *Dangerous Prisoners (Sexual Offenders) Act* came into force in Queensland, Australia, and enabled criminal justice authorities for the first time to detain indefinitely sex offenders who are assessed to be manifestly and continually dangerous. This is not uncommon legislation. In the United States, for example, a prediction of "future dangerousness" is the basis for indefinite treatment and detainment in specialized treatment facilities such as the Wisconsin Sex Offender Treatment Facility, where dangerous sex offenders are moved once they have completed their prison sentence. Such civil commitment laws are now operating in thirty-nine states across the country. Similarly, in the UK the *Criminal Justice Act 2003* enables those assessed with future dangerousness to be detained after completing the sentence for their initial sexual crime.[46] These various pieces of legislation, some civil and some criminal, predict the future dangerousness of a convicted sex offender via an individual clinical diagnosis of paraphilia, personality disorder or mental abnormality.[47]

In contrast, the *Sex Offenders Bill*, passed in the UK in 1997 and then subsumed under the *Sexual Offences Act* of 2003, required all those convicted of Schedule 1 sex offences, upon release from prison, to notify the police in person of any change in address within fourteen days. Conviction of serious sex offences of more than thirty months' imprisonment meant a lifetime requirement to notify the police, while lesser sentences required decreased periods of time on the register. Most interesting for this discussion was the inclusion on the register of those who had only ever been cautioned with a sex offence, while those offences excluded from the requirement to register included bigamy, abduction, soliciting by a man, incest by a woman and indecent exposure. By 2003, there were more than 15,000 individuals recorded on the register.[48] In this second example, there is no clinical diagnosis of dangerousness. In fact, these prisoners have been released precisely because they are not perceived to be dangerous in the future. They are, however, a population deemed "at risk" (of both reoffending and being offended against).

Thus, while selective incapacitation ensures that dangerous offenders are expunged from public space in ways reminiscent of what Foucault calls "the great confinement",[49] sex offenders who complete their sentences but are not predicted to be dangerous still face a range of restrictions on their movements in public space. Depending on the local legislation, sex offenders can be subject to a range of techniques that "mark" their bodies as sites of governance in public spaces. This can be enabled by community-notification statutes that employ strategies such as leaflet drops, community meetings, media reporting of addresses, and telephone hotlines, to name just a few.[50]

All these approaches have been trialled in various parts of the western world, and are a clear attempt to manage the risk posed by sex offenders by making them visible in public space. Such visibility becomes a powerful regulatory mechanism that surveils the spaces sex offenders inhabit in their local communities. Indeed, in some approaches, the general public become a form of "moral police", ensuring that sex offenders are kept at an appropriate distance from (morally) respectable society. Interestingly, community-notification techniques like these have been found to be ineffective in shoring up the safety of the community,[51] while more telling is research demonstrating how the stigma of community-notification processes "may inadvertently increase the likelihood of recidivism among some sex offenders ... by making it more difficult to achieve meaningful stability in important areas of their lives and facilitate positive relationships".[52] Gaining and maintaining employment is also seriously hampered by employers' attitudes to known sex offenders.[53] Moreover, the moral panic underpinning community notification has been found to increase the probability of recidivism.

However, the rise of risk did not supplant the older idea of dangerousness, but rather widened its ambit to a larger population, much in the same way as dangerousness simply worked with the older model of immorality. With sex offender registers in their various guises, we have a form of regulation of an at-risk population which sits easily with religious ideas of moral worth and fear of dangerous individuals. Perhaps more interestingly, given our previous discussion about the changing nature of both sex and sexuality, in the exponential rise of sex offender legislation we also see an outcome of the shift to passive female sexuality and active male sexuality. It will not be surprising to note, for example, that it is men who are the most likely to be identified as either dangerous sex offenders requiring indeterminate incapacitation and/or "at-risk" sex offenders placed on public registers, while women and female children are most likely identified as victims of such offences.[54]

The moral panic about children and sex discussed in some detail in chapters 2 and 3 is also relevant to current ideas about the risk of sex offenders. Much more than property offences, or even physical assaults, "sex offences against persons are considered to be violations that damage the very core of victims".[55] The more sacred, pure or innocent the victim, the more profane the violation and the offender. Children are the most innocent group in contemporary society, and because of this are also perceived as the most vulnerable, out of all proportion to reality. For example, at the end of the twentieth century, the number of sex offences against adults in the UK was reported as 37,492, of which 6000 were rapes and the remainder indecent assaults. In contrast, indecent assaults against girls under sixteen numbered 2116, and against boys, 476.[56]

Despite these low numbers, much of the impetus for the increased public surveillance of sex offenders is motivated by calls for public safety, especially of children. Residency restrictions exemplify how governmental authorities maintain moral and spatial distance between children and sex offenders by legislating the physical distances sex offenders may reside from spaces where children congregate. This may include proximity to schools, child care centres, shopping centres, playgrounds, skating rinks, neighbourhood centres, gymnasiums and youth centres. However, if we consider for a moment the number of child care centres alone in a local community, we begin to understand how residency restrictions work to further isolate and exclude sex offenders from society. An American study by Zandbergen and Hart[57] used geographical information system data to calculate how much housing would be unavailable to sex offenders in the area of Orange County, Florida, due to residence restrictions. They found "23% of the 137,944 properties zoned for residential use were located within 1000 feet of schools and 64% fell within 2500 feet, reducing the number of available residences to 106,888 and 50,108 respectively".

Other studies have noted the continuum of negative outcomes for the lives of sex offenders, from lack of access to housing to living homeless long term.[58] Perhaps the most powerful element of residency restriction legislation, though, is that it can apply for between ten and fifteen years after the sex offender has completed their sentence and been released from prison. Moreover, given that many people are defined as sex offenders for very minor crimes, including public exposure, or conducting a consensual sexual relationship with a person who is only just under the age of consent, such management techniques seem harsh in the extreme. This has been exacerbated through the use of global positioning systems (GPS), which ensure perpetual surveillance of sex offenders.[59] Such mechanisms have been implemented in various parts of the United States, Britain and Australia, for example, through electronic monitoring anklets and bracelets. These have already proved useful in serving breach notices related to this legislation and in having sex offenders re-incarcerated. More importantly, though, these forms of regulation restrict free movement to the point where regulation becomes "punishment in the absence of any evidence of wrongdoing".[60]

CONCLUSION

This chapter has charted how we have come to think about sex offenders as morally perverted and dangerous predators, a personhood that legitimates their enduring regulation in public space. In this contemporary context, an offender such as Arthurs is legitimately incarcerated for life on the basis that he is too morally and psychologically different to be able to coexist safely with the rest of society. Should Arthurs ever be released, his movements and time will inevitably be surveilled for the remainder of his life. His is marked as a body of sin and danger, one that reflects and justifies public panic and demands to ensure child sexual safety. That our contemporary perceptions about sex offenders have developed only recently, based on changes in understandings of sex and public space, illustrates just how intolerant society is of sexual deviance, regardless of whether there is any real basis for concern. We explore public discourses on other kinds of sexual deviance in order to demonstrate how contradictory these discourses are to contemporary perceptions that we, as an advanced and sexually experienced society, entertain a more liberal attitude towards sexuality.

NOTES

1   Liza Kappelle and Andrea Hayward, 2007, "Sofia's killer jailed for life over toilet murder", www.news. com.au/sofias-killer-jailed-for-life-over-toilet-murder/story-e6frfkp9-1111114822414 (accessed 29 September 2011).

2   Supreme Court of Western Australia, 2007, *Arthurs v. The State of Western Australia*, WASC 182, 31 July. www.austlii.edu.au/cgi-bin/sinodisp/au/cases/wa/WASC/2007/182.html (accessed 29 September 2011).

3   Terry Thomas, 2005, *Sex Crime: Sex Offending and Society*, 2nd edn. London, Willan Publishing, p. 18.

4   Thomas, 2005, p. 1.

5   James F. Quinn, Carla R. Forsyth and Craig Mullen-Quinn, 2004, "Societal reactions to sex offenders: a review of the origins and results of the myths surrounding their crimes and treatment amenability", *Deviant Behaviour*, 25(3), 219.

6 Steve Garton, 2004, *Histories of Sexuality: Antiquity to Sexual Revolution*. London, Equinox.

7 Gail Hawkes and John Scott (eds), 2005, *Perspectives in Human Sexuality*. Melbourne, Oxford University Press, p. 8.

8 William Naphy, 2002, *Sex Crimes: From Renaissance to Enlightenment*. Stroud, UK, Tempus Publishing, p. 9.

9 Steven R. Morrison, 2007, "Creating sex offender registries: the religious right and the failure to protect society's vulnerable", *American Journal of Criminal Law*, 35(1), 38.

10 Tim Hitchcock, 1997, *English Sexualities 1700–1800*. London, Macmillan, p. 5.

11 Hitchcock, 1997, p. 5.

12 Gail Hawkes, 2004, *Sex and Pleasure in Western Culture*. Cambridge, Polity Press, p. 66.

13 Hitchcock, 1997, p. 5.

14 Tim Hitchcock, 2002, "Redefining sex in eighteenth century England", in Kim Phillips and Barry Reay (eds), *Sexualities in History: A Reader*. New York, Routledge, p. 191.

15 Jeffrey Weeks, 1989, *Sex, Politics and Society*, 2nd edn. London, Longman.

16 Hitchcock, 1997, *op. cit.*, p. 99.

17 Laura Agustin, 1988, *Sex at the Margins*. London, Zed Books.

18 William Mayhew, 1851, cited in Agustin, 1988, p. 99.

19 Hitchcock, 1997, *op. cit.*, p. 99.

20 Hitchcock, 1997, p. 100.

21 Hitchcock, 1997, p. 100.

22 Hitchcock, 1997, p. 15.

23 Hitchcock, 1997, p. 101.

24 Thomas, 2005, *op. cit.*, p. 40.

25 Hawkes, 2004, *op. cit.*, p. 91.

26 Naphy, 2002, *op. cit.*, pp. 84–85.

27 John D'Emilio and Estelle Freedman, 2002, "Family Life and the Regulation of Deviance", in Kim Phillips and Barry Reay (eds), *Sexualities in History: A Reader*. New York, Routledge, p. 141.

28 Marjorie McIntosh, 1998, *Controlling Misbehaviour in England, 1370–1600*. Cambridge, Cambridge University Press.

29 Philip Jenkins, 1998, *Moral Panic: Changing Concepts of the Child Molester in Modern America*. New Haven, CT, Yale University Press, p. 26.

30 Michel Foucault, 1976, *The History of Sexuality: An Introduction*. London, Penguin.

31 Kim Phillips and Barry Reay, 2002, "Introduction", in Phillips and Reay, *op. cit.*, p. 13.

32 Mona Lynch, 2002, "Pedophiles and cyber-predators as contaminating forces: the language of disgust, pollution, and boundary invasions in federal debates on sex offender legislation", *Law & Social Inquiry*, 27, 557.

33 Jenkins, 1998, *op. cit.*, p. 22.

34 Jenkins, 1998, p. 12.

35 Morrison, 2007, *op. cit.*, 44–45.

36 Jenkins, 1998, *op. cit.*, p. 21.

37 Laura J. Zilney and Lisa A. Zilney, 2009, *Perverts and Predators: The Making of Sexual Offending Laws.* Lanham, MD, Rowman & Littlefield, pp. 66–67.

38 Estelle B. Freedman, 1987, "'Uncontrolled desires': the response to the sexual psychopath, 1920–60", *Journal of American History*, 74(1), 84.

39 Thomas, 2005, *op. cit.*, p. 15.

40 Foucault, 1976, *op. cit.*, p. 43.

41 Michael Petrunik, 2003, "The hare and the tortoise: dangerousness and sex offender policy in the United States and Canada", *Canadian Journal of Criminology and Criminal Justice*, 43(1), 43.

42 Robert Castel, 1991, "From dangerousness to risk", in Graeme Burchell, Colin Gordon and Peter Miller (eds), *The Foucault Effect: Studies in Governmentality.* London, Harvester, p. 283.

43 Gordon Tait, 2000, *Youth, Sex and Government.* Peter Lang, New York, p. 115.

44 David McCallum, 2001, *Personality and Dangerousness.* Cambridge, Cambridge University Press, p. 34.

45 Tait, 2000, *op. cit.*, p. 114.

46 Thomas, 2005, *op. cit.*, p. 121.

47 Petrunik, 2003, *op. cit.*, p. 44.

48 Thomas, 2005, pp. 156–58.

49 Michel Foucault, 1961, *Madness and Civilization: A History if Insanity in the Age of Reason.* London, Routledge, p. 55.

50 Thomas, 2005, pp. 220–24.

51 Australian Institute of Criminology, 2007, *Is Notification of Sex Offenders in Local Communities Effective?* Canberra, AIC; Bob E. Vásquez, Sean Maddan and Jeffrey T. Walker, 2008, "The influence of sex offender registration and notification laws in the United States: a time-series analysis", *Crime and Delinquency*, 54(2), 175–92.

52 Michelle L. Meloy, Yustina Saleh and Nancy Wolff, 2007, "Sex offender laws in America: can panic-driven legislation ever create safer societies?", *Criminal Justice Studies*, 20(4), 438.

53 Kevin Brown, Jon W. Spencer and Jo Deakin, 2007, "The reintegration of sex offenders: barriers and opportunities for employment", *Howard Journal of Criminal Justice*, 46(1), 32–42.

54 Petrunik, 2003, *op. cit.*, p. 44.

55 Petrunik, 2003, p. 43.

56 Thomas, 2005, *op. cit.*, p. 4.

57 Paul A. Zandbergen and Timothy C. Hart cited in Jill S. Levenson, 2008, "Collateral consequences of sex offender residence restrictions", *Criminal Justice Studies*, 21(2), p. 155.

58 Jill S. Levenson, Kristen Zgoba and Richard Tewksbury, 2007, "Sex offender residence restrictions: sensible crime policy or flawed logic?", *Federal Probation*, 71(3), 2–9.

59 Julian C. Roberts, Loretta J. Stalans, David Indermaur and Michael Hough, 2003, *Penal Populism and Public Opinion: Lessons from Five Countries.* Oxford, Oxford University Press.

60 Roberts, Stalans, Indermaur and Hough, 2003, p. 141.

CHAPTER 3

OUT OF PLACE

The Moral Geography of Sex and Deviance

SHARON HAYES

BELINDA CARPENTER

ANGELA DWYER

INTRODUCTION

In an episode from the popular television series *Seinfeld*,[1] the main character—Jerry—enters a train carriage on his way to work one day and takes a seat near the door. After several stops, the train soon becomes crowded. It's early, and Jerry succumbs to the rhythmic shunting of the wheels on the tracks and the stuffy atmosphere, and falls asleep. When he awakens some time later, he is surprised to find that he is alone, except for another man sitting across from him, who is reading a newspaper. However, further investigation—it takes Jerry some time to wake up properly—reveals that the carriage isn't empty at all; rather, its occupants have crowded down either end of the carriage, leaving otherwise empty the space occupied by himself and the man with the newspaper. This in itself is surprising, given the sheer number of people present, but Jerry is even more surprised when he realizes that the reason for this strange evacuation of the centre of the carriage is that the man sitting opposite him has disrobed and is now completely naked.

This scenario points up the absurdity of the average person's response to public nudity. The man with the newspaper sits nonchalantly, disregarding the fear and offence expressed through the actions of the other commuters. Jerry is caught in a situation where he is exposed to something commonly regarded as wrong—even illegal—and must decide what to do. It is clear that the other passengers are disturbed by the man's nudity because they have distanced themselves from it as much as possible. The following exchange between Jerry and the man is instructive:

JERRY: Oooo-Kay. You realize, of course, you're naked?
NAKED MAN: Naked, dressed, I don't see any difference.

JERRY: You oughta' sit here. There's a difference.

NAKED MAN: You got something against the naked body?

JERRY: I got something against yours. How about a couple of deep knee bends, maybe a squat thrust?

NAKED MAN: Who's got time for squat thrusts?

JERRY: All right, how about skipping breakfast. I'm guessing you're not a "half-grapefruit and black coffee" guy.

NAKED MAN: I like a good breakfast.

JERRY: I understand, I like good breakfast[.] … .

NAKED MAN: I'm not ashamed of my body.

JERRY: That's your problem, you should be.

NAKED MAN DROPS HALF OF HIS NEWSPAPER.

JERRY: Don't get up. Please, allow me.

This short exchange is interesting for several reasons. First, Jerry demonstrates a relatively socially "appropriate" response to the man's nakedness: "You realize, of course, you're naked?" The question is rhetorical because it is obvious to the viewer and to Jerry that the man knows he is naked. But the fact that Jerry makes a verbal observation about the man's nakedness—albeit sarcastic—indicates that he is both surprised and disturbed by the man's apparent disregard of social and legal niceties. So, why doesn't Jerry flee to the end of the carriage with the other passengers? The answer lies partly in the fact that this event occurs in the context of television comedy, where the different and the ridiculous evoke laughter as a way of countering discomfort. But we suggest that the other reason Jerry does not flee is that the writers of the episode seek to challenge viewers' instinctive reactions to public nudity. Jerry is surprised and possibly disturbed, but not alarmed at the man's nudity. Should he be? Jerry's response to the man's inquiry, "You got something against the naked body?" indicates he is more disturbed by the man's body size and aesthetic than he is by the fact of his nudity. The man's body apparently disgusts Jerry because he is overweight by common standards. Would Jerry have been completely undisturbed by the nudity if the man had been slim and/or muscled? If the naked person had been an aesthetically appealing woman? Clearly, the exchange challenges our instinctive discomfort about public nudity as well as sending up our entrenched attitudes concerning body size and shape. But why are such challenges regarded as comedic? In this section, we explore the concept of the public and what is considered to be acceptable in the public realm, with a view to challenging some of our common assumptions about, and attitudes towards, sexual deviance, illustrated through crimes of indecency and public offence. It also examines the differences between public and private space, how public space affects the criminalization of certain sex acts, and how the criminals associated with these acts are governed.

THE CONCEPT OF MORAL SPACE

In this chapter, we aim to trace the historical development of the notion of space and unpack the rationale behind how spaces at large are governed, particularly with respect to sexual behaviour. We suggest that geographical space in our society is governed by heteronormative discourses and practices which are hostile to non-traditional sexualities and non-traditional sexual behaviour. In this context, public space is characterized as areas in which people do not have a choice about what they are exposed to—in other words, they are reliant on the discretion of others in determining what visible, tactile and audible experiences they will encounter. Because of the heteronormative nature of public morality, which privileges traditional institutions such as families and hetero-sexual marriage, public spaces are governed by legislation preventing individuals from engaging in acts considered as offensive to those ideals.[2] This chapter examines the nature and socio-historical development of those ideals, and challenges their claim to dominance.

As we saw from our example above, one of the most entrenched attitudes surrounding public space is the fear of public nudity. Public nudity generally is considered to be inappropriate or wrong, and in many cases is also illegal. People do not expect to see naked bodies in public space and are affronted when exposed to them without warning. Nudity is acceptable under certain cir-cumstances, in certain spaces (mostly private) and with prior notice. The notion of public nudity is therefore linked to the notion of consent, a concept examined in more detail in Part 3. In contrast, this section focuses on geographies of sex, which appear to be dyadically delineated into public and private. This dualism also extends to sexuality—public spaces must, for the most part, be heterosexual spaces. There are very limited public spaces for non-traditional sexualities, and those that exist are hidden, or, if occupying visible public space, tend to be subcultural, rendered non-threatening by heteronormative laws and conventions. For example, the practice of "cottaging"—where sex between men occurs in public lavatories and similar spaces—is commonly frowned upon, and known "beats" are usually patrolled by police. Similarly, non-heterosexual displays of love and affection, even where participants are fully clothed, often are considered offensive and policed under "public obscenity" or "public nuisance" laws.[3] Heterosexual partners who engage in such public displays are more often tolerated, depending on the extent of the display. However, irrespective of the sexual preference, public sex is illegal and members of the general public are affronted when faced with such displays. This policing of sex and nudity in public spaces is far-reaching across cultures and ethnic boundaries, and doubly discriminates against non-heterosexuals, but the concept of space as a context for regulating sex is itself relatively new.

In the late eighteenth and early nineteenth centuries, space for the first time was seen by carto-graphers and geographers as something to be investigated, mapped and classified. Space was an "objective physical surface with specific fixed characteristics upon which social identities and categories were mapped out".[4] Subsequently, scientists began to see space as more complex—as a social experience with interwoven layers of social meaning. Marxism and radical approaches to geography also "began to see space as the product of social forces, observing that different societies use and organise space in different ways and to explain the processes through which social differences become spatial patterns of inequalities".[5] More recently, Doreen Massey[6] has defined space as:

> the product of the intricacies and the complexities, the interlockings and non-interlockings, of relations of the unimaginably cosmic to the intimately tiny. And precisely because it is the product of relations, relations which are active practices, material and embedded, practices which have to be carried out, space is always in a process of becoming. It is always being made.

Sexual geography, therefore, is a dynamic web of relationships circumscribing how people interact with sexual practices and displays, whether in public or private, and how such sexual practices are governed. Significantly, sexual practice is not neutral, but is embodied in heteronormative interpretations of gender and sexuality, as well as the proper constitution of a relationship and what that stands for. This is most obvious in how children's sexuality is governed in terms of spaces.

Recent ethnographic research has found, for example, that parents, in relaying messages about sexual threats while also trying to maintain children's innocence, give out the erroneous message that public space is dangerous, while private space is safe.[7] Where children were able to roam the streets and play freely with each other in times past, they are now more often locked behind closed doors, and both play and school time is closely regulated to ensure they are protected from anything sexual—including, but not limited to, naked bodies, sexual intercourse, and the display of erotic images and scenes. This moral governance of the risk of sex for children in large part determines where and when nudity and sexual practices may occur. Think back to our discussion of classification boards and television viewing codes in chapter 4. Such moral governance also determines the timeframe for sex—sex has become associated with the night, and so where public spaces are allocated to "adult entertainment", they are temporally confined to darkness. Needham comments that daylight is always associated with and reserved for families, because children in particular have access to the realm of the public during the day.[8] Thus anything to do with sex or non-heteronormative values and ideals must be hidden away from them, and only brought out when it is safe to do so. Hence we find television content regulated so that shows offering content over and above a PG rating must be held back until the relevant watershed time—usually 8.30 or 9pm, when all children are safely tucked into bed. Similarly, adult entertainment must be confined not only to spaces where families are unlikely to congregate, but also temporally to the night time, following the television watershed or even later. This ensures not only that the unsavoury activities conducted in these venues will occur outside family time, but also that they are covered by darkness, rendering them less visible and thereby less threatening to wholesome heteronormative values.

Foucault comments on the regulation of public spaces in his work on madness and prisons. Prisons discipline populations within confined spaces through an interweaving of medical, policed, urban and national spaces.[9] This facilitates the "careful organisation of time, space, bodies and action"[10] and "condones particular associations but not others between different classes of people, specific forms of sexual encounter, and certain spaces and times for the 'doing' of the sex acts in question".[11] Similarly, Philo argues that there is a "collision of population, sex and space—an interest in the spaces of sex acts, sex work, sex workers, sexual diseases, sexual health and sexual policies" that governs the way in which sex is enacted in society.[12] While some theorists advocate ridding society of regulatory practices concerning sex, Philo acknowledges the doubtful success of such a move:

> Many would doubtless feel uncomfortable with such an outcome, wherein sex escapes its regulatory framing, and where the spaces that matter become those of the chance encounter, embodied performance and the very immediacy of bodily shape, form, reach and position.[13]

The way in which sex is regulated, then, speaks to a fear of embodied sex in real life and real situations, which in turn creates an artificial moral category of sexual deviance focused on indecency and offence.

THE GEOGRAPHY OF DECENCY

In our society, prohibitions abound against activities such as nude sunbathing, flashing, streaking, solitary or mutual masturbation, fellatio, and vaginal and anal intercourse in public.[14] Specific criminal charges against offenders include "indecent exposure", "public indecency" and "lewd conduct". The concept of moral decency stems from deeply entrenched heteronormative ideals such as family, monogamy and marriage, and implies, as Johnson states, that "impersonal, casual and anonymous sexual encounters have negative connotations ... as they stand in contrast to ideals of romantic love, monogamous relationships, and long term commitments".[15] Discussions of nudity and sexuality are loaded with moral subtexts that speak to public judgments about what constitutes a moral space and how that space is governed.

Regulation of prostitution and adult entertainment in public spaces is a case in point. Strip clubs and brothels must be kept apart from areas where families and children congregate. Bernstein notes that urban renewal often relegates these venues, which originally tended to spring up in inner-city areas where adults congregate at night to seek entertainment, to marginal areas so that families will be encouraged and welcomed to frequent these previously morally inappropriate public spaces.[16] The same situation occurs with beats, which are strongly policed to the point where public toilets may be dismantled or moved to areas that provide more surveillance. The moral geography of sex precludes the pairing of sex with families in public spaces. Public toilets are for use by families and are not to be used as sexual spaces, regardless of how surreptitious or discreet the encounter. This causes a problem for non-heterosexuals, who may by necessity be forced out of private spaces in order to find sexual experiences. Sex is a private relation, and where it is offered publicly, it must be hidden or separated. Thus men cannot have sex together in public toilets and prostitutes cannot solicit in public spaces, because both represent a threat to the heteronormative construction of urban/suburban life.

Panoptic devices such as closed-circuit television, patrols, lighting and architecture are used to maintain surveillance of public spaces deemed at risk for illicit activity—either sexual, or criminal, or both. Legg notes that "these geographies can include the organisation of the home, the comportment and performance of a walker in the street, the sexual spaces of a community, the drilling of subterranean water channels, [and] citywide administration",[17] to name just a few. Public spaces are thereby arranged in such a way as to confine risky areas to fully regulated spaces subject to ongoing surveillance and control.

An interesting outcome of all this geographical surveillance and renewal is that cities now are creating what Bell and Binnie have termed "commodified gay spaces".[18] Spaces are set apart for gay clubs and they become publicly identified as gay spaces. Gay clubs and other spaces occupy their own territory, but such spaces are still policed to ensure that activity is restricted to congregating and does not extend to sexual activity.[19] Indeed, it is just because gays and lesbians (and intersexed and transgendered individuals, etc.) are identified by their sexuality that they become a "danger" in need of regulating. The essentialized association of "gay" with "sex" means that gay spaces are *necessarily* viewed as sexual spaces, regardless of whether actual sex is occurring in them. This leads to the view that such spaces must be monitored closely to ensure they do not impinge upon wholesome heteronormative individuals without their consent. Moreover, although public discourses about sexuality are becoming more and more tolerant, and even accepting, they continue to serve to confine non-heterosexualities, a phenomenon discussed in some detail in chapter 7.

SEX AND MORAL DISTANCE

Returning to our example of the naked man on the train, we can see how moral decency requires that individuals put distance between themselves and the indecent. Further examination of the exchange between Jerry and the naked man reveals some interesting observations about how people deal with indecency in public spaces. As the scene continues, Jerry picks up the man's newspaper and the scene cuts away to one of the other characters. Several scenes later, the other passengers are still jammed at either end of the carriage, but Jerry and the naked man are nonchalantly discussing baseball.

NAKED MAN: They still have no pitching. Goodin's a question mark. ... You don't recover from those rotator cuffs so fast.
JERRY: I'm not worried about their best pitching. They got pitching. ... They got no hitting.

NAKED MAN: No hitting? They got hitting! Bonilla, Murray. … They got no defence.

JERRY: Defence? Please. … They need speed.

NAKED MAN: Speed? They got Coleman. … They need a bullpen.

JERRY: Franco's no good. … They got no team leaders.

NAKED MAN: They got Franco! … What they need is a front office.

JERRY: But you gotta like their chances.

NAKED MAN: I LUV their chances.

JERRY: Tell you what. If they win the pennant, I'll sit naked with you at the World Series.

NAKED MAN: It's a deal!

By this stage, Jerry and the naked man seem to be completely disregarding the latter's state of undress and are carrying on the kind of normal conversation any two fairly well-socialized heterosexual men might have. They engage in a kind of camaraderie during this part of the exchange, and Jerry even jokes about being naked himself. Meanwhile, the other commuters are regarding this strange pair with some fear. The physical distance between the other commuters and these two speaks to the importance of space in two ways. First, individuals in our society feel threatened by public nudity in direct relation to how close they are to it. Second, a train carriage is a public space, and failure to observe the rules of public space require immediate withdrawal from that space. Given that the passengers are a captive audience, they have no option but to put as much distance as possible between themselves and the perceived threat.

In his influential work on offence and harm, Feinberg[20] examines some hypothetical situations in which behaviour such as public nudity may be regarded as offensive. The scenario for Feinberg's discussion is a crowded bus, on which we, the readers, are invited to imagine ourselves sitting. He asks if there are "any human experiences that are harmless in themselves yet so unpleasant that we can rightly demand legal protection from them, even at the cost of other persons' liberties".[21] In particular, Feinberg is interested in sexual acts performed in public and why such acts, which are acceptable in private, suddenly become offensive when performed in public.[22] He notes that "[o]ur culture, of course, is far more uptight about sexual pleasures than about 'harmless' pleasures of any other kind".[23] How would we feel, he asks, if the seat opposite us on the bus were occupied by a young couple who were engaged in kissing? It might make us feel slightly uncomfortable, but we would probably dismiss it as youthful ardour, and discreetly look away, perhaps occupying ourselves with reading or looking out the window. But what if the couple were of the same sex? What if they were fondling each other under their clothes as well? What if the couple proceeded to have oral sex or sexual intercourse on the seat across from us? Our reaction would most likely be similar to the reaction of the other passengers on Jerry's train—our disgust would warrant that we remove ourselves as quickly as possible.

Feinberg speculates that this discomfort about sex in public derives "from the danger in, and harmful consequences of, sexual behaviour in the past—disease, personal exploitation, unwanted pregnancy, etc.—and the intricate association of sexual taboos with rules of property transfer, legitimacy, marriage, and the like".[24] Public nudity and public sexual behaviour are, he concludes, complicated psychological phenomena leading to vicarious embarrassment and public shame.

> [N]ude bodies and copulating couples … have the power of pre-empting the attention and absorbing the reluctant viewer, whatever his preferences in the matter. The presence of such things in one's field of perception commands one's notice … Moreover, the problem of coping, for many persons as least, is a bit of a difficult one, not insurmountable, but something of an unpleasant strain.[25]

Why is this the case? Feinberg argues that nudity and sex acts draw us to thoughts that are normally repressed, eliciting unresolved conflict between instinctual desires and cultural taboos. There is a temptation to see, to savour, to become sexually stimulated, which triggers the "familiar mechanism of inhibition and punishment in the form of feelings of shame".[26] He argues that acts such as homosexual sex and bestiality are "immediately and powerfully threatening. … [L]ower-level sensibilities are shocked so that a spontaneous disgust arises. Male homosexual acts violate powerful taboos in our culture; they also threaten the 'ego ideals' of heterosexual men."[27] And yet homosexual acts and acts of bestiality that occur in private pose no threat whatsoever, though some individuals may continue to believe such acts are morally wrong. The idea that offence occurs only when such acts are witnessed in public speaks to the heteronormative allocation of public space to the family and all its associated paraphernalia.

The scenario of our naked man on the train, however, takes an interesting turn that seems to question the validity of this widespread attitude. Several scenes later, the naked man has put on his clothes again, and he and Jerry are getting off the train together, still deep in conversation.

NAKED MAN: I haven't had a hotdog at Nathan's for 20 years.
JERRY: First we ride the cyclone.
NAKED MAN: Chilly out.
JERRY TAKES A DEEP BREATH.
JERRY: Aah, French fries.

The two men then head off to the Coney Island funfair together. Clearly, the man's nudity has become passé and a friendship of sorts has formed out of their brief exchange. It might even be suggested that the man's nudity, and Jerry's eventual disregarding of it, has created some kind of bond between the two men. The message here is that people may be different, have different views about things such as nudity, but these may be overlooked or disregarded when the people in question share other interests. In the end, then, the writers of this episode are quite radically challenging viewers to question their beliefs about, and attitudes towards, public nudity and the people who engage in it. The fact that public nudity is incongruous and threatening makes the episode humorous, and yet we are left with the distinctly uncomfortable feeling that we would probably act in the same way as those passengers who fled to the back of the train.

THE NEXUS OF TIME AND SPACE

Discourses abound on the risk of public spaces, evidenced by the proliferation of institutions for managing the daily lives of children and those who interact with them. As we saw in Part 1, discourses on childhood have changed considerably over time, and the notion of childhood itself is therefore a social construction. Valentine[28] describes two contrasting narratives about the way we think about children. On the one hand, children are wild, possessed of primal instincts, and the road to adulthood is paved by learning to overcome or harness these instincts for social good. On the other hand, however, is the view—originally proposed at the end of the seventeenth century by the Cambridge Platonists—that children are born with innate goodness and have the potential to be corrupted by an evil world.

The eighteenth century saw these two views hotly debated,[29] with the second eventually becoming dominant.[30] This, as we have seen in Part 1, led to child labour reform, among other things. By the nineteenth century, education was seen as a way of instilling discipline—schools became "moral hospitals"—at the same time as the notion of the juvenile delinquent developed. The twentieth century then paved the way for the domination of family and the role of the mother in nurturing children. "Mothers in the UK are expected to be guardians of liberal-democracy by bringing their children up to be self-regulating."[31]

This view was reinforced in the late twentieth century through public discourses on "stranger danger" and other risks, exacerbated by the invention in the 1950s of the "teenager",[32] a category of social, emotional, sexual and physical development that further extended childhood into the second decade of life. During this time, and continuing on into the late twentieth and early twenty-first centuries, parental fears for children developed from a belief that children's safety in public spaces has deteriorated since their own youth. And yet the statistics indicate that the number of children killed each year by strangers in the UK hasn't changed over the past thirty years, "despite the fact that the numbers of people charged or cautioned for child pornography offences has risen by 1500 per cent since 1988, largely due to the increase in material available on the internet".[33] A similar picture has been found in North American research.

Parental fears about children and public space are therefore largely misguided. As Valentine notes, "children are more at risk in private space" and "from people they know ... yet parental fears imagine a geography of danger from strangers in public space".[34] The social construction of childhood as a period of innocence and vulnerability has led to the strongly held and widespread belief that children are more at risk in public spaces than adults, and that those risks are "inherently more serious".[35] Negotiating parenthood and raising children have thus become focused on managing risk. This attitude is encouraged by the media, who delight in reporting failures in the moral regulation of sex and children.[36] Katz[37] labels this media coverage as "terror talk" and claims that such "terrorizing contentions concerning violence against children in the public arena—from abductions and molestations to armed assaults and murders—weigh heavily on the public imagination".

City spaces are also seen as much more dangerous than rural spaces.[38] The concentration of populations in cities is seen to exacerbate the risks to children, not least through the allocation of public city spaces to erotica, adult entertainment and sexual commerce, all of which are much less visible in rural areas, which tend to be more family-oriented. The privatization of children's play and the "decline in children's independent use of space" have become *de rigueur* as media reports of child sexual abuse and child pornography continue to increase.[39] This constant surveillance of children and teens means they have very little privacy. The tendency of parents to create domestic tensions around home rules and to allocate different rooms to different purposes creates order along strong domestic boundaries. Teens, however, like disorder and weak boundaries,[40] and tend to rebel against the regulation of private spaces.

School, too, is a highly regulated public space, which teens experience as an acute lack of freedom. There is little in the way of public amenities for teens in both Australia and the UK,[41] with teens tending to be governed through sport and other extra-curricular activities, all of which attempt to occupy the teen's time and space in such a way as to dissipate risk. The teenager who chooses not to engage in such pursuits is frowned upon and regarded as "at risk"—either of "dropping out" or of becoming delinquent, both of which are seen as an *entrée* to a lifetime of moral risk and debauchery. Again, the media exacerbate this trend by creating moral panics around examples of "at-risk" behaviour, often exaggerating the causes and effects of such behaviours and events and placing them strategically within certain feared spaces such as "the street".[42] The moral geography of the street positions young people who frequent them as "out of place"—the acceptable geography of a teenage existence is delimited by heteronormative institutions such as school, sport, clubs, church and family. To step outside this bounded existence is to threaten the very fabric of the heteronormative imperative.

Virtual space, or cyberspace, is even more challenging to that imperative, creating as it does a new kind of public space, one that presents new risks and panics, especially regarding children.[43] Cyberspace has challenged the accepted view of public space, making it globalized and therefore extremely difficult to legislate. Identities may be hidden, adopted, or obliterated in the space of seconds or minutes, leading practices such as sexual commerce and adult entertainment to take on a whole new meaning. The fact that people may engage with cyberspace within the privacy of their own homes, and are able to disguise their identities, makes cyberspace a dangerous place.[44]

Actual space also overlaps with cyberspace to create even more risk for the vulnerable and innocent. Hayes and Ball[45] note that young and old alike use cyberspace to explore sex and sexuality. Indeed, the exploration of sexuality in virtual space is much easier than in "real life" thanks to the creation of virtual identities and the suppression of real identities, which allows individuals to access sexually explicit material, both educational and pornographic, without fear of detection. This virtual anonymity also may encourage young people to try out sexualities and sexual practices they would otherwise not have access to, and this fact has created another moral panic, this time surrounding children and cybersex.[46] Child pornography is more easily distributed in cyberspace, which by association becomes a sinister public space which authorities are anxious to control and monitor.

Cyberspace is an especially dangerous place for children and teens, and therefore must be governed in order to preserve childhood innocence. Cyberspace is highly threatening because it encompasses everything that constitutes a public space and yet is all but non-legislatable. The internet escapes the net of moral geography because it avoids the usual panoptic regulation imposed upon public spaces by heteronormative institutions of governance. It is, in other words, a space of resistance *par excellence* to heteronormative values and ideals. For young people, this is a double-edged sword, because the trade-off they make in exchange for cyber-freedom and the self-managing of identity is exposing themselves to genuine danger, even if the likelihood of being victimized is relatively low.

CONCLUSION

The burgeoning of virtual space over the past few decades has challenged accepted notions about the duality of the public and the private. Where physical public space has been sanitized so that it is acceptable to families, it has created a series of sexual subcultures that are identifiable and governable outside that heteronormative public space. However, the virtually ungovernable character of cyberspace has allowed the divide between the public and private to all but disappear, at least in terms of the internet. This ungovernability of virtual space has created a veritable moral panic that has led to further and more strenuous efforts at governing, leading to a burgeoning of policies and legislation regulating sex and children's exposure to it. The fact that such policies and legislation do not work has not forestalled such efforts.

In chapter 6, we examine how the effects of the panic about sex and children spill over into the governing of private lives through the regulation of sex offenders. In that chapter, we explore the vigilante nature of the public response to sex offenders and challenge some long-standing assumptions underlying the treatment of these criminals. Chapter 7 interrogates how deviant sexualities are positioned in the public realm, and identifies several inherent contradictions in the way we think about sexuality and non-heterosexual practices and identities. In this way, we hope to destabilize current acceptance of the duality of the public and private, and the way those spaces and associated crimes are regulated.

NOTES

1   The following excerpts are from "The Subway", episode #313 of *Seinfeld*, written and produced by Larry Charles, originally aired on NBC, 8 January 1992. Transcript quoted from www.seinfeldscripts.com (accessed 29 September 2011).

2   Judith Halberstam, 2005, *In a Queer Time and Place: Transgender Bodies, Subcultural Lives*. New York, New York University Press.

3 Joel Feinberg, 1988. *The Moral Limits of the Criminal Law, Vol.* 2. Cambridge, Cambridge University Press.

4 Gill Valentine, 2004, *Public Space and the Culture of Childhood.* Aldershot, Ashgate Publishing, p. 8.

5 Valentine, 2004, p. 8.

6 Massey, cited in Valentine, 2004, p. 8.

7 Massey, cited in Valentine, 2004, p. 12.

8 Gary Needham, 2008, "Scheduling normality: television, the family and queer temporality", in Gary Needham and Glyn Davis (eds), *Queer TV: Theories, Histories, Politics.* New York, Routledge, pp. 143–58.

9 Chris Philo, 2005, "Sex, life, death, geography: fragmentary remarks inspired by Foucault's population geographies", *Population, Space and Place,* 11(4), 326.

10 Philo, 2005, p. 329.

11 Philo, 2005, p. 330.

12 Philo, 2005, p. 330.

13 Philo, 2005, p. 330.

14 M. Lisa Johnson, 2004, "Way more than a tag line: HBO, feminism, and the question of difference in popular culture," *The Scholar and the Feminist Online,* 3.1 (Fall), 1.

15 Johnson, 2005, p. 1.

16 Elizabeth Bernstein, 2007, *Temporarily Yours: Intimacy, Authenticity, and the Commerce of Sex.* Chicago, IL and London, University of Chicago Press.

17 Stephen Legg, 2005, "Foucault's population geographies: classifications, biopolitics and governmental spaces", *Population, Space and Place,* 11(4), 144.

18 David Bell and Jon Binnie, 2000, *The Sexual Citizen: Queer Politics and Beyond.* Cambridge, Polity Press.

19 Bell and Binnie, 2004.

20 Joel Feinberg, 1985, *The Moral Limits of the Criminal Law. Volume One: Offence to Others.* New York, Oxford University Press.

21 Feinberg, 1985, p. 10.

22 Feinberg, 1985, p. 1.

23 Feinberg, 1985, p. 17.

24 Feinberg, 1985, p. 17.

25 Feinberg, 1985, p. 17

26 Feinberg, 1985, p. 17.

27 Feinberg, 1985, p. 20.

28 Valentine 2004, *op. cit.,* pp. 1–2.

29 For example, see Rousseau's *Emile,* 1762.

30 Valentine, 2004, p. 3.

31 Anne Phoenix and Ann Woollett, 1991, cited in Valentine, 2004, p. 5.

32 Valentine, 2004, p. 6.

33 Valentine, 2004, p. 18.

34 Valentine, 2004, p. 18.

35 Valentine, 2004, p. 20.

36 John Holt, 1974, *Escape from Childhood—The Needs and Rights of Children.* New York, E.P. Dutton and Co., p. 222.

37 Cindi Katz, 2006, "Power, space and terror: social reproduction and the public environment", in Setha Low and Neil Smith (eds), *The Politics of Public Space.* New York, Routledge, p. 3.

38 Valentine, 2004, *op. cit.*, p. 23.

39 Valentine, 2004, pp. 69–74.

40 Valentine, 2004, p. 83.

41 Valentine, 2004, p. 84.

42 Valentine, 2004, p. 89.

43 Marcel Henaff and Tracey B. Strong (eds), 2001 *Public Space and Democracy.* Minneapolis, MN, University of Minnesota Press.

44 Johnson, 2005, *op. cit.*, p. 10.

45 Sharon Hayes and Matthew Ball, 2009, "Queering cyberspace: fan fiction communities as spaces for expressing and exploring sexuality", in Burkhard Scherer (ed.), *Queering Paradigms.* Oxford, Peter Lang.

46 Clare Madge and Henrietta O'Connor, 2005, "Mothers in the making? Exploring liminality in cyber/space", *Transactions of the Institute of British Geographers*, 301, 83–97.

CHAPTER 4

THE SEX OFFENDER

An Introduction

RUDA FLORA
MICHAEL L. KEOHANE

OVERVIEW

During the past four decades the sex offender population has exploded on an international front, attracting public fear and outrage. Problems are reported with sex offenders in Australia, Canada, China, France, Germany, India, Norway, Russia, Sweden, the United Kingdom, and the United States. Other countries also report difficulties with this patient group. Sex offenders present difficult clinical problems that challenge accustomed methods of arrest, intervention, and treatment.

A fast-growing trend now exists in social policy to render services to this new patient phenomenon. However, many criminal justice, human service, and mental health professionals are unfamiliar with this population due to limitations in experience and specialized training. Meanwhile, convicted sex offenders are encountering insufficiently trained professionals and outdated systems at an increased rate.

As sex offenders continue to grow as an identified patient population, the need for more skilled professionals is expected to increase. There appears to be a major lack of understanding among policy makers regarding sexual crimes. The United States is the leader in incarceration of sex offenders, yet only those who are convicted of a sexual crime, which is less than 16%, are being monitored (Greenfeld, 1997). The majority of the 84% remain active and unmonitored. Harris-Perry (2013) and RAINN (2007) report that more than half (54%) of the victims of sexual assault in the United States do not report the offense.

The number of victims is alarming. Amnesty International USA (2013) and Ensler (2012) found that one in three women worldwide is abused, beaten, or raped sometime during her lifetime.

In the United States, more than 80,000 children are sexually abused each year, according to the American Academy of Child and Adolescent Psychiatry (2011). The National Society for the Prevention of Cruelty to Children reports over 17,000 sexual crimes involved children in England and Wales during a 2010–2011 study (NSPCC, 2013; Chaplin, Flatley, & Smith, 2011). A report in Australia during a 2012 review found up to 30% of all children experienced some type of sexual abuse (Ogloff, Cutajar, Mann, & Mullen, 2012). Country after country is reporting more and more sexual violence against adult women and children—a major concern for lay persons and professionals, as well as victims, and for society.

Many professionals who work directly with sex crimes and victims remain overworked and underpaid. Staff shortages and high case loads are common with limited operating budgets. In addition, many of these system providers report limited or no training with sex offenders. Such complaints are voiced in the United States as well as in Europe. This is the community's front line.

Grubin (2007) put forward three suggestions regarding the sex offender treatment problem: (1) a revision of sexual disorders that is more useful (as most identified are passive in form, with the exceptions of Pedophilia and Sexual Sadism), (2) neurobiological research into sexual behaviors of offenders, and (3) improved trials of medication that limit sexual aggression.

More studies on sexual offending are important. Allowing research money to be appropriated for sex offender research would open doors for more cost-effective ways to manage this social and legal problem. Sexual crimes impact the victim, family, and community in a psychological manner that other mental disorders and violent acts do not. Established institutional systems are overwhelmed and the need for more help by trained professionals has increased. Improved methods of intervention are required.

In many instances, criminal justice, human service, and mental health professionals operate in isolation from one another. Transfer of knowledge is often limited and impaired by interagency regulations. A more unified approach is required. Many sex offenders are able to avoid detection, prosecution, treatment, and incarceration as the result of system conflict. Overall, there appears to be a lack of information sharing and networking among disciplines about sexual offenders at the present time. Such situations lead to confusion and inappropriate methods of intervention. Communities and future victims remain at risk as additional solutions are sought.

Sex offenders are a difficult clinical population for criminal justice, human service, and mental health professionals. Some system providers question whether sex offenders even merit treatment. This question, although challenging in concept, does not address the rising cost of services, recidivism rate, and tragic toll sexual deviance takes from those involved. A number of complex physical and mental disorders can be present that are difficult to treat or resolve.

The purpose of this book is to serve as a reference guide for persons planning to work or who are now working with sex offenders in the criminal justice, human service, and mental health professions. This book explores those systems that offer services and how they function and provides information about assessment, intervention, and treatment of sex offenders.

DEFINITIONS

The National Sexual Violence Resource Center (2010) reports sexual crimes are traumatic to the victim. Sexual violence is defined as someone who forces or manipulates another person into engaging in sex by rape or sexual assault. In addition, a sexual offense may be defined as a criminal action of a sexual nature that is committed against another individual. Such sexual behavior may be used to display anger, control, domination, hostility, and power toward a person. Victims may be coerced, forced, or manipulated into engaging in sexual activity. Individuals who are unable to render informed consent as the result of mental incompetency or who are deemed minors are also considered victims of a sexual offense. Incidents may range from acts of voyeurism to rape. Other situations may include children sexually used in a passive or a forcible manner by another minor or an adult as well as spousal/partner rape (O'Connell, Leburg, & Donaldson, 1990). In recent years states have also been including electronic methods of sexual deviance such as sexting, webcams, and IM.

Coleman *et al.* (1996) reported that a sex offender is an individual who commits a sexual crime that violates cultural morals or laws. Laws may vary by locality, but most cultures have certain sexual behaviors they define as inappropriate and unacceptable.

The majority of offenders are male; however, over the last decade more female offenders have been reported. Throughout this book offenders will be referred to in a gender-neutral manner whenever possible.

Sexual offenders are heterogeneous. Offenders exist among both the employed and unemployed and within all income groups. Some sex offenders may be college educated while others may be high school dropouts. Sex offenders may be married, involved in a relationship, or single at the time of the reported offense. Offenders may be acquainted with the victims or strangers to them; some offenders are members of the victim's immediate family. Many sex offenders have a paraphilia disturbance. Many have offended on multiple occasions before their offense is discovered.

SEX OFFENDERS AND U.S. SOCIAL POLICY

Through the years, sex offenders have been impacted by social policy changes in the United States. Laws for the special commitment of sex offenders first appeared during the 1930s. Offenders were believed to be at a high risk for relapse; but at the same time, they were seen as good candidates for treatment services. The American Psychiatric Association (1999) reported the first sex offender laws were designed to accomplish two goals: (1) reduce recidivism among registered sex offenders in a shorter time than if incarcerated and (2) protect the community from persons believed to be sexually dangerous.

More than half of all states eventually enacted sex offender commitment laws in some form. They are known as "sexual psychopath laws," "sexually dangerous persons acts," and "mentally disordered sex offender acts." However, by the 1970s a number of these laws had lost endorsement as hope of "curing" sex offenders declined. By 1990 all but 12 states and the District of Columbia had changed or reversed earlier sex offender commitment laws.

Most clinical professionals who work with this specialized population know that reducing recidivism rates by way of treatment is the focal point in protecting the community. The lay community and many policy makers believe that treatment is ineffective for sex offenders. Those not familiar with this issue incorrectly assess their ability to detect sexual predators. Current laws do well with sex offenders who are already registered; however, due to the heterogeneous nature of this population it is often difficult to identify a sex offender by social, economic, stereotypical, or media-influenced markers.

Contrary to misinformation and sensationalism, research and empirical data rates for sexual reoffense are not nearly as high as the public's perceptions of these rates. Levenson, Brannon, Fortney, and Baker (2007) conducted a study to find out how much the general public knew about sex offender recidivism rates. They found that 74% of the 191 individuals who filled out his or her questionnaire believed that sex offenders go on to commit a new sex offense. However, sexual offenders as a population are the least likely of any criminal population group to commit new crimes (Levenson *et al.*, 2007).

The U.S. Department of Justice found that only 5.3% of the 9,000 sex offenders reviewed committed a new sexual crime within three years of their release from prison (Bureau of Justice Statistics, 2003). Hanson and Bussière (1998) completed a quantitative review of recidivism rates on more than 23,000 sex offenders and found that after five years, the average recidivism rate was 13.4%.

Harris and Hanson (2004) reviewed data across ten follow-up studies with a combined sample of 4,724 adult male sex offenders. Their results showed that after 15 years 73% of the sample had no new sexual reoffense charges or convictions. Three factors for increased risk included: (1) male victims, (2) prior sexual offenses, and (3) young age. Each one of these risks increases the recidivism rate; however, the rate of reoffense decreases the longer the offender avoids the behavior. The recidivism rate of a person leaving prison is higher within the first two years than between years 10 and 12.

The desire for sex offenders to be civilly committed has resurfaced. Several states have adopted new indeterminate commitment statutes; several other states have similar laws pending. A different policy has evolved, within these new laws, that is slanted toward the commitment of a sex offender only after incarceration in prison.

These new laws do not reflect the earlier belief that sex offenders can be successfully treated and "cured." As a result, a shift has started to occur in which offenders are now being referred to the mental health system for inpatient treatment services. If believed to be a danger to others, newly released sex offenders are being involuntarily committed to state psychiatric facilities.

Mental health is not and never has been a perfect science. As a discipline, it should be noted that the treatment of sex offenders is in the early stages of development. Social policy makers may desire to withhold assumptions until more empirical data are obtained. All treatment programs are said to possess failures; substance abuse programs may be cited as an example in which relapse may occur in many cases while others succeed in refraining from further drug and alcohol abuse.

Unlike substance abuse programs where relapse may be part of the recovery, relapse for sex offenders has detrimental consequences for a new victim, his or her family, the offender's family, and the community.

Communities are requesting more comprehensive services that address safety concerns. Rights advocate groups have changed the way both offenders and victims are treated. Victims are now more likely to report a sexual offense than in the past. Parole boards are becoming more reluctant to discharge a sex offender back to the community if they have the option to continue incarceration; in some cases, they will withhold release.

INTRODUCTION TO THE U.S. FEDERAL REGISTRATION

The first federal law requiring a registry for sex offenders was called the Jacob Wetterling Crimes against Children and Sexually Violent Offender Act of 1994, or the Wetterling Act of 1994 for short. Jacob Wetterling was abducted in 1989 at the age of 11. He has never been found. It was discovered later in the criminal investigation that there was a nearby halfway house where sex offenders often stayed. Law enforcement believe if they had known about the sex offenders in the area they could have saved valuable time in the investigation. The Wetterling Act of 1994 required individuals who commit violent sex offenses against children to register with law enforcement for ten years.

In May of 1996, the Wetterling Act was amended to include Megan's Law which requires community notification of sex offenders released from prison. Megan Kanka was a seven-year-old girl who was raped and murdered by a man in her neighborhood who was unknown to her parents. Megan's parents argued that had they known about this man's sexual offense history they would have talked to their daughter about staying away from this man (CNN, US, 1997).

The Children's Safety Act of 2005 incorporated "Dru's Law" which was officially called the Dru Sjodin National Sex Offender Public Registry (NSOPR); it was later changed to the National Sex Offender Public Website (NSOPW). The law was in response to Dru Sjodin, a 22-year-old female who was abducted, raped, and murdered by a man who had been on the sex offender registry. NSOPR joined web-based state registries to a single federal online registry that is available to the public (www.nsopw.gov). Sex offenders on the registry are required to update their contact information. A violation of this law would result in a felony and possible prison time.

Title I of the Adam Walsh Child Protection and Safety Act of 2006, known as the Sex Offender Registration and Notification Act (SORNA), became a federal law on July 27, 2006. It absorbed the Wetterling Act, Megan's Law, and Pam Lychner Sexual Offender Tracking and Identification Act requirements; includes Dru's Law; and sets a national standard for how each state is to register convicted sex offenders. It includes penalties and imprisonment for Internet crimes including child exploitation and/or "knowingly embedding words or digital images into the source code of a website with the intent to deceive a person into viewing material constituting obscenity" (Public Law 109-248, 2006, p. 648). The law requires more extensive information for registration and a felony offense of up to 20 years for failure to register as a sex offender. SORNA also requires a three-tiered system to classify sex offenders.

SORNA requires retroactivation for sex offenders convicted of any sexual offense before SORNA became law. Juveniles as young as 14 years of age who have been convicted of a sexual offense as an adult are also placed on the registry. SORNA also requires that states be in compliance with federal laws or risk losing federal money.

HOW THE CURRENT SYSTEM WORKS

It is important for all agency professionals to have a protocol in place that quickly identifies possible sex offenders or an allegation of sexual abuse, to reduce the number of victims assaulted by an offender.

Child Sexual Abuse

For child sexual abuse the initial child abuse report is routinely filed with the local department of human or social services. Child protection service workers will evaluate the complaint and then determine whether an investigation should be conducted. Often, social service departments are among the first agencies contacted.

Child abuse complaints may come from a variety of sources including family members, neighbors, or other acquaintances. Other reports or complaints may be filed by physicians, nurses, school teachers, guidance counselors, and mental health workers prompted, in part, by duty-to-report laws.

Cumming and McGrath (2005) note that most social service agencies have an established policy for the investigation of child sexual abuse allegations. A child protective service (CPS) worker or other similarly titled professional is assigned to investigate the report. A CPS worker will inform law enforcement officers, the district prosecuting attorney, and the child sexual abuse team (if one exists in that locality) of the complaint. Some children found to be at risk may need to be removed from the home; a CPS worker usually coordinates this process. In cases where the allegation is found to be serious and perhaps life-threatening a police officer may be asked to accompany the CPS worker to the residence. An officer may remain active in the case.

Cumming and McGrath (2005) also note that in the sexual abuse complaints of a child the primary role of the law enforcement officer is to prevent additional incidents of harm and to provide protection if necessary. The officer is also expected to investigate the allegation for possible criminal prosecution, gather evidence, and notify the prosecuting or district attorney of the incident. Referrals of child sexual abuse to police departments usually come from CPS workers. Police and CPS workers share the responsibility of arranging the investigation and may conduct joint interviews. In the event that the complaint is filed first with law enforcement, police officers are responsible for notifying social services of an allegation. Police officers must establish probable cause of a criminal offense to take action. Cooperation with other agencies is important. Such agencies may include the District Attorney's office, hospital, probation department, mental health center, and local school.

Adult Sexual Abuse

An adult victim reports sexual assault to the police. A sexual assault team or special victims unit is summoned to make contact with the victim. Adult protection services (APS) may become involved in cases in which the victim may not be legally competent or has a mental illness. Victims often are in shock, appear disoriented, and are confused. To avoid additional trauma many law enforcement departments assign male and female teams or have access to a rape counselor for assistance. In some cases adult sexual assault cases are first encountered by health care professionals.

General Procedures

All reported victims are referred to a physician for a medical examination. Most hospital staff are well versed in rape and sexual assault situations. A chain of custody of any medical evidence is required. The physician will attempt to establish the possibility of sexual abuse, diagnose, and treat the victim. The medical examination should occur as soon as possible after the report.

The District Attorney (DA) is responsible for the possible prosecution of the sex offender and the protection of the child or adult victim. Most DAs work closely with CPS and APS workers and police officers during the investigation of a sexual abuse complaint. A DA well versed in sex crimes may meet with members of a sexual assault team and the victim several times during an investigation. Evidence is reviewed; potential witnesses are interviewed if an arrest is expected.

Sex offenders usually elect by this point (if they have not already done so) to engage the services of a defense attorney. In some situations an offender will employ an attorney during the interview and investigation stage, prior to the filing of a possible arrest warrant. This is a difficult time for both the victim and the offender. Stress levels during this period can be exceptionally high. Most offenders will initially deny the offense, display defense behaviors that connote innocence, and be the image of a law-abiding citizen. Professionals associated with the investigation process may be confronted with a number of behaviors including anger, attack, denial, minimization, personalization, rage, and rationalization.

Some offenders will blame the victim; others will attempt to organize family and friends in an effort to protect their welfare. Victims may sometimes be exposed to the offender's denial of the incident. Both offender and victims often will display fear and withdrawal during this period. Some victims will become confused, blame themselves, and may recant their testimony. Offenders will sometimes attempt to threaten or manipulate victims or withhold information about the crime from the police. Police officers should carefully limit the offender's access to the victim during the investigation process.

Commonly, the last individual to be interviewed in a sexual abuse complaint is the sex offender; this is a part of most agencies' protocol when investigating sexual abuse situations. All available information should be obtained before confronting the offender. An informal meeting may be agreed upon with the suspect. The DA is consulted prior to such a session.

In child abuse cases, after the interview and related investigation, the human service agency will then rule if the complaint is founded, if there is reason to suspect, or if the allegation is unfounded. The working of these rulings varies by state. Evidence indicating a founded ruling results in the case being referred to law enforcement for a criminal investigation and potential criminal prosecution. During this period the situation usually increases in intensity; if the child is believed to be in danger, his or her safety may be evaluated. Law enforcement officers will continue to gather information and share their findings with the district or prosecuting attorney.

An arrest warrant may be filed against the offender if law enforcement officers believe there is sufficient evidence. The offender is then formally arrested and can be incarcerated. A bail or bond hearing or arraignment is then held, depending upon the laws of the particular locality; the suspect may be released pending a court hearing.

Child and adult victims are often referred to mental health professionals for treatment services after an allegation of sexual assault. A variety of behaviors may be exhibited by the victim. Victims might not seek out therapy until after the shock of the event has subsided. Some victims might seek out clinical services immediately; others never enter therapy. Child victims are sometimes reluctant to enter treatment. Some may protest or resist help. Mental health professionals who offer clinical services to a victim may expect to be summoned to court to provide testimony. Most courts need to hear the extent of the psychological harm experienced by the victim. Other professionals may be summoned to offer testimony in court regarding sexual assault cases.

Criminal Justice System Involvement

In most states an arraignment is usually held after the arrest. During this process the arrest warrant is reviewed with the defendant. In cases in which the accused is unable to obtain the services of an attorney a public defender is appointed by the court. A DA will usually request that the offender not be permitted to have contact with the victim. In cases where the victim is a child and a family member is the suspect, the DA may ask the court to order the accused out of the home. In emergency situations a child may be taken into temporary custody and placed in a foster home.

A court hearing is scheduled for the defendant. In many cases the offender has been released from jail prior to the hearing. This situation is fairly commonplace across the United States as the result of crowded court dockets, scheduling of witnesses, and the particular nuances of sex cases. Unfortunately, this can be extremely difficult emotionally for the victim and his or her family and sometimes impairs testimony.

Initially, a lower court will hear a case involving a sexual abuse complaint. Child sexual abuse cases are first heard in a family court before a judge; the courtroom is closed and the public cannot attend the proceedings. Adult sexual crime offenses are referred to a general or district court.

These courts are open to the public unless the presiding judge requests that the hearing be closed. Witnesses may be asked to remain outside of the courtroom until their testimony is required. Many lower courts do not keep a record of testimony unless requested.

Both the prosecution and defense are permitted to present witnesses. Usual witnesses may include the CPS or APS worker, police officer, physician, mental health professional, and other collateral witnesses. Family members, friends, co-workers, and possible witnesses to the crime may also be summoned to testify. Both the victim and the accused offender are permitted to present information. A lower court proceeding tends to be informal and permits attorneys, offenders, victims, and witnesses a certain amount of latitude in an effort to present evidence for an adjudication or finding. Most courts will permit child and adult victims to be questioned in detail but are careful that the behavior of counsel is not overly harmful to any party. The defendant is usually questioned at length, unless he or she declines to offer testimony. A victim's prior sexual history is not allowed to be addressed in court proceedings in most states.

Sentencing

In the event that the case is adjudicated and a guilty verdict is found, sentencing sometimes may be withheld pending additional information. The court may order an evaluation of the offender by a mental health professional. A report by a probation officer may also be requested. Misdemeanor sex crime cases may be resolved by the lower court. Some felony offenses are reduced to a misdemeanor or are plea bargained to a lesser charge by the prosecuting attorney and defense counsel. Offenders may be sentenced to jail or committed to an inpatient psychiatric hospital for treatment. Others may be placed on probation with a suspended jail sentence and ordered to attend outpatient therapy. Court fines, court costs, and victim restitution may be requested. An offender has the right to appeal a sentence which is then referred to a higher court.

A felony offense is referred to a higher court for final adjudication and sentencing. These venues include a judge and a jury, if requested; they are considered to be courts of record, with all testimony transcribed or recorded in some fashion. Most higher courts are in session for several months at a time, with a prospective list of possible jurors. Higher courts are more formal in their proceedings. Again, all witnesses, the victim, and the offender are summoned to reappear to offer testimony. Sentencing is usually more severe for a felony. Incarceration is usually ordered. However, in certain cases only probation supervision is requested. A presentence report by a probation officer may be ordered. Mental health evaluations are sometimes sought. Final adjudication can include treatment on an inpatient or outpatient basis by the court. An offender can be committed to a psychiatric facility. Federal and state laws will affect the type of sentencing imposed.

Sex Offender Incarceration

Normally, sex offenders who are incarcerated will be referred first to a type of holding center for an assessment before placement in a correctional facility. Staff evaluate each new inmate for placement. Eventually, the offender is placed in a correctional institution. Some states offer treatment for sexual offenders during incarceration. Other correctional facilities possess only limited services and prefer that clinical treatment options be managed by mental health providers after parole occurs. Some states place sex offenders at specialized facilities.

Parole expectations for sex offenders have changed. Several states now request sex offenders to attend treatment programs while in prison. Early release may be used as an incentive. Offenders who do not volunteer to participate in treatment programs usually are required to complete their full sentence. Many sex offenders are now serving all or most of their complete sentence as the result of changes in parole standards. Sex offenders who are paroled are referred to probation and parole departments for follow-up services. Parole conditions may include a mandate that the offender participate in a sex offender treatment program. Offenders who resist treatment services may be returned to prison.

Certain offenders who have completed their prison sentence are now being committed involuntarily to state psychiatric hospitals for a period of time. Such offenders are viewed as dangerous and a risk to the community. This form of treatment is still being debated. A review hearing is required on a regular basis. Discharge is dependent upon the individual's clinical status.

SUMMARY

Sex offenders are a growing patient population group in the United States and across the globe. Criminal justice, human services, and mental health professionals have found themselves on the front line in treating this growing patient population group. Research shows that sex offenders have a lower risk to reoffend compared to the general criminal population group.

CHAPTER 5

SEX OFFENDER CHARACTERISTICS

RUDA FLORA
MICHAEL L. KEOHANE

OVERVIEW

Sex offenders are found to cross all diagnostic and demographic groupings. Such individuals may be family members, neighbors, or acquaintances rather than strangers to the victims. Age, race, gender, employment status, income, religious affiliation, sexual preference, and criminal history may not always serve as possible variables in assessing sexual deviancy. Whitaker and Wodarski (1989) correctly point out that the general consensus of the mental health community is that sex offenders do not form a homogeneous group; they are a combined heterogeneous population of several groups of persons, each of whom represents some type of abnormal sexual behavior which is harmful to another person.

Clinically, this assessment is attractive, but the premise sometimes impairs and often confuses professionals in criminal justice, human service, and health care in assessment, intervention, and treatment program modality development. Sexual disorders, like any clinical problem such as substance abuse or a thought disorder, possess many subgroups or specific problem features.

Research is beginning to identify certain behaviors that can be directly correlated with a particular sexual disturbance. As with most problems, when sexual disorders are examined closely in a scientific context, they tend to lose a certain amount of their mystery. More material is expected to surface as further study occurs with sex offenders.

However, current evidence supports that certain basic characteristics or behaviors may be found in sex offenders as a group. These generalizations appear worthy of examination and review.

SEX OFFENDERS VIOLATE LAWS

First, sex offenders share one very important characteristic: they have committed a sexual act that violates law. Sexual offending is a criminal action that interferes with the rights of another. The victim of the offense was found to be unwilling or was incapable due to age or mental capacity to provide consent at the time of the event.

Offenders are usually first identified by the type of sexual crimes they have committed. Crime classifications, depending upon the offense, may range from covert and nonphysical behaviors to severe forms of sexual assault.

Sexual incidents involving children, forcible rape, or exhibitionistic acts are examples of actions that well exceed accepted forms of appropriate sexual conduct and are considered violations of law. Some offenders who commit highly visible crimes are quickly arrested; others avoid apprehension for years. Unfortunately, there are some sexual offenders that avoid disclosure indefinitely. Most sexual offenders have committed multiple crimes prior to their first arrest (English, Jones, Pasini-Hill, Patrick & Cooley-Towell, 2000).

Knopp (1984) emphasizes that the criminal justice system occupies a significant role in who is determined to have committed a sexual crime and how they are processed through the system. This method can differ dramatically in law from state to state as to who is arrested, prosecuted, incarcerated, or referred to treatment services.

Social and cultural attitudes can influence a society's tolerance level for certain types of sexual behaviors and whether they are considered a criminal offense. An example of this mixed message is reflected by the age of consent to marry. Certain states permit minors to marry, while other states restrict marriages with an age limitation and consider consensual sexual relations between a minor and an adult to be unlawful.

SEX OFFENDERS AS A VISIBLE AND GROWING POPULATION

Second, sex offenders are a visible and growing population. As noted in Chapter 3, about 234,000 sex offenders are in some type of correctional care at any given time (Greenfeld, 1997). These figures do not account for offenders who have been released from prison, those who are on probation or parole, or those who have escaped prosecution. Using a conservative measurement, during the next decade the criminal justice system can expect to provide services for more than 2 million sex offenders. Also, the sex offender population is growing at a rapid rate within the penal system. Most states indicate that 10% to 20% of their prison population is sex offenders, while some states estimate as many as 28% are sex offenders (Velázquez, 2008). Such an increase in itself may not present concern; however, when considering that each one of these offenders may have harmed multiple victims, the proper perspective is given to community safety and the protection of future victims.

A SEXUAL OFFENSE CHAIN

A sexual offense chain displays common behaviors exhibited by offenders in periods before, during, and after an offense. Such information is helpful when working with a sex offender. A number of excellent diagrams have evolved through the years outlining possible sexual abuse cycles or scenarios. One such model is by Eccles and Marshall (1999). Based on the relapse prevention and cognitive behavioral diagrams, an offense chain for sexual offenders is summarized as follows:

1. There is an offense-free mood state.
2. An event occurs in some form and several possible incidents happen, such as seeing oneself as a victim.
3. There is a feeling of entitlement or right to sexual pleasure; the individual starts to regress.
4. Positive thoughts about offending are found.
5. High-risk behaviors and deviant fantasies begin.
6. Cognitively distorted thinking is reported (e.g. a woman deserves to be raped, a child is sexually provocative).
7. The individual makes victim contact and enters a cognitively distorted mood state.
8. He or she sexually offends a victim.
9. The offender engages in qualification and rationalization of the crime.

THE SEX OFFENDER PSYCHOLOGICAL PROFILE

Sex Offenders are Different

O'Connell *et al.* (1990) reported that sex offenders are different from other types of psychotherapy patients. Most people who enter therapy do so to resolve a problem or conflict that is impairing them in some manner. Such individuals are motivated to receive treatment services. However, most sex offenders do not seek help on a voluntary basis; instead they enter therapy as the result of an external stimulus, such as a ruling from the court or probation officer, the fear of incarceration, or the opportunity for parole. It is extremely rare for a sex offender to reveal his or her deviancy voluntarily without outside pressures. Many sex offenders do not see themselves as being a danger to others. They often report during interviews that they had no plan to harm children and that it "just happened." Sex offenders will attempt to hide behind the trappings of their family, job, and position within the local community. Some offenders distort reality to the extent that they themselves begin to believe that the offense did not occur.

Sex Offenders Possess Multiple Paraphilias

Research has found that most sex offenders possess multiple paraphiliac behaviors. Abel *et al.* (1988) found that only around 10% of paraphilia-disordered individuals had one diagnosis; most were afflicted by two or more paraphilias. This information is helpful for the mental health professional who has been asked to complete an evaluation of an offender.

Many sexual offenders can possess a passive-like disorder, such as a fetish, that does not directly lead to a situation of assault. However, this same individual may also suffer from pedophilia and will sexually molest children. Such an individual, for example, may use children's underwear, taken during a prior offense, as part of a fantasy and masturbation process. However, the pedophile's urge to reoffend will grow as the fantasy diminishes. Another victim is then selected and seduced in some fashion by the offender. To enrich the continuation of the fantasy process, the new victim's underwear is taken by the offender.

Sex Offenders and Onset

The majority of reported paraphilia disturbances are said to have started during childhood or adolescence. Reportedly more than 50% of all paraphilias, regardless of diagnostic category, began before age 18 (Sadock & Sadock, 2007a).

A significant psychosocial stressor may have occurred during the offender's childhood. This event may have been extremely traumatic for the offender, regardless of the relative severity. The offender may have been sexually abused as a child, accidentally witnessed a couple engaged in sexual intercourse or inappropriate sexual boundaries between parents, or experienced an erotic experience that is sexually deviant such as finding a magazine that displays women in a degrading and abusive manner.

The fantasies and behaviors associated with paraphilias may have their beginnings in childhood, but they become more defined and elaborate during adolescence and early adulthood. The reenactment of fantasies will become even more advanced in adulthood and may last over the course of an individual's lifetime (American Psychiatric Association, 2000).

Sex Offenders as Victims

Research continues to reveal that some offenders have experienced sexual trauma in some form during their formative years. In early studies, Groth (1990) noted that approximately one-third of rapists and child molesters had experienced some type of sexual trauma as a child. However, it was suspected that this number was rather conservative.

A survey conducted by Greenberg, Bradford, and Curry (1993) found that more than 40% of pedophiles and hebephiles had been victims of childhood sexual abuse. Most practicing clinicians have long suspected a connection between childhood sexual abuse and sex offending. The offender's crimes may be viewed as a form of reenactment of his or her own sexual abuse. However, there continues to be some disagreement among researchers as to the magnitude of this problem. The validity of offenders presenting accurate or misleading information is a concern. The percentage of those sex offenders who were also victims of sexual abuse is expected to continue to be a subject of debate. A number of sex offenders have experienced emotional and physical abuse. Additional studies are merited.

Education and Employment

Many sex offenders are well-educated and gainfully employed. In one study of 561 sex offenders, approximately 26% had graduated from high school, around 27% had attended one year of college, over 12% had graduated from college, and close to 8% had finished graduate school. Also, this same study found almost 65% were fully employed or attending school. Only around 9% of survey respondents were temporarily unemployed (Abel *et al.*, 1987).

Such findings are contrary to the stereotypes that have emerged regarding sex offenders. The image of a sex offender who is unemployed, has little education, and is socially impaired appears to be unfounded by clinical study results.

Sex Offenders and Relationships

Professionals should be careful about making hasty assessments involving sex offenders and relationships. A number of offenders are either married or involved in a serious relationship with an adult companion, challenging former stereotypes of sex offenders being rather disheveled and unable to form relationships with an adult partner. A sex offender with a paraphilia disturbance may seem a paradox.

During a survey in 1987 approximately 50% of all sex offenders interviewed (n=561) were found to be married or involved in a significant relationship (Abel *et al.*, 1987). All sexual offenses were represented in this study of offenders, including such clinical disturbances as exhibitionism, fetishism, frotteurism, pedophilia, sexual masochism, sexual sadism, transvestic fetishism, voyeurism, other paraphilias, and those with a history of rape.

Victim Empathy

Groth (1990) has reported that the rapist's most prominent defect is the absence of any close, emotionally intimate relationships with another person. Such impaired individuals show little capacity for warmth, trust, compassion, or empathy.

Hildebran and Pithers (1989) noted that sex offenders tend to display resistance even to developing victim empathy. Two factors are found to be significant to this phenomenon. First, the sex offenders are reluctant to stop fantasies that have been a source of pleasure for a number of years. Second, offenders may be seen as emotionally underdeveloped individuals.

O'Connell *et al.* (1990) have reported that it is rare to find a sex offender who initially displays empathy for his or her victim. Most therapists consider victim empathy a key element in the treatment process of sex offenders. Individuals who are unable to develop empathy remain at risk to reoffend. However, the prospect of developing empathy can also trigger fear, humiliation, and shame in many sex offenders, which are similar feelings that the offenders created in their victims. Learning empathy, therefore, can be a rather frightening or difficult experience for an offender.

Truthfulness and Honesty

Most criminal justice, human service, and mental health professionals cite the tendency to be dishonest as a typical behavior found among sex offenders.

O'Connell *et al.* (1990) has reported that sexual offenders are not usually willing to reveal information about their deviant actions. Such individuals have developed a set of defense mechanisms with which they will hide the truth and have become extremely adept at concealing information. It is rare for sexual offenders to report their sexual abuse of others voluntarily. Naturally, many fear their actions will lead to involvement with the criminal justice system. Offenders fear intervention, prosecution, and incarceration; others express social, familial, and occupational concerns.

Equally important during the treatment process is the need for an offender to be honest about his or her behavior. A treatment program is dependent upon offenders developing honesty with themselves and others. Many sex offenders have spent years lying to and misleading others. As a result, such individuals are also dishonest with themselves. Some will display this behavior by lying about an incident that could result in a reoffending situation. An offender who clings to denial and continues to be dishonest about their crime is not only delaying their own treatment progress, but also discredits the victim (English, Pullen, & Jones, as cited in Vanhoeck & Daele, 2011).

Acknowledgment and Responsibility

Almost all sex offenders will display a reluctance to acknowledge that an act of sexual abuse occurred. This should not be confused with the above category of truthfulness.

O'Connell *et al.* (1990) have reported that the offender's reluctance to acknowledge the offense is a defense mechanism used to avoid admitting that a criminal sexual act did occur. Offenders are typically resistant to acknowledging the full nature and extent of the deviant behavior. However, treatment can begin only when the sex offender is willing to acknowledge that a sexual offense occurred. Treatment should center on the offender's admission that (1) the problem is related to his or her behavior, (2) it has caused the victim harm, and (3) he or she gave permission to him- or herself to offend.

Offenders who are unwilling to acknowledge their behavior cannot be successfully treated. As with most disorders, the patient must first accept the illness in order to begin recovery. A patient who denies a clinical disturbance possesses a poor prognosis for recovery. The responsibility for the offense belongs to the offender (Vanhoeck & Daele, 2011). Accepting responsibility for behavior is an important element when working with sex offenders. The offender may acknowledge the sexual event but qualify his or her behavior by blaming the victim. An example would be offenders who complain that their abuse was produced by the provocative clothing worn by the victim.

Denial, Minimization, and Depersonalization

Denial, minimization, and depersonalization are three behaviors that a therapist should be alert to when treating a sex offender (Schneider & Wright, 2004). These behaviors are part of the defense mechanism system and should be viewed separately from the section on acknowledgment.

However, like acknowledgment, sex offenders who deny their offenses are not likely to benefit from therapy. An offender must admit to the offense in order to benefit from treatment services (O'Connell *et al.*, 1990). Research completed by Hanson (as cited in Vanhoeck & Daele, 2011) looking at subgroups of sex offenders who used denial, found that incest offenders who denied their offense had a sexual recidivism rate that was three times higher than incest offenders who admitted their offense.

An offender who minimizes or gives only token acknowledgment of the crime(s) will be difficult to treat. Offenders who occasionally justify, excuse, or rationalize their behavior can be used to an advantage in a treatment setting: such offenders are at least admitting that a sexual offense did occur. However, such behavior, if not resolved, will impair the treatment and the offender will remain at risk to reoffend.

As noted above, offenders who deny that a sex offense has occurred are at risk to reoffend if permitted to remain in the community. A more controlled environment may be more appropriate for such offenders. Incarceration should also be a consideration.

Defense Reactions

Lanning (2010) has noted that pedophiles will display several predictable behaviors when confronted about an abuse case. These reactions include: denial; minimization; justification; fabrication; sympathy; attack; guilty, but not guilty, after conviction; and suicide. They are, in part, as follows:

- *Denial*—Typically, a sex offender first denies the allegation and may appear astonished, confused, shocked, or even angry about the report. Family, friends, co-workers, or others may be used to avoid arrest.
- *Minimization*—An offender may attempt to rationalize or minimize the assault when the evidence against him or her rules out denial. The type of crime and number of offenses may be distorted.
- *Justification*—Child offenders will develop a rationalization system and believe that their behavior is misunderstood and that they are moral, caring persons.
- *Fabrication*—Some offenders invent stories to explain their behavior in an effort to hide the sexual abuse. Fabrication may include such reports as conducting a scientific study on children or teaching a child about sex.

- *Sympathy*—Offenders using this defense technique will display regret while noting their familial, civic, and community achievements and their own unrelated personal problems.
- *Attack*—The offender may develop a defense plan that includes a personal attack as an offense. A pedophile, for instance, may harass, threaten, or even bribe victims and witnesses, while attacking the reputations of the case professionals.
- *After conviction "cooperation"*—New information may be offered by a child offender (as another form of reaction) to law enforcement officers after a conviction regarding other molesters and crimes involving children. Law enforcement should be wary of the motives behind such spontaneous and free information. A polygraph test may be appropriate to ensure that the information is valid to minimize the amount of valuable law enforcement resources that are wasted.
- *Suicide*—A serious reaction in certain cases involving middle-class offenders is the risk of suicide attempt at any time after the arrest or court hearing.

It is important that the offender move from denial to acknowledgment, truthfulness, and eventually victim empathy; however, this progress should not be expected immediately in therapy. In fact, in treatment the therapist can expect that most offenders will only let go of the denial when there is no internal motivation to embrace it any longer. However, Langton *et al.* (as cited in Vanhoeck & Daele, 2011) found that if the offender continues to use denial throughout the length of treatment group, then high-risk offenders are potentially at a higher risk for sexual recidivism "because the underlying cognitive schemas and processes that produced them remain, neither monitored nor challenged by the offender when they arise later with unfolding offense chains" (p. 362).

Schneider and Wright (2004) have indicated that offender denial and accountability are linked and are two areas that the therapist should focus on as treatment goals rather than to treat the denial and lack of accountability as obstacles.

In relation to the offender's denial and lack of accountability, Schneider and Wright (2004) have further suggested that:

> Determining whether offenders' biased explanations stem from preexisting beliefs, self-serving information-gathering strategies, or justifications after the fact may be of less consequence than recognizing that effective interventions require a therapeutic approach to evaluating these explanations in order to find ways to change them. Even if we know that an offender is intentionally misrepresenting certain facts, understanding the lie from the perspective of the offender may be essential to developing strategies to modify it. (p. 16)

Additionally, Lord and Wilmot (as cited in Vanhoeck & Daele, 2011) conducted in-depth interviews with sex offenders who had once denied committing a sexual offense, but were willing to look back and discuss the reason behind the denial. Their research narrowed the results to three categories of deniers: motivational, intrinsic, and external.

Motivational deniers do not want to stop offending. This type of denier hopes that the denial will assist them to get away with the crime, so that they can actively pursue re-offending. Intrinsic deniers suffer from low self-esteem, no ego-strength, and little self-awareness and are afraid of being seen in a negative light. External deniers are more concerned of being held accountable for their offense and what other people will think of them if they find out about the offense that was committed (Lord & Wilmot, as cited in Vanhoeck & Daele, 2011).

OTHER BEHAVIORAL CHARACTERISTICS

A number of other behavioral characteristics in sex offenders are noted by the clinical and research community. These are as follows:

- Sex offenders usually possess a very rich fantasy life. Masturbation is usually reported as a part of the offender's sexual activity. Nearly all sexual offenders in treatment report being sexually aroused by fantasies of their current or past deviant activities, which they reenact during masturbation (Abel, 1989).
- Sex offenders evolve or graduate in their style of sexual aggression. Paraphiliac behavior is found to be pleasurable and is likely to be repeated if no consequence occurs (Abel, 1989).
- Sex offenders who possess a history of substance abuse are more likely to offend when using alcohol or drugs. More than 40% of rapists have substance abuse problems (Groth, 1990).
- Typically, sex offenders derive some pleasure from their sexual deviancy. Many have developed impaired forms of sexual expression that are a part of their lifestyle and commit acts of abuse because it makes them feel good (O'Connell *et al.*, 1990).
- Adult and child offenders display a lack of insight and judgment. Often they are unable to understand the full harm and consequence of their sexual aggression (Groth, 1990).
- Approximately 56% of all rapists in one survey were found to have some type of personality disorder (Groth, 1990).
- Rapists sometimes display problems with impulse control and a distorted belief system as well as a need for instant self-gratification (Groth, 1990).
- Sex offenders, including rapists, often view persons as objects, which is a form of depersonalization (Groth, 1990).
- Sex offenders (paraphiliacs) are usually male (Abel, 1989); women sex offenders are an increasing clinical population (Cortoni & Gannon, 2011; Duncan, 2010; Ford, 2010; Mayer, 1992).
- Rapists often display a pattern of reckless behavior as their deviancy progresses. Many fail to consider the consequences of their actions and will act many times without thinking (Groth, 1990).

- Sex offenders possess histories of disordered family systems. In general, the more dysfunctional the childhood experience, the more severe or problematic the paraphilia (Meyer, 1995).
- Sex offenders who experience a reduction in their testosterone levels can display improved behaviors with less acting out (Meyer, 1995).

SUMMARY

As indicated in this chapter and throughout this book, sex offenders come from all walks of life. However, all sex offenders share two commonalities: they create or take part in creating victims and they are a growing population. In addition, sex offenders share other behavioral characteristics that make it difficult for them to accept personal responsibility and demonstrate any type of victim empathy. In fact, most people convicted of sex offenses will often not come forward to seek help until after they are convicted. In most cases patients continue to need external motivations (court orders or probation rules) to enter treatment.

It is important to understand that sex offenders have used various defense mechanisms to create victims or to continue to engage in sexual offending behaviors. At times offenders may confess all that he or she has done; but most often, offenders will only divulge information that he or she thinks the professional is already aware of. It is only after they have fully admitted to what they have done and begin to accept responsibility that treatment can begin.

CHAPTER 6

FEMALE SEX OFFENDERS

RUDA FLORA

MICHAEL L. KEOHANE

OVERVIEW

Mary Kay Letourneau is a name that exploded onto the media landscape and into public dialogue in the late 1990s. Letourneau was a 34-year-old middle school teacher, wife, and mother of four children. Her victim was a 13-year-old student in a sixth-grade class where she taught. After a process of grooming/seducing, the relations between the two turned sexual. There are some people, then and now, who believed that a 13-year-old young man that has sexual intercourse with an older woman is developing "experience" and that the boy was "lucky"; however, these same people would probably not have the same view if it had been a 34-year-old man and a 13-year-old girl that engaged in sexual intercourse.

Studies on female sex offenders have been sparse and until recently the research community was divided on the likelihood of women committing offenses that were sexually motivated (Cortoni, 2010). Some researchers believed that it was impossible while others believed that the prevalence of sexually motivated offenses by women was and is underreported (Cortoni, 2010; Cortoni, Hanson, & Coache, 2010).

Criminal justice, human service, and mental health professionals have begun to acknowledge the existence of female offenders as a special population group. It is important to note that the female sex offender as a population is not a new phenomenon, but that this population is starting to become more recognized (Cortoni *et al.*, 2010; Ford, 2009; Poels, 2007). In the past, female perpetrators were underreported, hampering intervention services by system providers. In one report of victims, 5% of girls and 20% of boys had been sexually abused in some form by women (Mayer, 1992; Finkelhor & Williams, 1988).

Cortoni *et al.* (2010) looked at police and court records as well as victim surveys of women who were involved in sexual offenses in several different countries (Australia, Canada, New Zealand, the United Kingdom, and the United States). The results indicated that 4% to 5% of all sexual offenses are committed by females, suggesting that the ratio of females to males who sexually offend is 1 to 20.

Factors influencing the low reporting of female offenders include the following: females may conceal sexually deviant actions through socially appropriate behaviors; female offenders who commit incest are reported less than those who violate others in a sexual manner outside of the family; and boys sexually abused by adult women are reluctant to report an offense (Mayer, 1992).

Also, Mayer (1992) has reported that societal standards differ for men and women. Males are socialized to express aggression and to sexualize their feelings of rage and impotence. Females are perceived as vulnerable individuals who are incapable of harming others. It was thought that women could not sexualize relationships, eroticize anger, or associate power and control with sexual needs.

Culturally, females are stereotyped as physically and psychologically incapable of committing acts of sexual abuse. Due to the misinformation about female sex offenders, children who report that sexual abuse happened at the hands of a female may not be taken as seriously as those reporting sexual abuse against them by a male (Hislop, 2001). However, Logan (2008), in addressing this fallacy has said, "Women can and do sexually abuse—children, young people, and adults—and just because a woman does not have a penis, her potential to significantly harm is not reduced" (p. 499).

An example of the damage that can be inflicted by female sexual offenders on their victims can be found in a comprehensive study completed by Rosencrans (as cited in Duncan, 2010). This study looked at 93 women and nine men who were sexually abused as children by their mothers. In addition to the emotional and psychological trauma that was caused by this maternal incest, physical damage was also caused. Below is a list of some of the items that these women used to penetrate their victims:

- Enema devices
- Sticks
- Candles
- Vibrators
- Pencils
- Keys
- Hairbrush handles
- Light bulbs
- Knives
- Goldfish

- Lit cigarettes
- Scissors
- Religious medals
- Bottles
- Surgical knives
- Barbie dolls.

Denov (as cited in Saradjian, 2010) observed that before 1983 the Canadian Crime Classification code did not allow for a woman to be charged with rape or indecent assault nor could a male be the victim of such an offense. In some countries this gender-specific enigma of only males being offenders and only females being victims still exists (Saradjian, 2010; Hislop, 2001). This double standard has carried over to female sex offenders.

However, this view is now starting to change. Various global studies, as discussed in Duncan (2010), indicated women do commit an extensive array of sexual offenses across different cultures and societies.

A study completed in South Africa by Andersson and Ho-Foster (as cited in Duncan, 2010) surveyed more than 126,000 boys across 1,191 schools and nine provinces. The survey identified over 13,000 boys as having experienced forced sex during the year the survey was completed. Results found that the sexual assaults happened while they were at school and that women were predominantly the perpetrators of the sexual offenses. In fact, the boys in the study reported that women accounted for 42% of the sexual offenses; males were linked to 32% and the boys reported that they were sexually assaulted by both males and females 27% of the time.

Although fewer in numbers, women sexual offenders still have devastating effects on their victims. Ramsey-Klawsnik (as cited by Hislop, 2002) discussed that children of both genders that were sexually abused by females demonstrated a variety of emotional and behavioral problems to include nightmares, regressed behaviors, sexualized behaviors, or even preoccupation with death.

In the Rosencrans study (as cited in Hislop, 2002) 44% of 93 women who had been sexually molested as children by their mothers reported that it was the most damaging experience of their life. In fact, no one in the study reported that the experience hadn't been at least somewhat damaging.

SOME CLINICAL FEATURES

Current data indicate that women as sex offenders are increasing as a clinical population (Cortoni & Gannon, 2011; Duncan, 2010; Saradjian, 2010, Hislop, 2001). A large number of offenses involve same-sex molestation situations. Sometimes female molesters are coerced by their adult partners into committing a sexual offense against a victim. Many times the female molester has parental rights over the victim.

There are both similarities and differences between female and male sex offenders. Such factors may include how defense mechanisms are displayed, power and control issues, victims as objects, and histories of sexual victimization during childhood (Mayer, 1992).

Kaufman, Wallace, Johnson, and Reeder (as cited by Duncan, 2010) completed a research study comparing the offending patterns between 53 children sexually abused by women and 53 male children sexually abused by men. The study found that both male and female offenders sexually abused their victims in the same way (fondling, sexual contact without penetration, and oral copulation). However, the study found that the female offenders were more likely to penetrate their victim(s) with various items, allow other adults to abuse the victim(s), and force sexual acts between children and teenagers.

Male and female offenders share a common clinical theme in their role of power over a victim. This dynamic is significant in the sexual abuse. Women as well as men are influenced by the psychological or physical hold they may possess over a victim. The use of control and manipulation are themes that are found in female offenders.

Research compiled by Poels (2007) indicated that at least 15% of female sexual offenders would meet the Psychopathy Checklist–Revised (PCL–R) criteria for psychopathy and these women have a higher rate for recidivism than female sex offenders who don't meet these criteria. However, the PCL–R, like other clinical tools used to assess female sexual offenders, has come under scrutiny due to factors that are different between the genders (Poels, 2007).

Female offenders may be more likely to have a history of sexual abuse or other significant trauma than male offenders. Males are more likely to treat their victims as an object, rather than as a person, than a female offender. Women are much more likely to have a shared relationship with the victim. Anger, if present, is expressed in a different form in female offenders when compared to males. Female offenders tend to internalize their anger, as compared to male offenders, who externalize emotions. Sadism is extremely rare. Defense mechanisms for female offenders may also include devaluation of self, displacement, dissociation, isolation, repression, and undoing (Duncan, 2010; Matthews, 1998).

There are some researchers (Duncan 2010; McCarthy, 1986) who have indicated that female offenders may perpetrate the same types of sexual offenses that may have been committed on them as children. Duncan (as cited in Duncan, 2010) has also reported that the sexual trauma that female offenders experienced as children is transferred to self-injurious behaviors that allow them to recreate the same sexual suffering to their bodies due to overwhelming emotional pains of guilt and shame. However, Duncan (2010), speaking specifically about female offenders, has also stated:

> They may be reenacting the sexual offenses committed against them as children onto their child victims but for different reasons and motivations that may include rage or sexual arousal. Additionally, simply because "trauma reenactment" occurs in other victim groups does not mean that female sexual offending is trauma reenactment. (p. 25)

Weizmann-Henelius, Viemero, and Eronen (as cited in Poels, 2007) completed a national sample of 61 violent female sexual offenders in Finland. The results showed that compared to non-offenders the violent offenders reported more issues in their families of origin and more troubling "experiences in both childhood and adulthood, more often psychiatric care, substance abuse problems, a history of attempted suicide, a problematic relationship in the year preceding the index offence, personality disorders, and cognitive deficits" (p. 234).

The recidivism rates for female sexual offenders tend to be much lower than that of male sexual offenders. For example, meta-analysis research completed by Cortoni *et al.* (2010) looked at ten studies and 2,490 female sex offenders for a period of six and a half years. The studies were examined with weighted averages and split into three categories: sexual recidivism estimates, violent recidivism estimates, and any recidivism estimates. In the sexual recidivism analysis, the average recidivism rate for new sexual offenses was 1.5%. Violent recidivism (including sexual) estimates indicated a 9.3% increase and any recidivism rates were averaged at 23.5%.

Compare the above recidivism rates with meta-analysis research completed by Hanson and Morton-Bourgon (2004) among male sexual offenders looking at the same three categories over a five to six year period. Results showed sexual recidivism rates at 13.7%, violent offenses (including sexual) at 25%, and for any type of recidivism at 36.9%. Hanson and Morton-Bourgon (2004) also suggested that the percentages reported "should be considered to underestimate the real recidivism rates because not all offences are detected" (p. 8).

It appears that once female sexual offenders enter the criminal justice system many do not go on to commit additional offenses of any type, especially sexual offenses. Cortoni *et al.* (2010) stressed that "most female sexual offenders are not convicted of any new crimes, and of those who are, they are 10 times more likely to be convicted for a nonsexual crime than a sexual crime" (p. 396).

FEMALE OFFENDER TYPES

There are various typologies for male offenders that have been developed and empirically tested, but these typologies are limited in empirical data for female offenders. The typologies to describe female sexual offenders, however, are extremely important in assisting the clinicians that work with this population (Harris, 2010). It should be said at the outset that by no means should a clinician attempt to treat a female offender primarily by a typology. No typology will be able to fully measure the heterogeneous nature of any population; however, there are currently many gaps in the literature and a typology may be a useful tool.

Typologies are important in that they place offenders into subgroups based on offender characteristics (e.g., histories involving substance abuse, child abuse, violence), offense characteristics (e.g., location, motivation, recidivism), and victim type (e.g., age, gender) (Harris, 2010).

Matthews (1998) has noted three types of female offenders: (1) the teacher–lover who becomes involved with a minor male; (2) the predisposed, a victim also, who acts out her molestation with children; and (3) the male-coerced who sexually abuses children with a male companion, either in or out of the home.

The Teacher–Lover Offender

The teacher–lover female offender becomes involved in a relationship with a child as the result of a combination of interactions that eventually leads to a sexual relationship. These encounters usually are not forced; the victim usually becomes supportive of the relationship. The victim's position is raised to adult status and the relationship, although illegal, is considered consenting.

This type of offender may have power over the victim and hold a position of authority in some form. Victims tend to be acquaintances, male, and are preadolescent or adolescent. The initial incident may not be planned, but later actions are organized and scheduled. This subgroup is less likely than any other group to have been sexually abused; however, this subgroup does tend to have experienced more verbal and emotional abuse and may have distant or absent fathers (Harris, 2010). The sexual abuse may be a way of filling this emotional dissonance.

The Predisposed Offender

The predisposed offender may display paraphilia interests. Many of these female offenders have a history of severe victimization themselves. The offending may be seen as a reenactment of their sexual abuse. These women tend to experience chaotic family life as a child, low self-esteem, self-loathing or self-hatred, physical and sexual abuse by a partner as an adult, alcohol and/or drug addiction, extreme distrust of other people, paranoia, suicidality, and deviant sexual fantasies among other tendencies (Matthews, 1998).

The target population is often the offender's own children and the offender tends to act alone. The victim(s) may be male or female. A number of these victims may be female and can be pre-adolescent or adolescent in age. This type of offense is usually preceded by fantasy acting out. Most incidents are planned to some degree and follow a sexual abuse cycle pattern. Force is sometimes reported if the victim is reluctant to comply. In addition to the sexual abuse, victims are often physically and emotionally abused and neglected by the offender (Denov & Cortoni, 2006).

The Male-Coerced Offender

Male-coerced female offenders are involved in a relationship with an adult, either a husband or boyfriend. Substance abuse may be involved during the sexual assault. These female offenders are encouraged by the companion to engage in sexual relations with a child. Usually, the adult male will observe the offense or engage during a part of the sexual assault.

Target victims may be female or male, are preadolescent or adolescent, and can be a family member, acquaintance, or even a stranger. The initial offense can be unplanned by the offender who has been manipulated by the companion.

Additional offenses can be planned or scheduled, with some resistance or reluctance on the part of the female offender. Force and coercion may be used by the adult male companion on the female offender. In fact, the male-coerced female offender is thought to sexually abuse only in the presence of the male companion (Harris, 2010). In further discussing the points of force and coercion used by the male companion, Harris (2010) has stated "the woman is thought to act out of fear of physical punishment or sexual assault at the hands of her partner, or due to extreme emotional dependency on her partner" (p. 35).

The Male-Accompanied Offender

The male-accompanied female sex offender, which is a subgroup of this typology, is believed to be the exact opposite of the male-coerced female offender. Atkins (as cited in Harris, 2010) indicated that the male-accompanied female sex offender appears to be more engaged in the sexual offending and will begin offending independently of her partner in crime.

Duncan (2010) has indicated that the more that is understood about the female sexual offender, the more it appears that the female sexual offender will commit a sexual offense without an accomplice. Ferguson and Meehan (as cited in Duncan, 2010) evaluated case records of 279 female sexual offenders in the state of Florida who were convicted of 940 separate sexual offenses and they found that a little more than 97% of the women in the study acted alone when they committed their sexual offense. The case record analysis also found that 43% of women who were on probation or parole had prior sexual offenses.

TREATMENT

Ford (2009) has reported that traditional research methods employed with men using static (history) and dynamic (psychological) factors to create risk assessment tools don't necessarily work with different sexual offender populations, including females. These assessment tools are being questioned.

Cortoni (2010) has discussed that actuarial tools validated and designed for men to assess their risk of recidivism would be inappropriate to use with women as there are presently not enough empirical data to support them. Also, when looking at static and dynamic risk factors there are differences between the genders that can skew test results and overestimate recidivism rates among female sex offenders (Cortoni *et al.*, 2010). To further bolster this point, Cortoni (2010) has stated that "simply extrapolating from the male sexual offender literature to assess risk in female sexual offenders is likely to lead to invalid risk appraisal and unintended consequences" (p. 163).

Cortoni and Gannon (2011) have discussed various characteristics of female sexual offenders. Much like any other group they are heterogeneous in nature. As a group they tend to be younger than their male counterparts, education tends to be limited, and their socioeconomic status tends to be lower in all categories.

Also, according to the research female sexual offenders tend, as a group, to have a high prevalence of being sexually abused prior to onset of offending behaviors; this can measure as high as 50% to 80% among sample sizes (Cortoni & Gannon, 2011). However, this should never be used to excuse the offending behavior. There should be opportunities in treatment to assess and discuss mitigating circumstances.

As part of any comprehensive assessment for any population, psychiatric concerns should be evaluated when treating female sexual offenders. Most often mood disorders, anxiety disorders, personality disorders, psychotic disorders, and histories of substance, physical, emotional, and sexual abuse are reported in large numbers among female sexual offenders (Rousseau & Cortoni, 2010; Logan, 2008; Ford, 2009).

While holistically treating the female sexual offender is important, the main goal of working with female sexual offenders is to address issues as they pertain to their offending behaviors. Areas related to psychopathology should be addressed as they relate to the offender's life, but distinguished from how these issues are related to the offending behaviors (Rousseau & Cortoni, 2010).

A balance must be struck when working in sexual offender therapy. Too much time given to mental health and prior victimization can offset the responsibility that is required from the patient; too little time would jeopardize not only the treatment, but could also increase potential risk for reoffense. It is important that, in addition to addressing the psychiatric concerns and other important issues, key factors related specifically to the sexual offending behaviors, such as cognitive distortions, problematic relationships and intimacy deficits, and how sexual fantasies played a role in the sexual offense, are also addressed (Rousseau & Cortoni, 2010).

Matthews (1998) has reported that the first stage in providing treatment services for the female offender requires the clinician to see the patient as both a perpetrator and a victim. Both roles are interrelated. To treat only the perpetrator fails to acknowledge the humanity of the offender. To treat only the victim negates the harm the offender has done to another person.

Genuine empathy for the offender's victim cannot be expressed until the patient is able to understand her own emotional pain and destructive behavior. Female offenders have a history of suppressing their feelings. They have forgotten how to articulate their emotions in an appropriate way. Therefore, the natural progress in treatment is to empower the offender in voicing her own emotional pain, which, in turn, acts as a turning point in her recovery process. It is recommended that the patient meet the following therapeutic goals: acknowledge the sexual abuse, accept responsibility, define individual emotional and behavioral factors, address issues of self and their specific offending type, work on victim empathy, develop exit criteria, and develop a prevention and aftercare treatment plan. No female offender should ever be placed in a male group.

THERAPY GOALS

The therapy goals of treatment should be directly related to the type of offending typology that has been identified. A generic form of psychotherapy for all female offenders is not considered suitable.

The Teacher–Lover Offender

Matthews (1998) suggests that in working with the teacher–lover offender the most important goal is to have female offenders recognize the harm they did to another individual. Initially, such offenders report that they are angry because they have been held accountable for their actions while their victims are excused from prosecution. Some female offenders believe that the victim is equally to blame in this type of sexual relationship. Clinicians should help the perpetrators understand how their position of power influenced the sexual abuse of the victim. Also, it is important to help the offender understand that as an adult she was responsible for establishing boundaries. It is also beneficial to educate this type of offender in the developmental stages of a child or adolescent, the problems of role confusion, and sexual identity.

The Predisposed Offender

The predisposed patient presents the most clinically challenging of the three female offender typologies. These individuals have very few coping skills. Their ego functioning is often impaired. The id may contribute to problems of impulse control and sexual acting out. The superego displays many misconceptions regarding appropriate behaviors. Such patients can be provocative and permissive in their interactions with others. This patient is most likely a victim of childhood sexual abuse herself. The family is disengaged, chaotic, and unsupportive.

A primary goal will be to help this offender rebuild her self-confidence. Self-esteem must be elevated in order for the patient to realize that people care for one another. An adult need for validation must be met by other adults rather than by children. An important goal for clinicians with such patients is addressing childhood issues. These offenders may both love and hate their parents, desire but fear an adult partner. They can cling at times, and reject during other periods. Such offenders have difficulty trusting. Paraphiliac behavior will also be represented; offenders will need to explore their fantasy system, masturbatory practices, deviant behaviors, and cycle of offending.

The Male-Coerced Offender

The male-coerced female offender may have first started offending with the assistance or coercion of a male partner. As a result, a primary treatment goal for such patients is to decrease their issues of dependency. Self-esteem is important in the recovery process for this type of offender. Such patients should be helped in psychotherapy to become more independent. These offenders need to learn that they can function without a male partner. Assertiveness training or proper job search skills may be helpful.

The male-coerced offender usually has been involved in an abusive relationship that has eventually led to the sexual abuse of a child. This type of offender fears abandonment and will do almost anything to keep the relationship with her husband or companion intact. Initially, the companion will introduce the female to alternative forms of sexual misconduct, which may include affairs or group sex. Later, the sexual behavior becomes more bizarre, and then a child is introduced and is sexually assaulted.

Individual, Family, and Group Treatment Suggestions

The treatment format for a female sex offender should be given serious consideration before psychotherapy is introduced. Individual, family, and group formats are all considered usable therapy formats for female offenders.

Hollin and Palmer (as cited in Ford, 2009) have recommended caution when assuming that the similar offending behaviors between male and female sexual offenders represent the same type of treatment needs. The authors further point out that "even if common areas of need are identified, the association between that particular need and offending may not be the same for both genders" (p. 477).

Also, Blanchette and Brown (as cited in Ford, 2009) have recommended that clinicians looking at treatment modalities consider utilizing a strength-based approach as it may be a more appropriate addition to a female sexual offender's treatment. This, of course, is not the only treatment approach, but considering that most female sex offenders also have a history of domestic violence or sexual abuse, utilizing an approach that empowers and strengthens the ego and looks at the qualities that the female sex offender does possess will assist in the overall treatment approach. Other types of treatment approaches that would complement the strength-based approach are person-centered therapy, cognitive behavioral, relapse prevention, eye movement desensitization and reprocessing (EMDR) (for trauma), and psychodynamic psychotherapy. Although there is a treatment structure, the therapist has flexibility to look at integrated therapies that enhances the female sex offender's treatment.

Group therapy is the preferred treatment model for female offenders. However, due to the limited number of female offenders referred for treatment, many clinicians have no option but to offer individual or family therapy services. Clinicians should never consider placing a female offender in a group with male offenders. This treatment is inappropriate and can place both the female offender and the group at risk. The dynamics of a female offender are too different for any benefit to be derived in a male group. Also, many female offenders are victims of sexual abuse; placement in a male group could be clinically harmful.

In therapy, men tend to forgive themselves much quicker than women do. Women will develop empathy for victims earlier in psychotherapy than men and will remain ashamed of their behavior for an extended period. Women tend to self-report abuse more often than men; those who do so are more likely to complete a program of therapy.

Mayer Treatment Model

Mayer (1992) outlined one suggested model of therapy for female sex offenders. This treatment protocol is both behavioral and supportive in approach. Supportive components are as follows:

1. Obtain disclosure by acceptance and trust building with the therapist.
2. Reduce or relieve stress by reassurance, validation, and development of improved insight.
3. Decrease isolation through group therapy.
4. Interrupt blocking by encouraging ventilation.
5. Listen, role-play, and write unmailed letters.
6. Improve self-esteem through group therapy.

Behavioral-environmental components are listed as follows:

1. Redirect behavior that is more socially acceptable.
2. Clarify beliefs about victimization, the cycle of abuse, and arousal patterns.
3. Enhance depressive mood states and anxiety problems by helping the offender develop a larger behavioral and emotional support system.
4. Offer relaxation and stress management techniques.
5. Increase emotional support through group therapy.
6. Suggest alternative behaviors for problems that would lead to offending.
7. Provide educational or medical referrals to other agencies.

SUMMARY

What the clinical community knows about female sex offenders is that more research is needed across the treatment spectrum. Ford (2010) has observed a need to understand why women offend and what they specifically need in treatment and how these variables may differ compared to the male sex offender population. Ford (2010) has also highlighted a need to continually examine "treatment approaches for women and how identified needs can be most effectively addressed through intervention. However, this must be underpinned by the development of theory which should guide us in these other aspects of our work" (p. 115).

This does not, however, mean that you throw out the proverbial baby with the bathwater. There are treatment interventions presently used that are clinically sound to use for both men and women; however, it should also be noted that research literature also indicates that many of the actuarial tools and much of what we know and use in female sexual offender group therapy has been adapted from the male offender population. Research is ongoing about more gender-specific techniques and treatments for female sex offenders.

It should also be noted that typologies can be useful and assist in the overall clinical assessment of the female sexual offender, but treatment goals should not be built on typologies alone. The heterogeneous nature of this population would prevent any one tool or intervention being successful.

Lastly, the female sexual offender does exist. This population can be and is as dangerous as their male counterparts. This population is not a new phenomenon, but is now more recognized; however, the cultures of some communities around the world, including the United States, do not perceive the danger to be as severe with female offenders as with male offenders. As long as a society believes that a teenage boy is fulfilling a rite of passage or that no harm comes from sexual exchanges between a 13-year-old boy and a 34-year-old woman, this issue will always be taken less seriously than it should be.

CHAPTER 7

PARAPHILIAS

RUDA FLORA

MICHAEL L. KEOHANE

OVERVIEW

The Merriam-Webster Dictionary (2012) defines *paraphilia* as a "pattern of recurring sexually arousing mental imagery or behavior that involves unusual and especially socially unacceptable sexual practices." Paraphilia is believed to have evolved from two separate Greek words: *para* referring to "the side of" or "beside" and *philos* meaning "love" (Sadock & Sadock, 2007a; Saleh, Malin, Grudzinskas, & Vitacco, 2010). The English translation of this term as we now know it originated in 1925 and was proposed by Stekel (as cited in Saleh *et al.*, 2010) in his book *Sexual Aberrations*. The word *paraphilia* first appeared in American psychiatric language in 1934 and was first used in the third edition of the *Diagnostic and Statistical Manual* (American Psychiatric Association, 1980) to extensively classify a subset of psychosexual disorders (Milner, Dopke, & Crouch, 2008). Sadock and Sadock (2007a) further defined *paraphilia* as sexual acts that incorporate "aggression, victimization, and extreme one-sidedness. The behaviors exclude or harm others and disrupt the potential for bonding between persons. Moreover, paraphiliac sexual scripts often serve other vital psychic functions. They may assuage anxiety, bind aggression, or stabilize identity" (p. 703).

Abel (1989) has reported that paraphiliac behavior is the extreme and exaggerated form of sexual activity. For instance, many persons may seek out erotic forms of entertainment in literature, theater, movies, and television without problem. Individuals will, on occasion, experiment sexually and may involve fantasy to enhance a relationship. A woman may wear lingerie or a man may wear a robe during a sexual encounter. A partner could seek out romantic or erotic literature from a privately owned or large chain bookstore and incorporate the ideas during sexual encounters.

These types of behaviors should not be confused with paraphiliac actions that include recurring rituals and fantasies or the involvement of a child or unwilling partner in order to achieve sexual gratification. Meyer (1995) has observed that the fantasy is believed to occupy the thought process in both a conscious and unconscious manner.

Individuals with a paraphilia commonly have three to five paraphilias either simultaneously or over their lifetime. The rate of occurrence of paraphiliac behavior appears to peak between the ages of 15 and 25 and then a decline will most likely occur. Most persons who suffer from one paraphilia disorder are likely to possess two or three other paraphiliac disorders (Holmes & Holmes, 2009; Neumann, Alley, Paclebar, Sanchez, & Satterthwaite, 2006; Abel, Becker, Cunningham-Rathner, Mittelman, & Rouleau, 1988).

The heterogeneous nature of the sex offender population requires a diverse knowledge about the maladaptive behavioral patterns that are incorporated into the offense cycle. These behaviors that sexual offenders often possess meet the criteria for one or more type of clinical disorder as outlined in the current *Diagnostic and Statistical Manual of Mental Disorders* (*DSM-IV-TR*; American Psychiatric Association, 2000). Numerous studies have discovered a psychosexual disturbance in certain individuals.

Outside of the United States, countries refer to the *International Classification of Diseases* (*ICD*) (World Health Organization, 2011) to diagnose a variety of clinical issues to include psychosexual disturbances. The diagnostic information is similar to what is found in the *DSM-IV-TR*. The sexual disorders in the *ICD* fall under the category of *Disorders of Sexual Preference* (code F65) and includes Fetishism, Fetishistic Transvestism, Exhibitionism, Voyeurism, Pedophilia, Sadomasochism, Multiple disorders of sexual preference (combination of psychosexual disorders), and Other disorders of sexual preference (includes frotteurism and psychosexual disturbances found under "Paraphilia Not Otherwise Specified" in the *DSM-IV-TR*) (World Health Organization, 2011).

This chapter offers readers a review of current recognized paraphilia disorders, features of each diagnosis, and examples of how these problems impact individuals.

CLASSIFYING PARAPHILIAS

There are clinical discussions about the direction in which the new *DSM* should go when classifying paraphilias. At the heart of the clinical debate is the discussion of paraphilia as a mental disorder (Shindel & Moser, 2011). Two of the paraphilias that are under scrutiny are sexual sadism and sexual masochism. Individuals who engage in behaviors linked to BDSM (Bondage/ Discipline, Dominance/Submission, Sadism/Masochism) must also show current distress, disability, or increased risk of harm in order to be herded into a paraphiliac diagnosis (Shindel & Moser, 2011).

A person having unusual sexual interest may violate social norms and morals; however, these behaviors do not necessarily constitute a clinical disorder. It should also be said that any sexual conduct "including BDSM, can involve non-consenting participants; the perpetrators of these acts are criminals and not necessarily mentally disordered. The difference between consensual coitus and rape is consent; similarly the difference between consensual BDSM and sexual violence is consent" (Shindel & Moser, 2011, p. 928).

People on both sides of the spectrum (to include special interest groups) are debating the clinical nature of paraphilias. Time and empirical data will determine how this argument unfolds. There are clearly individuals that would fit the pathology that was intended behind the diagnostic information as outlined in the *DSM-IV-TR* (American Psychiatric Association, 2000); however, there are also people who engage in these sexual behaviors that don't easily fit within the criteria ascribed.

Wright (2010), in discussing clinical language used to describe paraphilias has said, "Separating sexual behaviors (paraphilias) from the mental disorders (Paraphilic Disorders) is the first step to depathologizing consensual alternative sex. The second step is defining what exactly constitutes clinically significant distress" (p. 1230).

Nevertheless, until the next *DSM* is released the information that clinically exists will be presented from this point forward. To delve further into an area not yet present would be speculation and would detract from the information that we do have thus far.

PARAPHILIAS

According to the American Psychiatric Association (2000), a paraphilia is a condition that involves compulsive sexual behaviors comprising "recurrent, intense sexually arousing fantasies, sexual urges or behaviors" (p. 566). The problematic behavior may incorporate children or non-consenting adults, and in some cases, humiliation of a companion is a part of the conduct. The psychosexual condition must be an ongoing problem for at least six months with actions that cause clinical distress or negatively impact the person's life in areas of social, family, or occupational functioning for it to be classified as a paraphiliac disturbance.

Paraphilias may be divided further into three separate categories. *Paraphilia* is found when a certain target object is sexualized such as a child, article of clothing, or even an animal; *sexual deviation* is present when behavior occurs that is not commonplace to a particular culture, as in men who cross-dress for erotic arousal; and *perversion* is an aberrant sexual behavior or desire acted upon in which a central theme is enhanced and eroticized leading to sexual gratification (e.g. partialism, a common example being a foot fetish) (Meyer, 1995). Money (1993) compiled a list of the most well-known paraphilias that are believed to exist at the present time. Several of these paraphilias may be a part of a cluster grouping, overlap, exist independently, or may be a reciprocal reaction. (Money's list of paraphilias, in part, is in Appendix H.)

Current research appears to be divided into several different camps as to whether paraphiliac behaviors are exclusive or nonexclusive. In the exclusive form, only paraphiliac behaviors would promote arousal; while in the non-exclusive form, the patient may be stimulated by both para-philia and other types of stimuli. Some researchers believe most paraphiliacs can perform other sexual acts without the associated behaviors. Those who cannot experience sexual gratification without paraphilia behaviors are few in number.

THEORIES OF ATTRIBUTION

Sadock and Sadock (2007a) have reported that a number of theories may be attributed to a para-philiac dysfunction. These may include castration anxiety, childhood sexual abuse, developmen-tal impairment, narcissism, trauma, oedipal conflict issues, overly strong identification with the opposite sex, and powerlessness with issues of control. Other theories have included behavioral and biological problems, courtship and intimacy deficits, medical difficulties, and personality and psychiatric pathology.

Other findings about paraphilia include the following:

- More than 40 types of paraphilias have been found to exist, but are not included in the *DSM-IV-TR* (Holmes & Holmes, 2009; Money, 1993).
- Approximately 10% to 20% of all children have been molested by age 18 (Meyer, 1995).
- More than 50% of all paraphilias have their onset before age 18 (Abel, Rouleau, & Cunning-ham-Rather, 1986).
- Individuals with a paraphilia problem rarely seek help on their own without intervention by criminal justice, human service, or mental health systems (American Psychiatric Associa-tion, 2000).
- The majority of children molested by sexual offenders were found to fall into two significant categories: young boys outside of the home by strangers and young girls inside the home by family members. More offenses occur against boys than girls (Abel *et al.*, 1987).

CLINICAL STUDIES

Abel *et al.* Study

A landmark study in 1987 and one that has not been completed was conducted on paraphiliac behaviors in sex offenders. A total of 561 subjects were interviewed for the project. The study involved individuals who were not incarcerated. High-frequency acts were found to include exhi-bitionism, frottage, masochism, transvestitism, and voyeurism (Abel *et al.*, 1987).

Many stereotypical assumptions were challenged. Most of the sex offenders surveyed were found to possess a moderate amount of education and were usually employed. About 40% of the respondents had completed one year of college while 64% were fully employed or enrolled in college. Approximately one-half of the subjects in the study had a relationship with another adult partner in a significant relationship in some form including marriage (Abel *et al.*, 1987).

Child molestation results were found to be of significant interest. Pedophiles who abused female targets in non-incest situations had a mean average offense rate of 23.2 acts and a median average of 1.4 offenses. Pedophiles who abused male targets had a mean average offense rate of 281.7 in non-incest situations and a median average of 10.1 offenses. The study found that paraphiliacs who offended young boys outside the home committed the highest number of crimes in this category. Pedophiles involved with children outside the home were found occasionally to reoffend the same victim, particularly men who molest boys.

Pedophiles who commit incest involving female victims had a mean average of 81.3 acts and a median of 4.4 acts. Pedophiles who commit incest crimes involving male victims had a mean average of 62.3 acts and a median of 5.2 acts.

Rapists involved in the study were reported to commit a mean average of 7.2 offenses with a median average of 0.9 offenses. Approximately 126 rapists were involved in the study.

Exhibitionists had a reported mean average of 504.9 offenses and a median average of 50.9 offenses. Additionally, it was reported that exhibitionists and rapists usually commit one act per victim.

Voyeurs, with 62 respondents, committed a mean average of 469.9 offenses and a median average of 16.5 acts. Voyeurs were found to sometimes reoffend the same individual.

Also, in a separate study in 1988, it was found that only 10.1% of the paraphiliac respondents possessed only one diagnosis. Most were found to have two or more diagnoses of some type of paraphilia dysfunction. Approximately 19.2% of the respondents were found with two diagnoses of paraphilia, 20.6% had three diagnoses, and 11.5% had four diagnoses. The other 37.6% surveyed were found to possess five to ten different types of paraphiliac behaviors (Abel *et al.*, 1988).

Dietz, Cox, and Wegener Study

In another clinical study, Dietz, Cox, and Wegener (1986) reported some significant findings for exhibitionists. Based on arrest records, it was found that the highest number of exposure incidents occurred in the spring during the months of April, May, and June. Exposure incidents occurred less often during the months of December, January, and February. Most incidents of indecent exposure occurred during the daylight hours and in public outdoor places.

Bradford and Gratzer Study

Several similar clinical features appear to exist in these disorder groupings. Paraphilias are often found to be intrusive, and involuntarily repetitive with a compulsive component. Comparable features are found to exist in impulse control disorders and obsessive-compulsive disorder. A biological explanation for sexual offending behavior is being explored.

Bradford and Gratzer (1995) report that a possible relationship or parallel feature may exist between impulse control disorders and paraphilias. Research completed by Raymond, Coleman, Ohlerking, Christenson, and Miner (1999) noted that 29% of their sample had a co-occurring psychiatric disorder of impulse control and 64% had a co-existing Axis I diagnosis of anxiety (social phobia 38% and PTSD 33%).

Many sexual offenders often report problems that include compulsive urges, obsessive-like thoughts about sex, and difficulty managing their desires and impulses. A sex offender may now be seen not only as an individual who desires to harm another, but also as someone who is impaired and acts out those sexual urges and needs as a result of impulse control problems and obsessive-compulsive behaviors.

Available findings may help lessen offending incidents, which in turn can reduce the number of individuals assaulted. Additional studies are being continued by a number of researchers.

EXHIBITIONISM

Exhibitionism is a disorder which involves the recurring urge and sexual desire to expose one's genitals to another person. Usually the victim is an unsuspecting stranger (American Psychiatric Association, 2000).

Typically, exhibitionists have a desired target population and location as part of the offending cycle. Such places may include public areas such as mall parking lots, public parks, and playgrounds where the intended victims may be found, all with easy access for the exhibitionist to escape. Many exhibitionists will use a car; they drive around hunting for potential victims.

Consider a married, middle-aged Caucasian male, father of two prepubescent daughters, who has a history of exposing his penis to adult women. His target population may be slender brunette Caucasian females in their early twenties. Such an offender will fantasize about exposing his genitals to a potential victim prior to the offense. His cycle of offending may include cruising in his car during the evening hours after work, searching for victims outside of his own community.

The sexual excitement occurs in the anticipation of the exposure. Masturbation may occur prior to, during, or after the event has occurred. Usually, no attempt at further sexual activity with the victim is made. There is a desire to shock, frighten, or surprise a victim. Some offenders experience a fantasy in which the victim will also become sexually aroused. There is some debate about the effectiveness of therapy on recidivism among this population, but when therapy is utilized addressing the underlining personal issues of trust, shame, and impulse control related to immediate gratification can increase the likelihood of a positive outcome (Holmes & Holmes, 2009).

Exhibitionism Quick Facts

- Found mostly in males (Sadock & Sadock, 2007a; Shaffer & Penn, 2006).
- Typically begins in the teenage years (Holmes & Holmes, 2009; Murphy & Page, 2006).
- Most common of paraphilias leading to contact with the criminal justice system. One-third to two-thirds of all reported sexual crimes involve some form of exhibitionistic behavior (Marshall, Eccles, & Barbaree, 1991).
- Exhibitionists who are in the criminal justice system represent a small portion of actual exhibitionist behavior reported (Murphy & Page, 2006).
- Extremely diverse in the methods of exposing themselves to victims: some operate vehicles, driving while exposing their genitals; others will use an elevator or walk on a street with a portion of their pants open. Reports occur in which some offenders will leave curtains or blinds open or doors to bedrooms and bathrooms ajar (Carnes, 2001).
- One study showed 23 out of 25 patients diagnosed with exhibitionism also met the criteria for an Axis I diagnosis (Marsh *et al.*, 2010).
- Account for approximately one-third of relapsing sex offenders (Murphy & Page, 2006; Rooth, 1973).
- Exhibit passive personality styles. The opportunity for men to expose themselves reduces the potential for them to resort to a more harmful type of sexual dysfunction (Holmes & Holmes, 2009; Rooth, 1973). However, a small group of exhibitionists (10% to 30%) can escalate to hands-on offenses (Murphy & Page, 2006).
- Exhibitionism toward children increases the likelihood of eventually sexually abusing children (Murphy & Page, 2006).
- Believed to be the most treatable of the paraphilias (Marshall *et al.*, 1991; Murphy & Page, 2006).

FETISHISM

A fetishism disorder exists when a person is sexually aroused on a recurrent basis by certain nonliving objects. These objects represent a special meaning to the fetishist and evoke strong sexual feelings. Sexual activity is associated with the particular objects that have been eroticized (American Psychiatric Association, 2000).

In some reported cases, the fetish disorder can be acted out in a passive manner by the individual, such as working in a shoe store, selling female lingerie, styling hair, or other socially acceptable forms of behavior. The identified object of sexual attraction will play a role in the individual's fantasy process. Such a person may masturbate with the object, observe the item while masturbating, or use the object in some fashion during a sexual encounter. Sometimes such individuals will relive the fantasy, replaying the event (e.g., selling a pair of shoes to a woman, touching her foot, and then later masturbating while thinking of the experience).

Other fetish behavior can be acted upon with a consenting sexual partner. A man who has sexual intercourse with his wife only if she wears black high heels may suffer from a fetish disorder. Such behaviors should not be confused with typical fantasy behavior and sexual play. For the behavior to be deemed a fetish-level disorder, the person must have recurrent urges to experience a particular sexual event in a certain way. Sexual gratification, when a fetish is present, is often linked with the object that has special erotic meaning. Behaviors or thoughts can be incorporated into a fetish system.

Fetishism Quick Facts

- First coined by French psychologist Binet in 1887 (Weinberg, Williams, & Calhan, as cited by Konrad-Torres & Nickchen, 2006).
- Primarily found in males, and is rare in females (Kunjukrishnan, Pawlak, & Varan, 1988).
- Sexual focus is on nonliving objects, such as shoes, underwear, pantyhose, or stockings (Sadock & Sadock, 2007a; Konrad-Torres & Nickchen, 2006).
- Usually starts in adolescence, although in some cases as early as childhood. This disorder is chronic in duration (Sadock & Sadock, 2007a).
- Fetish object is somehow linked to someone from the offender's past or childhood (Sadock & Sadock, 2007a).
- Often found in men who practice autoerotic activities, bondage, and transvestism behaviors (Byard, Hucker, & Hazelwood, 1990).
- Considered to be a displacement behavior (Kunjukrishnan *et al.*, 1988).
- Fetishists usually do not encounter problems with the criminal justice system (Meyer, 1995).
- Fetishism behavior should only rise to the level of meeting the criteria as a paraphilia when the interest is so extreme that the fetish object must be present before sexual gratification can be met (Weinberg *et al.*, as cited in Konrad-Torres & Nickchen, 2006).

TRANSVESTIC FETISHISM

Transvestic fetishism is a disorder that is revealed by a male's recurrent desire to cross-dress for sexual arousal. This disorder is found only in heterosexual males. Men who cross-dress will masturbate while fantasizing about themselves and a certain female or related object of sexual interest. The male will imagine himself to be in both roles of man and woman in the sexual fantasy. Presently, the *DSM-IV-TR* does not include transvestic fetishism in individuals with a gender identity problem (Wheeler, Newring, & Draper, 2008; American Psychiatric Association, 2000).

An example of this disorder may be a man who will, on occasion, cross-dress in women's clothing including a dress, underwear, and stockings. While masturbating he will fantasize about himself and a woman in a sexual situation. He may be married and on occasion act out his fantasy with his sexual partner. A small number of individuals may experience gender dysphoria and attempt to live permanently as a female or seek surgery. This disorder begins in childhood or adolescence.

Transvestic Fetishism Quick Facts

- Magnus Hirschfield is credited for first describing and using the word transvestism in the early 1900s. His research looked at 16 men and one woman that were cross-dressers. He concluded that the transvestic behavior began in childhood, increased in adolescence, and didn't change into adulthood (Bullough & Bullough, as cited in Heasman, Johnson, & Chau, 2006).
- Cross-dressing behavior generally starts when a child is between six and nine years old (Heasman *et al.*, 2006).
- It should be noted that there is a difference between transvestic and transsexual. Transvestic fetishists derive pleasure from the sexual organs. Transsexuals are repulsed by the sexual organs (Buhrich & McConaghy, as cited in Heasman *et al.*, 2006).
- The male when not cross-dressed is usually masculine in manner. Some men may wear female attire that is hidden or concealed (American Psychiatric Association, 2000).
- Transvestites are generally married and have children (Wheeler *et al.*, 2008).
- Transvestic fetishism occasionally leads individuals into conflict with the criminal justice system in disturbing the peace situations if cross-dressed in a public area (Meyer, 1995).
- Only a small percentage of men with transvestic fetishism disorders seek treatment (Wheeler *et al.*, 2008; Wise, 1990).
- The majority of those seeking treatment or volunteering for research studies with transvestic fetishism problems were found to be Caucasian, well-educated, married or previously married, highly successful, and well-integrated members of the community. They also started cross-dressing before age 12. Marital problems are most often the contributing psychosocial stressor leading patients into treatment since transvestic fetishism is a chronic disorder (Brown, 1995).

FROTTEURISM

Frotteurism comes from the French word *frotteur* meaning to brush or rub (Neumann *et al.*, 2006). More formally, frotteurism is a disorder in which an individual is sexually stimulated by touching, rubbing, or having physical body contact with another individual. The offending behavior is usually carried out in a public location where victims are fairly easy to access, such as a crowded room, mall, or subway. Victims are non-consenting and usually unknown to the offender. The perpetrator will fantasize that he has a special relationship with the victim during the encounter. Escape is important to avoid detection and to avoid possible prosecution (Holmes & Holmes, 2009; American Psychiatric Association, 2000).

A case of frotteurism may be illustrated by an adult male who selects elevators in high-rise office buildings to act out his sexual need. This individual will place himself near potential victims in an elevator that is crowded and intentionally bump or touch passengers. Incidents appear to be accidental, and the perpetrator will often offer an excuse for the clumsy behavior. Victims are sometimes unaware of the offense. This type of behavior is often perpetrated in crowded public places where accidental bumping can be excused. Most acts of frottage are believed to take place during adolescence and early adulthood (15 to 25 years of age); they then will decline in frequency as the offender becomes older (Holmes & Holmes, 2009; American Psychiatric Association, 2000). Although frotteurism (like all of the psychosexual disorders) crosses socioeconomic boundaries, Holmes and Holmes (2009) have noted that people with this clinical disorder are generally found in middle and higher classes.

Frotteurism Quick Facts

- Found mostly in male offenders (Holmes & Holmes, 2009; Sadock & Sadock, 2007a).
- Frotteurs are usually intelligent and often have additional paraphilias (Holmes & Holmes, 2009).
- Victims often do not report the crime for fear of reprisal or that their complaint will not be taken seriously (Meyer, 1995).
- Arrests are rare because the act often goes without notice by the victim (Meyer, 1995).
- The average frotteur may have over 800 incidents before coming to the attention of the criminal justice system (Neumann *et al.*, 2006).
- One theory offered suggests that the frotteur may be a "timid rapist" that has not advanced in ego strength or assertiveness; however, like most other paraphilias, given time and opportunity, the frotteur could graduate to more sexually deviant motives and behaviors (Horley, as cited in Neumann, 2006).

PEDOPHILIA

Pedophilia is a disorder characterized by sexual attraction to or sexual activity with a child. Features include fantasies, sexual urges, and possible sexual behavior with a prepubescent child. Out of all the paraphilias, pedophilia is the most documented and discussed in forensic and clinical research (Seto, 2008; American Psychiatric Association, 2000).

There is no statistical evidence to show the rate or frequency of pedophilia, but data on male pedophilia represent over 90% of what is in the literature at this time (Seto, 2008). With such a high percentage there is significant evidence to indicate that men are more likely than women to be sexually attracted to prepubescent children (although some women are pedophiles) (Seto, 2008). However, as more clinical and forensic research is completed and data collected, the number of women pedophiles may be more significant than once believed (Holmes & Holmes, 2009).

Persons diagnosed with this disorder cannot be diagnosed before the age of 16 and must be at least five years older than the child in which they have a sexual interest. For adolescents between the ages of 16 and 19 years old with such a problem, no age is specified and clinical judgment in assessment is encouraged (American Psychiatric Association, 2000).

Pedophiliac behavior may differ in action depending upon the individual. Certain persons may meet their sexual needs by viewing child pornography videos while maintaining a sexual relationship with an adult. Others may find sexual gratification only through actual sexual encounters with children. The sexual behavior may appear rather passive in manner and consensual by using bribery. More severe forms of this disorder may result in threats of force, coercion, or actual physical assault of victims including rape.

There are times that people will use or understand the terms *pedophilia* and *child molester* to describe the same kind of person. It is important to note that not all pedophiles are child molesters and not all child molesters are pedophiles. The terms don't necessarily describe the same offenders, although often the boundaries between the two types are crossed (Lanning, 2010).

Pedophilia is a psychiatric diagnosis and specifically describes a person that is attracted to, fantasizes about, and sexually prefers prepubescent (13 years or younger) children, sometimes exclusively. However, unless he or she acts on the preference or fantasies they are not a child molester (Lanning, 2010).

A child molester, on the other hand, is an offender of opportunity. If there is a chance for the child molester to sexually offend a child then he or she may, especially if he or she has no adult partners; however, his or her focus is not exclusively on children (Harrison, McCartan, & Manning, 2010; Lanning, 2010; McAnulty, 2006).

To further distinguish between pedophiles and child molesters or people who sexually offend a child, Seto (2008) has stated, "Having pedophilia is not illegal, whereas an adult having sexual contact with a prepubescent child usually is. 'Pedophilia' refers specifically to a sexual preference for prepubescent children" (p. 164).

Another word that is often confused with pedophilia is *hebephilia*. Although the age range may be close, the hebephiliac offender's victim target population is a little older. Hickey (as cited in Litton, 2006) remarks that the confusion may be due to "closeness in the age range required for the diagnosis of a pedophile. The pedophile is attracted to children aged from pubescent to [13], while hebephiles' victims' ages range from [13] to [16]" (p. 311).

An illustration of a pedophile may be a single male who is active in church youth groups. He is a college graduate and works full-time in addition to his volunteer services. He is sexually attracted to prepubescent females and seeks out this target population in locations frequented by young girls. The sexual abuse may first be displayed in a covert manner with the offender only engaging in frottage behaviors in which his body "accidently" touches the girls' during church youth volleyball games. Later, a potential target victim is selected and a more premeditated form of sexually offending behavior is initiated, with the offender offering to transport a young girl home after games, befriending both the victim and her parents. Oftentimes the offender will choose a victim from a single-parent home or a home where the youth is in a dysfunctional relationship with the parents. The offender will then take time to groom the parents. Once he has convinced the parent(s) that he can be trusted he will then focus his attention on developing the relationship with his potential victim. As the relationship develops a more seductive and aggressive approach is started by the offender, such as fondling the victim's breasts. This sexual behavior advances; soon the offender is regularly fondling the child, which includes genital contact while she is clothed, oral sex, and unclothed vaginal activity. The girl may have first been informed by the offender that the behavior was appropriate. Later, the girl may be subjected to forms of manipulation, bribery, and threats of harm. Such offenders often take part in positions in a community in which they will have an opportunity to encounter potential victims.

Research completed by Bogaert, Bezeau, Kuban, and Blanchard (as cited in Litton, 2006) reports that pedophiles as a group prefer female victims over male victims more than 60% of the time. However, earlier research completed by Ames and Houston (as cited in Litton, 2006) reports that pedophiles are attracted to both genders of children.

Murray (as cited in Litton, 2006) reported that when the victim is a female the offender is more likely a relative and the sexual offense tends to happen in the victim's home; whereas, with a male victim, the offender tends to be a stranger and the sexual offense happens outside of the home.

Those with a pedophilia disorder may report a sexual attraction to children of a specific age range and gender. Those found to be attracted to females usually report an interest in young girls between the ages of eight to ten, while those who are sexually aroused by males are more inclined to select children that are slightly older (Murray, as cited in Litton, 2006; American Psychiatric Association, 2000).

As a clinical group, pedophiles are characterized as being introverted, passive, lacking self-confidence, having social skill deficiencies, and are less intimidated by children (McAnulty, 2006). Murray (as cited in Litton, 2006) also indicates that pedophiles targeting male or female victims older than nine years old are more likely to have lower self-esteem.

Pedophilia Quick Facts

- As a clinical group, pedophiles are heterogeneous (Harrison *et al.*, 2010; Seto, 2008; McAnulty, 2006).
- Pedophiles tend to live at home or alone, be introverted and suffer from depression (Litton, 2006).
- Pedophiles commonly engage in other paraphiliac behavior (Seto, 2008).
- Approximately 20% of all females and 10% of all males have been sexually molested prior to 18 years of age (Abel & Osborn, 1995).
- It is estimated that 50% of pedophiliac victims are children ten years old and under (25% are under six years old and 25% between the ages of six and ten years old) and approximately 50% are between 11 and 13 years old (Erickson, Walbek, & Seely, as cited in McAnulty, 2006).

- Sexual activity with female victims is reported more than pedophilia involving male victims. However, homosexual pedophiles tend to have more victims then heterosexual pedophiles. Victims for a heterosexual pedophile may number as many as 20 separate children, while a homosexual pedophile may have as many as 150 victims (McAnulty, 2006; Abel *et al.*, 1987).
- Sexual interest is not limited to one sex. Some offenders may prefer males while others prefer females. Some offenders may be attracted to both sexes (McAnulty, 2006; American Psychiatric Association, 2000).
- Most cases of actual child molestation involve genital fondling or oral sex. Vaginal or anal sexual activity is infrequent except in cases of incest (Sadock & Sadock, 2007a).
- A large portion of adolescents committing sexual crimes, including acts of pedophilia, are often victims of sexual abuse themselves. Many also experienced emotional, sexual, or physical violence in the home (Seto, 2008; McAnulty, 2006).
- Pedophiles have usually experienced some interruption in their own developmental growth. Such persons may be at the same developmental level socially as the child (Carnes, 2001).

SEXUAL MASOCHISM

Sexual masochism involves the recurrent act of being "humiliated, beaten, bound, or otherwise made to suffer" in some way to achieve arousal and orgasm (American Psychiatric Association, 2000, p. 572). Fantasies may include being raped while being held or bound by others without means of escape. More aggressive forms of this disorder may be found in persons who will bind themselves, use pins to stick oneself for the purpose of inflicting pain, commit acts of self-mutilation, or endure forms of electric shock alone or with a partner. Masochistic acts that may be sought with a partner include bondage, blindfolding, paddling, spanking, whipping, beating, electrical shock, cutting, and other forms of humiliation, both verbal or physical (American Psychiatric Association, 2000).

This disorder may be evidenced by a male who requests that his partner humiliate him by using profane and derogatory language while striking his buttocks with a leather belt. Another example may be evidenced by a woman who requests to be tied to her bed and blindfolded with a scarf by a consenting partner during sexual intercourse. More severe forms of this behavior may include self-mutilation with a razor, encouraging a partner to batter him or her in an aggressive manner, or hypoxyphilia (also known as autoerotic asphyxiation or sexual asphyxia). This sexual practice involves cutting off the oxygen supply to the brain through some type of ligature around the neck, bag over the head, or some other type of oxygen-depriving method. This method creates a heightened state of sexual arousal that the person enters into while masturbating. The person may engage in this activity alone or they may have a partner. Due to any number of errors that can happen in this process, accidental death is possible (American Psychiatric Association, 2000).

Sexual Masochism Quick Facts

- Found in both males and females (American Psychiatric Association, 2000).
- Most masochistic behavior begins in adolescence (American Psychiatric Association, 2000).
- General population estimates for masochism ranges between 5% to 10%; however these estimates have increased over the last 20 years (Baumeister, as cited in Shaffer & Penn, 2006).
- Females are more likely to be introduced to sexual masochism, while males appear to discover this interest on their own (American Psychiatric Association, 2000).
- There is a hypothesis or probability that individuals engaging in sexual masochistic behaviors do not do as well in relationships where the partner does not share the interest.
- A survey of 182 persons with sadomasochistic interests revealed the following: 52.5% of men and 57.5% of women were married; 31.4% of men and 20% of women were college graduates; 38.5% of men and 13.3% of women had monthly incomes between $1,001 and $2,000 (Breslow, Evans, & Langley, 1985).
- Preferences of sadomasochistic interests have included the following for both sexes: spanking, master–slave relationships, oral sex, masturbation, bondage, humiliation, erotic lingerie, restraints, anal sex, pain, whipping, rubber and leather clothing, boots and shoes, stringent bondage, enemas, torture, golden showers by urine, transvestism, petticoat punishment, and toilet activities (Breslow *et al.*, 1985).

SEXUAL SADISM

Sexual sadism is a disorder that is characterized by individuals who obtain sexual pleasure through the psychological and physical suffering of others. The paraphilia is most often found in the male population. The behavior involves the desire to control others, devalue others, or inflict pain. Severe forms of this disorder may lead to emotional trauma, physical harm, or death for consenting and non-consenting partners (American Psychiatric Association, 2000).

This disorder may be expressed in a mild form when an individual is sexually aroused by acts in which a consenting partner is punished, spanked, whipped, or pinched. More serious forms of this disorder may lead to excessive features of brutality, inflicting serious physical harm to a victim as in sexual assault and rape or death (American Psychiatric Association, 2000).

Sexual Sadism Quick Facts

- Named after Marquis de Sade, an eighteenth-century French writer and military officer who committed violent acts of sexual behavior against women; he was imprisoned several times (Sadock & Sadock, 2007a).
- May include the use of restraints, whipping, blindfolding, paddling, spanking, pinching, beating, burning, electrical shock, rape, cutting, strangulation, torture, mutilation, or killing (American Psychiatric Association, 2000).

- Piquerism is a major form of sadistic behavior where the offender will usually stab a female victim in the breast or buttocks (Yates, Hucker, & Kingston, 2008).
- Other major forms of sadistic behaviors include lust murder, necrophilia, and stabbing (Yates *et al.*, 2008).
- Various research regarding sexual sadist serial killers indicate that all were male, many were Caucasian, had planned their offenses, did not know their victims; and in all cases there was evidence of physical torture present at the scene (Yates *et al.*, 2008).
- Sadistic rape is aggressive, eroticized with ritualistic acts involving the victim. The offender's mood state is often one of intense excitement and depersonalization. Sadistic rape may include language that is commanding, degrading, or alternately reassuring and threatening. Weapons can be used to capture the victim, along with methods of restraint and possible forms of torture. Victim selection for sadistic rape is determined by specific features or symbolic representation (Groth, 1990).
- Less than 10% of rapists would be categorized as sadistic rapists (Baker, as cited in Johnson, 2006).
- Associated characteristics include childhood physical abuse, and a history of cross-dressing, peeping, obscene telephone calling, or indecent exposure incidents. Clinical history may include marriage, military experience, education beyond high school, established reputation as a solid citizen, and an incestuous relationship with a son or daughter (Gratzer & Bradford, 1995).
- Sexual sadism and offending characteristics have included careful planning of the offense, victim taken to preselected location, unemotional or detached affect during the offense, intentional torture, victim beatings, and sexual dysfunction during the offense (Gratzer & Bradford, 1995).
- Sexual sadism disorder patients should have a two-prong approach of psychological services: group or individual counseling involving modified cognitive behavioral therapy (CBT) and relapse prevention (RP) model and anti-androgens (drugs to reduce libido) to reduce the risk of recidivism and for public safety (Marshall & Hucker, 2006; Kingston & Yates, 2008).
- Scoring a sexual sadist on an actuarial tool may not reveal the true danger that may be associated with that person (Marshall & Hucker, 2006).

VOYEURISM

Voyeurism is a disorder in which a person derives sexual pleasure and gratification by secretly watching individuals, usually strangers, who are undressing, naked, or participating in some form of sexual activity (American Psychiatric Association, 2000).

This disorder may be expressed, for instance, in the form of peeping in a window and viewing a couple who are engaged in sexual intercourse. Although not always the case, pools and public rest areas are opportunity areas for voyeurs.

When this disorder is present it is most often found in males; however, this demography has been questioned. Two such questions that the clinicians should consider: Is it that women don't engage in voyeurism or is it that women are not approached in the same manner about this specific paraphilia? Clinically, when ruling out potential voyeurism, an individual should not be precluded due to gender (Mann, Ainsworth, Al-Attar, & Davies, 2008).

Voyeurism Quick Facts

- Another formal name for voyeurism is scoptophilia; not to be confused with scatophilia (obscene phone calls) (Holmes & Holmes, 2009; Shaffer & Penn, 2006).
- A layman's term to describe a voyeur is "Peeping Tom."
- The act is limited to only looking, with no other sexual activity sought. The individual may masturbate and reach orgasm during or after the incident. The onset of voyeuristic behavior is before age 15 and tends to be chronic (American Psychiatric Association, 2000; Neumann, 2006).
- Voyeurs who are arrested are usually charged with trespassing. Voyeurs enjoy their behavior and enter treatment only if arrested, for fear of being caught, or if the behavior is impacting other areas of their lives (Neumann, 2006; Smith, 1976).
- Studies seem to indicate that voyeurism is co-morbid with other paraphilias and could potentially lead to more sexually aggressive or deviant behavior (Neumann, 2006).
- Sexual voyeurism without any other type of paraphilia rarely comes to the knowledge of the clinical or criminal justice system due to its secret nature. Knowledge about sexual voyeurism is usually uncovered when other sexual or non-sexual offenses are discovered or treated (Mann *et al.*, 2008).
- Computer voyeurism is a newer behavior that needs additional research. Research completed by Cooper, Morahan-Martin, Mathy, and Maheu (as cited in Neumann, 2006) found that people who engaged in online sexual activity (OSA) were usually married males in their thirties.
- The prevalence of sexual voyeurism among the general population is not presently known (Mann *et al.*, 2008).
- The research on voyeurism is sporadic and no clear treatment modality has been proven to be effective or able to reduce recidivism; however, combining treatment modalities and possible pharmacological approaches may assist in treatment (Mann *et al.*, 2008; Neumann, 2006).
- An accompanying paraphilia of voyeurism is troilism which generally involves a couple and a third party. One member of the couple (troilist) becomes sexually aroused by watching the other member engage in sexual activity with the third party member. One member of the couple may be hidden or they may videotape or photograph themselves engaged in sexual activity. They can be a party of two or three couples who engage with each other or any variation of behavior that allows the troilist to watch (Holmes & Holmes, 2009).

- Research suggests that most often it is the man that wants to engage in a troilist lifestyle than the woman, but it is the woman that wants to maintain the lifestyle after the man wants to discontinue it (Holmes & Holmes, 2009).
- Another associated paraphilia related to voyeurism is candaulism in which the male exposes his partner or her pictures to other people in order to fulfill voyeuristic fantasies or sexual arousal. Coercion into troilism may occur if the partner is unwilling to fulfill the voyeur's candaulist fantasies (Holmes & Holmes, 2009).

PARAPHILIA NOT OTHERWISE SPECIFIED

According to the American Psychiatric Association (2000), Paraphilia Not Otherwise Specified (NOS) may include (but are not limited to) telephone scatologia (obscene phone calls), necrophilia (corpses), partialism (exclusive focus on part of a body), zoophilia (animals), coprophilia (feces), klismaphilia (enemas), and urophilia (urine). Paraphilia (NOS) is considered more of a residual grouping of sexually aberrant behaviors less frequently observed by clinicians, criminal justice, and human service professionals.

Sadock and Sadock (2007a) report that the category of Paraphilia (NOS) includes a varied number of paraphilias that do not qualify for other sexual disorders. Included are hypoxyphilia (hanging, suffocation, or strangulation to achieve orgasm) and masturbation (when found to be compulsive or preferred to intercourse) in addition to those listed by the American Psychiatric Association (2000).

SUMMARY

Sexual offenders often present paraphiliac disorders that may meet the criteria as outlined in the *DSM-IV-TR*. However, it should be noted that there are many paraphilias that meet the criteria but are not in the current manual.

Various clinical findings appear to indicate that some sexually related behaviors can be attributed to biomedical, psychiatric, or psychological types of illnesses or disorders. However, other research has demonstrated that certain sexual behaviors are related to early childhood and family events, developmental factors, behavioral experiences, and trauma. It should be noted that research is not conclusive about what triggers the existence of a psychosexual disturbance in certain individuals.

Although there are paraphilias that are clinically understood to be related to men, newer research is starting to question whether some paraphiliac behavior can also be related to women.

When completing an assessment it is important to measure clinical sexual disorders regardless of gender.

Finally, when looking at the paraphilias, the *DSM-IV-TR* recognizes eight clinical sexual disorders in addition to Paraphilia (NOS). In addition, research appears to indicate that it is not uncommon for individuals to have co-occurring paraphilias. However, it is important when assessing the client that the therapist is aware there may be other clinical disorders that are nonsexual, but may still influence the patient's treatment.

CHAPTER 8

THE ROAD AHEAD: THE IDENTIFICATION AND ENFORCEMENT OF THE LAW FOR SEX OFFENDERS IN THE INTERNET AGE

STEPHEN T. HOLMES

BRYAN M. HOLMES

UNIVERSITY OF CENTRAL FLORIDA

INTRODUCTION

Understanding sex offenders remains one of the most important things that academics and those who work with the offenders attempt to do. Long gone are the days when we could ignore sex offenders or bury our heads in the sand thinking the problem would go away. In the days of 24-hour news programing, every station in just about every city is looking for a new headline and—few stories attract an audience like sex offenders. Whether it is a stranger trolling the streets exposing themselves to kids or a school teacher sleeping with students, sex offenders capture the attention of the American public.

Just what is it about these offenders that draws our attention? Are we looking at others as a way to judge our own behavior? That is likely part of the calculus. Or are we afraid of them? Afraid of them not only preying upon our friends, family and neighbors but also the threat they pose to the values and cultural traditions that we have been brought up with. Clearly, we can all agree that it is a little of both. We are concerned for our safety and the safety those around us, but we are also concerned that their behavior (no matter how it is treated in the news media) has to be universally condemned—even if it is a behavior the majority of people engage in. For instance, in Olympia, Washington, a Department of Social and Health Services employee was fired from his job for looking at porn while at work (KIMAtv.com, 2016).

Would this have made news if the individual was not a state employee? Probably not. Would the individual have been fired or had his name and reputation tarnished if he had not viewed these images at work? Probably not. But when you look at the offense, you begin to understand that this individual was terminated for doing something that a majority of men in this country do monthly, weekly and some daily. Therefore it is often the context in which the event occurs that matters.

While these types of cases are interesting, what matters most to others are not those that engage in nuisance sexual behavior but those that push the envelope a bit further and engage in acts and activities that can be dangerous to either the participant or victim. The acts can be dangerous either physically or psychologically for the victim. These are the true sex offenders—or at least the ones that most citizens care about—not those individuals that look at pornography or engage in salacious sexual behavior with consenting partners.

TYPES OF SEXUAL OFFENDERS

Defining the persons and behaviors that we are concerned about it is one of the most difficult challenges we face. Because when we discuss the topic of sex offenders and try to understand the future of enforcement, we all too often paint offenders and their offenses with a broad brush. So in attempting to define our population of interest we typically divide sex offenders into one of two types: those who engage in deviant, yet not criminal, behavior (nuisance offenders) and those who engage in behavior that is dangerous to victims and even the participants themselves (serious and/or dangerous offenders). It is these dangerous offenders that we are most concerned about. These are the offenders that are likely to make the evening news and harm those we care most deeply about.

The Futility of a Search for a Cure for Most Sex Offenders

Regardless of the type, we as a society must come to accept that for many of these offenders their behaviors or fantasies cannot be "cured" in the traditional sense. Once a person is attracted to an act, a type of individual or an object, no amount of treatment is going to "turn off" that interest or fantasy or attraction to the object of their affection. Treatment may, however, allow an individual to contextualize their actions and understand individual and societal repercussions. But treatment is only as good as the individual and their desire for positive behavioral change. Often forced or court ordered intervention strategies are not indicative of an offender's true wish for change.

If most treatment strategies fail or are doomed to fail because the offenders typically have no investment in the treatment plan, just what can we as a society do? The answer to that question is not an easy one, and it is often a tough pill to swallow for many people. The only true answer is to focus our efforts on those that we can help, and of course make sure those that are a danger to others are not allowed the freedom and mobility to engage in these types of offenses.

THE NEW REALITY

This type of effort and recognition does come at a cost. First we must come to the realization that the behavior of nuisance sex offenders, while offensive to some, is not and should not be treated as criminal. We have to understand the boundaries of normal and appropriate sexual behavior and that some behavior, while socially undesirable, is not serious enough to warrant the intervention of the legal system. However, that does not mean that informal sanctions or means of social control should not be used to censure inappropriate behavior.

The Utility of the Criminal Sanction in Low-Level Offenses

That being said, law enforcement and others involved in the justice system must recognize that, as in minor drug possession cases, the criminal sanction is not one that should be purposely employed against those that engage in nuisance sexual behavior. Of course, it is the context of the act that may determine whether it is serious or a nuisance. For instance, public nudity represents one such act. If an individual decides to disrobe in a public place, there typically is no harm unless there are children nearby or the intent is to garner sexual pleasure from the display. Individuals that engage in the former type of behavior (maybe sunbathing or just having a bit too much fun at a party) just need a firm talking to or warning by others or a justice system representative. However, those that go too far or engage in salacious acts in front of children or for their own pleasure may need the justice system to go one step further and invoke the power of arrest. It is, after all, these offenders that we are most concerned with.

A DIFFERENT APPROACH AND EMPHASIS

One may ask what is different between this approach and what currently happens in the justice system today where police have the discretionary power of arrest and courts often choose lesser sanctions for those that engage in first-time offenses. The answer is not much. However, the approach being called for is one that formally recognizes the power of the criminal justice system and the actors that occupy seats within it. Since the police are often the closest agency to those that break the law and engage in socially forbidden behavior, it is their behavior and reactions that matter. If the police enforced the criminal law as written, the justice system would become overburdened and, for all practical purposes, break down. Thus, the utilization of discretion by the police and others in the justice system is an integral part of this process. But we are not only talking about individual officer discretion; just as important is the recognition by agencies and bureaus of their role in creating cultural and informal expectations about what types of crimes they are going to enforce and what types of investigations and units they are going to fund with the limited resources available.

If one examines the response of the police over time and evaluates how they react to differing policies imposed upon them by external sovereigns, one can see clearly how much power law enforcement has. For instance, in jurisdictions across the country police routinely choose not to enforce the law regarding juvenile curfews, jay walking, minor alcohol or drug possession and even prostitution. In that way, the police have made it clear to the residents and even the criminal elements that these behaviors, while not fitting within the confines of what most would consider normal behavior, will not evoke a formal state authorized response. However, the threat of enforcement is what keeps the system and social boundaries intact. So, these informal rules don't always have to be formally communicated.

For instance, in one large county in one of the most populated areas in Florida, it is known by the police and unfortunately the criminals that the courts will not prosecute juveniles for car theft until they have at least five offenses on their record. Thus, while the police may arrest a youth, the judges will typically release the offender until there is a sufficient record for sentencing. The officers and kids all know the going rate. This means that these juveniles are free to keep stealing cars until they are caught the fourth time. It is at that point that these youthful offenders begin to contemplate other options for entertainment and making money. In this way, the court system has established its own rules; rules that are different that that the police use and of course different from the law. So, while the courts control the formal sanctions handed down, the police as the front-line agents control who is brought into the system. They control who is inconvenienced in terms of the loss of the liberty (even for a limited time). They control who will often have to pay a significant amount of capital to an attorney to defend themselves. And it is the police who are ultimately responsible for the number of auto thefts that occur in a given jurisdiction. Thus, while we typically think of the police as operating at a step lower than that of the Courts, their importance in enforcing the imperative moral codes of a society is of the most importance regardless of the future sanctions (if any) handed down by the state.

Hence, if we want to see the state get serious and really commit to prosecuting those we classify as true sex offenders and threats to our society, we must start focusing on the behaviors that the people (and those that are on the front line) believe are the most serious threats to society. And allow the police the discretionary power at the organizational level to focus its efforts in areas where the law is needed and can make a real impact on protecting our citizenry.

The emphasis here is on law enforcement—they are closest to the criminal element and the behaviors in question. Further, it is the police who can change enforcement strategies almost overnight through the use of situational discretion. The courts often take more time since they typically cannot act independently. Cases must be brought to the court's attention, a disposition must be read, and its intent must be interpreted and then placed into agency policy across the country. Thus, the police, as the front-line agents, have tremendous power in bringing offenders into the system.

Once we understand and accept that the state or (in this case) the police are not to be used as an agent of a subsection of the population to police moral crimes through the political process, they can then be freed to use the resources they have to begin addressing some of the major problems we face. And today, in the area of sexual offending, these major problems are generally considered to be offenses involving human trafficking and the use and abuse of women and children.

Crimes Against Children

The use of children by adults in procuring their own sexual satisfaction is a problem that has existed since the dawn of time. In ancient Rome, it was perfectly acceptable for adult males to take children in and become their mentors in both business and sexual behavior. In fact, families often competed with one another to place their children in the homes of prominent businessmen (Holmes and Holmes, 2009). However, those days are now gone. Today, in most Western nations children are seen as a protected class, and those that prey on them are the most vile criminals in the justice system. Even in prisons, child molesters and abusers occupy the lowest levels in the heirarchy of social status (Santos, 2007).

Today, law enforcement officials and even units at the state and federal level are increasing their efforts to protect children. They are hiring individuals that are tech savvy and understand not only the physical but virtual environments where kids congregate. Ten years ago, all law enforcement had to do was create a fictional identity in a chat room, but now kids and their predators are much more sophisticated. They hang out on Facebook, Twitter, Instagram, forums on gaming computers and just about anywhere else you can imagine. Law enforcement has to mirror this behavior to keep up with the criminals. Law enforcement not only has to keep their finger on the pulse of youth but also learn how to blend in with others to avoid detection.

The interesting thing about child predators is that many of them are normal in almost every other way except for their sexual interests. Further, the predators, who are often educated members of the community, know the risks of either meeting or electronically engaging with a child. They know that law enforcement is out there. They know that officers are in online forums posing as children. They know that when they meet a child in person, there is always the risk that they are being set up and will be taken down. They know that once caught, their lives will never be the same—they may lose their jobs, their friends and their social network. However, these risks often do not stop them. In this way, they are extremely dangerous; their crimes often do not fit the rational behavioral patterns that our justice system is based on (Greer, Estupinan and Manguno-Mire, 2000). Thus, no amount of proactive enforcement measures will lessen the propensity of those who have an interest in sexual relations with children.

Protecting our children, then, requires constant monitoring and enforcement. It demands an agency that consistently changes and evolves. Agencies are thus compelled to hire young adults that are able to fit in well and "talk and act" like other youth even in a virtual environment. And at the same time, the agency must employ seasoned officers to follow, supervise and assist those that are currently in sex offender lists and registries.

The Forgotten Role of Law Enforcement

Many actors within and those who study the justice system often overlook that law enforcement officials have been working with, monitoring and bringing to justice sex offenders. All too often we assume that taking a hard-line approach with the offenders at least in media accounts, creates a antagonistic relationship between these offenders to those assigned to watch and supervise them. This simply is not the case. While officers from sex crimes units are charged with investigating crimes but are also charged with following up with the offenders. That is, it is often their job to surveil the offenders. Officers must verify that the offender is employed, living in the home that they claim and fulfilling the conditions of release. And the best of these officers develop a personal relationship with the offenders. In this sense, they assume a role not unlike modern day social workers. While the officers may find the offenders and their acts personally repulsive, but they understand that, if they want to control the offender and protect others, assisting these offenders often becomes of their unwritten duties. One deputy told the authors that they treat this part of their job as a game. He said:

> It is my job to watch over them—to pretend to be interested in them personally and their reintegration in the community. And it is their job to hide as much as they can from me. It's a cat-and-mouse game, and we both know we are playing a game. I can usually tell when suspects are up to no good, but have a hard time proving it. The best tool I have in my tool belt is the use of unannounced visits. (Anonymous, 2015)

These visits may be as simple as a wave from a car or as involved as a personal meeting at the offender's home. It is these meetings that often bear the most fruit in terms of determining whether an offender is meeting the conditions of release. Further, it is the officer's ability to relate one-on-one with the offender that will determine whether the offender is willing to share the intimate details of their crime and past criminal behavior. In some cases, we have seen officers take on not just the role of a formal agent of social control but also that of a therapist because there are few people that many of these offenders can talk to about their crimes. And when an officer can get an offender to open up, the offender can then begin to truly understand the patterns and motivations that have driven them in the past and potentially the future.

This secondary and often misunderstood role of police is one of the most important in monitoring sex offenders in the community. While it does involve officers taking on roles that were often reserved for probation and parole agents, it is also one that can bear a lot of fruit. Officers may receive information about previously unknown individuals with like propensities who are preying on the weak and helpless in their communities. For it is these offenders who know who the major players are that engage children in organized ways for exploitation in the form of pornography or sexual trafficking.

Human and Sex Trafficking

Just as it is important to focus law enforcement efforts on offenders that prey on children, it is also important to better utilize our agents of the law to investigate and arrest those that prey upon and exploit vulnerable populations for their own sexual or financial purposes. Until relatively recently, little was really known or written about human or sex trafficking in the United States. That has however changed in the past ten years. It now is being recognized as a major problem both here and worldwide (Hughes, 2000).

The Size and Extent of the Industry and Problem

It is estimated that up to 4 million people worldwide are trafficked, with about a quarter of them brought into the sex slave market. Some claim this number is much higher given that law enforcement has no idea how many individuals are brought into this nexus (International Organization for Migration, 2001). The business is so large that it is estimated that human trafficking is the third most profitable enterprise in the world behind only the sale and distribution of drugs and arms.

With profits so large and exceeding legitimate business interests, it is no wonder that this industry is growing rapidly. Involved in the trade are individual entrepreneurs, international businessmen and even established organized criminal enterprises.

One does not have to look far to see evidence of human trafficking and, more specifically, the sexual trafficking of women and children. One of the hotbeds of sex trafficking is the roadside massage parlors that litter many of our major expressways. Many of these establishments "employ" young women who are brought into this country illegally. They work at these "establishments" not only to earn their keep but to help pay off the debt bond for their travels to this country. For Asian women, this debt can be anywhere from $6,000 to $35,000. For women from Russia, the price is considerably lower (Human Rights Watch, 2000). In any event, the amount of the debt bond promised by the transporter is typically quoted low and then drastically inflated upon arrival. Relatively few girls will ever make enough to pay off their debt.

In order to avoid detection, these women are rotated to different locations across jurisdictional boundaries. This "rotation of stock" also serves as a control mechanism and prevents them from getting to know others in the community outside of the organization.

Law enforcement experts that investigate these establishments will tell you that the shops are owned by large criminal enterprises who join with other loosely organized groups to keep "talent" coming into the country. They then dispose of those that are no longer useful to the organization (Finckenauer and Schrock, 2003).

Even more alarming is that many sold into servitude in these enterprises are young (usually below the age of 15) and promised a better life with freedom once they have served their time. Unfortunately, that rarely happens without strings or the ability to report those in charge to the authorities.

It is important to note that the victims of sexual trafficking in the United States are not only persons brought into this country illegally. Instead, law enforcement is increasingly finding that young women and children born in the United States are brought into the trade by independent entrepreneurs. This can happen in numerous ways—it most commonly happens when children run away from home. Runaways are usually drawn to cities they view as glamorous or where they believe there is enough work for them to make it on their own. Typically, these cities are tourist destinations such as Orlando, Miami, New Orleans, Los Angeles or New York.

Once they arrive in these cities, not only do they often not have a place to stay but they discover that work is difficult if not impossible find without a permanent address, a phone number, transportation and a means of cleaning what clothes they have. Thus, many are forced into the sex trade to make ends meet. Once in the trade, they are usually taken in and under the wing of a "pimp" who arranges their meetings with paying customers, transports them to their destination and of course provides needed protection from being ripped off or, even worse, physically assaulted.

Creating Dependency

Increasingly law enforcement has seen that pimps are not only part of an organized group but that they use the same tactics to bring the girls in and make them dependent on the organization for their survival. For instance, they typically use highly addictive drugs such as heroin to get the girls (or young men) dependent on the pimps not only for the roof over their head, food and spending money, but for the drugs they need in order to get through the day. One offender stated that "they only need to give the girls about six doses of heroin to get them right where they need them." And since heroin is so cheap, it is the most efficient and cost effective way to ensure that the girls will not flee despite their living or work conditions.

Once chemically dependent, the typical process is to keep forcing the victims to increase their production until their utility is used up. Reports of women being forced to work 6 days a week and service up to 25 men a night is not out of the ordinary (Gardiner and Monohan, 2001). They are then sold to another solicitor typically in another town. The price generated for the victims of the sex trafficking trade can vary from a low of approximately a couple hundred dollars to upwards of $20,000, with the prime determiner of the price being the condition and age of the victim. Typically, younger girls and those in better physical condition draw higher values on the open market.

Human sex trafficking is very different than the traditional prostitution rings of years past. True, there have always been pimps and those that use the threat of violence to keep their brood in line. And it is also true that drugs have also been used as a means to control the flock. However, what has changed is the availability of cheap, highly addictive drugs, the large multinational networks that control the distribution and trade of the victims and of course the lucrative dollars that are associated with this trade. While we don't have accurate figures for the United States, it is estimated that the sex trade accounts for between 2 to 4 percent of the GDP in Indonesia, Malaysia, the Philippines and Thailand (Perry and Sai, 2002).

What makes human and sex trafficking such a large problem for law enforcement and government alike is not only the harm done to the victims, but the problems associated with investigating and policing this type of crime.

Investigation of Human Trafficking Cases

As mentioned previously, the availability of women who are willing to sell access to their bodies and men who are willing to pay for it is not new. In fact, prostitution has been labeled the world's oldest profession. But what makes this more complicated today is not only the accessibility of the victims but the huge profits available to those that engage in this type of criminal activity.

The Internet has done many wonderful things for the world. It brings people closer together, it opens new world markets but it also allows those that engage in the trafficking of individuals to advertise to a larger and even worldwide audience. Not only can they advertise, but they can do so with relative impunity. The risk of being caught or investigated by agencies across jurisdictional lines is minimal. Further, the risk that the women or children being trafficked will come forward once brought into a foreign country is low—they rarely speak the native language, their passports have been confiscated by the traffickers, they do not want to be shipped back to their home country and they often believe that the faster they pay back their debt, the sooner they will be allowed the leave the organization.

Further, most of the women involved in the trafficking trade come from countries where there are no written laws regarding human trafficking specifically. So, it is difficult for law enforcement to make a case against those who send the victims abroad. The only recourse law enforcement has is to attempt to prosecute the women locally, which often results in them being held by ICE for possible deportation back to their own country, while the traffickers go free because the victims are afraid to testify.

Some have even stated that criminals participating in human and sex trafficking engage in a calculus recognizing the financial lucrativeness of trafficking humans versus drugs. What they typically find is that both offenses offer huge financial payoffs, but human trafficking often carries little risk of being caught, much less convicted (Orhant, 2001).

THE ROAD AHEAD

As discussed in this article, the focus on and prosecution of sex offenders is a topic that has captured the attention of people worldwide. While we commonly think of sex offenders as those that prey on our children, family and friends, the scope of individuals that engage in these types of offenses is much larger —there are individuals, groups of people and even multinational enterprises dedicated to this criminal activity.

Today, law enforcement simply does not have the resources to investigate and prosecute everyone who engages in these criminal enterprises. Thus, they must prioritize where and in what areas they may be able to make a difference. The politicians and other governmental bodies who control the laws will always want the police to enforce all the laws on the books, especially those that violate the morality of the most populous sections of the voting public. That task, however, is just not possible. As those closest to the people and the criminal enterprise, law enforcement must decide who the biggest threats are and where to place their limited financial and human capital. And for all appreciable purposes, their attention should primarily be turned to investigating and prosecuting those that engage in crimes against children and those that prey on vulnerable populations (as in the case of human trafficking).

As a nation, we need to come to grips with human and sexual trafficking. For too long people in the United States have believed that this type of activity simply couldn't be occurring here. Of course, the evidence has been right before our eyes for years; we just didn't want to admit it.

In the coming years, we need to empower government, and law enforcement specifically, to go after those that traffic in humans and enslave them for sexual purposes. Laws need to be strengthened, enforcement efforts need to be ramped up and, most importantly, people need to become aware of the reality of the situation—right now it is just too easy for the perpetrators of this crime to get away with it. Cheap drugs are readily available, making it easy to create chemically dependent victims, and the penalties do not meet the damage done by those who commit the crime.

As we move forward into the next decade we need to stop focusing on the nuisance sex crimes that make national headlines and begin focusing on crimes that are truly harmful to victims and those that offend the dignity of human life.

REFERENCES

Finckenauer, J. and J. Schrock (2003). "Human Trafficking: A Growing Criminal Market in the US." Washington, DC: National Institute of Justice.

Gardiner, S. and G. Monohan (2001). "The Sex Slaves from Mexico: Teenagers Tell of Forced Prostitution." Newsday.com, March 12. Available at http://www.newday.com/news/local.newyork/ny-smuggled-mexico.story (7 pp.).

Greer. J., L. Estupinan, and G. Manguno-Mire (2000). "Empathy, Social Skills, and Other Relevant Cognitive Processes in Rapists and Child Molesters." *Aggression and Violent Behavior*, 5 (1), 99–126.

Holmes, S. and R. Holmes (2009). *Sex Crimes: Patterns and Motivations*. Thousand Oaks, CA: Sage.

Hughes, D. (2000). "The Natashia Trade: The Transnational Shadow Market of Trafficking in Women." *Journal of International Affairs* 53 (Spring): 625–651.

Human Rights Watch (2000). Owed Justice: Thai Women Trafficked into Debt Bondage. (September).

International Organization for Migration (2001). "New IOM Figures on the Global Scale of Trafficking." *Trafficking in Migrants: Quarterly Bulletin 23 (April)*.

KIMAtv.com (2016) http://kimatv.com/news/offbeat/washington-state-employee-fired-for-watching-hours-of-porn-at-work)

Orhant, M. (2001). "Sex Trade Enslaves Eastern Europeans." Available at http://fpmail.friends-partners.org/pipermail/stop[traffic.

Perry, A. and Mae Sai (2002). "How I Bought Two Slaves to Free Them." *Time* March 11: 7.

Santos, M. (2007). *Inside: Life Behind Bars in America*. New York: St. Martin's Griffin.

CHAPTER 9

ABERRANT FORMS OF SEXUAL BEHAVIOR

THOMAS S. WEINBERG

From a symbolic interactionist perspective, the label "aberrant" is problematic, because such a label and its application are dependent upon some social audience with the power to make it stick. In turn, how these labelers see behavior is reliant upon the social context, which changes over time and from place to place. For example, the psychiatric profession is one of our society's most powerful labelers. The American Psychiatric Association's *Diagnostic and Statistical Manual of Mental Disorders* (*DSM*) defines many psychiatric behaviors. Yet, these definitions have changed over the years and through several editions of the *DSM*. At one time, for instance, homosexuality was defined as pathological. Later, at a meeting of the APA in 1974, it was decided to remove homosexuality from the *DSM*. Nymphomania, first defined as a form of mental illness in 1882 by the physician E. C. Abbey (Abbey 1882) and discussed in Richard von Krafft-Ebing's *Psychopathia Sexualis* four years later (Krafft-Ebing 1965 [1886]), is no longer in the *DSM*. Instead, there have been discussions about adding a category of sexual addiction or hypersexuality to the next edition.

There is a section on paraphilias in the fourth, revised edition of the *DSM*. Included in this section are exhibitionism, fetishism, frotteurism, pedophilia, sexual masochism, sexual sadism, transvestic fetishism, and voyeurism. There is also a category for "paraphilia not otherwise specified," which includes less common paraphilias, such as necrophilia, zoophilia, and others. These categories, closest to the label of aberrant sexuality, have been devastatingly critiqued by Moser and Kleinplatz (2005), who question the categorization of the paraphilias as mental disorders by the *DSM*. By so doing, they attack the underlying psychoanalytic assumptions of the paraphilia section.

In their analysis, Moser and Kleinplatz make a number of important points. They begin by using a social constructionist approach to point out that conceptions of mental disorders are made within a sociocultural context, thus making scientific definitions of healthy sexual behavior difficult to find. They deny that the paraphilias are mental disorders, noting that research has not provided data in support of this classification. In fact, they emphasize that non-clinical studies of individuals with unusual sexual interests do not distinguish them from those with conventional sexual interests. Additionally, Moser and Kleinplatz point out inconsistencies and contradictions within the *DSM* classification. They also provide specific instances in which statements appearing as fact in the section are not supported by research, including assertions about the sex ratio among masochists, the extent of injuries stemming from this behavior, and the prevalence of certain sexual practices. Claiming that the paraphilia section is not consistent with the current state of knowledge, they assert that criteria for such diagnoses rest on unproven and untested assumptions. Similarly, Reiersol and Skeid (2006) critique the usefulness of the classification of fetishism, fetishistic transvestism and sadomasochism in the *International Classification of Diseases* of the World Health Organization.

Traditionally, discussions of aberrant sexuality have taken a clinical approach, seeing these behaviors as individual psychopathology and utilizing case histories to validate their assertions (Caprio 1955; Chideckel 1963 [1935]; Krafft-Ebing 1965 [1886]; Stekel 1964 [1930]). However, many of these behaviors are also subcultural, which fundamentally alters how we view and understand their origins and practice. The advent of the internet, with its plethora of blogs, chat-rooms, web pages, and the like illustrates the subcultural nature of many of these forms of non-normative behavior.

Keeping these caveats in mind, this paper will discuss a few behaviors presently labeled as "aberrant."

SADOMASOCHISM

Like many other forms of aberrant sexual behavior, sadomasochism, the eroticization of dominance and submission, has traditionally been viewed as an individual psychopathology (Freud 1938, 1953 [1905], 1959 [1924], 1961 [1920]; Krafft-Ebing 1965 [1886]; Ross 1997; Stekel 1965 [1929]). It was only four decades ago, beginning with the pioneering work of anthropologist Paul Gebhard (1969), that a more comprehensive view of this behavior as subcultural began to develop. Scores of articles on various social aspects of sadomasochism have been published since Gebhard's seminal paper, employing a variety of methodologies, including content analyses, survey research, in-depth interviews, and ethnography, and utilizing various theoretical perspectives, including symbolic interactionism, frame analysis, and postmodernism. Writers have noted that rather than being an isolated subculture, aspects of sadomasochism have found their way into popular culture and fashion (Falk and Weinberg 1983; Weinberg and Magill 1995). Social science research in sadomasochism over the past four decades indicates that this is a complex social phenomenon, not easily or accurately summed up by psychoanalytical perspectives. Contrary to the psychoanalytical view that SM is an individual psychopathology, sociological, social psychological, and anthropological studies see SM practitioners as emotionally and psychologically well balanced, generally comfortable with their sexual orientation, and socially well adjusted.

Characteristics of Sadomasochism

Sociologists and social psychologists have identified a number of defining characteristics of sadomasochism. It is about the ritualization of dominance and submission and not necessarily about pain. SMers often consider their behavior to be a power exchange (Ernulf and Innala 1995; Hoople 1996; Moser 1988). SM is recreational or play-like behavior (Moser 1998), which is set aside from other aspects of life. Sadomasochistic behavior thus involves fantasy in varying degrees. Frequently, sadomasochistic scenarios are scripted; individuals play designated roles during their interaction. This serves to confine the behavior only to that episode, keeping it from spilling over to other aspects of life. Using fantasy, sadomasochistic scenes are framed by social definitions that give the behavior a specific contextual meaning (Weinberg 1978). It is this fantasy frame that allows participants to engage in behaviors or roles that are usually not permitted in everyday life, enabling them to enjoy themselves without feeling guilt (Weinberg 1978).

Sadomasochistic scenes are both consensual and collaboratively produced (Newmahr 2008; Weinberg 1978, 1987, 2006; Weinberg and Falk 1980). What may appear to the uninitiated observer to be spontaneous behavior is often carefully planned. Forced participation is not acceptable within the subculture; it is only the *illusion* that individuals are coerced that is approved by sadomasochists. Participants must agree on what will take place during the scene and carefully discuss limits to the interaction, as well as specific fantasies or scenarios (Moser 1998), insuring that both derive pleasure from their participation. Moser (1998) notes, however, that when SMers know each other well, this discussion may not always take place. Kamel (1980) points out that risk is reduced through agreement on norms and values within the subculture.

Sadomasochistic behavior is highly symbolic; a variety of devices, such as clothing (Brodsky 1993), the use of language, the utilization of restraints, and so forth, serve to indicate a participant's role, either dominant or submissive, in the interaction.

Sadomasochistic identity

Kamel (1980; see also Kamel and Weinberg 1983) demonstrated that for gay leathermen, becoming a sadomasochist was part of an interactive process or "career," during which the individual becomes aware of role expectations and is socialized into the community. The first sadomasochistic experience often, but not always, precedes "coming out," which refers to the process of coming to terms with a sadomasochist self-identity and entry into the subculture (Moser and Levitt 1987). There may be gender differences in this process, although the literature on coming out is unclear. Some people who have not previously recognized any SM interests become involved in sadomasochism through a variety of relationships. Breslow *et al.* (1985) found that another person had introduced over 60% of the women they studied to SM. While Breslow *et al.* found that men reported first developing an interest in SM on average six years earlier than females (14.99 years versus 21.58 years), Moser and Levitt (1987) found that women and men came out and participated in sadomasochistic behavior at about the same age. Coming out in the Moser and Levitt sample occurred at 22.9 years for males (Moser and Levitt 1987) and 22.7 years for females (Levitt *et al.* 1994). Bezreh (2009: 28) found that "13 of 20 respondents reported that they were aware of fantasies or feelings related to SM by age 15. Seven respondents reported that awareness by age ten."

Sadomasochistic Subcultures

It is inaccurate to speak generically of the sadomasochistic subculture. There are many different sadomasochistic worlds organized around sexual orientation, gender, and preferred activities. For example, there are heterosexual, gay male "leathersex," and lesbian subcultures. There are more specialized subcultures devoted to bondage and discipline (B & D), which is used to describe the combination of restraint and control with punishment or humiliation, and body modifications like genital piercing, branding, burning, and cutting. Some SM practitioners make distinctions between sadomasochism, dominance and submission, and bondage and discipline. Often, however, there are blendings and overlaps among these subcultures, and a variety of practitioners may interact in parties or clubs (Moser 1998).

Sadomasochists enter their subcultures in a variety of ways. In addition to being introduced to these practices by another person, they meet others by placing and responding to advertisements in specialized publications, through chat-rooms on the internet, and by joining formally organized SM clubs, such as the Eulenspiegel Society and the Society of Janus. These societies function as support groups and agents of socialization into SM. They provide information about sadomasochistic practices and develop and maintain justifications, ideologies, and neutralizations, which allow members to engage in these activities while avoiding a deviant self-identity. There are also SM bars in which sadomasochists can find one another and engage in sadomasochistic scenes. Additionally, sadomasochists hold private parties, sometimes with more than 500 participants (Moser 1998).

FETISHISM AND PARTIALISM

Fetishism is sexual arousal by an inanimate object, while partialism refers to the generation of sexual excitement by a body part. Both of these behaviors have been traditionally dealt with as clinical aberrations. Caprio (1955: 265), for example, defines fetishism as "a form of sexual deviation in which the person's libido becomes fixated to something that constitutes a symbol of the love-object." Stekel (1964 [1930]: 3) notes that:

> The personal form of sexual attraction varies with different persons on the basis of a kind of fetishism, i.e., everyone prefers certain characteristics or attributes in his sexual objects … We call them normal fetishes. They become pathological only when they have pushed the whole love object into the background and themselves appropriate the function of a love object.

Many of the erotic attractions of fetishists are learned within the larger culture and reflect knowledge of culturally learned symbols of sexuality. For instance, the fascination large female breasts hold for some men may have its roots in popular culture. The 1950s icon Dagmar, for example, was a celebrity so well known for her mammary endowment that car bumpers of the day were named after her. Women undergo breast enhancement partly because of the societal norm that larger breasts are more attractive. Some fetishes seem to be traceable to the era in which fetishists grew up. For example, preoccupation with separate garter belts and stockings in an earlier era appears to have been replaced with erotic attraction to pantyhose.

As with many other sexual variations, there are subcultures for fetishists and partialists. The advent of the internet not only facilitates communication among fetishists but provides materials for their satisfaction. Both pay and free internet sites enable fetishists to indulge their fantasies. There are, for example, sites for those interested in shoes, feet, smoking, face-sitting, pantyhose, cheerleaders, hairy women, female body builders, and so on.

Weinberg, Williams, and Calhan (1995) used mailed questionnaires to study a non-clinical sample of 262 gay and bisexual men who belonged to a mail organization catering to foot fetishists. They found that "it does not appear that our group of fetishists is much different in the extent of their psychological problems than wider populations … fewer than one in four clearly fit the picture of the psychologically troubled fetishist found in the literature" (Weinberg, Williams, and Calhan 1995: 24).

FROTTAGE

Frottage, also called frotteurism, the rubbing of one's genitals against another's body for sexual gratification, has barely been noted in the sociological literature. It may be either consensual or non-consensual. Consensual frottage was discussed by Paul Cressey (1968 [1932]) in his study of taxi-dance halls. Some of the female employees in these halls engaged in "sensual dancing," allowing their paying dance partners to rub their genitals against them. This was one of several techniques used to increase their customer base and, hence, their earnings. Generations of teenagers have practiced "dry humping" as a way of avoiding actual sexual intercourse. Sexual rubbing is also engaged in by gay men and women.

Non-consensual frottage is a form of sexual assault. It occurs in crowded public situations like bars, subway trains, and buses:

I was seated in a crowded streetcar with standing room only during rush hour. An elderly man, probably in his mid-seventies, climbed aboard. Almost immediately, he found a spot behind a young woman, reaching over her to grasp the hanger. As the streetcar lurched forward, he pressed against her backside. I would not have paid much attention to this except that he maintained his position, even when additional space became available.

After several blocks had passed, the young woman exited the streetcar. Quickly, the man found another young woman and positioned himself similarly behind her. After this woman left the car, he once again found a young woman and pressed against her. Finally, he left the streetcar.

(Author's field notes)

This episode is instructive as an example of how one frotteur selected his victims and was able to carry out his private sexual aberrance within a very public setting. First, all of his victims were similar in appearance, although two were Caucasian and one was Asian. They were young, probably in their late teens or early twenties, petite, slim, and had long, straight hair. Second, the man used the ambiguity of the situation—a crowded vehicle that swayed back and forth, starting and stopping abruptly—to conceal his deviant motives. By selecting young women, he was probably assuming that they would be somewhat naive and less likely to confront him than an older, more experienced individual. He also used the possibility that the setting provided for multiple explanations of his behavior, which may have made the women reluctant to confront him and cause a public scene. He could, if challenged, use the ambiguity of the setting to proclaim his innocence.

While frottage is an individual behavior, there is some indication of the beginning of a formation of a subculture of frotteurs. For instance, there is an anonymous web group called "I Like Frottage" (www.experienceproject.com/groups/like-frottage/230720). However, it claims only three members and has no posts.

BESTIALITY AND ZOOPHILIA

Sexual contact with animals (bestiality) and sexual preference for animals (zoophilia) are depicted in myth and legend (Cornog and Perper 1994; King 2002; Rathus, Nevid, and Fichner-Rathus 2008). They have also been the subject of films and plays (*Equus*, 1977; *Futz!*, 1969). Yet, sex researchers other than psychiatrists (Caprio 1955; Krafft-Ebing 1965 [1886]) have not paid much attention to these forms of sexuality, and as Williams and Weinberg (2003) point out, even sexuality texts devote little space to this behavior. There are exceptions to the general avoidance of this topic, however. In Alfred Kinsey's pioneering studies (Kinsey, Pomeroy, and Martin 1948; Kinsey, Pomeroy, Martin, and Gebhard 1953), he presented data indicating that a small percentage of both men and women engaged in sex with animals. Hunt (1974) also found a small proportion of men and women in his sample had had sexual contacts with animals. In August B. Hollingshead's classic study of *Elmtown's Youth* (1949: 416), he describes contact between young men and farm animals:

> During these early adolescent years a considerable proportion of these boys develop a behavior pattern which brings them into contact with farm animals on a scale that has only recently been emphasized. Young farm boys have relations with animals more frequently than the town boys, but town boys often visit friends in the country and in the course of their play a visit to the barn is not unusual. Twenty-six boys admit that they have had intercourse with animals at one time or another—calves most frequently, but mares, sows, and ewes are included.

Sexual contact with animals is not confined to youths. In July 2009, a 50-year-old South Carolina man was arrested and charged with having sex with a horse. This was the second time he had been arrested for the same offense with the same animal. The horse's owner had installed a surveillance camera in the stable and caught him *in flagrante*. He had previously been ordered to undergo psychiatric treatment and had been given medication (Associated Press 2009).

Sex with animals remains controversial. Wisch (2008) notes that 30 states have passed legislation that prohibits sexual contact between humans and animals. Beirne (2001) makes a strong case that human–animal sex is wrong because it involves coercion, produces pain and suffering, and violates the rights of another being.

The definitive work on zoophilia to date has been done by Williams and Weinberg (2003). They studied a sample of 114 self-identified zoophile men, obtained through an internet website and snowball sampling. Additionally, they attended a gathering of some of these men and conducted face-to-face and telephone interviews. The men were well educated, most of them were single and had never married, and many were working in technical fields. Their median age was 27. The subjects made a distinction between bestiality and zoophilia, noting that the former simply indicated having sex with animals, while the later indicated real love and affection for them. The major reason for having sex with animals, according to these men, was the desire for affection and pleasurable sex. They saw animals as more honest and unconditionally loving than humans. Williams and Weinberg emphasize the importance of the internet in bringing zoophiles together as a subcultural community.

CONCLUSION

This brief survey of a few types of aberrant sexual expression indicates that these behaviors have to be explored sociologically as well as psychiatrically to be fully understood. They are not merely individual behaviors but socially reinforced and supported by subcultural groups, which provide their members with accounts, justifications, rationalizations, and neutralizations, enabling them to normalize their desires and behaviors and make them appear to be acceptable. The ubiquity and accessibility of the internet facilitates contact among like-minded individuals, thus promoting the formation of these subcultures.

REFERENCES

Abbey, E. C. (1882) *The Sexual System and Its Derangement*, Buffalo, NY.

American Psychiatric Association (2000) *Diagnostic and Statistical Manual of Mental Disorders*, 4th rev. edn, Washington, DC: American Psychiatric Association.

Associated Press (2009) "Stable owner catches man having sex with horse," July 29. Online. Available at: www.chron.com/disp/story.mpl/bizarre/6553012.html (accessed September 29, 2009)

Beirne, P. (2001) "Peter Singer's 'heavy petting' and the politics of animal sexual assault," *Critical Criminology* 10:43–55.

Bezreh, T. (2009) "The dilemma of disclosure: developing resources for 'coming out' about sadomasochism," unpublished thesis, Emerson College.

Breslow, N., Evans, L., and Langley, J. (1985) "On the prevalence and roles of females in the sadomasochistic subculture: report on an empirical study," *Archives of Sexual Behavior* 14: 303–317.

Brodsky, J. I. (1993) "The mineshaft: a retrospective ethnography," *Journal of Homosexuality* 24(3/4): 233–251.

Caprio, F. S. (1955) *Variations in Sexual Behavior*, New York: Grove Press.

Chideckel, M. (1963 [1935]) *Female Sex Perversions: The Sexually Aberrated Woman as She Is*, New York: Brown Book Company.

Cornog, M. and Perper, T. (1994) "Bestiality," in V. L. Bullough and B. Bullough (eds) *Human Sexuality: An Encyclopedia* (pp. 60–63), New York: Garland.

Cressey, P. G. (1968 [1932]) *The Taxi-Dance Hall: A Sociological Study in Commercialized Recreation and City Life*, New York: Greenwood Press.

Ernulf, K. E. and Innala, S. M. (1995) "Sexual bondage: a review and unobtrusive investigation," *Archives of Sexual Behavior* 24: 631–654.

Falk, G. and Weinberg, T. S. (1983) "Sadomasochism and popular Western culture," in T. Weinberg and G. W. L. Kamel (eds) *S and M: Studies in Sadomasochism* (pp. 37–144), Buffalo, NY: Prometheus Books.

Freud, S. (1938) *The Basic Writings of Sigmund Freud*, trans. A. A. Brill, New York: Modern Library.

—— (1953 [1905]) "Three essays on sexuality," trans. J. Strachey, in J. Strachey (ed.) *The Standard Edition of the Complete Psychological Works of Sigmund Freud*, vol. VII (pp. 135–230), London: Hogarth Press.

—— (1959 [1924]) "The economic problem in masochism," trans. J. Riviere, in E. Jones and J. Riviere (eds) *Sigmund Freud, Collected Papers*, vol. II (pp. 255–276), New York: Basic Books.

—— (1961 [1920]) *Beyond the Pleasure Principle*, trans. J. Strachey, New York: Liveright.

Gebhard, P. (1969) "Fetishism and sadomasochism," in J. H. Masserman (ed.) *Dynamics of Deviant Sexuality* (pp. 71–80), New York: Grune & Stratton.

Hollingshead, A. B. (1949) *Elmtown's Youth: The Impact of Social Classes on Adolescents*, New York: John Wiley & Sons.

Hoople, T. (1996) "Conflicting visions: SM, feminism, and the law, a problem of representation," *Canadian Journal of Law and Society* 11(1): 177–220.

Hunt, M. (1974) *Sexual Behavior in the 1970s*, Chicago, IL: Playboy Press.

Kamel, G. W. L. (1980) "Leathersex: meaningful aspects of gay sadomasochism," *Deviant Behavior: An Interdisciplinary Journal* 1: 171–191.

Kamel, G. W. L. and Weinberg, T. S. (1983) "Diversity in sadomasochism: four S&M careers," in T. Weinberg and G.W. L. Kamel (eds.) *S and M: Studies in Sadomasochism* (pp. 113–128), Buffalo, NY: Prometheus Books.

King, B. M. (2002) *Human Sexuality Today*, 4th edn, Upper Saddle River, NJ: Prentice- Hall.

Kinsey, A. C., Pomeroy, W. B., and Martin, C. E. (1948) *Sexual Behavior in the Human Male*, Philadelphia, PA: W. B. Saunders.

Kinsey, A. C., Pomeroy, W. B., Martin, C. E., and Gebhard, P. H. (1953) *Sexual Behavior in the Human Female*, Philadelphia, PA: W. B. Saunders.

Krafft-Ebing, R. von (1965 [1886]) *Psychopathia Sexualis*, trans. F. S. Klaff, New York: Stein & Day.

Levitt, E. E., Moser, C., and Jamison, K. V. (1994) "The prevalence and some attributes of females in the sadomasochistic subculture: a second report," *Archives of Sexual Behavior* 23: 465–473.

Moser, C. (1988) "Sadomasochism," *Journal of Social Work and Human Sexuality* 7(1): 43–56.

—— (1998) "S/M (sadomasochistic) interactions in semi-public settings," *Journal of Homosexuality* 36: 19–29.

Moser, C. and Kleinplatz, P. J. (2005) "*DSM-IV-TR* and the paraphilias: an argument for removal," *Journal of Psychology & Human Sexuality* 17(3/4): 91–109.

Moser, C. and Levitt, E. E. (1987) "An exploratory-descriptive study of sadomasochistically oriented sample," *Journal of Sex Research* 23: 322–337.

Newmahr, S. (2008) "Becoming a sadomasochist, integrating self and other in ethnographic analysis," *Journal of Contemporary Ethnography* 37: 619–643.

Rathus, S. A., Nevid, J. S., and Fichner-Rathus, L. (2008) *Human Sexuality in a World of Diversity*, 7th edn, Boston, MA: Allyn & Bacon.

Reiersol, O. and Skeid, S. (2006) "The ICD diagnoses of fetishism and masochism," in P. J. Kleinplatz and C. Moser (eds) *Sadomasochism: Powerful Pleasures* (pp. 243–262), New York: Harrington Park Press.

Ross, J. M. (1997) *The Sadomasochism of Everyday Life*, New York: Simon & Schuster.

Stekel, W. (1964 [1930]) *Sexual Aberrations*, New York: Grove Press.

—— (1965 [1929]) *Sadism and Masochism: The Psychology of Hatred and Cruelty*, vol. II, New York: Grove Press.

Weinberg, M. S., Williams, C. J., and Calhan, C. (1995) "'If the shoe fits . . .' exploring male homosexual foot fetishism," *Journal of Sex Research* 32: 17–27.

Weinberg, T. S. (1978) "Sadism and masochism: sociological perspectives," *Bulletin of the American Academy of Psychiatry and the Law* 6: 284–295.

—— (1987) "Sadomasochism in the United States: a review of recent sociological literature," *Journal of Sex Research* 23: 50–69.

——(2006) "Sadomasochism and the social sciences: a review of the sociological and social psychological literature," in P. J. Kleinplatz and C. Moser (eds) *Sadomasochism: Powerful Pleasures* (pp. 17–40), New York: Harrington Park Press.

Weinberg, T. S. and Falk G. (1980) "The social organization of sadism and masochism," *Deviant Behavior: An Interdisciplinary Journal* 1: 379–393.

Weinberg, T. S. and Magill, M. S. (1995) "Sadomasochistic themes in mainstream culture," in T. Weinberg (ed.) *S & M: Studies in Dominance and Submission* (pp. 223–230), Amherst, NY: Prometheus Books.

Williams, C. J. and Weinberg, M. S. (2003) "Zoophilia in men: a study of sexual interest in animals," *Archives of Sexual Behavior* 32(6): 523–535.

Wisch, Rebecca F. (2008) "Overview of state bestiality laws," East Lansing, MI: Animal Legal & Historical Web Center. Online. Available at: www.animallaw.info/articles/art_details/print.htm (accessed October 19, 2009).

CHAPTER 10

INVESTIGATING SEXUAL DREAM IMAGERY IN RELATION TO DAYTIME SEXUAL BEHAVIOURS AND FANTASIES AMONG CANADIAN UNIVERSITY STUDENTS

DAVID B. KING

TERESA L. DECICCO

TERRY P. HUMPHREYS

Abstract: This study aimed to qualitatively assess the content of sexual dreams and determine their relationship to waking life sexual experience and fantasy. Dream reports were collected from 97 female and 33 male university students with a mean age of 20.6 years who, in addition to reporting their most recent dream with sexual content, completed the Index of Sexual Fantasy (Hurlbert & Apt, 1993), the Sexual Daydreaming Scale (Giambra, 1978), and two surveys to account for sexual and orgasmic behaviour and experience. Reports of sex dreams were dominated by references to clothing and emotion, with the most common targets of sexual relations being friends and/or acquaintances. Aggression was present in 19% of the collected dreams and 8% contained direct references to rape. Men were observed to report greater daytime sexual fantasizing with more frequent reports of multiple partners, sexual propositions, and sexual thoughts in their dreams. Findings offer partial support for the continuity hypothesis of dreaming (Hall & Nordby, 1972) in relation to human sexuality, at least within the current subsample of young men. It is suggested that many sex dreams may serve as an outlet for sexual fantasies and desires. Limitations and suggestions for future research are discussed.

Correspondence concerning this article should be addressed to David King, Department of Psychology, 2136 West Mall, University of British Columbia, Vancouver, BC V6T 1Z4. Email: dbking11@psych.ubc.ca

INTRODUCTION

Although research supports a physiological relationship between sex and sleep (e.g., Branchey, Branchey, & Nadler, 1973; Empson & Purdie, 1999; Ho, 1972; Manber & Armitage, 1999; Shin & Shapiro, 2003), little is known of the relationship between sex and dreaming. Freud (1900/1950) argued that all dreams contain sexual content (in either latent or manifest form) and that dream images often symbolize sex organs. He also claimed that much of dream imagery represents repressed sexual instincts or desires. Subsequently, Hall (1953) suggested that dreams are filled with impulse gratification, and that this is especially true of dreams with sexual content. Since the proposal of these theories, however, literature on sexual dream content has been sparse. A PsycINFO database search revealed 38 articles containing the words sex and dream in their titles since 1953. Excluding those which referred to sex differences and gender roles, only 10 related specifically to dreams and human sexuality. Of these, only six were interested in either latent or manifest content of sexual dreams.

An early study by Husband (1936) reported that married people dreamed less of sex and that men were more likely to dream of someone other than their current partner. The Kinsey studies of the 1940s and 1950s found that two-thirds of women reported having dreams with overtly sexual content, compared to 100% of men. By 45 years of age, 37% of women reported having had a sexual dream with orgasm (Kinsey, 1953). Within the male sample, 83% reported having nocturnal emissions with or without dreams, with the highest incidence occurring in the late teens (Kinsey, 1948). A later study of male outpatients found that sex dreams declined following traumatic paraplegia (Comarr, Cressy, & Letch, 1983). LaBerge (1985) investigated sex dreams which were lucid in nature, finding that lucid dream sex is common and induces strong physical reactions similar to waking sex. Although women reported more orgasms in lucid dreams, men reported more sex dreams overall (LaBerge, 1985).

Recently, Schredl, Sahin, and Schafer (1998) confirmed earlier findings that men have more sexual content in their dreams compared to women. Stankovic, Zdravkovic, and Trajanovic (2000) investigated the sex dreams of university students in Yugoslavia, finding that men and women differed significantly in the content, frequency, and emotion of their sex dreams. Some gender differences in sex dreams were confirmed in an extensive investigation by Zadra (2007), who found that men's sex dreams were more likely to involve multiple partners and to take place outdoors. This was in contrast to women's sex dreams that were more likely to contain public figures and celebrities. In spite of these and other differences, frequencies of sex dreams were equal among men and women (approximately 8% of dreams were sexual), as were frequencies of orgasm in sex dreams (approximately 4% of sex dreams). Regardless of content, sexuality appears to be one of the most frequently self-reported dream themes among Canadian university students (others were related to school, falling, being chased, and arriving late) (Nielsen et al., 2003). For the males in this study, sexual experiences were the most frequently reported theme, while they were the second most frequent for females.

Although Zadra (2007) proposed that gender differences were likely due to differences in waking life sexual attitudes and behaviours, the relationship between sexual dream content and daytime sexual activity has not been investigated. In spite of the accumulated support for Hall and Nordby's (1972) continuity hypothesis of dreaming (see Domhoff, 1999a; Schredl, 2003), which contends that dreams reflect waking life, the continuity hypothesis has not been explored in relation to dreams with sexual content. Furthermore, of the recent literature available on sexual dreams (Schredl et al., 1998; Stankovic et al., 2000; Zadra, 2007), only that by Zadra (2007) is based on a North American sample. There is a need for supplementary and innovative research on this topic. Such research would more generally contribute to our understanding of the relationship between sexuality and sleep, of which dreaming is a critical aspect (Domhoff, 1999a; Van de Castle, 1994).

The Current Study

The purpose of the current study was to investigate the relationship of sexual dream content to daytime measures of sexual behaviour, sexual fantasizing, and sexual daydreaming. In accordance with Hall and Nordby's (1972) continuity hypothesis, it was expected that significant positive relationships would be observed between sexual dream imagery and sexual characteristics during waking life. In particular, we hypothesized that individuals who reported higher frequencies of daytime sexual behaviour would also report higher frequencies of sexual interactions in their sex dreams. This hypothesis is consistent with findings by Erlacher and Schredl (2004) of some-what direct links between dream content and daytime concerns and preoccupations (e.g., sport students dream more often of sports compared to psychology students). Hence, individuals who reported greater daytime sexual fantasizing and daydreaming were also expected to report higher frequencies of sexual interactions in their sex dreams. Although this hypothesis was based largely on the notion of continuity between daytime preoccupations and dream content, limited previous research has suggested potential links between daydreams and nocturnal dreams. For example, Soper (1999) observed similar reports of perspective-taking across both types of dreams. The present study sought to test these hypotheses within the context of sex dreams alone in order to draw better conclusions regarding theme-specific variability in dream content.

METHODS

Participants

Dream reports were obtained from an initial sample of 117 female and 44 male university under-graduate students. However, since dream reports of less than 50 or more than 300 words are not recommended for use in such studies of dream content (Domhoff, 2000), dream reports that fell outside of this range were excluded from all subsequent analyses. A final sample of 97 female and 33 male participants was thus the source of the 130 dream reports for this study. The mean age of the participants was 20.55 years (SD = 3.69, range = 17 to 50 years). No significant age difference was observed between men and women. The majority of participants were Caucasian (88.5%), followed by 3.8% Asian and 3.8% African or Caribbean, with the remainder of other descent. Approximately half were in a monogamous relationship (49.2%) at the time of participation, while 32.3% were single, 15.4% were casually dating, and 3.1% were married. Reported sexual orientation was 85.4% heterosexual, 12.3% heterosexual with incremental homosexual experience, .8% homosexual, and 1.5% homosexual with incremental heterosexual experience. The majority had only completed one year of university (61.5%).

Measures

Demographic information. A one-page survey was used to gather basic demographic information on sex, age, sexual orientation, ethnicity, relationship status, and level of education.

Sexual Experiences Questionnaire. Information on frequency of participation in different sexual behaviours was derived from a 25-item questionnaire that asked "How often do you participate in the following sexual behaviours in your waking life?" Questions were modeled loosely on Zuckerman's (1973) Human Sexuality Questionnaire, with removal of dated language and an amalgamation of homosexual and heterosexual behaviours so that one sexual orientation was not favoured over others. Many of the usual behaviours in the original questionnaire were retained including kissing, hand stimulation of partner's genitalia, mouth stimulation of genitalia, and penile-vaginal intercourse; items added to these included anal stimulation, anal intercourse, stimulation using vibrators and sex toys, and sexual activity with multiple partners. Responses were based on a 7-point scale: 0 = "never," 1 = "less than once a year," 3 = "once a month," 4 = "once a week," 5 = "2-5 times a week," and 6 = "more than 5 times per week" with the mid-range response being ("Once a month"). Total possible scores for individual items were 0-6 with a possible total score range of 0-150 and a midpoint of 75. Higher scores indicated greater total sexual experience.

Orgasmic Experiences Questionnaire. Information on frequency of orgasmic experience from different behaviours was derived from a 13-item questionnaire that asked "How often do you experience orgasm through the following behaviours?" Items were drawn as above for total sexual behaviour and included orgasm through "masturbation, alone or with a partner," "oral stimulation of your genitals by someone else," "heterosexual intercourse, vaginal penetration," "homosexual relations or intercourse," "dreams (nocturnal emissions, i.e. wet dream)," and "fantasy alone without masturbation or stimulation of genitals." Responses were based on a 7-point scale from 0 = "never" to 6 = "more than 5 times a week" and were worded exactly as the total experience scale above. Possible scores for individual items were 0-6 with a possible total score range of 0-78 and a midpoint of 39. Higher scores indicated greater total orgasmic experience.

Total lifetime number of sexual intercourse partners. Participants indicated their total number of lifetime sexual intercourse partners in response to a question that asked "With how many partners have you had sexual intercourse (penile-vaginal or anal)? (over your entire lifespan; please estimate if uncertain)." Due to the low mean age of the participants, this estimation was expected to be fairly accurate.

Index of Sexual Fantasy (Hurlbert & Apt, 1993). This is a 24-item questionnaire that measures a person's degree of comfort with and enjoyment of sexual fantasies during their waking life. Participants were asked to "Please read each statement carefully and indicate the extent to which it is true for you by circling one of the following numbers." Items such as "I think sexual fantasies are healthy," "I am easily aroused by thoughts of sex," and "I feel uncomfortable telling my partner my sexual thoughts" were rated on a five-point scale as follows: 0 = "never," 1 = "rarely," 2 = "some of the time," 3 = "most of the time," 4 = "all the time." Individual item scores ranged from 0-4 and the possible total score range was 0-96, with higher scores indicating greater comfort with and enjoyment of sexual fantasies. Validity was supported by Hurlbert and Apt (1993). An alpha of .89 was observed in the current study.

Sexual Daydreaming Scale (Giambra, 1978). This 12-item scale was used to assess frequency and type of sexual daydreaming during one's waking life. Participants were asked to respond as follows: "Please read each statement carefully and indicate the extent to which it is true for you by circling one of the following numbers." Statements included "While working intently at a job, my mind will wander to thoughts about sex," "Whenever I am bored, I daydream about attractive people," "While reading I often slip into daydreams about sex or making love to someone," and "My daydreams tend to arouse me physically." Items were rated on a five- point Likert scale from 0 = "definitely not true of me," 1 = "usually not true for me," 2= "usually true for me," 3 = "true for me," to 4 = "very true of me." Individual item scores could range from 0-4 and the possible total score range was 0-48 with higher scores indicating higher frequency of sexual daydreaming. Validity and reliability of the scale have been supported across multiple studies (e.g., Giambra, 1978). An alpha of .88 was observed in the current study.

Sexual dream content during sleep and content analysis. Each participant was asked to write down, in as much detail as possible, his/her "most recent dream with sexual content." The Most Recent Dream technique is one of two popular and statistically validated techniques currently employed in dream research, the other being the collection of dream journals (Domhoff & Schneider, 1998). The goal of the present study was not to examine the frequency of sex dreams as a proportion of all dreams, but rather to survey the frequency of sexual imagery within such dreams. As such, the Most Recent Dream technique was deemed appropriate and was modified to address dreams of a sexual nature. This technique made it possible to accumulate a large pool of dream reports which contained sexual references, whereas dream journaling may or may not have revealed a sufficient number of sex dreams to meet our research purposes. Dream journaling is also very time-consuming and long-term participant commitment is required (Domhoff & Schneider, 1998). Participants responded to the following question: "Write your most recent dream with sexual content in the space below. Use as much detail as possible. Write in consecutive sentences, as you recall the dream." In addition, they were asked to rate the tone of their sexual dreams as positive, negative, or neutral/unsure.

Dreams were analyzed, in part, using the Hall and Van de Castle (1966) system of content analysis. This is a nominal coding system for dream content used to identify the frequency or occurrence of a large variety of dream images, figures, actions, emotions, and conflicts. Individual dreams are read and scored for categories of interest according to rigidly established rules and guidelines. Normative data are available based on a sample of 1000 dreams from male and female university students, to which novel findings can be compared (Hall & Van de Castle, 1966). This qualitative system of dream analysis has been deemed reliable and valid in multiple studies (see Domhoff & Schneider, 1998; Krippner & Weinhold, 2002) and normative data have been consistently replicated (Domhoff, 1999b; Domhoff, 2000).

The current analyses focused on the Sexual Interactions subcategory of Social Interactions, which is comprised of five subclasses (sexual thoughts, propositions to dream characters, kissing, petting/ fondling, and attempted or actual intercourse). Although subclasses were independently examined and reported, variance within each subclass was lacking (thereby violating parametric assumptions), leading to the examination of total number of sexual interactions (which is a sum of all subclasses) for correlational purposes. For descriptive purposes, the number of sexual partners was summed for each dream, while the primary target of the sexual interaction(s) was identified as one of the following: stranger, friend/acquaintance, family member, or past/current romantic partner. Dreams were also examined for the presence or absence of references to rape, aggression, positive and negative affect, nudity, clothing, and body parts. This was in order to better account for the type of imagery observed in the current sample of sexual dreams.

All dreams were coded by two researchers trained and experienced in content analysis. Inter-rater reliability was calculated by dividing the total number of agreements between analysts by the total number of observations (Domhoff, 1999b; Spata, 2003). This method was recommended by Hall and Van de Castle (1966) for determining inter-rater reliability in content analysis (for a more detailed explanation see Domhoff, 1999b). Resulting reliability was above 90%, which surpasses the minimum required value of 70% (Spata, 2003). Disagreements between coders were resolved by discussion with a senior faculty member also trained in content analysis and mutually agreed upon. In each dream, totals were summed for each of the afore-mentioned themes, providing frequency counts of sexual dream images within each respondent.

Procedure and Data Analyses

This study was advertised to all first-year undergraduate psychology students at Trent University. All participants were volunteers who received a bonus credit towards their introductory psychology course, as per standard departmental policy. Participants were made aware of the nature of this study prior to participation and were asked to sign a detailed consent form, guaranteeing full privacy and informing them of their right to withdraw at any time without consequence. Participation lasted approximately 45 minutes and occurred in a research laboratory at the university which was equipped with private kiosks for confidential responding. Basic demographic information was collected first, followed by the dream report and all other aforementioned questionnaires. Participants were provided with an envelope in which to seal all responses when completed, ensuring full privacy of any information which might be deemed sensitive. Full debriefing occurred with each participant, in which they had the opportunity to voice concerns and/or ask questions about the study. No harms, risks, or concerns were observed in the current sample.

All data were analyzed using SPSS 17.0. One-tailed tests were employed where hypotheses were directed. All other significance testing (including tests of group differences) employed two-tailed tests. Although multiple comparisons were employed, a Bonferroni- type correction was deemed inappropriate due to the study's exploratory nature (Peres-Neto, 1999; Perneger, 1998), as the relationship between sexual dream content and waking sexual characteristics has not been previously investigated. Furthermore, correcting for multiple comparisons increases the risk of committing Type II error and potentially leads to reduced power and loss of valid information (Nakagawa, 2003; Perneger, 1998). As such, all significant results should be regarded as preliminary and require replication in subsequent studies.

RESULTS

Based on the 130 dream reports obtained (one per participant), the average word length for the entire sample was 116.35 words per dream $(SD = 61.14$, range $= 50{-}300)$. Males displayed an average of 102.03 words $(SD = 45.95$, range $= 50{-}222)$ while females displayed an average of 121.22 words $(SD = 65.00$, range $= 50{-}300)$ per dream. A two-tailed t- test for unequal group sizes revealed no significant sex difference in word length of written dream reports. A bivariate analysis (Pearson product-moment correlation) revealed no significant relationship between number of words and number of sexual interactions in dream content, $r = .069$ $(p = .44$, 2-tailed), suggesting that frequency of sexual dream content was not confounded by word length of dream reports in the current sample.

Daytime (Waking) Sexual Behaviour Variables and Dream Content Variables

The wide range of participant responses on each of the five daytime sexual behaviour variables (Table 1) reflects the variability needed in a study seeking to determine the association between dream content and waking behaviour. Sex differences were noted for all five measures. Specifically, men had higher total scores on the sexual experience scale, $t = 2.55$ (128) $(p = .01)$ and the orgasmic experience scale, t (128) $= -3.54$ $(p < .001)$. Men also had significantly higher total scores on the sexual fantasy scale, t (128) $= -2.59$ $(p = .01)$ and the sexual daydreaming scale, t (128) $= -2.26$ $(ip = .03)$ and reported more lifetime sexual partners, t (128) $= -3.27$ $(p = .001)$ than did women. The average number of lifetime sexual intercourse partners for the total sample was 4.63 $(SD = 7.24$, range $= 0{-}60)$.

For both sexes, total scores for sexual experience and orgasmic experience appeared to be notably below the scale mid-points of 75 and 39 respectively; however, this may be misleading due to the high number of "never" responses (scored as 0) for some items. For example, one of the 13 items on the total orgasmic experience scale asked about orgasm during dreaming; 48.5% of male and 58.8% of female participants reported that they had never experienced an orgasm

Table 1 Sex differences in daytime sexual behaviour variables and dream content variables

Daytime sexual behaviour variables (range for all participants)	Females (n = 97) M (SD)	Males (n = 33) M (SD)	p
Total sexual experience (1–128)	45.78 (24.11)	57.87 (21.35)	*
Total orgasmic experience (0–59)	18.53 (11.37)	26.55 (10.86)	***
Number of sexual partners (0–60)	3.46 (3.67)	8.06 (12.43)	**
Sexual fantasy total score (17–95)	64.53 (15.05)	71.90 (10.90)	*
Sexual daydreaming total score (1–48)	24.24 (8.99)	28.11 (6.88)	*
Dream content variables (range for all participants)	M(SD)	M (SD)	p
Number of sexual partners (0–5)	1.03 (.47)	1.33 (.99)	*
Number of sexual interactions (0–14)	3.07 (1.99)	3.76 (3.01)	ns

Note. All *t*-tests are two-tailed and account for unequal sample sizes. Possible score ranges (and mid-points) for the scales above are: total sexual experience 0-150 (75); total orgasmic experience 0-78 (39); sexual fantasy total score 0-96 (48); and sexual daydreaming total score 0-48 (24). *p < .05, **p < .01, ***p < .001

as the result of (or during) a dream while 6.8% of men and 6.2% of women experienced orgasm once a week or more (4—7 on the scale) as the result of dreams. Men and women did not differ significantly on this specific item. Among the sexual behaviour variables, total scores for sexual fantasy and sexual daydreaming fell at or above the midpoint level for both sexes.

The two dream content variables reported in Table 1 show that men reported an average of 1.33 sexual partners in their dreams and women reported an average of 1.03. Men reported significantly more dream partners, $t (128) = -2.34$ $(p = .02)$ within a range of 0-5 for the total sample. The number of sexual interactions in dreams did not differ by sex.

Frequency of Different Categories of Sexual Behaviour in Sex Dream Reports

The sex dreams reported by all participants included an average of 3.25 $(SD = 2.30)$ references to sexuality or sexual interactions. The number of sexual references across dreams totalled 422. Among these, 41.7% concerned attempted or initiated sexual intercourse, 19.7% involved petting or fondling, 19.7% were references to kissing, 16.7% concerned sexual propositions, and only 2.2% referred specifically to sexual thoughts or fantasies.

The findings regarding these measures for males and females are presented in Table 2 as are the Hall and Van de Castle (1966) norms for comparison. Z-tests calculated for males and females independently revealed that the "sexual thoughts and fantasies" category in the dream reports of males significantly differed from the Hall and Van de Castle (1966) norms, $z = 2.78$ $(p < .05, 2$-tailed).

Table 2 Subtypes of sexual interaction in dream reports and comparisons to Hall and Van de Castle (1966) norms

Subclass of Sexuality	Females (n=97)	H/V Norms	Males (n=33)	H/V Norms
Sexual intercourse	45.3%	26%	30.4%	27%
Petting/fondling	19.2%	26%	21.4%	18%
Kissing	20.9%	21%	16.1%	11%
Sexual propositions	12.8%	16%	28.6%	30%
Sexual thoughts/ fantasies	1.7%	11%	3.6%	14%

Note. H/V Norm = Hall and Van de Castle (1966) normative data. Percentages represent proportion of each subclass to number of sexual interactions.

No other subtypes of sexuality were found to differ significantly from normative data in the current sample. Similar tests revealed that females reported a significantly higher proportion of direct references to sexual intercourse compared to males, $z = 2.75$ ($p < .05$, 2-tailed), while males displayed a significantly higher proportion of sexual propositions than females, $z = 3.78$ ($p < .05$, 2-tailed).

Dream Ratings and Content

Based on dreamer ratings, 42.3% of participants rated their sex dreams as positive, while 18.5% rated them as negative and 39.2% described them as neutral or were unsure. A chi-square test of independence demonstrated that these frequencies in dream ratings did not differ between males and females. Of the 130 dreams collected, 18.5% contained aggression, although the dreams often remained positive (e.g., a female respondent described sex with her boyfriend while he was tied to a four-post bed, blindfolded, with his clothing removed). In terms of emotions, 23.8% contained happiness, 23.1% contained apprehension, 7.7% contained anger, 4.6% contained confusion, and 3.8% contained sadness. In total, 49.2% of sex dreams contained some emotional material.

References to body parts were quite common, with 43.1% of dream reports containing at least one direct reference, the head being the most common (followed by extremities and sex organs). Direct references to nudity or being naked occurred in 25.4% of sex dreams. Clothing was described in 38.5% of the sex dreams, with some involving quite detailed descriptions of attire and, in some cases, costumes (e.g., a male respondent described his girlfriend wearing a French maid's outfit, tickling his scrotum with a duster; another respondent described wearing overalls, a tool belt, and army boots during foreplay and intercourse).

In terms of targets of sexual interactions in dreams, 41.6% described friends or acquaintances, 26.9% described past or current romantic partners, 24.6% described strangers, 4.6% were alone or observing others, and 2.3% described family members. Some interactions were romantic in nature (e.g., one female respondent carefully described being out for dinner with her boyfriend, drinking wine and being fed cheesecake, which was followed by caressing, passionate kissing, and eventually sex) while others were more direct and straight to the point (e.g., "We went in the back of his jeep and had sex. After we were finished we went back to his cottage").

Interestingly, only 20 of 68 participants (29.4%) in committed relationships (i.e., married or monogamously coupled) reported a sex dream with their current partner as the target. Descriptions of multiple partners occurred in 8.4% of sex dreams, while homosexual interactions occurred in 6.2% of dreams. Only one dreamer reported a celebrity as the target of her sexual interactions. Finally, 7.7% of dreams contained direct mentions of rape or forced sexual interactions (e.g., "They were chasing me everywhere. When they did catch me, they had sex with me. I had to pretend that I liked it, so that they would not kill me"). All mentions of rape occurred in the dreams of female respondents, and three of these dreams involved the dreamer's father as the aggressor. One dream involving rape ended with pleasurable feelings and sexual satisfaction on the part of the dreamer.

Settings also varied, from indoors to outdoors, and from the mundane (e.g., "I was in my room at my residence. My girlfriend and I were having sex. She was on top smiling at me") to the more imaginative (e.g., "I was in my boat at the cottage at night. My girlfriend was with me. We started having sex on the carpeted floor. The sex was great in [the] missionary position. Right before I finished the boat ran ground preventing me from reaching climax"). In a small number of cases, respondents reported witnessing sexual activity but having no direct involvement (e.g., one dreamer reported looking for her boyfriend, eventually finding him in his room having sex with another male and two females).

Gender was an issue that arose in the content of only two dreams. One was reported by a pre-op male-to-female transsexual, who described being "out of his body" and flying amidst other males. In his dream, his body "fell into" the other male bodies, merging with each of them and producing feelings of warmth and sexual pleasure. The other involved a female participant who reported the following dream: "I was at my friend's house, and we were having sex. It was weird because she is a girl and so am I, however, she did have a penis. When we were finished she became my boyfriend."

Correlational Analyses of Dream Content and Waking Sexual Behaviour

Significant correlations were observed between sexual interactions in dream content and waking life measures (Table 3). Those with more sexuality in their sex dreams reported slightly higher levels of orgasmic experience, sexual daydreaming, and sexual fantasy in their waking lives. Significant positive correlations were also observed among waking life measures, supporting the validity of their current assessment.

Due to the significant gender differences observed across the majority of waking life measures, as well as in the number of sexual partners reported in dreams, correlations were repeated independently for males and females. These differential analyses indicated no significant correlations between waking life measures and sexuality in dreams among women (i.e., sexual interactions in dream content) (Table 4). Among men, however, daytime sexual fantasy scores and sexual daydreaming scores displayed moderate and significant positive correlations with sexuality in

Table 3 Correlations among daytime variables and partial correlations with sexual interactions in dream content

Daytime Variable	1	2	3	4	5	SI
Total sexual experience (1)	—	.60***	.10	.29***	.09	.08
Total orgasmic experience (2)		—	.12	.42***	.33***	.15
Number of sexual partners (3)			—	.12	.10	−.01
Sexual fantasy score (4)				—	.48***	.20*
Sexual daydreaming score (5)					—	21**

Note. N = 130. SI = sexual interactions in dream content. All correlations among daytime variables are one-tailed (Pearson product-moment). Partial correlations between sexual interactions in dreams and daytime variables control for word count. Possible score ranges (and mid-points) for the scales above are: total sexual experience 0-150 (75); total orgasmic experience 0-78 (39); sexual fantasy total score 0-96 (48); and sexual daydreaming total score 0-48 (24).
*p < .05, **p< .01, *** p < .001

dreams (with marked increases from the grouped data). In order to control for potential confounding effects of dream length, all correlational analyses between daytime variables and sexuality in dreams utilized partial correlations which controlled for word count. Partial correlations did not differ significantly from those obtained via bivariate analyses (with most coefficients being identical across methods).

Table 4 Correlations among daytime variables and partial correlations with sexual interactions in dream content (according to sex)

Daytime Variable	Females (n = 97)						Males (n = 33)					
	1	2	3	4	5	SI	1	2	3	4	5	SI
Total sexual experience (1)	—	.62***	.26**	.31**	.10	.01	—	.42**	−.16	−.18	−.03	15
Total orgasmic experience (2)		—	.27**	.48***	.31**	.12		—	−.16	−.01	.21	.11
Number of sexual partners (3)			—	.13	.11	−.02			—	.01	.01	−.07
Sexual fantasy score (4)				—	.44***	.10				—	.55***	.39*
Sexual daydreaming score (5)					—	.14					—	.33*

Note. SI = sexual interactions in dream content. AU correlations among daytime variables are one-tailed (Pearson productmoment). Partial correlations between sexual interactions in dreams and daytime variables control for word count. Possible score ranges (and mid-points) for the scales above are: total sexual experience 0-150 (75); total orgasmic experience 0-78 (39); sexual fantasy total score 0-96 (48); and sexual daydreaming total score 0-48 (24).
* p < .05, ** p < .01, *** p < .001

DISCUSSION

Sexual Dreams and Dream Content

One fundamental purpose of this study was to explore the content of sexual dreams, as research on this topic remains quite limited among North American samples. Although conclusions cannot be made regarding frequency of sexual dreams and sexual dream content across the dreaming experience, the present findings contribute to our understanding of content that is specific to this understudied thematic niche. All subsequent observations on this theme reflect variability within sex dreams, as identified by the dreamers themselves.

In terms of the sexuality reported in these dreams, the percentage of Hall and Van de Castle (1966) subtypes did not differ significantly from normative data overall, with the exception that males were more likely to report sexual fantasies and thoughts in their dreams. This sex difference reflects the current findings more generally, as males also reported more sexual partners in their dreams (mirroring findings by Zadra, 2007) and more sexual propositions in their dreams than did females. These gender differences are in line with those observed for waking life measures, as males reported greater and more varied sexual experience as well as greater sexual fantasizing and daydreaming than did females. Despite these findings, and in contrast to those by Schredl et al. (1998), males and females did not differ significantly in overall frequency of sexuality in their dreams, suggesting that gender differences are more pronounced with regard to sexual fantasizing, both in dreams and in waking life. Furthermore, among males, sexual fantasizing and daydreaming demonstrated notable significant relationships with sexual dream content that were not observed in females. Taken together, the findings indicate a more explicit role of sexual fantasizing among males that spans both waking and dreaming experiences. Such observations of dream content reflect previous analyses of daytime fantasies by Wilson (1992), who discerned higher frequencies of group sex, multiple partners, and voyeuristic/fetishistic tendencies in self-reported sexual fantasies of males. As Wilson (1992) also suggested, however, sexual fantasizing on the part of males is more often the result of sexual frustration than sexual satisfaction. Such an inference is possible in the current sample, as no significant relationships were observed between daytime sexual activity and daytime sexual fantasizing for males. Such relationships were, however, observed for females, supporting previous claims that women who fantasize more have a more active and fulfilling sex life (Wilson, 1992).

Clothing and body parts were referenced quite frequently in the current sample of sex dreams. In many of the dreams, analysts noticed a greater focus on clothing than on body parts, reinforcing the critical role of clothing in sexuality and sexual interactions. Many dreamers described typical daily dress, while others described quite detailed costumes with a fantasy-like quality, representing a spectrum of possibilities that was further reflected in settings, partners, and sexual acts. Nearly half of the sex dreams collected also contained emotional content, suggesting potential underlying affective associations with sex manifesting in dreams. Happiness and apprehension were the most common emotions, again representing a range of content that was primarily rated as positive or neutral by dreamers.

Although negative content did not dominate, aggression occurred in approximately one fifth of the dreams, with nearly half of these dreams containing direct references to rape or forced sexual relations. Such imagery was exclusively reported by females, reflecting previous observations of daytime fantasies by Wilson (1992), who found greater frequencies of rape in the sexual fantasies of women than in those of men. While the histories of these female participants are unknown, this is an area that deserves greater attention, in order to determine the factors in one's waking life that might contribute to potentially negative content. Previous research has indicated that women with greater sexual experience may be more likely to fantasize about rape (e.g., Pelletier & Herold, 1988); however, it has also been demonstrated that women who fantasize about rape are no more likely to have experienced rape in their lifetime (e.g., Gold & Clegg, 1990; Kanin, 1982). Furthermore, some rape fantasies are perceived positively and therefore may be more accurately interpreted as seduction fantasies (Kanin, 1982). This suggests that many dreams of rape may be reflections of sexual experience and fantasy alone rather than negative waking life experiences.

The incidence, however small, of father figures as aggressors in sex dreams suggests that latent content of such dreams may be quite complex, involving subject matter that is not limited to sex or sexuality alone. This further speaks to the utility of examining sex dreams in psychotherapeutic settings. In spite of these limited findings, the most common target of sexual relations was a friend or acquaintance, with another quarter of dreamers reporting a stranger as the target, further suggesting that sex dreams may be a common outlet for the expression of sexual fantasies and desires. This lends partial support to Hall's (1953) claim that impulse gratification is common in dreams with sexual content. This claim is further supported by the finding that only 29% of participants in committed relationships dreamed of their current romantic partner.

Sex Dreams and Waking Sexual Behaviour: Testing the Continuity Hypothesis

Hypotheses regarding continuity were partially supported in the current study. In regards to the first hypothesis, only orgasmic experience was related to the sexual content of reported dreams, and this relationship was non-significant for males and females independently. While this lack of support is discouraging, future research may benefit by examining a greater range of dream content that is less directly related to sexuality. Nevertheless, current findings do suggest that the relationship between waking life sexual experience and sexuality in dreams is weak at best and likely indirect (that is, waking life sexuality may be manifesting itself in less obvious forms of dream content; for example, characters or settings). In regards to the second hypothesis, low but significant correlations were observed between sexual dream content and daytime sexual fantasizing and sexual daydreaming. When examined independently by sex, these relationships strengthened for males and became non-significant for females, offering support for the second hypothesis among males only. Such differential findings among males and females highlight the importance of independently examining sexual dream content by gender.

Limitations

It should be emphasized that findings from the current study are limited to the demographic employed (i.e., Canadian university students in their late teens and early twenties). Nevertheless, Domhoff (2000) notes that the Hall and Van de Castle (1966) norms have been replicated in multiple adult samples and appear not to differ significantly from norms based on university samples, suggesting that current findings may indeed generalize to adult populations. This is further supported by the current observation that proportions of sexuality subtypes in dreams did not differ significantly from normative data (excluding a higher number of sexual thoughts and fantasies in the dreams of males). Although Domhoff (2005) states that research has revealed very little change in dream content from the late teens to old age, further research is needed in order to confirm if this is also the case with continuity between daytime sexuality and sexual dreams. In spite of the potential stability of dream content over the lifespan, changes in sexual activity over the course of human adulthood (see Bee & Bjorklund, 2004) may contribute to changes in continuity with waking life. Whether or not these findings are generalizable beyond a Western context should also be investigated.

The current study also depended on retrospective recall of dream reports, introducing the problem of memory distortion. Due to the lack of information on when reported dreams actually occurred, the current analyses did not control for elapsed time since dream, potentially contributing to inaccurate dream reporting and increased error. Information is restricted to the assumption that reported dreams were the most recent dreams experienced by participants. Although the Most Recent Dream method has been previously validated (Domhoff & Schneider, 1998), it was slightly modified in the current study to address dreams of a sexual nature, limiting conclusions regarding validity. One potential source of error associated with retrospective recall is variation in length or detail of dream reports (Domhoff, 2000). While the current sample of dreams varied considerably in number of words, this factor was controlled for and found not to relate to dream content variables which were of interest to the current study. Nevertheless, retrospective recall remains a problematic source of error, as it has been demonstrated that memory and recall of dreams are dependent on their emotionality and bizarreness, among other factors (Cohen & Conway, 2008).

Future studies may limit some of these problems by utilizing diary reports of dreams or laboratory recall methods, although the relative validity of these methods over and above the Most Recent Dream technique is inconclusive (Domhoff, 2000). Continuity would be more accurately assessed by means of repeated measures or daily diary designs, as cross-sectional research is quite limited in its ability to capture the potential effects of daily sexual experiences on same- or subsequent-night dream content. Although a number of significant differences were observed between the sexes, future research would benefit from larger and more comparable groups of men and women.

Current findings add to the empirical understanding of dreams with sexual content, an area of research which is quite limited in both the human sexuality and dreaming fields of psychology.

Based on dream reports alone, this study offers important insights regarding variability of content within sexual dreams. It appears that, although not representative of the majority, some sexual dreams may contain information about clinically relevant issues related to human sexuality, including violent sexual experiences, familial relationships, and gender identity. The majority, however, qualitatively seem to serve as an outlet for sexual fantasies and desires, lending some support to early theories by Freud (1900/1950) and Hall (1953). This was especially the case for the young men who comprised the current sample, and it is within this subsample that the greatest support for continuity between waking life sexuality and sexual dream content was observed. Preliminary gender-specific support can be extended to Hall and Nordby's (1972) continuity hypothesis in relation to human sexuality. Additional research is needed in order to confirm such continuity and elaborate on its scope and boundary.

REFERENCES

Bee, H.L., & Bjorklund, B.R. (Eds.). (2004). *The journey of adulthood* (5th ed.). Upper Sadler River, NJ: Pearson Education.

Branchey, L., Branchey, M., & Nadler, R.D. (1973). Effects of sex hormones on sleep patterns of male rats gonadectomized in adulthood and in the neonatal period. *Physiology & Behavior,* 11, 609–611.

Cohen, G., & Conway, M.A. (Eds.). (2008). *Memory in the real world* (3rd ed.). New York: Routledge.

Comarr, A.E., Cressy, J.M., & Letch, M. (1983). Sleep dreams of sex among traumatic paraplegics and quadriplegics. *Sexuality and Disability,* 6,25–29.

Domhoff, GW. (1999a). Drawing theoretical implications from descriptive empirical findings on dream content. *Dreaming, 9,* 201–210.

Domhoff, G.W. (1999b). New directions in the study of dream content using the Hall/Van de Castle coding system. *Dreaming, 9,*115–137.

Domhoff, GW. (2000). Methods and measures for the study of dream content. In M. Kryger, T. Roth, & W. Dement (Eds.), *Principles and Practices of Sleep Medicine: Vol. 3* (pp. 463–471). Philadelphia, PA: W.B. Saunders.

Domhoff, G.W. (2005). The content of dreams: Methodologie and theoretical implications. In M.H. Kryger, T. Roth, & W.C. Dement (Eds.), *Principles and Practices of Sleep Medicine* (4th Ed., pp. 522–534). Philadelphia, PA: W.B. Saunders.

Domhoff, G.W., & Schneider, A. (1998). New rationales and methods for quantitative dream research outside the laboratory. *Sleep, 21,* 398–404.

Empson, J.A.C., & Purdie, D.W. (1999). Effects of sex steroids on sleep. *Annals of Medicine, 31,* 141–145.

Erlacher, D., & Schredl, M. (2004). Dreams reflecting waking sport activities: A comparison of sport and psychology students. *International Journal of Sport Psychology, 35,* 301-308.

Freud, S. (1950). The interpretation of dreams. (A.A. Brill, Trans.). New York: Modem-Random House. (Original work published in 1900)

Giambra, L.M. (1977-1978). Adult male daydreaming across the lifespan: A replication, further analyses, and tentative norms based upon retrospective reports. *International Journal of Aging and Human Development, 8,* 197–228.

Gold, S.R., & Clegg, C.L. (1990). Sexual fantasies of college students with coercive experiences and coercive attitudes. *Journal of Interpersonal Violence, 5,* 464–473.

Hall, C.S. (1953). A cognitive theory of dreams. *The Journal of General Psychology, 49,* 273–282.

Hall, C.S., & Nordby, V.J. (1972). *The individual and his dreams.* New York: Signet.

Hall, C.S., & Van de Castle, R.L. (1966). *The content analysis of dreams.* New York: Appleton Century Crofts.

Ho, M.A. (1972). Sex hormones and the sleep of women. *Dissertation Abstracts International, 33,* 1305.

Hurlbert, D.F., & Apt, C. (1993). Female sexuality: A comparative study between women in homosexual and heterosexual relationships. *Journal of Sex and Marital Therapy, 19,* 315–327.

Husband, R.W. (1936). Sex differences in dream contents. *The Journal of Abnormal and Social Psychology, 30,* 513-521.

Kanin, E.J. (1982). Female rape fantasies: A victimization study. *Victimology, 7,* 114–121.

Kinsey, A.C. (1948). *Sexual behaviour in the human male.* Philadelphia, PA: W.B. Saunders, Bloomington, IN: Indiana University Press.

Kinsey, A.C. (1953). *Sexual behaviour in the human female.* Philadelphia, PA: W.B. Saunders, Bloomington, IN: Indiana University Press.

Krippner, S., & Weinhold, J. (2002). Gender differences in a content analysis study of 608 dream reports from research participants in the United States. *Social Behavior and Personality, 30,* 399–410.

LaBerge, S. (1985). *Lucid dreaming.* New York: Ballantine Books.

Manber, R., & Armitage, R. (1999). Sex, steroids, and sleep: A review. *Sleep: Journal of Sleep Research & Sleep Medicine, 22,* 540–555.

Nakagawa, S. (2004). A farewell to Bonferroni: The problems of low statistical power and publication bias. *Behavioral Ecology, 15,* 1044-1045.

Nielsen, T.A., Zadra, A.L., Simard, V., Saucier, S., Stenstrom, P., Smith, C., et al. (2003). The typical dreams of Canadian University students. *Dreaming, 13,* 211–235.

Pelletier, L.A., & Herold, E.S. (1988). The relationship of age, sex guilt, and sexual experience with female sexual fantasies. *Journal of Sex Research, 24,* 250–256.

Peres-Neto, P.R. (1999). How many statistical tests are too many? The problem of conducting multiple ecological inferences revisited. *Marine Ecology Progress Series, 176,* 303–306.

Pemeger, T.V. (1998). What's wrong with Bonferroni adjustments? *British Medical Journal, 316,* 1236–1238.

Schredl, M. (2003). Continuity between waking and dreaming: A proposal for a mathematical model. *Sleep and Hypnosis, 5,* 38–52.

Schredl, M., & Hofmann, F. (2003). Continuity between waking activities and dream activities. *Consciousness and Cognition, 12,* 298–308.

Schredl, M., Sahin, V., & Schafer, G. (1998). Gender differences in dreams: Do they reflect gender differences in waking life? *Personality and Individual Differences, 25,* 433–442.

Shin, K., & Shapiro, C. (2003). Menopause, sex hormones, and sleep. *Bipolar Disorders, 5,* 106–109.

Soper, B. (1999). A comparison of daydream and dream perspectives. *College Student Journal, 33,* 217–218.

Spata, A.V. (2003). *Research methods: Science and diversity.* New York: Wiley.

Stankovic, M., Zdravkovic, J., & Trajanovic, L. (2000). Comparative analysis of sexual dreams of male and female students. *Psihijatrija Danas, 32,* 227–242.

Van de Castle, R.L. (1994). *Our dreaming mind.* New York: Random House, Inc.

Wilson, GD. (1992). *The great sex divide: A study of male-female differences.* Washington, DC: Scott-Townsend Publishers.

Zadra, A. (2007). 1093: Sex dreams: What do men and women dream about? *Sleep, 30,* A376.

Zuckerman, M. (1973). Scales for sex experience for males and females. *Journal of Consulting and Clinical Psychology, 41,* 27–29.

CHAPTER 11

PEDOPHILIA, CHILD PORN, AND CYBERPREDATORS

ETHEL QUAYLE

O ur understanding of pedophilia and its relationship with child pornography has become more critical with the advent of technology-mediated offending. The internet has led to an overall increase in the availability of all pornographic materials, and sexually related online activities have become routine for many adults and young people in the Western world (Döring 2009). This has also led to concerns, from professionals and public alike, about the effect of pornographic materials on society (Diamond 2009) and on young people in particular (Perrin *et al.* 2008). However, Cassell and Cramer (2008: 70) have argued that throughout history there has been a recurring moral panic about the potential danger of communication technologies (particularly for young women) but that when investigated it is less the technology that appears to be to blame, but rather the potential sexual agency of young women, parental loss of control, and the 'specter of women who manifest technological prowess'. Much of the debate has been about whether there is a causal relationship between viewing child pornography and the commission of a contact offense against a child (e.g. Endrass *et al.* 2009) and whether those who view images of children are inevitably pedophiles (Seto *et al.* 2006; Seto 2009).

PEDOPHILIA

In the sex offender literature, internet offenders are often called pedophiles (Durkin 1997) however, *The Diagnostic and Statistical Manual of Mental Disorders* (*DSM*; APA 2000) criteria used to diagnose pedophilia have in more recent times been extensively criticized. Studer and Aylwin (2006) argued that the category adds little to our understanding of a person, beyond being a description of their behavior and that the pedophilia diagnosis actually subsumes a 'continuum' of sexual responses rather than dichotomous or exclusive groups. They concluded that the criteria are too broad to allow for any meaningful discrimination between child molesters and pedophiles, and too narrow where arousal by adult–child sex is ego-syntonic and not acted upon, a more relevant point with the huge increase in child pornography available on the internet (Quayle 2008).

The *DSM* (APA 2000) defines pedophilia as the erotic preference for prepubescent children. Blanchard *et al.* (2009) point out that if taken literally this would exclude from diagnosis a proportion of those men whose strongest sexual feelings are for physically immature persons. A review by these authors of the relevant evidence suggests that pubescent children are generally those aged between 11 and 15 years, and as the modal age for victims of child sexual abuse in the United States is 14 years, this would imply that the majority of offenders would not meet the criteria for pedophilia. One conclusion from this is that we should either expand the criteria for pedophilia to include children who are pubescent, or add a separate diagnosis of hebephilia, which would specify a preference for pubescent children.

Authors such as Hall and Hall (2007) have also pointed out that pedophiles may engage in a wide range of sexual acts with children, including exposing themselves to children (exhibitionism); undressing a child; looking at naked children (voyeurism); masturbating in the presence of children; rubbing their genitalia against a child (frotteurism); fondling a child; engaging in oral sex with a child; or penetrating the mouth, anus and/or vagina or a child. Seto (2009) has suggested that the prevalence of pedophilia in the general population is unknown as there have been no large-scale epidemiological studies, and we know very little of this population outside of clinical or correctional settings. However, a recent study by Goode (2010) draws on research with self-identified pedophiles living ordinary lives in the community who may or may not have been involved in criminal activity. The existence of such people is clearly evidenced in the number of internet communities who draw support from online fora (O'Halloran and Quayle 2010), which may lead us to conclude that the number of people with a sexual interest in children exceeds those within the criminal justice system. A related debate with regard to pedophilia is whether it should be classified as a mental disorder (e.g., Tromovitch 2009).

In general, most people who are classified as pedophilic are male, although more recently there has been growing literature about women who commit sexual offenses against children. Gannon and Rose (2008: 458), in their review of published literature, concluded that while female child sex offenders are a heterogeneous group, it appears that they

> are more likely to offend in the company of a male, are highly likely to have experienced both childhood and adulthood victimization at the hands of men, and are likely to display some profound disturbances in their ability to seek and maintain appropriate adult intimate relationships … relationships, personality traits, and perceptions of men and boys are relatively immature, profoundly disturbed, and inextricably linked to their offending behavior.

To date, there have been very few reports of women whose offenses relate to child pornography, although in the UK the case of Vanessa George, a female nursery worker who admitted sexually assaulting very young children in her care and making and distributing indecent photographs of them through a social networking site, has been the cause of great concern (*Times Online* 2009).

CHILD PORNOGRAPHY

Child pornography is not a new phenomenon, and there are historical accounts that would suggest that sexualized images of children became both available and collectable with the advent of photography (Taylor and Quayle 2003). While the term child pornography is used widely across most jurisdictions (Akdeniz 2008), more recently concerns have been expressed as to whether this reflects actual content or implies consent (Quayle 2009b). The term 'abusive images' is now widely used by those who advocate for children's rights in relation to sexual abuse through photography (Jones and Skögrand 2005) although it might be argued that such terms fail to capture the wide array of material depicting abusive and exploitative sexual practices towards children in the online environment (Quayle *et al.* 2008). The criminalization of such practices has led to an increase in the number of people within the criminal justice system who have been given the label of 'internet sex offender'. In the UK by 2005, internet-related sexual offenses accounted for one-third of all sexual convictions (Middleton *et al.* 2009).

Clearly not all sexualized images of children demonstrate the same degree of sexually abusive or exploitative practices, nor are all of these images illegal across many jurisdictions. If we look at the material found in the collections of offenders, the pictures range from images of clothed children, through nakedness and explicit erotic posing, to sexual assault. We can make some objective sense of this by thinking of the pictures in terms of a continuum of increased deliberate sexual victimization (Taylor *et al.* 2001). This continuum ranges from everyday and perhaps accidental pictures involving either no overt erotic content or minimal content (such as showing a child's underwear), at one extreme, to pictures showing rape and penetration of a child or other gross acts of obscenity, at the other. Taking this perspective focuses attention not just on illegality as a significant quality of pictures, but on the preferred type of pictures selected by the collector, and the value and meaning pictures have to collectors (Taylor and Quayle 2003).

In trying to understand the ways in which children are victimized within the images, Taylor *et al.* (2001) generated a typology based on an analysis of publicly available images obtained from newsgroups and websites (made possible under Irish law). This 'COPINE Scale' had ten levels, ranging from indicative images to those depicting sadism or bestiality. In 2002, in England and Wales, the Sentencing Advisory Panel (SAP) published its advice to the Court of Appeal on offenses involving child pornography. The SAP believed that the nature of the material should be the key factor in deciding the level of sentence, and adapted the COPINE Scale to five levels. It dropped Levels 1 to 3 completely, arguing that nakedness alone was not indicative of indecency.

The proposed structure was therefore that COPINE Levels 5 to 6 constitute Sentencing Level 1, and COPINE Levels 7 upwards each constitutes an individual sentencing stage (Gillespie 2003). One consequence of using such a measure has been that it provides a means of communication about the images without, for most people, the images ever having been seen (Quayle 2009a).

INTERNET SEX OFFENDERS

In relation to people convicted of internet sexual crimes against children, there are demographic consistencies between study samples, the most notable of which relate to gender and ethnicity. Wolak *et al.* (2005), in their study of internet crimes against minors, reported that 99 percent of their sample was male. This is similar to the findings of other studies (Sullivan 2007; Finkelhor and Ormrod 2004; Seto and Eke 2005; Webb *et al.* 2007; Bates and Metcalf 2007; Baartz 2008). The majority of offenders are not only male but white Caucasians (Sullivan 2007; O'Brien and Webster 2007; Wolak *et al.* 2005). Webb *et al.* (2007) indicated that their internet-related offenders were predominantly white, which appeared different from their child molester sample within the same study that came from a more mixed ethnic group. Within an Australian sample, the majority of internet sex offenders were identified as Caucasian (86 percent), with minimal representation in the Asian, Mediterranean and Aboriginal ethnic groups (Baartz 2008). Coward *et al.* (2009), in their analysis of an ongoing US research project, examined 405 cases made up of 277 convicted offenders with no known or reported internet sex offenses who had access to the internet and 128 with a charge or arrest for an internet sex offense. Ninety-two percent of the internet sex offenders were Caucasian males, compared to 73 percent in the comparison group (which had a higher proportion of African Americans and Hispanics).

Given the volume of internet sex offenders, whose offenses largely relate to downloading, distribution and production of child pornography, it is unsurprising that there has been concern about the relationship between viewing abusive images, pedophilia and the commission of further offenses against children. Seto *et al.* (2006) studied a group of men whose offenses related to child pornography using a bio-signal measure of sexual arousal (penile plethysmography). Within their sample, 61 percent of child pornography offenders showed greater penile responses to stimuli depicting children compared to those depicting adults, and this was greater than those offenders who had committed contact offenses against children. Seto (2009: 396) has hypothesized that 'child pornography offenders with more child pornography images, a higher ratio of child to adult images, and images depicting younger children and both boys and girls are more likely to be pedophilic and thus more likely to seek sexual contacts with children'. However, there is still limited data to support this claim, and to date there are considerable differences across studies in the number of people convicted of child pornography-related offenses who have previous convictions for contact offenses against children (Hanson and Babchishin 2009).

Clearly, as yet, we have little information to indicate what risks are posed by internet offenders with no known history of sexual contacts with children, although a study by Seto and Eke (2005) indicated that child pornography offenders with any kind of prior criminal history were more likely to commit a contact offense, or an offense of any kind, during the study follow-up period of two and a half years.

CYBERPREDATORS

Child pornography offenses are not the only internet sex offenses committed against children. Television programs such as *To Catch a Predator* have alerted us to the fact that some people (usually men) go online in order to engage with children and young people in a sexual way, and that a proportion of these people will have sexual contact with that young person in the offline world. Clearly such activity may target adults as well as children, and such terms as 'cyber-predators' have been used to describe this type of behaviour (Philips and Morrissey 2004). Kierkegaard (2008) makes reference to the 'grooming' of children in relation to this, and there have been changes in UK law to reflect growing concerns about such online activity, as well as an increase in proactive 'sting operations' by police to interrupt the process before a child can be sexually assaulted. Research by Davidson and Martellozzo (2008) with the UK Metropolitan Police would suggest that such offenders demonstrate a tendency to minimize their intention to abuse a child sexually. Several of the offenders in their study claimed that the online communication was about sharing fantasies with people whom they thought to be adults.

However, researchers from the University of New Hampshire alert us to what they believe are the myths and realities of online 'predators' (Wolak *et al.* 2008). Their studies of American youth suggest that the publicity about online 'predators' who engage with naive children through trickery and develop a relationship with them that culminates in violence is largely inaccurate. Their data suggest that these encounters are often closer to models of statutory rape, rather than forced sexual assaults or pedophilic attacks.

Much of this research has come from two studies (YISS-1 and YISS-2), which conducted telephone interviews with national samples of young internet users (aged 10 to 17 years) in 2000 and 2005 (Finkelhor *et al.* 2000; Wolak *et al.* 2006). This US research suggests that most internet-initiated sex crimes involve adult men who use the internet to meet and seduce underage adolescents into sexual encounters. 'The offenders use Internet communications such as instant messages, e-mail, and chatrooms to meet and develop intimate relationships with victims. In the majority of cases, victims are aware that they are conversing online with adults' (Wolack *et al.* 2008: 112). The implication of this research is that we should be paying particular attention to those youths who are most vulnerable. This would include those with histories of sexual abuse, those with concerns about their sexual orientation, and those who have patterns of risk taking across all domains. The research would also support the idea of developmentally appropriate prevention strategies that acknowledge normal adolescent interests in romance and sex.

The Internet Safety Technical Task Force (2008) argued that, although they are frequently reported in the media, US internet sex crimes against minors have not overtaken the number of unmediated sex crimes against minors, nor have they contributed to a rise in such crimes. The report states that the increased popularity of the internet in the United States has not been correlated with an overall increase in reported sexual offenses. Evidence is cited from the US that, overall, sexual offenses against children have declined in the last 18 years (National Center for Missing and Exploited Children 2006), with research indicating a dramatic reduction in reports of sexual offenses against children from 1992 to 2006 (Calpin 2006; Finkelhor and Jones 2008). What is still not known is whether we will continue to see a decrease in sexual offenses against children across other countries, and whether this will be paralleled by an eventual increase in technology-mediated sexual crimes.

REFERENCES

Akdeniz, Y. (2008) *Internet Child Pornography and the Law: National and International Responses*, Aldershot: Ashgate.

American Psychiatric Association (APA) (2000) *The Diagnostic and Statistical Manual of Mental Disorders*, 4th rev. edn, Washington, DC: American Psychiatric Association.

Baartz, D. (2008) *Australians, the Internet and Technology-Enabled Child Sex Abuse: A Statistical Profile*, Canberra:Australian Federal Police.

Bates, A. and Metcalf, C. (2007) A psychometric comparison of internet and non-internet sex offenders from a community treatment sample, *Journal of Sexual Aggression*, 13, 1: 11–20.

Blanchard, R., Lykins, A.D., Wherrett, D., Kuban, M.E., Cantor, J., Blak, T., Dickey, R. and Klassen, P.E. (2009) Pedophilia, hebephilia, and the *DSM-V*, *Archives of Sexual Behaviour*, 38: 335–350.

Calpin, C.M. (2006) *Child Maltreatment*, US Department of Health and Human Services. Available: www. acf.hhs.gov/programs/cb/pubs/cm06/cm06.pdf (accessed 5 June 2007).

Cassell, J. and Cramer, M. (2008) High tech or high risk: moral panics about girls online, in T. McPherson (ed.), *Digital Youth, Innovation, and the Unexpected*, John D. and Catherine T. MacArthur Foundation Series on Digital Media and Learning, Cambridge, MA: MIT Press.

Coward, I.A., Gabriel, A.M., Schuler, A. and Prentky, R.A. (2009) Child internet victimization: project development and preliminary results, paper presented at the Annual Conference of the American Psychology-Law Society, San Antonio, March.

Davidson, J.C. and Martellozzo, E. (2008) Protecting vulnerable young people in cyberspace from sexual abuse: raising awareness and responding globally, *Police Practice and Research*, 9, 4: 277–289.

Diamond, M. (2009) Pornography, public acceptance and sex related crime: a review, *International Journal of Law and Psychiatry*, 32: 304–314.

Döring, M. (2009) The internet's impact on sexuality: a critical review of 15 years of research, *Computers in Human Behavior*, 25: 1089–1101.

Durkin, K. (1997) Misuse of the internet by pedophiles: implications for law enforcement and probation practice, *Federal Probation*, 61, 2: 14–18.

Endrass, J., Urbaniok, F., Hammermeister, L.C., Benz, C., Elbert, T., Laubacher, A. and Rossegger, A. (2009) The consumption of internet child pornography and violent and sex offending, *BMC Psychiatry*, 9: 43–49.

Finkelhor, D. and Jones, L. (2008) *Updated Trends in Child Maltreatment, 2006*, Crimes Against Children Research Center. Available: www.unh.edu/ccrc/Trends/index.html (accessed 11 January 2009).

Finkelhor, D., Mitchell, K. and Wolak, J. (2000) *Online Victimization: A Report on the Nation's Youth*, Alexandria, VA: National Center for Missing and Exploited Children.

Finkelhor, D. and Ormrod, R. (2004) *Child Pornography: Patterns from the NIBRS*, Washington, DC: US Department of Justice Programs, Office of Juvenile Justice and Delinquency Prevention.

Gannon, T.A. and Rose, M.R. (2008) Female child sexual offenders: towards integrating theory and practice, *Aggression and Violent Behavior*, 13: 442–461.

Gillespie, A.A. (2003) Sentences for offences involving child pornography, *Criminal Law Review*, February: 80–92.

Goode, S.D. (2010) *Understanding and Addressing Adult Sexual Attraction to Children*, Abingdon: Routledge.

Hall, R.C.W. and Hall, R.C.W. (2007) A profile of pedophilia: definition, characteristics of offenders, recidivism, treatment outcomes, and forensic issues, *Mayo Clinic Proceedings*, 82, 4: 457–471.

Hanson, R.K. and Babchishin, K.M. (2009) How should we advance our knowledge of risk assessment for internet sexual offenders?, paper presented at the Global Symposium for Examining the Relationship between Online and Offline Offenses and Preventing the Sexual Exploitation of Children, Chapel Hill, NC, April.

Internet Safety Technical Task Force (2008) *Enhancing Child Safety and Online Technologies: Final Report of the Internet Safety Technical Task Force to the Multi-State Working Group on Social Networking of State Attorneys General of the United States*, Cambridge, MA: Berkman Center for Internet and Society, Harvard University.

Jones, V. and Skögrand, E. (2005) *Position Paper Regarding Online Images of Sexual Abuse and other Internet-Related Sexual Exploitation of Children*, Copenhagen: Save the Children Europe Group.

Kierkegaard, S. (2008) Cybering, online grooming and age play, *Computer Law and Security Report*, 24: 41–55.

Middleton, D., Mandeville-Norden, R. and Hayes, E. (2009) Does treatment work with internet sex offenders? Emerging findings from the internet Sex Offender Treatment Programme (i-SOTP), *Journal of Sexual Aggression*, 15, 1: 5–19.

National Center for Missing and Exploited Children (2006) *CyberTipline Annual Report Totals*. Available: www.cybertipline.com/en_US/documents/CyberTiplineReportTotals.pdf (accessed 4 June 2007).

O'Brien, M.D. and Webster, S.D. (2007) The construction and preliminary validation of the Internet Behaviours and Attitudes Questionnaire (IBAQ), *Sex Abuse*, 19: 237–256.

O'Halloran, E. and Quayle, E. (2010) A content analysis of a 'Boy Love' support forum: revisiting Durkin and Bryant, *Journal of Sexual Aggression*, 16, 1: 71–85.

Perrin, P.C., Madanat, H.N., Barnes, M.D., Corolan, A., Clark, R.B., Ivins, N. *et al.* (2008) Health education's role in framing pornography as a public health issue: implications, *Promotion and Education*, 15: 11–18.

Philips, P. and Morrissey, G. (2004) Internet cyberstalking and cyberpredators: a threat to safe sexuality on the internet, *Convergence: The International Journal of Research into New Technologies*, 10: 66–79.

Quayle, E. (2008) Internet offending, in D.R. Laws and W. O'Donohue (eds), *Sexual Deviance*, New York: Guilford Press.

Quayle, E. (2009a) Assessment of internet sexual abuse, in M.C. Calder (ed.), *Complete Guide to Sexual Abuse Assessments*, 2nd edn, Lyme Regis: Russell House.

Quayle, E. (2009b). Child pornography, in Y. Jewkes and M. Yar (eds), *The Handbook of Internet Crime*, Cullompton: Willan.

Quayle, E., Lööf, L. and Palmer, T. (2008) *Child Pornography and Sexual Exploitation of Children Online*, Bangkok: ECPAT International.

Seto, M. (2009) Pedophilia, *Annual Review of Clinical Psychology*, 5:391–4079.

Seto M.C., Cantor, J.M. and Blanchard, R. (2006) Child pornography offenses are a valid diagnostic indicator of pedophilia, *Journal of Abnormal Psychology*, 115: 610–615.

Seto, M.C. and Eke, A. (2005) The criminal histories and later offending of child pornography offenders, *Sexual Abuse: A Journal of Research and Treatment*, 17, 2: 201–210.

Studer, L.H. and Aylwin, A.S. (2006) Pedophilia: the problem with diagnosis and limitations of CBT in treatment, *Medical Hypotheses*, 67, 4: 774–781.

Sullivan, C. (2007) *Internet Traders of Child Pornography: Profiling Research*, New Zealand: Censorship Compliance Unit.

Taylor, M. and Quayle, E. (2003) *Child Pornography: An Internet Crime*, Brighton: Routledge.

Taylor, M., Holland, G. and Quayle, E. (2001) Typology of paedophile picture collections, *The Police Journal*, 74, 2: 97–107.

Times Online (2009) Child abuse: the camera doesn't lie, 25 October. Available: www.timesonline.co.uk/tol/news/uk/crime/article6886186.ece (accessed 26 October 2009).

Tromovitch, P. (2009) Manufacturing mental disorder by pathologizing erotic age orientation: a comment on Blanchard *et al.* [Letter to the editor], *Archives of Sexual Behavior*, 38, 3: 328.

Webb, L., Craissati, J. and Keen, S. (2007) Characteristics of internet child pornography offenders: a comparison with child molesters, *Sex Abuse*, 19: 449–465.

Wolak, J., Finkelhor, D. and Mitchell, K.J. (2005) *Child-Pornography Possessors Arrested in Internet-Related Crimes: Findings from the National Juvenile Online Victimization Study*, Alexandria, VA: National Center for Missing and Exploited Children.

Wolak, J., Mitchell, K. and Finkelhor, D. (2006) *Online Victimization: 5 Years Later*, Alexandria, VA: National Center for Missing and Exploited Children.

Wolak, J., Finkelhor, D., Mitchell, K.J. and Ybarra, M.L. (2008) Online 'predators' and their victims: myths, realities, and implications for prevention and treatment, *American Psychologist*, 63, 2: 111–128.

CHAPTER 12

CHILD MOLESTATION

DANIELLE A. HARRIS

INTRODUCTION

Sexual abuse of children is a deeply complex phenomenon. It is 'steeped in contradiction, confusion and emotion' (Innes, 1997:63), 'violates the norms of almost every culture' (Ryan, Metzner & Krugman, 1990:260) and has been considered the most hated crime in the criminal justice system (Briggs, 1995). When public interest intersects with correctional philosophy this particularly abhorrent offense becomes a 'highly charged issue guided less by sound information than by emotion-laden attitudes and rhetoric' (Broadhurst & Maller, 1992:54; Samenow, 1984). In the past, these concerns have confounded an academic criminological comprehension of child sexual abuse. Borrowing from psychology however, allows for the useful application of behavioral and cognitive-behavioral theories. This chapter is concerned only with sexual offenders who abuse children (hereafter called child molesters). The major focus is on adult males because this reflects the emphasis of the field. However, recently there has been an increased interest in research and treatment on female and adolescent child molesters. Therefore, these offenders are discussed where appropriate.

The term, 'child molester' is used in this chapter to describe offenders who abuse extra-familial children exclusively. Importantly, this is distinguished from incest offenders who offend within the context of family and abuse their own biological, foster, adoptive, or step children. Incest will not be discussed in this chapter and any mention of child abuse shall refer only to extra-familial children. It is important to note there are substantively significant differences between incest offenders and child molesters and therefore, automatic comparisons between the two should not be drawn.

Child sexual abuse is often used to illustrate the concept of the dark figure of crime because the exact number of offenders, offenses and victims is unknown and underestimated (Grant, 2000; Lee, 1993; Morrison, 1999). Definitional variance across jurisdictions regarding offense type, age of consent, age of adulthood and age of criminal responsibility, for example, obscure these data also. One might measure how many members of the population have been victimized, how many members of the population have offended (prevalence), how many offenses an average offender might commit (incidence) or how many offenses a particular victim might experience.

Using official statistics to gauge the extent of child sexual abuse is perhaps the most unreliable measure of its actual prevalence. While it is necessary to provide some overview of the problem, it is with hesitation that the following statistics are offered. The most commonly cited prevalence data estimate that one in five women and one in 11 men has been sexually victimized (Finkelhor, 1984). Sex offenders (not delineated by offense type) make up approximately 4.7 percent of the total national correctional population with approximately 60 percent of these convicted offenders living in the community (Bureau of Justice Statistics, 1997).

Sexual abuse of children typically occurs secretly, usually within an existing relationship (Lee, 1993) where there is a marked disparity of power (Ryan, Metzner & Krugman, 1990). A victim's subsequent disclosure therefore becomes unlikely, dangerous, or even impossible (Lee, 1993). For these reasons estimates of child molestation are likely to be understated (Lee, 1993; Mathews, 1997; Worling, 1995a). Disclosure is even less likely for victims of incest and/or female offenders.

OFFENDER CHARACTERISTICS

A broad review of the emerging knowledge from international literature reveals that extra-familial child molesters share common and identifiable characteristics. These include chaotic family environments, (Stenson & Anderson, 1987) inconsistent parenting, and significant marital discord (Friedrich & Luecke, 1988), little or no contact with fathers (Ford & Linney, 1995; Graham, 1996), physical or sexual parental abuse, witnessing domestic violence (Higgs, Canavan & Meyer, 1992), chronic isolation from same age peers (Ford & Linney, 1995) difficulty making friends (Prentky & Knight, 1993), early childhood sexualization and prior victimization (Veneziano, Veneziano & LeGrand, 2000).

Seriousness of Child Sexual Abuse

The inherent social conscience of the average citizen is sufficient to accept unconditionally the gravity of this phenomenon. This however makes it particularly necessary to illustrate the effects of abuse and the likelihood of recidivism from a scholarly and empirical standpoint.

Effects of Abuse: The negative effects of child sexual abuse are well documented and include feelings of betrayal, powerlessness, stigmatization, traumatic sexualization, depression, guilt, substance abuse, suicidal ideations, anxiety, somatic complaints, phobias, and severely impeded emotional development (Friedrich & Luecke, 1988; Grant, 2000; Bartol, 2002; Worling, 1995a). The impact of abuse depends heavily on the child's age at the time, the number of perpetrators, their relationship to the child, the type of abuse, its frequency and duration and whether force was used (Friedrich & Luecke, 1988). Abuse is particularly traumatic where bodily penetration and aggressiveness are combined, as the experience is more likely to be "split off" (or denied) by the child, who is unable to integrate the experience and make sense of it (Friedrich & Luecke, 1988; Prentky & Knight, 1993).

Likelihood of Recidivism: The high probability of sex offender recidivism has been supported by numerous clinical results (Hanson, 2002) and this finding has informed much legislation. Sexual Predator laws, for example, allow for the civil commitment of violent sexual offenders (Andrews & Bonta, 2003) and Megan's Law and other iterations of community notification and registration require that individuals be informed of a child molester residing in their neighborhood (Bartol, 2002).

Sex offender criminal activity differs from the offending of many other offender types. For many other offenders, the age crime curve clearly describes their criminal careers (Gottfredson & Hirschi, 1983). As the offenders get older they age out of crime. The reality of sexual offending against children is dramatically different. While early onset age is evident (Prentky & Knight, 1993), 'unlike other juvenile delinquents who typically grow out of their offending' (Erooga & Masson, 1999:4) many child sexual abusers continue offending and 'get better' or 'grow into it' with time (Grant, 2000; Stenson & Anderson, 1987). The sexual experience has a positively re-inforcing physical element and when this occurs at an early age, (sometimes even in the context of victimization) it may lead to repetitive and ingrained deviant patterns of arousal (Elliot & Smiljanich, 1994; Graham, 1996).

THEORETICAL PERSPECTIVE

Child molestation as a topic for research and theory has typically not been a focus of traditional criminologists. Most work in this area has been done by the 'helping professions' of psychology, psychiatry and social work (Gelles & Wolfner, 1994). American criminology was born mostly out of schools of sociology. This perspective has lead to a rejection of the psychological ideas of offender typologies and classifications. The very title of this book however, indicates an appreciation for crime specific theory; a new approac h for traditional criminology.

Box 5.1

In the News

'Expecting a school district and a police department to be on guard against female teachers in their 30's out to ravish 12-year-old boys is like expecting a weather bureau to be on the watch for showers of frogs'[1]

An exhaustive search for mention of female sexual offenders in international press over the last five years yields extremely little. What *is* reported however, reveals an extreme dearth of insight, research and understanding which generally perpetuates uninformed or worse, ill-informed public perception. This perception evidently influences the way in which these individuals are treated by the media and by all levels of the criminal justice system.

Society's general reluctance to accept that women can commit sex crimes against children[2] is documented in articles that describe the 'prevailing sentiment that it's not a big deal'[3] and the belief that it is 'more of a fluke of nature than a miscue by authorities.'[4] Not surprisingly, various criminal justice personnel are repeatedly quoted with their arms in the air saying 'it's very shocking … you just don't see things like that'[5] and 'I never could have imagined it … I have never heard of such a thing.'[6]

The well-publicized case of Mary Kay LeTourneau (the 34-year-old Seattle married mother of four who bore two additional children to a 12-year-old male student and was recently released after serving a seven and a half year prison sentence for child rape) is doubtless the most well-known and is referred to by almost all journalists in their discussions of this phenomenon.

In the press coverage of her case, LeTourneau is described as 'America's most infamous female child molester,'[7] a 'randy Miss,'[8] 'a nut, out in the ozone layer,'[9] and 'a troubled person whose list of psychiatric difficulties goes well beyond delusions that

---

[1] Hall, May 24, 2002.
[2] Stanley, June 9, 2002; Taylor, April 1, 2002.
[3] Adamson, June 16, 2002.
[4] Hall, May 24, 2002.
[5] Stanley, June 9, 2002.
[6] Hall, May 24, 2002.
[7] Haskell, March 29, 2002.
[8] Flynn, April 5, 2002.
[9] O'Reilly, May 29, 2002.

Box 5.1, *continued*

she is romantically in love with a 12-year-old boy.'[10] Interestingly, her 12-year-old *victim* is described as 'her grade school lover.'[11] The 'couple' were reported to be 'tangled in an intimate relationship'[12] that was described by one journalist as a 'steamy 18-month affair,'[13] The abuse was defined as a relationship by four additional writers,[14] and was once considered to be 'torture' rather than 'true love.'[15]

Curiously, two separate journalists describe LeTourneau and Tanya Hadden (a 33-year-old teacher who was found with her 15-year old student in a Las Vegas hotel room[16]) as 'blonde'[17]—an interesting choice of adjective given that the hair color of a male sex offender is rarely considered significant enough to report.

This skewed public perception is best displayed by the recent case of Pamela Diehl-Moore, 43, who abused a 13-year-old boy in New Jersey,[18] where Judge Bruce Gaeta made the following statements during her trial: 'It's just something between two people that clicked beyond the teacher-student relationship[19] … I really don't see the harm that was done here[20] … people mature at different rates[21] … certainly society doesn't need to be worried[22] … it was simply an opportunity for the boy to satisfy his sexual needs.'[23]

The point is repeatedly made that had the genders been reversed, public reaction, legal responses and media coverage would have been very different.[24] Thus, when compared to their male counterparts these women received incredibly disproportionate sentences. For example, 'in 1993 in Virginia, a male teacher who had sex with three teenage female students was sentenced to 26 years in prison—while the next day [in the same jurisdiction] a female swimming coach who had an "affair" with an 11-year-old boy and sexual encounters with two others got 30 days.[25] Additionally, when LeTourneau received her initial sentence of six months probation [which she broke upon falling pregnant for a

---

[10] Hall, May 24, 2002.
[11] Radue, May 6, 2002.
[12] Gold and Dirmann, May 3, 2002.
[13] Flynn, April 5, 2002.
[14] Giles, May 19, 2002; Gold and Dirmann, May 3, 2002; Mitchell, May 15, 2002; Young, June 3, 2002.
[15] Mitchell, May 15, 2002.
[16] Gold and Dirmann, May 3, 2002.
[17] Giles, May 19, 2002; Flynn, April 5, 2002.
[18] Young, June 3, 2002.
[19] Associated Press (AP), May 24, 2002.
[20] Adamson, June 16, 2002; Young, June 3, 2002.
[21] AP, May 24, 2002.
[22] Adamson, June 16, 2002; AP, May 24, 2002; Young, June 3, 2002.
[23] Young, June 3, 2002.
[24] Mitchell, May 15, 2002.
[25] Young, June 3, 2002.

Box 5.1, *continued*

---

second time to the same boy] at the same time in Seattle, there was another case where a male teacher was caught with a female student and received four years in prison.[26] Further, in reporting LeTourneau's case, Flynn's recent article is titled, 'See me after History Class … and I'll Strip!' One gets the feeling that this headline would be considered in extremely poor taste if gender roles were reversed.

While the incidence of female perpetrated abuse is under-reported, the popular explanations given in the media have disastrous reinforcing qualities in terms of public perception. These include: 'some boys may see sexual contact at the hands of an older woman not as molestation but as early initiation,'[27] the boys 'who are usually willing partners, do not consider themselves victims,'[28] a boy is 'going to enjoy this, and it's going to be the fantasy of a lifetime,'[29] young boys dream about 'experienced older women,'[30] 'in some way it is difficult to blame frisky teachers.'[31]

---

[26] O'Reilly, May 29, 2002.
[27] Kluger, April 1, 2002.
[28] Stanley, June 9, 2002.
[29] O'Reilly, May 29, 2002.
[30] Peters, June 9, 2002.
[31] Adamson, June 16, 2002.

It is difficult to use criminology theories to understand the phenomenon of child molestation. Psychoanalytic perspectives that dominated psychology for many years also seem inadequate. Child molestation may perhaps be best understood as both a criminological and psychological problem and theories must combine both perspectives.

This chapter pays particular attention to behavioral and cognitive-behavioral theories. When behavioral theory is applied to sexual offending, the emphasis is on learning sexual deviations as part of masturbation fantasies. As its title suggests, cognitive-behavioral theory attaches the assumption that thoughts and feelings mitigate one's actions (Schwartz & Cellini, 1996).[1]

Behavioral Theory

Consistent with some features of criminological learning theories, behavioral theory assumes that sexual deviation is 'another form of learned behavior' (Schwartz & Cellini, 1996:2-14). Classical conditioning is a relevant consideration 'in which a repetitious or traumatic pairing of sexuality and some negative experience, produces some type of intensive emotional response that distorts subsequent sexual gratification' (Schwartz & Cellini, 1996:2-14).

Clinicians use the tenets of behavioral theory to explain the unconscious compulsion to re-enact the abuse or gain mastery over the abusive experience (Wyatt & Johnson-Powell, 1988; Worling, 1995a). Also known as the 'vampire effect' (Veneziano, Veneziano & LeGrand, 2000) or the 'abused/abuser hypothesis' (Worling, 1995b) re-victimization (or inappropriate sexual acting out in a normative way) is considered a function of the individual's own sexual abuse victimiza-tion (Graham, 1996; Fagan & Wexler, 1988). When re-victimization occurs, one's past abuse is triggered and the compulsion to repeat produces the 'same tragic conditions for pleasure' (Miller, 1999:108). Sometimes, the behaviors in which they engage are often completely reflective of the offender's own victim experiences (Veneziano, Veneziano & LeGrand, 2000). The child molester re-enacts in literal and repetitive ways their own victimization (Elliot & Smiljanich, 1994).

This explanation assumes that all child molesters have histories of child abuse. To clarify, the broader umbrella of victimization encompasses early exposure to pornography, witnessing parental abuse, neglect and early sexualization. Importantly, there is an evident paradox that only a small proportion of the thousands of child sexual abuse victims become perpetrators (Blues, Moffat & Telford, 1999). One consistent interpretation of this data is that while victimization is a strong correlate of subsequent sexual offending, it is certainly not a causal factor.

Cognitive-Behavioral Theory

Cognitive-behavioural theory holds that individuals are affected not by events but by the views they take of them. In this sense, a child molester's thoughts and feelings allow them to become preoccupied with deviant fantasies (Schwartz & Cellini, 1996). The specific appeal of this approach to child molesters is its ability to describe the subtle manner in which an individual denies, mini-mizes, justifies and rationalizes his behavior. The criminological parallel of this perspective with which readers may be more familiar are the 'Techniques of Neutralization' described by Sykes and Matza (1957). These techniques include 'denial of responsibility,' 'denial of injury,' 'denial of victim,' 'condemnation of the condemners' and 'appeal to a higher loyalty.' They are used to describe the way in which an individual is able to overcome certain internal and external inhibi-tors and commit an offense.

The cognitive-behavioral approach implies that sexual arousal to abusive or deviant acts can develop over time (Veneziano, Veneziano & LeGrand, 2000) and that severe sexual abuse in child-hood might contribute to a 'predilection for sexually aggressive behavior' in later life (Friedrich & Luecke, 1988:159). Operant conditioning offers a similar explanation where reaching orgasm (even in the context of abuse) is a powerful behavioral reinforcement, particularly when paired with relevant thoughts and emotions. So arousal (if any) stems not from sadism or sexual devi-ance, but is instead a product of the way the offender has 'processed' his own abuse. The victim comes to 'regard these behaviors as appropriate, normal and worthwhile' (Burton, Nesmith & Badten, 1997:160). Sometimes, inappropriate sexual behavior might also be rewarded with a level of intimacy that is otherwise lacking in the child's relationships (Erooga & Masson, 1999).

TREATMENT/PREVENTION

Consistent with the discussed theoretical perspective, cognitive-behavioral therapeutic techniques are considered to be the most appropriate for child molesters. Importantly, while surgical, pharmacological and purely behavioral treatments (outlined in Box 5.2) exist, research is conflicting at best. The strongest research with the most rigorous methodologies and most promising conclusions are drawn from cognitive-behavioral programs.

In the following sections, the objectives and difficulties of sex offender treatment are outlined and the characteristics of cognitive-behavioral therapy are illustrated. A short review of past and existing attitudes towards sex offender treatment will follow with a discussion of the effectiveness of treatment programs. Finally, to answer the all important question of determining 'what works,' recent meta-analyses will be reviewed and discussed.

Box 5.2 outlines the important link between theory and practice (treatment). The goal of behavioral theory is summarized and the treatment modalities that have been informed by this perspective are detailed. These include (but are not limited to) aversion therapy, covert sensitization, masturbatory satiation therapy and shame therapy. For more detail on these specific treatment types, readers are referred to the footnoted citations.

The goals of cognitive-behavioral theory are also provided in Box 5.2. In addition, the widely applicable treatment modalities of this perspective are discussed. Contemporary cognitive-behavioral treatment is probably best represented in the form of Relapse Prevention techniques. This is the most common and well regarded treatment option today. Other treatment options with cognitive behavioral components include sexual education, social skills training and reducing cognitive distortions. It should be noted that unlike the behavioral approaches in the table, the cognitive-behavioral approaches are most often provided in concert with each other.

Despite our acknowledgement of the detrimental effects of abuse and the high likelihood of recidivism, there is little public currency and even less political will to promote or fund necessary programs for child molesters. Effective treatment is further hindered by the absence of a solid theoretical basis for this work. And finally, it is especially hard to change entrenched sexual arousal and deviant sexual preferences in an adult who has likely spent years 'refining' and 'hiding' his behavior (Hanson & Bussiere, 1998).

Cognitive Behavioral Therapy

Cognitive-Behavioral Therapy (CBT) is the historically favored approach for adult offender treatment (Orr, 1991). Its consistent application in the field and its evident relationship to cognitive-behavioral theory makes it an appropriate choice for the present discussion. According to CBT, the most effective change is said to come from recognizing the connection between thoughts, emotions and beliefs about offending and actual offending behavior (Lakey, 1994; Whitford & Parr, 1995).

Box 5.2

Treatment Goals, Components, Definitions and Findings from Behavioral and Cognitive-Behavioral Perspectives

Theoretical Influence	Goals	Treatment Type and Components	Treatment Definition and Description	Advantages, Disadvantages and Evaluative Findings
Behavioral Theory	Aims to reduce deviant arousal or remove libido	Aversion Therapy[1]	Pairing a noxious stimuli with images of the target behavior (can include nausea inducing agent, electrical shock, foul odor)	Mixed results. Very little empirical evidence. The most rigorous meta- analyses have found temporary advantages only.
		Covert sensitization[2]	Pairing an imagined aversive consequence with deviant thoughts to eliminate that thought or behavior	
		Masturbatory Satiation Therapy[3]	Continuation of masturbation during the unresponsive period immediately following orgasm while repeatedly evoking deviant fantasies	
		Shame Therapy[4]	Client acts out his molestation a mannequin in front of staff family members who do not respond to produce a feeling of extreme anxiety and shame	
Cognitive Behavioral Theory	Aims to increase self control and reduce the cognitive distortions that allow offending to occur	Relapse Prevention[5]	Focuses on deviant arousal, lapses are deviant, controllable and stoppable— addresses cognitive distortions that lead to offending	Is widely applicable. Metaanalyses con- sistently support the relapse prevention model. Limitations include that it requires high verbal intelligence and admission of the offense.
		Sexual education and social skills training[6]	Teaching appropriate sexual arousal patterns and pro-social attitudes	
		Reducing cognitive distortions[7]	Examining minimizations, denial and justifications of offending	

[1] Righthand and Welch, 2001.
[2] Righthand and Welch, 2001.
[3] Righthand and Welch, 2001.
[4] Schwartz and Cellini, 1996.
[5] Pithers in Schwartz and Cellini, 1996.
[6] Perkins et al., 1998.
[7] Perkins et al., 1998.

The paramount goal of all sex offender treatment is the prevention of further victimization and the cessation of sexually inappropriate behavior (Orr, 1991; Perkins et al., 1998). CBT achieves this by employing the relapse prevention model to circumvent 'the build up to inappropriate sexual gratification' (Thomas, 1999:6) and to alter negative thoughts and cognitive distortions (Gabor & Ing, 1991:43). CBT focuses primarily on the individual's criminality in a confrontational and non-sympathetic manner, pays direct attention to abusive behaviors (Orr, 1991) and is characterized by logical, straightforward and highly structured techniques (Gabor & Ing, 1991). An additional advantage of CBT is its cost. It is less expensive and more flexible than some of the more invasive behavioral techniques as well as those that might require surgical expertise.

Importantly, because CBT requires 'a high level of cognitive ability on the part of the client,' (Gabor & Ing, 1991:50) its relevance for special populations including adolescents and developmentally delayed offenders has been questioned.

Sex Offender Treatment Program Evaluation

The paramount question of 'what works' and 'how do we know?' should be answered by rigorous research evaluations. Unfortunately, evaluative research of Sex Offender Treatment Programs (SOTPs) is still considered to be extremely problematic (Perkins et al., 1998). This is most often attributed to methodological weaknesses in research design, such as lack of randomization, use of small unmatched samples, variation in treatment approach and absence of control groups (Polizzi, MacKenzie & Hickman, 1999; Rasmussen, 1999; USGAO, 1996). Further, no two studies of SOTPs are directly comparable (Perkins et al., 1998).

Martinson's now legendary 1974 conclusion that 'nothing works' evidently shook the foundations of criminology and has had lasting effects on the level of commitment shown to offender rehabilitation. Despite psychology's dedication to treatment and rehabilitation ideals, the sexual abuse field was similarly devastated over a decade later. In a landmark meta-analysis of existing SOTPs, Furby, Weinrott, and Blackshaw (1989) came to their own damning conclusions that treatment had no effect on sexual recidivism. Researchers have spent the last fifteen years lamenting the effects of Furby et al. (1989) on the field and professional ideas have been contaminated by an echo of 'nothing works.'

Selected Sex Offender Treatment Program Evaluations Meta-Analyses

Treatment can be evaluated on a number of dimensions such as integrity, intermediate impacts, costs and outcome (Perkins et al., 1998). Since outcome measures of recidivism are the most accessible, most telling and most commonly provided, they will be used here. It is important to consider the re-offending rates of untreated offenders as a baseline against which to judge treatment effects (Perkins et al., 1998). Hanson and Bussiere (1998) achieve this in their meta-analysis of recidivism rates in the absence of treatment. The research findings and conclusions cited in this chapter come from a selection of recent meta-analyses and qualitative reviews conducted in the field. The three major evaluations that are outlined in Box 5.3 are described below.

The most noticeable obstacle to comparing different programs is the inconsistent definition and measure of recidivism. Recidivism has been operationalized as reconviction, re-arrest, failure of a polygraph, or violation of probation or parole (Hanson et al., 2002). Some studies delineate by sexual or nonsexual and violent or non-violent re-offense, and others use general re-offending regardless of offense type. Further, the measure of recidivism and data collection techniques that are employed range from police records to self report data, family interviews and community records.

Hall (1995) reviewed all treatment studies published since Furby et al.'s (1989) damning review in 1989. Perhaps in an attempt at neutralization, his conclusions are curiously positive. While treatment providers and professionals in the field of sexual abuse evidently appreciated this perspective, his findings have more recently been interpreted with caution.

Gallagher et al.'s (1999) meta-analysis of 25 sex offender treatment programs has been considered the most comprehensive and technically sophisticated review available (Hanson, 2002). The biggest advantages of this study are its international focus; attention to both published and unpublished treatment initiatives and its ability to delineate by offense type.

Hanson et al. (2002) provide the most recent and most highly anticipated and definitive meta-analytic review of psychological treatment for sex offenders to date. These researchers share all of the advantages that Gallagher and colleagues offer but boast a larger sample size, longer follow-up periods and inclusion of studies that randomly assigned cases to non-treatment control groups.

What Works in Sex Offender Treatment?

The summary provided here is drawn from the conclusions of various meta-analyses and qualitative reviews of sex offender treatment programs over the past 15 years. Clinical findings from various treatment programs are mostly consistent with theoretical predictions. However, because clinical significance does not equate to statistical significance, it is impossible to tell to what degree CBT is effective. Evidence suggests that a combination of group treatment and individual therapy works better than either in isolation; residential community programs are more effective than custodial programs for incarcerated offenders and the most promising results are coming from programs catering specifically to adolescents (Hall, 1995). Given a youth's greater capacity for change and the established advantages of early intervention, this is not surprising.

Box 5.3

Comparison of the Three Most Important Meta-Analyses of Sex Offender Treatment Programs in the Last Decade

	# studies	total n of SOs	Published or not published	# CM # R # all or mixed	Dominant Treatment type	Follow up period	Definition of recidivism	Data source	Average Treatment recidivism	Average control recidivism	Characteristics of programs with strongest treatment effects
Hall 1995	12	1,313	Published since Furby et al. (1989)	R (6) CM (10) mixed (5)	Not specified	Mean 6.85 years (SD 5.95)	Reconviction (2); other (10)	Official records (5); self-report (3); combination (4)	SRO 19%	SRO 27%	CBT over hormonal programs; longer follow ups; adolescent programs; community over institutional;
Gallagher et al. 1999	25	N/A	Both	R (13) CM (22) mixed (12)	CBT	N/A	Reconviction (3); re-arrest (18); other (4) (1)	Official records (18); combination (6); not specified	N/A	N/A	CBT; surgical castration;
Hanson et al. 2002	43	9,454	Both	N/A	CBT	12 months – 16 years (median 46 months)	Reconviction (8); Re-arrest (11); Parole violation, community reports and readmission (20)	CJ records (26); state records (19) self-report (9); not specified (6)	SRO 12.3% NS 27.9%	SRO 16.8% NS 39.2%	unpublished; when compared to alternative treatment than to untreated group; community over institutional;

SOs: sex offenders; # CM: number of programs for child molesters; # R: number of programs for rapists
all: number of programs for both child molesters and rapists, or programs that did not specify their clientele
CBT: Cognitive-Behavioral Therapy; SRO: sexual re-offense; NS: non-sexual re-offense

Other Populations

Discussions of female and adolescent populations are too often considered exclusively by a last minute paragraph before the conclusion. And regretfully, they are also addressed here.

In recent years, attention has turned to the reality of sexual abuse of children that is perpetrated by adolescents. At least one-half of the adult males who are known to have sexually offended against children admit to having started their offending before the age of 16. Findings from retrospective self-report surveys administered to sexually aggressive adults indicate a need to focus on the likelihood of juveniles to continue offending across the life course (Grant, 2000).

The number of adolescents who sexually abuse children as a percentage of all child sexual abusers is unknown (Grant, 2000; Erooga & Masson, 1999). Self-report studies with adult and adolescent offenders and their victims give some indication of the actual figures. Generally, it has been found that adolescent perpetrators are responsible for between one fifth and one third of all child sex offenses (Cavanagh-John-son, 1988; Ford & Linney, 1995; Morrison, 1999; National Clearinghouse on Family Violence, 1997; Ryan, Metzner & Krugman, 1990; Stenson & Anderson, 1987). Some studies have found the figure to be well over 50 percent (Elliott & Smiljanich, 1994; James & Neil, 1996).

Sexual offending by females is less understood than offending by males. They are generally considered to make up 5 to 10 percent of all sexual offenders (Hislop, 2001). Female child molesters are often described in one of three ways. The *teacher/lover* offender non-violently instructs the child (usually a prepubescent boy) in love-making. The *male coerced* offender is directed into the abusive role by a persuasive male (Higgs, Cana-van & Meyer, 1992; Briggs, 1995:138). The third type is the *predisposed* offender who usually has a transgenerational history of sexual abuse and may have had previous psychiatric diagnoses or treatment (Higgs, Canavan & Meyer, 1992). It is unclear whether female child molesters begin offending in adolescence, one study found that a conservative estimate of 75 percent had engaged in age inappropriate sexual behavior by the time they entered adolescence (Saradjian, 1996:66).

The official responses to females who sexually abuse are seldom consistent (Blues, Moffat & Telford, 1999; Elliott, 1993). Women criminals are consistently 'perceived to be either not women or not criminals' (Worrall, 1990:31). They are treated either with forgiving lenience or severe harshness. Exhibitionism by a female for example, might 'more readily be labeled promiscuity than viewed as a legal offense such as indecent exposure' (Fehrenbach & Monastersky, 1988:150). Consistent with the chivalry thesis, Miller et al. (1995) assert that most judges are reluctant to place girls in correctional settings. Prosecution for a sexual offense is a crucial step in acknowledging victim harm and in providing the offender with a chance to take responsibility for her behavior and seek treatment. Despite this, prosecutors have a tendency to decriminalize sexual offenses committed by women (Elliott, 1997:105). 'By discounting the existence of female offenders, researchers have invalidated the experience of hundreds of thousands of victims and denied female offenders the help they might have received in treatment' (Turner & Turner, 1994:11).

While women and girls have very specific treatment needs (Miller et al., 1995) they are considered better candidates for treatment than men and boys. It has been found that offending girls are less likely to deny their offense, blame the victim, or describe it incorrectly as 'love' (Cavanagh-Johnson, 1989). Further, they are far more likely to feel that their behaviour was wrong and to assume total responsibility for the incident (Fromuth & Conn, 1997). Importantly, therapy for female sex offenders is particularly beneficial when there is an opportunity to address their own victim/survivor issues (Blues, Moffat & Telford, 1999; Hirshberg & Riskin, 1996).

Box 5.4

Why Females Are Less Likely to Be Identified as Sex Offenders

Male victims seldom disclose abuse by females. Male conditioning teaches that sexual initiation by an older female is 'the ultimate beneficial educational experience for boys' (Briggs, 1993:36). The victim is generally assumed to be "lucky" because she made the first move (Cavanagh-Johnson, 1989:572). This leads to traumatic sexualization, which is one of the effects of child sexual abuse that Finklehor (in Saradjian, 1996) identified.

Boys are socialized to be the initiators of sexual activity and it is therefore quite difficult for them to admit to 'sexual subjugation'. This situation is 'magnified if the abuser is a woman' (Saradjian, 1996:16).

Briggs (1995:138) describes how the women's movement was at the 'forefront of publicizing the abuse of female children by men' and pioneered the establishment of women's shelters and help lines and survivor groups across the western world. These developments 'gave women the courage to reveal childhood abuse, which they had previously kept secret. In the meantime there was no similar recognition by male society of the existence and needs of abused boys' (Briggs, 1995:138). Regardless of their offender's sex, male victims 'have a long way to go to get past the resistance and backlash' that still exists (Mathews, 1997:58).

CONCLUSION

There are still a number of questions remaining about treatment. Future research should examine three issues. One relates to whether deniers should be admitted into a treatment program with admitters. Some argue that acceptance is the first step to recovery and having admitters and deniers in the same group can be disruptive. A second important topic for research is whether mandatory attendance should be required. While treatment is often required by court order, some treatment providers argue treatment is useless unless it is voluntary. The third issue concerns the importance, necessity or likelihood of family reunification. This is considered to be particularly relevant for incest offenders.

Traditional criminology fails to provide a theoretical understanding of sexual offending against children. Sources of official statistics, which are mostly accepted by criminologists, are equally inadequate since this crime is so rarely identified, disclosed or discussed. The knowledge we have garnered instead from clinical samples and psychological perspectives is useful in furthering our understanding of child molestation. Whether the offense is considered a modeled behavior, an alternative sexual preference or a rational act of criminality, behavioral and cognitive-behavioral theories hold that there is some level of learning (conscious or unconscious, intended or not) that encourages, disinhibits, and reinforces this behavior. The cognitive-behavioral perspective offers the most consistent explanation of child molestation and cognitive-behavioral therapy specifically, offers the best approach for individual therapy, group treatment and overall management of this troubled and troubling population.

NOTE

[1] In regard to sexual offending, Finkelhor's (1984) four factor model integrates both of these perspectives and remains one of the most frequently cited theories in the field.

REFERENCES

Adamson, R. (2002). "Don't Turn a Blind Eye When Boys Are Sexually Exploited by Women." *Ottawa Citizen*, (June 16):A14.

Andrews, D. and J. Bonta (2003). *The Psychology of Criminal Conduct,* Third Edition. Cincinnati, OH: Anderson Publishing Co.

Associated Press (AP) (2002). "New Jersey Teacher Who Had Sex with 13-Year-Old Student Gets Probation." *AP State and Local Wire* (May 24).

Bartol, C. (2002). *Criminal Behavior: A Psychosocial Approach.* New Jersey: Prentice Hall.

Becker, J. (1988)."The Effects of Child Sexual Abuse on Adolescent Sexual Offenders." In R. Wyatt and G. Johnson-Powell (eds.) *Lasting Effects of Child Sexual Abuse.* London: SAGE Publications.

Blues, A., C. Moffat, and P. Telford (1999). "Work with Adolescent Females Who Sexually Abuse: Similarities and Differences." In M. Erooga and H. Masson (eds.) *Children and Young People Who Sexually Abuse Others: Challenges and Responses,* London: Routledge.

Briggs, F. (1995). *From Victim to Offender.* Sydney: Allen and Unwin.

Broadhurst, R. and R. Maller (1992). "The Recidivism of Sex Offenders in the Western Australian Prison Population." *British Journal of Criminology*, 32(1):54–80.

Bureau of Justice Statistics (1997). http://www.ojp.usdoj.gov/bjs

Burton, D., A. Nesmith, and L. Badten (1997). "Clinician's Views on Sexually Aggressive Children and Their Families: A Theoretical Exploration." *Child Abuse and Neglect,* 21(2):157–170.

Cavanagh-Johnson, T. (1988). "Child Perpetrators: Children Who Molest Other Children—Preliminary Findings." *Child Abuse and Neglect,* 12:219–229.

Elliott, D. and K. Smiljanich (1994). "Sex Offending among Juveniles: Development and Response." *Journal of Pediatric Health Care,* 8(3):101–105.

Erooga, M. and H. Masson (eds.) (1999). *Children and Young People Who Sexually Abuse Others: Challenges and Responses.* London: Routledge.

Fagan, J. and S. Wexler (1988). "Explanations of Sexual Assault among Violent Delinquents." *Journal of Adolescent Research,* 3(3):363–385.

Finkelhor, D. (1984). *Child Sexual Abuse: New Theory and Research.* New York: The Free Press.

Finney, D. (2002). "Breaking the Silence: Sexual Abuse of Kids Causes Untold Misery." *Omaha World-Herald,* (April 7): LIVING, 1.

Flynn, B. (2002). "See Me after History Class … and I'll Strip!" *The Sun,* (April 5).

Ford, M. and J. Linncy (1995). "Comparative Analysis of Juvenile Sex Offenders, Violent Nonsexual Offenders, and Status Offenders." *Journal of Interpersonal Violence,* 10(1):56–70.

Friedrich, W. and W. Luecke (1988). "Young School-Age Sexually Aggressive Children" *Professional Psychology: Research and Practice,* 19(2):155–164.

Fromuth, M. and V. Conn (1997). "Hidden Perpetrators: Sexual Molestation in a Non-Clinical Sample of College Women." *Journal of Interpersonal Violence,* 12(3):456–465.

Furby, Weinrott and Blackshaw (1989). "Sex Offender Recidivism: A Review." *Psychological Bulletin,* 105:3–30.

Gabor, P. and C. Ing (1991). "Stop and Think: The Application of Cognitive-Behavioral Approaches in Work with Young People." *Journal of Child and Youth Care,* 6(1):43–53.

Gallagher, C., D. Wilson, P. Hirschfield, M. Coggeshall, and D. MacKenzie (1999). "A Quantitative Review of the Effects of Sex Offender Treatment on Sexual Reoffending." *Corrections Management Quarterly,* 3(4):19–29.

Gelles, R. and G. Wolfner (1994). "Sexual Offending and Victimization: A Life Course Perspective." In A. Rossi (ed.) *Sexuality Across the Life Course.* Chicago: University of Chicago Press.

Giles, D. (2002) "Pupil 'Kidnapped.'" *Perth Sunday Times,* (May 19).

Gold, S. and T. Dirmann (2002). "Teacher Held in Kidnapping; Police Discover 33-year-old Woman in a Las Vegas Hotel Room with a 15-year-old Boy from Her Science Class. She Faces Felony Charges." *Los Angeles Times,* (May 3):CALIFORNIA METRO, 1.

Graham, K. (1996). "The Childhood Victimization of Sex Offenders: An Underestimated Issue." *International Journal of Offender Therapy and Comparative Criminology,* 40(3):192–203.

Grant, A. (2000). "The Historical Development of Treatment for Adolescent Sex Offenders." *Trends and Issues in Crime and Criminal Justice,* 145:1–6.

Hall, B. (2002). "Of Course, the Police Didn't Suspect LeTourneau." *Lewiston Morning Tribune,* (May 24):12A.

Hall, G. (1996). *Theory-Based Assessment, Treatment and Prevention of Sexual Aggression*. New York: Oxford University Press.

Hall, G. (1995)."Sex Offender Recidivism Revisited: A Meta-analysis of Recent Treatment Studies." *Journal of Consulting and Clinical Psychology*, 63(5):802–809.

Hanson, K. and M. Bussiere (1998)."Predicting Relapse: A Meta-Analysis of Sex Offender Recidivism Studies." *Journal of Consulting and Clinical Psychology*, 66(2):348–362.

Hanson, K., A. Gordon, A. Harris, J. Marques, W. Murphy, V. Quinsey, and M. Seto (2002). "First Report of the Collaborative Outcome Data Project on the Effectiveness of Psychological Treatment for Sex Offenders." *Sexual Abuse: A Journal of Research and Treatment*, 14(2):169–194.

Haskell, D. (2002). "Analysis: Molesters Lurk Anywhere." *United Press International*, (March 29):GENERAL NEWS.

Higgs, D., M. Canavan, and W. Meyer (1992). "Moving from Defence to Offence: The Development of an Adolescent Female Sex Offender." *The Journal of Sex Research*, 29(1):131–139.

Hirschberg, D. and K. Riskin (1994)."Female Adolescent Sexual Offenders in Residential Treatment: Characteristics and Treatment Implications." Available at http://www.germainelawrence.org/web/fasort.html

Hirschi, T. and M. Gottfredson (1983). "Age and the Explanation of Crime." *American Journal of Sociology*, 89:552–584.

Hislop, J. (2001). *Female Sex Offenders: What Therapists, Law Enforcement and Child Protective Services Need to Know*. Washington: Issues Press.

Innes, M. (1997). "Commentary." *Journal of Child and Youth Care*, 11(1):63–64.

James, A. and P. Neil (1996)."Juvenile Sexual Offending: One Year Period Prevalence Study within Oxfordshire." *Child Abuse and Neglect*, 20(6):477–485.

Kluger, J. (2002)."Why Do They Target Kids?: The Molesters' Mind-Set." *Time*, (April 1):37.

Lakey, J. (1994). "The Profile and Treatment of Male Adolescent Sex Offenders." *Adolescence*, 29(116):755–761.

Lee, R. (1993). *Doing Research on Sensitive Topics*. London: SAGE Publications.

Mathews, F. (1997)."The Adolescent Sex Offender Field in Canada: Old Problems, Current Issues and Emerging Controversies." *Journal of Child and Youth Care*, 11(1):55–62.

Martinson, R. (1974). "What Works? Questions and Answers about Prison Reform." *The Public Interest*, 36:22–54.

Mitchell, M. (2002). "LeTourneau's Relationship with Boy 'Torture Not True Love' Lawyer Says." *AP State and Local Wire*, (May 15).

Morrison, T. (1999)."Is There a Strategy Out There? Policy and Management Perspectives on Young People Who Sexually Abuse Others." In M. Erooga and H. Masson (eds.) *Children and Young People Who Sexually Abuse Others: Challenges and Responses*. London: Routledge.

National Clearinghouse on Family Violence (1997). "Adolescent Sex Offenders." Available at http://www.hc-sc.gc.ca/hppb/familyviolence/html/adosxof.htm.

O'Reilly, (2002). "Back of the Book." *The O'Reilly Factor*, (May 29).

Orr, B. (1991). "Male Adolescent Sex Offenders: A Comparison of Two Treatment Approaches." *Journal of Child and Youth Care*, special issue:87–101.

Perkins, D., S. Hammond, D. Coles, and D. Bishopp (1998). *Review of Sex Offender Treatment Programmes*— prepared for the High Security Psychiatric Services Commissioning Board (HSPSCB) Department of Psychology, Broadmoor Hospital.

Peters, B. (2002) "Sex with an Adult Just as Harmful for Boys." *Lewiston Morning Tribune*, (June 9):1A.

Polizzi, D., D. MacKenzie, and L. Hickman (1999)."What Works in Adult Sexual Offender Treatment? A Review of Prison and Non-Prison Based Treatment Programs." *International Journal of Offender Therapy and Comparative Criminology*, 43(3):357–374.

Prentky, R. and R. Knight (1993)."Age of Onset of Sexual Assault: Criminal and Life History Correlates." In G. Nagayama Hall, R. Hirschman, J. Graham, and M. Zaragoza (eds.) *Sexual Aggression: Issues in Etiology, Assessment and Treatment*, Washington: Taylor & Francis.

Radue, A. (2002). "Students Address Teacher-Student Relationships in Light of Area Cases." *Milwaukee Journal Sentinel*, (May 6):4E.

Rasmussen, L. (1999). "Factors Related to 'Recidivism Among Juvenile Sexual Offenders." *Sexual Abuse: A Journal of Research and Treatment*, 11(1):69–85.

Righthand, S. and C. Welch (2001). *Juveniles Who Have Sexually Offended: A Review of the Professional Literature*. Washington: Office of Juvenile Justice and Delinquency Prevention.

Riley, R. (2002)."Sex with Kids Illegal for the Right Reasons." *Detroit Free Press*, (May 29).

Ryan, G., J. Metzner, and R. Krugman (1990). In K. Oates (ed.) *Understanding and Managing Child Sexual Abuse*. Sydney: Harcourt Brace Jovanovich Publishers.

Samenow, S. (1984). *Inside the Criminal Mind*. New York: Time Books.

Sapp, A. and M. Vaughn (1990)."Juvenile Sex Offender Treatment at State-Operated Correctional Institutions." *International Journal of Offender Therapy and Comparative Criminology*, 34(2):131–145.

Saradjian, J. (1996). *Women Who Sexually Abuse Children: From Research to Clinical Practice*. Chichester, West Sussex, England: John Wiley and Sons.

Schwartz, B. and R. Cellini (eds.) (1996). *The Sex Offender: New Insights, Treatment Innovations and Legal Developments*. New Jersey: Civic Research Institute.

Sefarbi, R. (1990). "Admitters and Deniers among Adolescent Sex Offenders and Their Families: a Preliminary Study." *American Journal of Orthopsychiatry*, 60(3):460–465.

Stanley, S. (2002)."Reports of Sex Abuse by Women Increase: Experts Say Attacks Not as Rare as Thought." *The Times-Picayune*, (June 9):METRO, 1.

Stenson, P. and C. Anderson (1987). "Child Care Commentary: Treating Juvenile sex Offenders and Preventing the Cycle of Abuse." *Journal of Child Care*, 3(2):91–101.

Sykes, G. and D. Matza (1959)."Techniques of Neutralization: A Theory of Delinquency." *American Sociological Review*, 22.

Taylor, P. (2002)."Beyond Myths and Denial: What Church Communities Need to Know about Sexual Abusers." *America*, 11(186):7.

United States General Accounting Office (1996). *Sex Offender Treatment: Research Results Inconclusive About What Works to Reduce Recidivism.* Report to the Chairman, Subcommittee on Crime, Committee on the Judiciary, House of Representatives. (GAO/GGD-96–137)

Veneziano, C., L. Veneziano, and S. LeGrand (2000). "The Relationship between Adolescent Sex Offender Behaviours and Victim Characteristics with Prior Victimization." *Journal of Interpersonal Violence,* 15(4):363–374.

Ward, T. and S. Hudson (1998). "The Construction and Development of Theory in the Sexual Offending Area: A Meta-Theoretical Framework." *Sexual Abuse: A Journal of Research and Treatment,* 10(1):47–63.

Weisburd, D. (2000). "Randomized Experiments in Criminal Justice Policy: Prospects and Problems." *Crime & Delinquency,* 46(2):181–193.

Whitford, R. and V. Parr (1995). "Uses of Rational Emotive Behavior Therapy with Juvenile Sex Offenders." *Journal of Rational-Emotive and Cognitive-Behavior Therapy,* 13(4):273–283.

Worling, J. (1995a). "Adolescent Sex Offenders against Females: Differences Based on the Age of their Victims." *International Journal of Offender Therapy and Comparative Criminology,* 39(3):276–293.

Worling, J. (1995b). "Adolescent Sibling-Incest Offenders: Differences in Family and Individual Functioning When Compared to Adolescent Non-Sibling Sex Offenders." *Child Abuse and Neglect,* 19(5):633–643.

Young, C. (2002). "The Bias against Male Victims." *The Boston Globe,* (June 3):A13.

CHAPTER 13

WHAT ARE THE EFFECTS OF ABUSE?

EDWARD L. ROWAN

S urvivors of rape, child sexual abuse, domestic abuse, natural disaster, terrorism, hostage-taking, and war—all situations in which a person is rendered helpless by overwhelming forces—may show the characteristic manifestations of posttraumatic stress disorder (PTSD). The American Psychiatric Association's Diagnostic and Statistical Manual (DSM IV) identifies three clusters of symptoms that characterize PTSD: persistent reexperience of the traumatic event, persistent avoidance of stimuli associated with that trauma and numbing of general responsiveness, and persistent symptoms of increased agitation. Reexperience may be manifest as recurrent and intrusive recollections or flash backs of the event, recurrent distressing dreams of the event, and psychological or physiological distress when exposed to internal or external cues that resemble an aspect of the traumatic event. Avoidance and numbing are seen as efforts to avoid thinking, feeling, or talking about the trauma, to avoid activities, people, or places associated with the traumatic event, and to be unable to recall certain aspects of that event. The traumatized individual shows decreased interest in significant activities, feels detached from others, and has a restricted range of affective responses and the sense of a foreshortened future. Increased arousal takes the form of difficulty in falling or staying asleep, irritability and outbursts of anger, difficulty in concentrating, hypervigilance, and an exaggerated startle response.

A diagnosis of complex post-traumatic stress disorder proposed for DSM V emphasizes that chronic abuse and abuse in childhood result in additional symptoms. These include difficulty with regulation of emotion, dissociative symptoms, and somatization or related physical complaints. Such individuals experience a damaged sense of self, chronic guilt and shame, feelings of ineffectiveness, and a chronic sense of despair and helplessness. They may idealize the perpetrator, have difficulty in establishing and maintaining trusting relationships, and display a tendency to be revictimized or to victimize others.

Harvard psychiatrist Judith Herman, M.D., summed this up by noting that such traumatic events may produce profound and lasting changes in physiologic arousal, emotion, cognition, and memory as well as in the integration of all these functions. Survivors are "disconnected from the present" and continue to react to life experiences as if they were anticipating, experiencing, or responding to the earlier trauma.

The nature and severity of symptoms may vary depending upon the age at which the trauma occurred. Younger children with fewer defenses and underdeveloped coping strategies are more susceptible to negative aftereffects and may even show significant impairment in personality development. More frequent or severe abuse, especially the trauma of penetration, sadistic abuse for the arousal of the perpetrator, extended time of abuse, a close relationship to the abuser, and the experience of multiple abusers may all increase the negative impact.

Study of the neurobiology of post-traumatic stress disorder is still in its infancy, but animal studies and limited human studies suggest that it is a discrete illness with specific physical manifestations. The human body responds and adapts to stressful events. The nervous and endocrine systems play a key role in this.

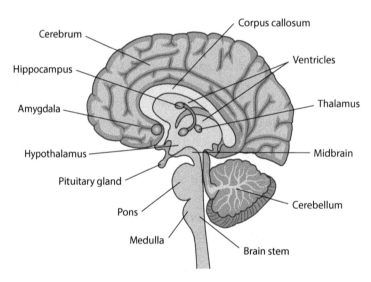

Figure 13.1 Cross-section of Brain

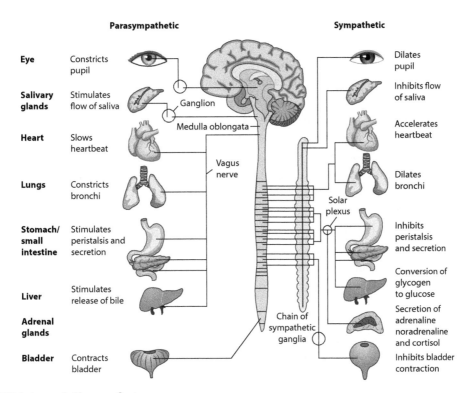

Figure 13.2 Autonomic Nervous System

First, we need to review basic neuroanatomy. The central nervous system consists of the brain and spinal cord. The peripheral nervous system carries incoming sensory input and outgoing motor responses to the rest of the body. The autonomic nervous system serves internal organs and has cells within the central nervous system. The autonomic nervous system has two parts: the sympathetic nervous system responds when the body needs to react with "fight or flight," and the parasympathetic nervous system takes over during periods of rest and restoration. The brain consists of three parts: the most primitive innermost layer, the brain stem, is responsible for basic functions such as heart rate and respiration; the central limbic system regulates affect and emotion; and the outer neocortex governs thought and language.

The neuroendocrine system sends chemical messages (hormones or neurotransmitters) to start or stop responses. The hypothalamus in the brain stem controls the endocrine glands via the pituitary gland. In response to pituitary regulation, the adrenal medulla (inner part) secretes the catecholamines adrenalin (epinephrine) and noradrenalin (norepinephrine) and the adrenal cortex (outer part) releases cortisol, a glucocorticoid. The locus coeruleus (literally, "blue place") in the brain stem and sympathetic fibers themselves also produce catecholamines. Serotonin is also a catecholamine and neurotransmitter whose role is uncertain in the stress response but appears to modulate the norepinephrine effect.

The catecholamines stimulate the sympathetic nervous system to increase heart rate, blood pressure, oxygen consumption, and blood sugar, all of which mobilize the body for action. The glucocorticoid cortisol elevates metabolism and blood sugar but also exerts negative feedback on the hypothalamus and pituitary so that a high level of cortisol closes the loop and shuts off the mobilization of catecholamines.

When a potentially stressful event occurs, the neocortex interprets and coordinates incoming stimuli and plans a response. This input is filtered by the hippocampus and amygdala. They are located in the medial temporal lobe, but are directly connected to the limbic system via the Papez circuit. The hippocampus receives the motor and sensory input and puts it into historical context. It provides relational memory and also determines if information should be stored in longterm memory or be forgotten. The amygdala assigns emotional significance to the input. The amygdala also contains many opiate and benzodiazepine receptors which, if blocked, can interfere with the conditioned emotional response. If assessment determines that "fight or flight" is indicated, the locus coeruleus releases catecholamines, the adrenal glands are stimulated via the hypothalamic-pituitary axis to release both catecholamines and glucocorticoids, and the body is activated to respond.

In most people, the stressful event ends and all these processes return to homeostatic, or balanced, baseline function. This is not true for individuals with post-traumatic stress disorder. Their systems continue to be sensitive to external stimuli and they are in a state of permanent alert, prepared for further attack. Atlanta researcher J. Douglas Bremmer, M.D., has reported changes associated with this condition in the hypothalamic-pituitary-adrenal (HPA) axis and noradrenergic systems as well as in benzodiazepine, opiate, dopaminergic and various neuropeptide systems that modulate function in the hippocampus, amygdala, and prefrontal cortex of the brain. Neuroimaging studies have shown that post-traumatic stress disorder is associated with a decrease in hippocampal volume. (It is not currently known if the hippocampus actually shrinks or if individuals susceptible to PTSD have smaller hippocampi to begin with. Neuroimaging studies have not been done on pre-morbid, asymptomatic individuals.) Without feedback about past experience and current context, the amygdala has exaggerated activation and attaches additional emotional significance to the incoming stimuli. Catecholamines are mobilized and full sympathetic arousal occurs. In individuals with post-traumatic stress disorder, cortisol is also mobilized but is quickly metabolized and does not reach a level sufficient to turn off catecholamine production. This state of hyperarousal causes hypervigilance and increased startle responses. Activation of the amygdala is associated with activity in the visual cortex that may be the basis for flashbacks and nightmares. One small aspect of the original trauma—a look, a sound, a smell, or a feeling—may trigger the whole memory picture along with all the negative emotional responses that accompanied the original event.

Boston psychiatrist Bessel Van der Kolk postulates that the extreme arousal associated with trauma floods the brain with neurotransmitters, "stamping in" vivid sensory memories of the event. These events may take the form of fragmented images that, when stimulated by present emotion, produce a vivid "reliving" of the past trauma in the present. The emotional memory system is housed in the amygdala and operates independently of cortical control. The system operates in a rapid response mode and this hypervigilance may produce sustained fear. These responses become automatic and beyond conscious control.

The overall effects may be so powerful and painful that the survivor becomes overwhelmed and cannot deal with them. Detachment, numbness, and passivity may extend to a complete denial of reality. It is not uncommon for a victim of abuse to describe the sensation of being outside the body, sometimes floating in the air, and dispassionately observing what is going on. Some theorists believe that depersonalization may progress to somatization disorder (formerly called hysteria), borderline personality disorder, and dissociative identity disorder (formerly called multiple personality disorder). The sense of disconnection may be so great that the survivor resorts to self-injury to feel something—anything. Paradoxically, the sight of one s own blood may be soothing and experienced without pain. The survivor is ultimately unable to integrate the multiple levels of response and finally assigns them to different selves rather than acknowledging that they are part of the same complex emotional reaction. Identity may be fragmented, but the individual is able to survive and to present a superficially normal façade to the world.

The world does not feel like a safe place for the sexually abused child and adult survivor. Basic trust is shattered. This is especially true when the perpetrator is a member of the family. The victim is often isolated from friends and other family members and has to deal with an often unpredictable abuser. The child may think, "Will they be angry, or drunk, or act as if I were special?" When other supposedly caring family members passively ignore—or worse, actively enable the abuse—basic trust is eroded even further. This can be devastating to potential future relationships, especially to sexual relationships. Intimacy and sexuality are often split. A survivor may want closeness but fear sexual contact and avoid both.

Debra Kalmuss, Ph.D., from the Columbia School of Public Health, defines *sexual health* as the ability to "derive pleasure from and make decisions about ones sexual and reproductive behavior and identity in a manner that respects ones own sexual rights and desires as well as those of others." For someone on whom sex was first imposed on terms dictated by another more powerful person and not associated with pleasure, sexual health may be an unrealized dream. Sexual dysfunctions including low desire, inability to experience orgasm, vaginal muscle spasm (vaginismus), and painful intercourse are common. Sexual behavior is learned, and imposed sex is not a positive experience.

University of Nevada–Reno psychologists Leah Leonard and Victoria Follette have suggested two theories to explain the relationship between child sexual abuse and sexual dysfunction. One is experiential avoidance, a process that includes an unwillingness to reexperience painful thoughts, feelings, and memories associated with the experience of sexual abuse. The other is emotional avoidance, a process where sexual intimacy is associated with emotional pain. Both must be addressed as part of the therapeutic process.

Unwanted sexual activity may result in physical trauma, bleeding, infections, vaginal discharge, itching, urinary tract infections, abdominal pain, or pregnancy. Some clinicians have suggested that early sexual activity causes an increase in sex hormone levels, hypersexuality, and early puberty. Statistics do confirm that survivors of child sexual abuse engage in consensual sexual activity at an earlier age than do their non-abused peers. They are also less likely to use barrier forms of contraception such as condoms and are therefore more at risk of contacting sexually transmitted diseases including HIV/AIDS. They have more partners, more pregnancies, and more abortions and are more likely to be victimized in the future. Some survivors may prostitute themselves in order to have more control over who has access to their bodies and to make their partners pay for it.

Self-doubt as a result of early victimization is common.

The child asks, "What did I do to deserve this?" The perpetrator often tells a female child that she is bad or just like mother and does indeed deserve the abuse. The confusion is compounded if there is any erotic aspect to the abuse, such as involuntary sexual arousal. Rewards from the abuser in the form of treats or privileges also lead to conflicting emotions. Negative feelings may make the survivor more susceptible to self-medication with drugs or alcohol, or the negativity may be converted to physical symptoms requiring relief by prescription medication. Self-identification as a 'victim" or "damaged goods" may result in low self-esteem and create a pattern of self-destructive behavior.

Overall, the victims, and then the survivors, lose faith in what is supposed to be the natural order where children are cherished and protected, and where they are safe in the family and community. For them the world becomes unjust.

Young children who are abused may not express themselves verbally, but may demonstrate disorganized or agitated behavior as well as highly sexualized play, inappropriate sexual knowledge, or sexually aggressive behavior. They may act out in their play what they are unable to verbalize. They may have nightmares, but these may not be specifically sexually oriented. They may regress developmentally and wet the bed, suck their fingers, or bang their heads. If the perpetrator was a stranger, the child may demonstrate separation anxiety. All are warning signs of possible abuse. Symptoms of trauma or infection would have few other explanations. Undeveloped psychological defenses and intellectual abilities make it difficult for these victims to understand that they are not responsible, and basic issues in trust and gender identity may be compromised.

Adolescents have multiple developmental tasks to accomplish. They must become independent of parental control, achieve mature sexual expression, develop the capacity for intimacy and understand how it differs from sexuality, choose an adult role, and crystallize their personal value systems. Sexual abuse complicates each of these tasks. If the abuser was a parent, the conflicting feelings of attachment and hostility must be worked through or else there is great potential for future negative relationships and revictimization. Mature sexual expression gives way to aversion to sexual behavior, sexual identity confusion, and sexual dysfunction. Promiscuity—the seemingly opposite behavior—is also common. For girls, a history of sexual abuse is associated with increased teen pregnancy. Such a pregnancy is often accompanied by stress, substance abuse, and the birth of small, poorly developed babies. Teenage girls who sexually abuse younger children are likely to report a history of sexual abuse themselves. The capacity for intimacy is compromised by an inability to trust others. Adult role choices may be limited as the perception that the world is a safe place is shattered. Self-image may include worthlessness, shame, and guilt.

Any issues unresolved in adolescence will carry over into adulthood, and the resulting behavior patterns become harder to change. The intimate invasion of personal space leaves many survivors with an inability to trust other people to be close to them. The bodily invasion also seems to predispose survivors to focus on somatic responses and to develop a wide range of physical complaints. Not surprisingly, the complaints often involve lower abdominal or pelvic pain, bladder dysfunction, irritable bowel syndrome, premenstrual dysphoria, painful menstruation, chronic fatigue syndrome, and headache. It is also not surprising that women with these complaints are reluctant to seek gynecological services including Pap tests for cervical cancer screening. When they do see a physician, the often vague nature of the complaints results in a disproportionate number of surgical procedures. They may also avoid dental care. A recent Australian study has shown that, among a group of adult women treated for depression, those with a history of child sexual abuse showed more deliberate self-harm and were more likely to have been recent victims of violence than were their depressed peers. Long-term physical consequences of abuse can become manifest in a great many ways.

According to Gelinas, low self-esteem and guilt are characteristic of the grown-up parentalized female child. These women had no rights as children and feel that they have no rights as adults. They blame themselves for being victimized and do not believe that they deserve better. (Interestingly, abused younger sisters of the parentalized child show all the traumatic effects but not the low self-esteem and guilt. They know they were not responsible.)

These women have problems with parenting; it is difficult for them to balance discipline and affection, especially after their children start to talk and make demands. Children learn to use guilt and feel entitled to have their demands met. Husbands are still needy. Often the new mothers parents continue to make demands on her as well. As she tries to deal with all these demands, she feels progressively more inadequate and withdraws. She may then begin to lean on her oldest daughter, and the cycle continues.

Such a woman may lead a life of quiet desperation until some external event triggers symptoms; promotion or selection for a position that presumes a level of competence she doesn't feel or her daughter reaching the age at which she was abused are examples. She may not demonstrate classic post-traumatic stress disorder but a disguised presentation such as chronic depression, impulsive acting out, or confusion. These women will not spontaneously report their history of abuse, and may not even realize that there is a cause-and-effect relationship. They will disclose if asked.

Progression of the psychological effects of child sexual abuse is associated with particular personality disorders. "Association" is the operative word here because, although a large number of people with these disorders report a history of child sexual abuse, many abused individuals do not develop those patterns of behavior.

Depersonalization, dissociation, and dysphoria are key elements of PTSD and are characteristic of somatization disorder, borderline personality disorder, and dissociative identity disorder as well. A person will not show all these disorders at once or sequentially, but will settle into one pattern over time.

To meet the DSM IV criteria for somatization disorder, a person must have had multiple physical symptoms beginning before age thirty and lasting a number of years. These must include pain symptoms in at least four different sites or functions, two different gastrointestinal complaints, one sexual or reproductive symptom other than pain, and one pseudoneurological symptom, none of which can be explained by a known medical condition such as an arthritic joint, an ulcer, a uterine tumor, or nerve damage.

People with borderline personality disorder have problems with relationships, self-image, affect, and impulse control. They may do anything to avoid perceived abandonment, have intense and unstable interpersonal relationships, struggle with poor self-image, feel chronically empty, demonstrate inappropriate and intense anger, and they may dissociate. Many of these symptoms are carried over from the relationship between victim and abuser.

Individuals with dissociative identity disorder take this defense to an extreme. They have two or more distinct personality states with different and enduring patterns of perceiving, relating to, and thinking about the environment and themselves. These different identities recurrently control that persons behavior, and things that happen to one identity may not be accessible to the memory of another. A history of a helpless child leaving conscious memory behind in the face of overwhelming force seems very relevant.

While the physical, sexual, and psychological consequences of child sexual abuse are generally the same for boys and girls, boys may deal with them differently. First, a boy is less likely to report abuse. If the perpetrator is female, he may not want to acknowledge that he was overpowered or controlled by a woman. He may also feel that the experience of having sex with an older woman is positive, but his subsequent behavior might indicate that this is not the case. If the perpetrator is male, the child may feel shame, embarrassment, a sense of emasculation, or the fear of being labeled as gay by others. Male anger may be expressed in acts of aggression or criminal behavior. While abused males show the same patterns of reckless and dysfunctional sexual behavior as abused females, they are more susceptible to sexual identity confusion. This is particularly so for prepubescent victims. There seems to be a statistical association between the experience of child sexual abuse and adult male homosexuality. The operative word again is association. Boys who are most attractive to male perpetrators may show effeminate behavior, lack secondary sex characteristics such as facial and pubic hair and a deepening voice, and have no peer support or strong male figures with whom to identify. These factors may contribute to a homosexual identity formation without the complicating factor of sexual abuse, but the experience of sexual activity with an older male may serve to crystallize such an identity. The same does not appear to be true for postpubescent males who may already have identified themselves as committed heterosexuals. No information is available about sexual identity distortion in girls who are abused by older women.

The effects of child sexual abuse on parenting behavior are variable. The boundary violations of abuse could result in survivors exhibiting a range of punitive, permissive, or overprotective behaviors toward their own children. They may reject or mimic their own parents' model of the parent-child relationship.

CHAPTER 14

COMMON FORMS

Sex Trafficking

KIMBERLY A. MCCABE

A cross the nations and throughout a variety of cultures is the criminal activity of human trafficking. Victims of human trafficking include men, women, and children. These victims are deceived, coerced, and abused—all for profit. This chapter recognizes human trafficking as a transnational criminal enterprise as it reaches far beyond geographic boundaries and flourishes from the victimization of individuals for profit. This chapter is organized to provide an overview of human trafficking, to discuss some of the causes, victims, and offenders of sex trafficking, and to explain some of the reasons human trafficking continues to thrive. In a nutshell, through this chapter, readers will become more aware of the problem of human trafficking and the issues surrounding sex trafficking.

CHAPTER LEARNING OBJECTIVES

Learning objectives for this chapter include the following:

- Understand some of the reasons that humans are trafficked.
- Know two major US Acts prohibiting human trafficking.
- Understand the phrase "severe forms of human trafficking."
- Understand how the Push–Pull Theory of Migration helps explain human trafficking.

DEFINING HUMAN TRAFFICKING

The United Nations has defined human trafficking as the recruitment, transfer, harboring, or receipt of persons by threat or use of force. The US State Department's Trafficking Protection Act (2000) further identifies severe forms of human trafficking as: (1) sex trafficking in which a commercial sex act is induced by force, fraud, or coercion, or in which the person induced to perform such an act has not attained 18 years of age; or (2) the recruitment, harboring, transportation, provision, or obtaining of a person for labor or services through the use of force, fraud, or coercion for the purpose of subjection to involuntary servitude, peonage, debt bondage, or slavery. However, defining a criminal activity is only the first step in the attempt to reduce the activity.

Individuals are usually trafficked for one of two main reasons: labor or sex. This chapter focuses on the trafficking of individuals for sex or, as commonly referred to, sex trafficking. However, it is acknowledged that individuals (oftentimes children) are also trafficked for reasons other than sex and labor, reasons such as adoption, soldiering, camel jockeying, marriage, or for their internal organs.

Oftentimes the criminal activity of human trafficking goes undetected. In many instances, it is misidentified as human smuggling or people smuggling. People smuggling implies enabling passage into a region where the person is not a resident and is common on the US/Mexico border. Human trafficking involves exploitation and crossing a national border is not a requirement as individuals may be trafficked within regions where they are residents. However, some cases of human smuggling may become cases of human trafficking if the initial consent for the victim to leave one country for another was achieved through deception or coercion. In these cases consent is irrelevant and human trafficking has occurred (McCabe, 2008).

Estimates on the revenue produced through human trafficking by the International Organization of Migration (IOM) in 2009 suggest that human trafficking now generates a 36 billion dollar enterprise. These criminal enterprises are often accomplished through criminal organizations. Most human trafficking organizations are small units of one to five individual person networks. These individuals are involved in the identification, transportation, housing, and victimization of the victims. However, some human trafficking organizations are larger with more than 50 individuals involved in the delivery of the human product (Raymond and Hughes, 2001). Nationally, it is suggested that human trafficking is the third most profitable criminal enterprise following only the trafficking of drugs and the trafficking of firearms.

Although individuals are trafficked for a variety of reasons, sex trafficking is the most publicized aspect of human trafficking. Media attention, as far as news reports, documentaries, and even movies suggest, tells us that sex trafficking occurs throughout the world and that everyday involvement in sex trafficking continues to increase. For the most part, this is correct. How individuals become involved in sex trafficking may be explained from both a personal perspective and an environmental perspective.

In sex trafficking, it is recognized that individuals are victimized through their forced participation in the sex industry. Sex trafficking is not simply pornography or simply prostitution. It involves traffickers, victims, and clients. For clarity, the United Nations has recognized the distinction between sex trafficking and prostitution and advanced the notion of participant-victim by their extension of the definition of sex trafficking to include payments or benefits to a person with control over another person for the purpose of exploitation; thus, recognizing the role of the trafficker in human trafficking (McGinnis, 2004).

In the criminal activity of sex trafficking, the trafficker controls both the sexual exploitation of his sex worker, his worker's "decision" to work or not work, and his worker's location for work. Note that although in this narrative the trafficker is referred to as "he" there are many cases, especially in the cases of the sex trafficking of children, where the trafficker is a female not a male. In the majority of the cases of sex trafficking in the United States, victims are prostituted through force on the part of their traffickers and the victims do not have the choice to decide to work or not. The United States government estimates that approximately 70 percent of the victims are female and approximately 50 percent of the victims are under the age of 18. Therefore, many children are involved in sex trafficking and research has suggested that one single trafficked child can net their trafficker up to 30,000 dollars (Kangaspunta, 2006).

Across the globe, sex trafficking is not limited to prostitution. Victims of sex trafficking are forced into a variety of forms of sexual exploitation to include prostitution, pornography, bride trafficking, and sex tourism. The common element in all forms of sex trafficking is the total control of the trafficker over his victim or the term "forced." Often, victims of sex trafficking are not only abused by their clients, they are abused by their traffickers; therefore, victims of sex trafficking face multiple situations of victimization—all for another's profit or pleasure. Victims of sex trafficking often face physical abuse, emotional abuse, health risks, and sexual coercion (McCabe, 2008). Victims of sex trafficking rarely receive proper food, safe shelter, or medical attention. They are often addicted to drugs and/or alcohol provided by their traffickers in an effort to more easily control them. In addition, members of the victims' families may be threatened, tortured, or killed if the victims do not participate in their sexual exploitation. For the victims of sex trafficking, the abuse appears to be never ending until they are freed or (most likely) die.

As stated sex trafficking, just as the case for drug trafficking, is extremely profitable. Without the possibility of recognition, with little interference from law enforcement, and essentially no pursuit from prosecutors, sex trafficking is perceived as a lucrative career track for those willing to victimize others with few risks or consequences for traffickers. The phrase "white slavery" is used today to describe the Eastern European women first perceived to be involved in sex trafficking in the United States. These white slaves were "prostituted" without the choice of participation and forcibly moved from city to city, state to state, and country to country for profit (McCabe, 2010). Of course, today it is not recognized that all victims of "white slavery" are not "white."

VICTIMS

It is impossible to document the first time sex trafficking occurred; however, in the 1980s globalization and technology facilitated the movements of individuals across international borders nonprofit organizations to help victims of sex trafficking have existed for over three decades (Guinn and Steglich, 2003).

The general demographic characteristics of the victims of sex trafficking are, of course, young and female (McCabe, 2008). Since sexual exploitation is the goal of the trafficking, the more "attractive" the product, the higher the sale price. Although specific ages of sex trafficking victims are unknown, research suggests that the average age of a sex slave in the United States is around 20 while the average age outside of the United States is approximately 12 years old (McCabe, 2008). Also ideal in the sex trafficking industry is the fact that many of the victims of sex trafficking do not speak the language of the host country. Researchers who have attempted to generate a profile of the child victims of sex trafficking suggest that the children come from families with four or more children, from families with few family members contributing to the household income, and from families that reside in extremely poor countries (Kangaspunta, 2006).

Victims usually become involved in sex trafficking through one of two ways. The first is through *force*, *fraud*, or *coercion* where victims do not choose to participate in their sexual exploitation. The second involves victims who *volunteer* to participate in prostitution, but who are later placed in a situation where they perform unanticipated, undesired, and non-consensual sexual acts under inhumane conditions (Tiefenbrun, 2002). The first group of victims—those forced into sexual exploitation—are sometimes kidnapped in their home country and brought into another country with false documentation or no documentation then forced to work in sexually exploitive occupations by their traffickers. In other cases of forced entry into sex trafficking, these victims are sold by an acquaintance or family member.

In the cases of victims who have agreed to prostitution, but are then trafficked, assistance from law enforcement is extremely difficult to obtain. The victims have willingly agreed to participate in an illegal activity (prostitution) and are unlikely to report their victimization for fear of being arrested. It is also this group of victims who are perceived by the public as unworthy of legal assistance as they voluntarily participated in criminal activities themselves. A 2009 UNICEF report confirms what others have noted: that country characteristics such as poverty, limited work opportunities, and lack of government response continue to fuel sex trafficking.

Regardless of the degree of victim involvement in sex trafficking, the destinations for most of the trafficking victims are cities with large commercial trade centers or areas with large military bases and where large/global sporting events are to be held (i.e., Olympics, World Cup, etc.). It is within these densely populated areas that victims of sex trafficking and their traffickers easily blend in and function. Just as the criminal activity of prostitution occupies a central position in the development of national and international capitalism, sex trafficking flourishes within the same governmental structure.

Bales (2004) suggested that over 200,000 individuals were enslaved as prostitutes across the world at the turn of the twenty-first century. The US Department of State estimates that approximately 50,000 victims of trafficking are in the country today. Researchers who study sex trafficking suggest that the movement of these victims may be on a group or individual basis. These movements are generally based upon the relationship between the traffickers and the brothel owners, the size of the traffickers' networks, and the need for a certain type of victim. For example, in Central Asia, a blonde female from Sweden is very profitable for her trafficker.

In addition to the movement of victims based upon client preferences victims of sex trafficking are moved to avoid relationships, for variety, and to provide location confusion (McCabe, 2008). Relationships that may occur between a victim and a client may lead the client to attempt to rescue the victim from their traffickers. By moving the victim from location to location with only days at each location, these relationships are avoided. The work of a victim of sex trafficking is endless, brutal, and sometimes deadly. It is suggested that the trafficking of victims for the purpose of sexual exploitation is more dangerous to the victim than trafficking for labor. Victims of sex trafficking are exposed to physical violence, sexual violence, sexually transmitted diseases, and confinement. The mortality rate for victim of sex trafficking is 40 times higher than the national average (Sulaimanova, 2006). Of course, when one victim dies, another victim is easily obtained as a replacement.

EXPLAINING SEX TRAFFICKING

In attempting to explain how sex trafficking can occur, one of the earliest explanations is founded in Lee's (1966) Push–Pull Theory of Migration. Just as with migration in general, characteristics of both the host and destination countries facilitate human trafficking. Specifically, characteristics of the host country push its natives out and conditions of the destination country pull the immigrants into the country. One common method of recruiting women for sex trafficking is by placing an advertisement in local newspapers for nanny or waitressing jobs in a country that is more resourced than their own (sometimes the United States). Once the women have been recruited, they are transported to the destination country where their travel documents are confiscated, they are imprisoned by their traffickers and forced to repay their debts (i.e., cost of their transportation, food, clothing, and shelter).

A second explanation for human trafficking is military presence. Farr (2004) suggests that in areas with a strong military presence, there are often women engaging in prostitution (some of whom may be trafficking victims). The prostitution serves both the military members and to a lesser extent the women involved in prostitution. When the military vacates the area, that demand for prostitution no longer exists; thus, the women in the area are without work. It is these women who become the targets for traffickers interested in victims for sex trafficking. Research that supports this notion is the finding that many sex-trafficked adults are simply aged prostitutes who have chosen to relocate for prostitution (Raymond and Hughes, 2001). Again, these women will endure the abuse of a trafficking victim and resist being arrested for fear of being sent back to a country where they cannot secure work.

A third explanation for sex trafficking suggests that human trafficking thrives on extreme poverty. This is especially true for victims of inequality (McCabe, 2010). In many countries, women and children are seen as property and disposable. It is these persons who will be recruited for human trafficking. In many cases, even women who enter the sex industry as strippers may become victims of sex trafficking by being prostituted against their will. Thus, one cannot discount the link between prostitution and sex trafficking when attempting to explain human trafficking. In addition, with sex tours (the rotation of victims throughout geographic areas for sexual exploitation) increasingly becoming more popular, the relationship between prostitution and sex trafficking is even stronger.

A fourth and often under-reported explanation of human trafficking is family involvement. Just as a family member often perpetrates the abuse of a child, a family member is often responsible for a women or child involved in sex trafficking. In exchange for money or even a television set, a family member will sell or trade their loved-one into the world of sex trafficking (Farr, 2004). As the family member has allowed and even profited from the victimization of this person, the sex trafficking victim cannot return to the family for fear of punishment by their traffickers or that same family member.

A fifth explanation of sex trafficking is related to spousal prostitution and the mail-order bride industry. Cullen (2002) has reported that often the mail-order bride becomes trapped in the climate of slavery and prostitution. A young woman, who wishes to escape the poverty and depression of her home country, may choose to become a mail-order bride to a man in a "better" country. Of course, the mail-order bride feels that this decision will lead to a secure environment in which her basic needs will be met and she may even perhaps discover love. Unfortunately this is rarely the case as the mail-order bride business is essentially unregulated (McCabe, 2010). Instead, these women are perceived as any material purchase—replaceable or even disposable. To give some perspective on the magnitude of this problem, there are over 200 mail-order bride businesses operating in the United States with over 5,000 women entering the United States each year as a potential bride. The brokers of mail-order brides are not considered traffickers; however, they are often regarded as frauds for not disclosing all of the facts of the transaction. In addition, McCabe (2007) presents *spousal prostitution* and the mail-order bride business as an element of sex trafficking because in these cases the husbands receive money or other goods in exchange for sex with their wives.

Finally, the emerging entrepreneurs in the area of sexual exploitation are those who utilize the Internet. The Internet is the newest avenue for those interested in sex trafficking. It can be used to distribute pornography produced with victims of sex trafficking or to arrange a sexual encounter. Just like with any online order, perpetrators interested in obtaining a victim for sexual exploitation may utilize the Internet and email or a website to facilitate their desire. Again, this mode of communication is very difficult to monitor and, often times, regulations go unenforced.

North America and, in particular the United States, is one of the most reported destination countries for sex trafficking as victims are transported to the United States and throughout the country for the purpose of sexual exploitation. The United States is perceived by many of the poorer countries as the land of opportunity and as such draws individuals from many places. Unfortunately, this appeal of the United States facilitates the criminal enterprise of sex trafficking.

OFFENDERS

One of the best ways to identify the offenders of sex trafficking is to identify the environment of the criminal action. Areas prone to sex trafficking are usually those areas prone to heavy-security establishments, including bars on the windows and strong locks on the doors. However, due to the secrecy of this criminal enterprise, offenders are often as hidden as their victims are.

In an attempt to identify the offenders of sex trafficking one must consider the multiple aspects of the criminal activity. The most obvious offenders are those involved in the sex trafficking of the victim; however, in most cases, there are multiple individuals involved in the trafficking of individuals. In addition, the client of the sex trafficking victim must also be considered the offender. However, in the area of sex trafficking, little research exists on anyone other than the victims of sex trafficking and much of that information is based upon very small samples (Raymond, 2004). Due to the secrecy of the criminal activity, many of those involved in sex trafficking remain unidentified with only general information available on their role in the crime of sex trafficking. As Kangaspunta (2006) has suggested, those involved exclusively in human trafficking are more likely to be organized around a small core group. Around this core group is a larger group of associates involved in a diversified array of criminal activities all to accomplish the trafficking of a person.

To identify the offenders involved in the actual movement or sex trafficking of a victim, one must first consider the individual who has introduced the victim to the criminal organization. As suggested, the individual that is often involved at the entry level of the victim is a family member, close family acquaintance, or boyfriend of the victim. With child victims of sex trafficking, the individuals most likely responsible for their entry into this type of victimization is a family member or family acquaintance who allows the child to enter into this arrangement of victimization. As discussed previously, some family members are tricked into believing that their child will receive a better life and more opportunities for success in another country whereas other family members, in need of money or in desire of some material good (such as a television set), may offer the child as trade. It is difficult to provide the demographic characteristics of these family members. Some researchers suggest that these family members are most often male as the family unit is male-headed. Others suggest it is the mother of the child who makes such arrangements for the good of the remaining children (McCabe, 2008).

Another person who is often involved in the entry of young women into the arena of sex trafficking is the boyfriend of the young lady. This boyfriend, much like a pimp in the arena of prostitution, begins to pursue the young woman with promises of love and security when in actuality he is a recruiter for the sex trafficking organization and will soon offer this young unsuspecting female to the criminal world of sex trafficking. In addition, and not to be overlooked, in many cases the recruiters of young women for sex trafficking are other young women who are themselves victims of sex trafficking (McCabe, 2008). These victims, to gain some sort of status with their traffickers, will bring other young women into the world of sex trafficking.

Also involved as offenders in the criminal activity of sex trafficking are the so-called middlemen who are responsible for a variety of activities in the trafficking of persons. These individuals include the persons who create the fake documents for travel or who arrange for the legitimate travel documents, the individuals who accompany the victim on the journey from source to destination countries, and the customs officials who allow "questionable" individuals to enter the destination country.

Similar to cases of counterfeiting and fraud, the individuals who arrange for the fake travel documentation are experienced in this area, are often acquainted with local government employees, and are known through the criminal network. The individuals who arrange for legitimate travel documents are also excellent at their position, are often trained in law or in some other aspect of government regulations, and carry with them a strong sense of identity within the criminal organization. Just as there exists some information on individuals involved in the smuggling of persons, there is some information on those individuals who travel with the victims of human trafficking. Those individuals who travel with the young adult female victims of human trafficking are often male and often posing as a family member of the victim. However, as stated, with the trafficking of children, it is not unusual for the accompanying traveler to be a woman with the responsibility of childcare (McCabe, 2008). In some extreme cases of child sex trafficking, these female accomplices travel with the very young children, care for the children until they are at an age to be profitable in the criminal activity, then offer the children to the trafficker for a fee.

Bales (2004) suggests that one identifying characteristic of a trafficker is an individual involved in a "respectable" business in addition to owning a brothel (perhaps through an investment club). The profits from sex trafficking are hidden under the red tape of legitimate business bureaucracy. These traffickers are most often male, they are most often involved in some sort of entertainment business, and they may in some cases have friends in high government positions (sometimes law enforcement).

Finally, as Kangaspunta (2006) has suggested, it is not unusual for many of the members of the sex trafficking criminal organization to share the nationality of the victim. The client, on the other hand, probably does not share the nationality of the victim. The motivation for the trafficker is profit. The motivation for the client is pleasure.

Sex trafficking can produce thousands of dollars for the criminal organization. As stated earlier, sex trafficking is one of the most profitable criminal enterprises occurring today. However, clients of the victims of sex trafficking are not interested in financial gain. In terms of the characteristics of the other offenders of sex trafficking (i.e., the clients of the sex trafficked victims), Raymond and Hughes (2001) report that solicitors are most often male and of all ages and all socio-economic statuses. Similar to individuals engaging in prostitution, clients of sex trafficking desire sexual gratification from their victims, are interested only in their immediate sexual need, and are often ignorant of uncaring about their victim's desire or willingness to participate. This is especially the case with child victims of sex trafficking as clients will pay hundreds even thousands of dollars to have sex with a child.

FUELING THE PROBLEM

As with any type of criminal activity, there are multiple explanations for its success. Sex trafficking is not unique in this respect in that sex trafficking is a multibillion dollar industry with an endless supply of victims (Farr, 2004). There will always be poor countries with little opportunity for women. There will always be individuals willing to exploit other individuals for personal gain and until governments gain more knowledge on sex trafficking and its impact on individuals and societies as a whole, sex trafficking will continue to flourish.

Investigative effort is one aspect of the problem of sex trafficking that remains a challenge in reducing sex trafficking and in many ways fuels the problem. Globally, resources for law enforcement and prosecutors to reduce sex trafficking or human trafficking as a whole are limited. With little training on the recognition of cases of sex trafficking and little experience in identifying or investigating cases of sex trafficking, few officers and even fewer prosecutors are able to distinguish cases of sex trafficking from cases of prostitution. Therefore, victims remain unidentified and traffickers remain unnoticed.

Limited penalties for sex traffickers are yet another aspect fueling the problem of sex trafficking. In particular, in comparing cases of human trafficking with cases of drug trafficking or firearms trafficking, the maximum penalty for sex trafficking is perhaps 10 years whereas distributing a kilo of heroin or stolen weapons could mean a life sentence (McCabe, 2010). Again, without the recognition of victims and without legislative penalties, sex trafficking continues.

Limited reports of sex trafficking by the victims are yet another reason this criminal activity continues to flourish. As suggested, many of the victims of sex trafficking are from countries outside of their destination country. Hence, language is a barrier in reporting abuse. In addition, many of these victims have enter the destination country illegally or have had their travel documents taken from them by their traffickers. These victims are often from counties with negative perceptions of law enforcement and, in many cases, they fear law enforcement, and are unwilling to speak with officers even to report their own victimization. For those victims who do not fear the corruption of law enforcement, the fear of being returned to their home country causes victims to resist reporting their victimization to law enforcement. Without a victim to report an abuse, efforts by law enforcement to end that abuse are nonexistent.

Finally, one cannot underestimate the impact of the Internet in the trafficking of persons for sexual exploitation. It is not uncommon for traffickers to be discovered with filming equipment and computers to create and distribute pornography (McGinnis, 2004). Many law enforcement organizations now have specialized investigators to pursue cases of child pornography and, in some rare instances, cases of sex trafficking are identified. However, with few law enforcement officers focusing on crimes via the computer and none specializing in sex trafficking via the Internet, this new type of cyber-exchange is fueling the sex trafficking industry.

LEGISLATIVE RESPONSES TO SEX TRAFFICKING

Although cases of sex trafficking have been known to exist for years and NGOs that provide assistance to victims of sex trafficking have existed for years, when asked about the problem of sex trafficking, most individuals have no idea that the criminal activity exists. In their minds, slavery was a problem of the past, but not today.

During the twentieth century, there was no single department or agency responsible for collecting data on human trafficking (McCabe, 2010). However, in 2004, the US Department of Justice estimated that approximately 45,000 people were trafficked into the United States on an annual basis and efforts were initiated to reduce human trafficking.

Surprisingly, it was not the human rights groups or even public opinion that began to recognize this injustice but rather is was the business industry, concerned for the competition of labor, who prompted the awareness of the problem of human trafficking for labor (Bales, 2004). Later, when then Secretary of State Colin Powell announced that monies acquired through human trafficking were used to support the activities of the 9-11 hijackers, legislative acts and law enforcement efforts began focusing on human trafficking (McCabe, 2008).

In 2000, with an estimate of nearly 700,000 individuals trafficked annually worldwide, the United States Congress passed the Victims of Trafficking and Violence Protection Act of 2000, P.L. 106-386, commonly referred to as the Trafficking Victims Protection Act (TVPA). The TVPA mandated that the Secretary of State submit a report on severe forms of human trafficking to Congress on June 1 of that year. This report began to identify countries as source, transit, and/or destination countries and has continued to be produced annually citing not only cases of human trafficking but also a list of countries and their rankings in the tier classification system (McCabe, 2010). Those countries that fully abide by the TVPA's minimum standards for "elimination of trafficking" are placed on tier one. Countries that did not fully comply, but were making efforts to do so are placed in either tier two or tier two-watch categories. Tier three countries are those countries not in compliance with the minimum of standards for the elimination of trafficking and are not making any significant efforts to do so.

After the 2000 TVPA, other countries began anti-trafficking efforts on a larger scale. In 2003, then president George W. Bush signed the amended Trafficking Victims Protection Reauthorization Act (TVPRA), which further supported government efforts to reduce human trafficking. In addition, and after the passing of the 2003 TVPRA, data began to be published in the annual Trafficking in Persons Report (on a limited basis) on cases of sex trafficking within various countries. Legislative efforts from various countries have continued as more and more geographic locations attempt to identify and reduce cases of human trafficking. In addition, information on the number of sex trafficking cases per country is available for some reporting countries.

SUMMARY

The United Nations has defined human trafficking as the recruitment, transfer, harboring, or receipt of persons by threat or use of force. The US State Department's Trafficking Protection Act (2000) identifies severe forms of human trafficking as: (1) sex trafficking in which a commercial sex act is induced by force, fraud, or coercion, or in which the person induced to perform such an act has not attained 18 years of age; or (2) the recruitment, harboring, transportation, provision, or obtaining of a person for labor or services through the use of force, fraud, or coercion for the purpose of subjection to involuntary servitude, peonage, debt bondage, or slavery. Individuals are usually trafficked for one of two main reasons: labor or sex. This chapter focused on the trafficking of individuals for sex or sex trafficking.

Victims of sex trafficking usually become involved in sex trafficking through either force of fraud. The destinations for most of the trafficking victims are cities with large commercial trade centers or areas with large military bases. It is within these densely populated areas that victims of sex trafficking and their traffickers easily blend in and function.

It is suggested that over 200,000 individuals were enslaved as prostitutes across the world at the turn of the twenty-first century. The US Department of State estimates approximately 50,000 victims of trafficking in the country today. Victims of sex trafficking are exposed to physical violence, sexual violence, sexually transmitted diseases, and confinement. Many victims of sex trafficking die during their period of victimization.

Explanation for sex trafficking include poverty, inequality, and family involvement. The United States is one of the most reported destination countries for sex trafficking as it is perceived by many of the poorer countries as the land of opportunity. Unfortunately, the appeal of the United States facilitates the criminal enterprise of sex trafficking.

CASE STUDY 7.1: SEX TRAFFICKING: AN ATYPICAL SITUATION

In 2010, two female college students from Europe excitedly searched the Internet for summer employment in the United States. Through Craig's List, they found work in the state of Pennsylvania. After securing the proper visas, the two boarded a plane and headed off on their journey. Their intention was to work during the week and to try to see as much of the United States as possible on the weekends during their summer abroad. The young women's plans came crashing down when the men posing as legitimate employers, met them at the airport and transported them to a home in a residential neighborhood where they proceeded to force the girls to have sex for money, money that the women never saw. After several months of being victimized, the women escaped. The women were assisted by the local FBI and the Southwestern Pennsylvania Anti-Human Trafficking Coalition and are now safely home with their families.

QUESTIONS:
- What makes this case unusual?
- What kinds of services do you think the Coalition needed to provide for the victims?

The offenders of sex trafficking include those involved in the sex trafficking of the victim and the client of the sex trafficking victim. Due to the secrecy of this activity, little research exists on anyone other than the victims of sex trafficking and much of that information is based upon only a few cases.

Poverty, inequality, and limited investigative efforts help to explain the increase in cases of sex trafficking. In addition, an unwillingness by victims to report sex trafficking and the use of the Internet continues to facilitate the activity.

Finally, after the 2000 TVPA, other countries began more focused anti-trafficking efforts on a larger scale. After the passing of the 2003 TVPRA, data began to be published in the annual Trafficking in Persons Report on cases of sex trafficking within various countries. In addition, legislative efforts from various countries have continued in an attempt to identify and reduce cases of sex trafficking. However, the activity of sex trafficking is still often misunderstood and misidentified; therefore, sex trafficking continues. Only through research and books such as this one will sex trafficking finally be understood, identified, and eliminated.

DISCUSSION QUESTIONS

1. If human trafficking is a problem in essentially all countries, why are law enforcement efforts so limited?
2. Why is there little public sympathy for adult victims of human trafficking?
3. Is it conceivable that a parent would allow one of their children to be a victim of sex trafficking to provide food for the others?
4. Why do you think sex trafficking continues and becomes even more profitable every year?
5. With so many crimes of concern in the United States, do we really have the time or the money to be concerned about a crime that largely occurs outside of the United States?

CHAPTER 15

FEMALE PROSTITUTION

MARY DODGE

P rostitution evokes a wide spectrum of images and vernacular but can be defined in the most basic terms as the performance of sexual activities in exchange for money. Prostitutes are referred to by various labels, including whores, hookers, street walkers, working girls, escorts, call girls, and ladies of the evening. Prostitution on a service continuum may range from drug-addicted crack whores waiting for johns (customers) on the street to chic, expensive, call girls operating at luxury hotels. References to prostitution are common in popular culture, which often romanticizes or parodies sex work. In the movie *Pretty Woman*, Julia Roberts' character was rescued from a life of prostitution after being hired by a handsome, serious-minded, and rich corporate tycoon played by Richard Gere. As a fairy-tale ending would predict, they fall in love and live happily ever after. *The Best Little Whorehouse in Texas* musical and comedy starred Dolly Parton as a madam and Burt Reynolds as a sheriff in the roles of star-crossed lovers on opposite sides of the law. The daily realities of prostitution, however, are not those portrayed in the movies or media-driven incidents of high-class call girls with rich, famous customers.

Public scandals involving the so-called sordid behavior of high-profile prostitute–client relationships are fodder for the media. Transactions with escort services often include madams who offer "quality" women at exorbitant costs. Sydney Biddle Barrows, labeled the "Mayflower Madam" because she was a member of an upper-crust family, provided expensive services to wealthy and powerful men. Her Cachet escort service operated in the late 1970s and early 1980s. After her arrest, Barrows pled guilty to promoting prostitution and published an autobiography, aptly titled *Mayflower Madam*. Heidi Fleiss became well known in the 1990s after news leaked that the Hollywood madam provided prostitution services to wealthy men. Clients allegedly paid from $1,500 to $1 million for high-end services. Fleiss, who spent a short time in prison for tax evasion, is now residing in Nevada and is planning to open a brothel for female customers. In 2008, a federal wiretap provided information that New York Governor Eliot L. Spitzer, also known as Client-9, allegedly arranged to pay $4,300 to a prostitute for a rendezvous at the Mayflower Hotel in Washington, DC. Spitzer who had built his reputation prosecuting white-collar criminals and prostitution rings, resigned from office. Although elite escort services are available to those who can afford them, most prostitutes use the Yellow Pages, local newspapers, and the internet to advertise. High-end call girls charge clients $300 to $500 an hour for services; the average street worker receives $30 to $50 an hour.

PROSTITUTION SERVICES

Prostitution services often hide under the guise of seemly legitimate businesses. Some massage parlors and private modeling agencies, for example, may offer hidden sex services. Bryant and Palmer (1974) identified four types of massage parlor. Genuine parlors found in health clubs, spas, and hotel resorts offer legitimate massage therapy. Rip-off parlors seduce customers with erotic promises, but merely provide inept massages and refuse to engage in physical sexual acts. Other massage parlors are actually brothels that offer a wide range of sexual services. And massage and masturbation parlors employ young women who describe themselves as "hand whores."

Prostitutes may specialize to accommodate customers who have a particular sexual penchant. Sadomasochistic clients, for example, take pleasure in inflicting or enduring pain or humiliation. Prostitutes may offer bondage, discipline, dominance, and submission. In clever marketing schemes, some have outfitted vehicles with restraints, cages, gags, chains, whips, and, of course, soundproofing. Prostitutes on wheels can quickly service specialized clients who, in some cases, require no actual intercourse. At the far end of the spectrum, some prostitutes will accommodate sadistic clients by enduring physical beatings for a substantial fee that also includes ensuing medical and dental treatment.

Prostitution is far more complex than a simple consensual economic exchange of goods and services for money. Deeply embedded controversies surrounding prostitution include moral, monetary, medical, and hegemonic issues related to basic sexual instincts. Sexual drives have created profitable illegal and legal markets in societies that hold diverse viewpoints on appropriate and inappropriate sexual behavior. Advocates, feminist theorists, law enforcement, and community members disagree on the form, function, and fit of prostitution in contemporary and sexually liberated cultures. The tenet that the subjugation and degradation of women sex workers undermine equality between the genders is a primary source of contention, though males, to a much lesser degree, also engage in prostitution. The somewhat sordid, yet intriguing, history of prostitution has resulted in a large body of research and perspectives that examine a wide variety of topics, including historical roots, myths and realities, violence, policing, and legislation.

THE FUNCTIONS OF PROSTITUTION

From a functionalist's perspective, prostitution may serve several purposes in society by providing an outlet for men who experience uncontrollable lust, thereby reducing rape and promoting healthy courtships and marriages. Meier and Geis (1997: 50) note that the absence of prostitution may result in sexually deprived men engaging in increased acts of "masturbation, more intense courtships or seduction patterns, sex by force, or behavior patterns that psychiatrists label as inhibitions and sublimations." A husband visiting a prostitute may alleviate the burden on a wife who is so overly taxed with home and childcare responsibilities that sex is a low priority for her. Sex for money may, in such a case, result in increased satisfaction levels for the husband and relief for the wife. Of course, such scenarios ignore the secretive nature and duplicity involved in sex-for-money transactions, especially considering the intricate nature of relationships between genders.

Men offer numerous reasons for engaging a prostitute. More often than not, they view such liaisons as mere business transactions. Puritanical notions of marriage and sexuality also influence encounters. In one case, a police officer asked an arrested, married john (slang for customer) why he had sought out a street walker's services. The man, who had paid for oral sex, responded, "I kiss my wife." According to some research, men indicated that they seek out prostitutes so that they can be with a woman who "likes to get nasty" (Weitzer, 2000). Men also noted the excitement and thrill of approaching a prostitute, the need to experience a variety of sexual partners, and the desire to have a different kind of sex or change from their regular partners. Weitzer says fellatio is the most common activity requested from a prostitute. Prostitution also offers men the opportunity to engage in sex without emotional investment, and a sex worker can be found in each and every socioeconomic level.

MOTIVATION FOR PROSTITUTION

Street-level prostitution often develops out of need and desperation as a means of survival for runaway teenagers and drug-addicted women. Street prostitutes may be pimp controlled or independent. In many cases, the women are addicted to crack or methamphetamine, and prostitution merely provides enough money to score another hit. In most major cities, prostitution areas are well known by johns and the police. Women will wait on the sidewalk or at truck stops for a customer to cruise by, known in England as kerb-crawling, and when approached will suggest that the transaction be conducted in the car or a nearby hotel room. Prostitutes on the streets are not "pretty women." Street-level prostitutes' lives are marked by violence, exploitation, and poverty which results in severe health issues that are often left untreated.

Prostitutes, according to many research findings, have frequently been subjected to sexual abuse at an early age. In most qualitative studies, a high percentage of juvenile and adult female prostitutes self-report unwanted sexual behavior before the age of sixteen (Earls and David, 1989).

Additionally, studies report a strong correlation between prostitution and running away from home. Young women who lack legitimate opportunities may believe that prostitution represents the only way to obtain substantial incomes. Indeed, many prostitutes report that money is their primary motivation for sex work.

But financial concerns represent only one of the many motivations that contribute to decisions to perform sex work. Women may engage in prostitution because legitimate opportunities are limited or unattractive. Alternative jobs for prostitutes are likely to offer low wages, consist of dull, routine tasks, and demand long hours (Hoigard and Finstad, 1986). Other researchers have identified behavioral characteristics such as promiscuity, disassociation, and isolation as motivating factors. Some prostitutes also enjoy the independence and excitement of sex work (Weidner, 2001).

The proposition that prostitution is a victimless crime is easily countered by research findings that show drugs, violence, and sexual diseases commonly affect sellers, buyers, families, and law enforcement. Research concerning violence against prostitutes often focuses on street-level workers who are controlled by pimps. Violence and exploitation by pimps includes physical, emotional, and financial abuse. In interviews with former prostitutes, Williamson and Cluse-Tolar (2002) discovered a pattern of violence by pimps including savage beatings used to exert control and dominance over the women.

Prostitutes are also targeted by violent customers and sometimes corrupt police officers. Sadistic customers perpetrate physical and sexual assaults. However, the illegal nature of sex work prevents victims from reporting such crimes. In some cases, when prostitutes do report crimes by customers, their victimization is trivialized by law enforcement officials and prosecutors who see the violent consequences as an expected "part of the job."

POLICING AND PROGRAMS

Generally, police focus on arresting individual women in stings using male undercover officers who pose as customers, though an increasing number of agencies are conducting reverse sting operations and cracking down on the customers in a bid to reduce demand. In the United States, however, only 10 percent of prostitution arrests are male customers (Weidner, 2001). In California, one prostitute appealed her conviction, claiming sexual discrimination by the police department. She noted that the more common use of male decoys compared with female decoys in police stings resulted in biased arrests. Court documents in this case revealed that 1,160 women were arrested for solicitation by male undercover officers in 1973 and 1974, compared to 57 men arrested in reverse sting operations (Kay, 1982). Supportive evidence was provided by Lefler (1999), who discovered that Boston courts arraigned 263 women in 1990 on charges of prostitution but no male customers. The California Superior Court denied the prostitute's appeal and outlined three reasons justifying the use of male officer decoys rather than female. First, a working prostitute will see several customers each night, hence committing several crimes, whereas a customer will typically hire only one prostitute for the evening and therefore commit only one crime. Second, arresting prostitutes is a stronger deterrent on other women in the business who communicate with each other as compared to male customers who are unknown to each other. Third, the use of female decoys is more expensive because of safety issues, equipment, and back-up teams that require the presence of male officers.

Creative policing and prevention programs have developed as law enforcement agencies struggle with improving practices and policies. Arrest patterns are troubling and police officers complain about repeat offenders who are granted bail and therefore return to the streets almost immediately. In San Francisco, police officers frustrated with the rapid release of a particular prostitute issued 54 citations over a three-month period for "obstructing the sidewalk," which eventually resulted in a 60-day jail sentence (Pearl, 1987). Some cities control street prostitution by implementing area restrictions that prevent a woman from being in a certain neighborhood. The likely result of such ordinances or statutes is merely the displacement of the activity. Other cities have established mandatory licensing for prostitutes which requires a background check and is renewable annually. Violations of licensing policies can result in one year in jail and a $1,000 fine. This approach is primarily a law enforcement tool to increase conviction options with low expectations that prostitutes and pimps will be lining up at the court house to purchase a license. Police argue that aggressively arresting johns and prostitutes will reduce drug crimes, sexual assault, robberies, and homicides.

Police agencies' focus on johns in the last ten years has increased the number of reverse sting operations and promoted innovative tactics to deter men from engaging in future transactions. Many major cities in the United States have programs designed to deter and humiliate customers, including driver's license revocation, john television, and vehicle seizure (Dodge *et al.*, 2005). John TV features mug shots of convicted offenders on local television stations or the internet. In some cities, billboards and paid newspaper advertisements expose customers to public scrutiny. Efforts to shame and humiliate customers are believed to serve as general and specific deterrence, though the effectiveness of such methods remains unknown. "John schools" have become popular. Customers are ordered by a court to attend the classes, where they learn of illicit sex dangers through graphic representations of sexually transmitted diseases and narratives from former prostitutes. However, law enforcement efforts that focus on johns remain futile because of the low number of overall male arrests.

Social programs for prostitutes strive to divert women from the profession to a more stable lifestyle. In Washington, DC, the Bridges Program offers education and therapeutic groups that address addictions and early childhood trauma. Salt Lake City's Prostitution Diversion Project (PDP) has shown some level of success for women who have been arrested. It keeps the women out of jail and offers networking in the community by employing a collaborative approach that emphasizes harm reduction through treatment, therapy, and abstinence. As one of the few projects designed specifically for commercial sex workers, the PDP appears to provide useful recovery services across community agencies and saves the city money (Wahab, 2006). Resource referrals give women information on substance abuse, domestic violence, rape, self-defense, housing, and welfare.

LEGALIZATION

In the United States, brothels (also known as houses of ill repute, bordellos, and cat houses) are legal only in rural counties of Nevada. These brothels operate under strict regulatory law, including licensing fees (ranging from $200 to $100,000), minimum age requirements (ranging from 18 to 21 years old), weekly checks for certain sexually transmitted diseases (gonorrhea and chlamydia), and monthly examinations for HIV and syphilis. Condoms are mandatory for oral sex and sexual intercourse. Additionally, any brothel prostitute with HIV who knowingly engages in sex work is subject to felony charges and may face ten years in prison or a $10,000 fine.

Researchers have identified and studied three types of violence in legalized brothels in Nevada: interpersonal violence against prostitutes; violence against community order; and sexually transmitted diseases as violence against the backdrop of government regulation that allegedly provides a safe and hygienic outlet for prostitution (Brents and Hausbeck, 2005). Legalization, according to Brents and Hausbeck, increases public scrutiny and official regulation, thereby decreasing all three types of violence. This "challenges assumptions that prostitution and violence necessarily and inevitably coexist in predictable ways," though a lack of sophistication in analysis fails to address the inherently oppressive nature of the commercial sex trade (Brents and Hausbeck, 2005: 294).

In Rhode Island, transactions involving sex for money are not defined as illegal, although brothels, pimping, and street prostitution are statutorily defined and carry legal sanctions. The "loophole" in the state's law that allows acts of prostitution to take place in private is relatively unknown except among sex trade workers, and efforts are being made in the legislature to introduce changes to criminalize all acts of prostitution. Politicians, including Providence Mayor David N. Cicilline, argue that the proliferation of indoor prostitution "spas" has a negative impact on quality of life in high-traffic neighborhoods and damages the city's reputation (Cicilline, 2009).

In 1973, Margo St. James, a former prostitute, founded COYOTE (Call Off Your Old Tired Ethics) as an organization to help end the stigma of sex work, further public education, and offer support groups and referrals to service providers. St. James became well known for her quip that "a blow job is better than no job." As noted by scholar and author Valerie Jenness (1993) the group's potential lay in its ability to represent disreputable causes and gain legitimacy for disenfranchised deviants, such as prostitutes, strippers, pornography actresses, and phone-sex operators.

The controversy over the efficacy of legalized prostitution is far from resolved. The arguments for decriminalization focus primarily on the heavy-handed tactics that infringe on a woman's civil rights and cause further oppression. Current laws encourage corruption, unfairly penalize prostitutes by forcing them to work on the streets, reinforce negative labeling, and waste taxpayers' money on prosecutions and imprisonment (Meier and Geis, 1997). The voices of women prostitutes are silenced by fears borne of "intimidation, terror, dissociation, and shame" (Farley, 2004: 117). Many commentators and scholars, however, argue against legalization or decriminalization. They contend that prostitution can be costly in terms of disease, drug addiction, and moral degradation, and assert that prostitution results in high rates of violence throughout the world, with between 60% and 94% of prostitutes reporting physical assault and rape, including in the Netherlands where prostitution is legal (Farley, 2004).

The division among feminist theorists also reflects a deep schism in the field. Jolin (1994) identified two primary approaches among feminist scholars that are inherently impossible to resolve. First, the sexual equality first (SEF) approach asserts that prostitution is dependent on the sexual subordination of women and, if allowed to continue, will prevent women from obtaining true equality. The SEF position is clearly articulated by the radical feminists Catherine MacKinnon and Andrea Dworkin, who suggest that all heterosexual sex demeans and subordinates women. The refusal by some feminists to accept prostitution as legitimate work marginalizes sex workers, though many adopt values aligned with the feminist movement, including "independence, financial autonomy, sexual self-determination, personal strength, and female bonding" (Kesler, 2002: 220). Second, the free choice first (FCF) approach gives women the freedom to choose with no restrictions or controls over decisions related to sexuality and reproductive rights. The catch-22, according to Jolin (1994: 77), is that "one can either believe that true equality for women will not exist so long as women sell their bodies to men or one can believe that true equality will not exist so long as women are prevented from exercising choice, including the choice to sell their bodies to men."

FUTURE FRONTIERS

In many ways, technology has transformed the business of prostitution and has resulted in women leaving the streets. Craigslist, for example, offers "erotic services" by city. In one Colorado case, an internet site offered potential customers full services from "nineteen-year-old Amanda." Monitoring by police employees of sites known to promote prostitution resulted in a sting and arrest after the girl was driven to a motel room by her pimp. In reality, Amanda was just fifteen years old. Nevertheless, she had already earned approximately $150,000 for her pimp, according to police reports. Meanwhile, Craigslist's erotic services came under fire after a masseuse was allegedly killed at the Marriott Hotel in Copley Square by a Boston University medical student, Phillip Markoff. Craigslist has promised to relabel its erotic services "adult services" and to prescreen the paid advertisements.

Child prostitution represents perhaps the most serious victimization problem. In America alone, according to the Department of Justice, an estimated 293,000 youth are at risk of being victimized by some form of commercial sexual exploitation. Juveniles who are recruited into sex work by force or pressure from parents are subjected to violence, drugs, and threats. Though little research is available, very young girls are involved in prostitution and pornography. Researcher and scholar James Inciardi (1990) interviewed nine girls between the ages of eight and twelve who were introduced into sex work by parents, siblings, or relatives. Known as "baby pros," these elementary school girls were living at home with parents or other relatives. They described performing masturbation and oral sex, and, in a few cases, engaging in sexual intercourse. Several of the girls worked in massage parlors as hand whores. Inciardi discovered that the girls participated because of fear of rejection by their parents or guardians and to gain attention from indifferent adults, in addition to covert coercion. However, they rightly and understandably expressed a deep disdain for the male clients.

REFERENCES

Brents, B. G, and Hausbeck, K. (2005). Violence and legalized brothel prostitution in Nevada: Examining safety, risk, and prostitution policy. *Journal of Interpersonal Violence*, 20(3), 270–295.

Bryant, C. D., and Palmer, C. E. (1974). Massage parlors and "hand whores": Some sociological observations. *Journal of Sex Research*, 11(3), 227–241.

Cicilline, David N. (2009). Mayor Cicilline urges RI Senate to pass prostitution legislation. Press release, May 18. Available at: www.providenceri.com/press/article.php?id=515 (accessed June 1, 2009).

COYOTE (n.d.). Website. Available at: www.coyotela.org/what_is.html#who_gets (accessed June 1, 2009).

Dodge, M., Starr-Gimeno, D., and Williams, T. (2005). Puttin' on the sting: Women police officers' perspectives on reverse prostitution assignments. *International Journal of Police Science & Management*, 7(2), 71–85.

Earls, C. M., and David, H. (1989). Male and female prostitution: A review. *Sex Abuse*, 2, 5–28.

Farley, M. (2004). Bad for the body, bad for the heart: Prostitution harms women even if legalized or decriminalized. *Violence Against Women*, 10(10), 1087–1125.

Gusfield, J. (1994). Making it work: The prostitutes' rights movement in perspective (book review). *Contemporary Sociology*, 23(3), 379–380.

Hoigard, C., and Finstad, L. (1986). *Backstreets: Prostitution, money and love*. University Park: Pennsylvania State University.

Inciardi, J. A. (1990). Little girls and sex: A glimpse at the world of the "baby pro." In C. D. Bryant (Ed.), *Deviant behavior: Readings in the sociology of norm violations* (pp. 303–310). New York: Hemisphere.

Jenness, V. (1993). *Making it work: The prostitute's rights movement in perspective*. New York: Aldine de Gruyter. Jolin, A. (1994). On the backs of working prostitutes: Feminist theory and prostitution policy. *Crime & Delinquency*, 40, 69–83.

Kay, H. H. (1982). *Sex-based discrimination: Test cases and materials* (2nd edn). St. Paul, MN: West.

Kesler, K. (2002). Is a feminist stance in support of prostitution possible? An exploration of current trends. *Sexualities*, 5(2), 219–235.

Lefler, J. (1999). Shining the spotlight on "johns": Moving toward equal treatment of male customers and female prostitutes. *Hastings Women's Law Journal*, 10, 11–35.

Meier, R.F., and Geis, G. (1997). *Victimless crime?* Los Angeles, CA: Roxbury.

Pearl, J. (1987). The highest paying customers: America's cities and the costs of prostitution control. *Hastings Law Journal*, 38, 769–800.

Wahab, S. (2006). Evaluating the usefulness of a prostitution diversion project. *Qualitative Social Work*, 5, 67–92.

Weidner, R. (2001). *"I won't do Manhattan": Causes and consequences of a decline in street prostitution*. New York: LFB Scholarly.

Weitzer, R. (2000). *Sex for sale: Prostitution, pornography, and the sex industry*. New York: Routledge. Williamson, C., and Cluse-Tolar, T. (2002). Pimp-controlled prostitution: Still an integral part of street life. *Violence Against Women*, 8(9), 1074–1092.

CHAPTER 16

MALE PROSTITUTION

RONALD WEITZER

T
raditionally, scholars have focused their attention on female prostitution and have ignored male and transgender prostitution, despite the fact that males and transgenders comprise a substantial percentage of the prostitutes in many cities (Weitzer 1999). In the past decade, however, a growing body of literature has examined male sex workers. Most male prostitutes sell sex to other men.

MALE PROVIDERS, MALE CUSTOMERS

There are some basic similarities as well as some important differences between male and female prostitution. For instance, there is a similar hierarchy in each—stratified by whether the worker sells sex on the street, in a bar or a brothel/club/massage parlor, through an escort agency, or as an independent call boy. Like female street workers, young men on the street often enter the trade as runaways or to support a drug habit, and they engage in "survival sex." Like upscale female workers, call boys and escorts possess social skills that allow them to relate to educated, upper-class customers, and they may develop emotional attachments to some of their regular clients (Smith *et al.* 2008; van der Poel 1992). And, like female workers in the mid- and upper-level tiers, similarly situated males are more likely than street workers to hold positive views of their work and themselves (Koken *et al.* 2010; West 1993). Interviews with 185 male prostitutes in three Australian cities found that two-thirds felt good about being a sex worker (Minichiello 2001). A study of male escorts reported that, as a result of being generously paid for sex, the escorts felt desired, attractive,

Ronald Weitzer, "Male Prostitution," *The Routledge Handbook of Deviant Behavior*, ed. Clifton D. Bryant, pp. 378-382. Copyright © 2011 by Taylor & Francis Group. Reprinted with permission.

187

empowered, and important; they also developed greater self-confidence and more positive body images over time (Uy *et al.* 2007). As a male brothel worker stated, it was "so wonderful to have love made to me by so many wealthy and socially elite men" (Pittman 1971: 23).

Economic motives are central for both male and female sex workers, but some males are also motivated by the potential for sexual adventure that prostitution may offer (van der Poel 1992). Differences in the ways male and female prostitutes experience their work are evident in the following areas. Males tend to be:

- involved in prostitution in a more sporadic or transitory way, drifting in and out of prostitution and leaving the trade earlier than women (Aggleton 1999; Weinberg *et al.* 1999);
- less likely to be coerced into prostitution, to have pimps, and to experience violence from customers (Aggleton 1999; Weinberg *et al.* 1999; West 1993);
- in greater control over their working conditions, because few have pimps (West 1993);
- more diverse as to their sexual orientation: some self-identify as gay; others as bisexual; and others insist that they are heterosexual despite engaging in homosexual conduct, an identity–behavior disparity typically not found among female prostitutes (Aggleton 1999);
- less stigmatized within the gay community (Aggleton 1999; Koken *et al.* 2010) but more stigmatized in the wider society because of the coupling of homosexuality and prostitution.

Like female sex workers, males draw boundaries around the services they are willing to perform. Some limit their activity to oral sex; some engage in penetrative but not receptive oral or anal sex; and others engage in all types. Some limit their encounters to sexual exchanges, while others are open to more comprehensive interactions, including cuddling, massage, and conversation. This has come to be known as the "boyfriend experience," a quasi-romantic, yet paid, encounter.

Although most research focuses on street prostitution, a thriving indoor market has been studied by some researchers. Male brothels are fairly rare, though a few have been studied (Pittman 1971). One hybrid brothel–escort agency, a business that provided services to about 200 clients per month, was studied by Smith, Grov, and Seal (2008). Most of the sexual encounters took place outside the agency, but some were "in-call," occurring in a designated room at the agency. Some of the workers even lived at the agency. When not working, some of the men engaged in social activities with other men at the agency, including the manager and friends of their fellow escorts. The manager served as a mentor to the escorts and was well liked by them. Like madams in female brothels, the manager screened clients and sought to ensure a safe and pleasant working environment for his employees. The benefits of working for this agency were that it provided a "sense of community" for the workers, "shielded escorts from potential stigma," and was "a source of positive support" for their work and lifestyle (Smith *et al.* 2008: 206, 208).

Most escort agencies do not double as brothels, resulting in much more social distance between the employees. Salamon's (1989) study of an escort agency in London that did not provide in-call services reported very little social interaction between the manager and the workers, and few workers knew any of the others.

Research on street prostitution offers a picture of a very different world—more risky for the workers but also potentially exciting. McNamara's (1994) ethnographic study of male street prostitutes in Times Square, New York, in the early 1990s found a community involved in selling sex on the street and at peep shows, gay bars, the bus terminal, and hotels. Most were Hispanic youths, and most of the clients were white men. The sex trade was remarkably well ordered: "very few problems occur either between the hustlers and the clients or among the boys themselves. In the vast majority of cases, the activities are completed without incident" (McNamara 1994: 62). The police generally left the prostitutes alone unless there was a disturbance.

Although most of the research on sex tourism centers on female prostitutes and foreign male clients, sometimes men travel abroad to meet and pay for sex with other men. Padilla's (2007) ethnographic study in the Dominican Republic provides a unique window into gay male sex tourism. Many of the workers do not self-identify as gay—in fact, many are married—and they service men simply because they comprise a much larger market than female sex tourists who are willing to pay for a sex encounter. Many sex tourists eroticize this, as it seems to accord with the fantasy of having gay sex with a heterosexual male. While some male prostitutes aim to avoid long-term or serial relationships with particular clients, due to the potential emotional risks involved, others cultivate long-term clients, develop affectionate feelings toward them, and await their next visit. The latter put a premium on meeting customers who will continue to send money or gifts after they return home. Padilla found a connection between the material and emotional aspects of these relationships: workers who received the most economic rewards were most likely to develop affectionate feelings toward a customer. Older clients were more likely to seek stable and more intimate relationships with a specific worker, while younger clients sought sex with multiple partners.

MALE PROVIDERS, FEMALE CUSTOMERS

Relatively little is known about male prostitutes who sell sex to women, and the few studies on this topic all center on tourist destinations. A handful of studies have examined contacts between affluent Western female tourists and young Caribbean men, who meet at clubs and on beaches (Phillips 1999; Sanchez Taylor 2001, 2006). There are some basic similarities between female sex tourism and male sex tourism (e.g., economic inequality between buyer and seller) as well as some differences (e.g., female sex tourists rarely act violently against male prostitutes). There is a profound economic inequality between the buyer and seller, and this gives the buyer a similar level of control over the worker, whether the latter is female or male. Like male sex tourists, female sex tourists use their economic power to buy intimate relations with local men, and during these encounters they assert control over the men. One study in the Caribbean concluded:

> The kind of control exercised in their relationships with local men is actually very similar to that exercised by male sex tourists in sexual economic relationships with local women … They are able to use their economic power to limit the risk of being challenged or subjugated.
>
> *(Sanchez Taylor 2006: 49–50)*

Female customers may become long-term companions or benefactors to the men, and in some cases this can lead to marriage.

Many of the female sex tourists do not define themselves as "customers" who buy sex from local men. Instead, they construct the encounters as "holiday romances" or "real love," and almost none describe their affairs as "purely physical" (Sanchez Taylor 2001: 755). The women do not see themselves as sex tourists and the men do not see themselves as prostitutes. However, the latter do receive material rewards for the time they spend with foreign women, including meals, lodgings, gifts, and money. According to Sanchez Taylor, these relationships therefore have all the hallmarks of sex tourism, irrespective of whether they are short or long term or whether money is exchanged, provided that the man receives at least some material benefits. Similarly, Phillips (1999: 191) argues that these transactions can be "easily fitted under the umbrella of prostitution," even though both the tourist and the provider do not perceive their liaison as such.

The "host club" in Japan is another example of male sex work involving female clients. Similar to the hostess clubs where women entertain male customers, host clubs are locations where women go to enjoy themselves in the company of attractive male hosts, which may include sexual encounters. Such bars have flourished in the past decade, with approximately 200 now operating in Tokyo alone. The hosts serve exorbitantly expensive alcoholic drinks to their clients and lavish praise, compliments, and advice upon the specific women to whom they attach themselves. The nature of this phenomenon is captured in the concept of "commodified romance" (Takeyama 2005), which involves nonsexual intimacy but may also include sexual services.

Why do women seek out these paid encounters? An ethnographic study of host clubs revealed that "customers claim that there are few other places in Japan's male-centered entertainment world where women can safely enjoy romantic excitement" (Takeyama 2005: 204). According to this study, the vast majority of hosts have had sex with at least some of their customers, although they prefer to avoid sexual intercourse in order to keep the woman coming back to the club and paying the high prices (the host gets a cut). Some hosts sleep with their customers without having sex with them.

CONCLUSION

Further research on male sex workers who service women will help address the question of whether the customer's gender influences the character and subjective meaning of the encounter.

To what degree, if at all, is gender inequality or domination present in exchanges between female customers and male workers? Do female customers engage in less objectification of the workers, or is objectification evident irrespective of the customer's gender? Do female customers expect more emotional involvement from sex workers than is true for male customers? When the customer is a woman, is there less likelihood of violence from either party? These questions have yet to be investigated, but such research would be invaluable in answering the theoretical question of whether prostitution has certain "fundamental" or "essential" qualities, irrespective of the gender of the worker and the customer, or whether it varies significantly according to the actors involved. To answer these questions, we need systematic examinations of male prostitutes who service men in comparison with those who service women, and of male and female prostitutes working in the same tier, such as the comparative studies by Koken *et al.* (2010) and Weinberg *et al.* (1999).

REFERENCES

Aggleton, P. (ed.) (1999) *Men Who Sell Sex*, Philadelphia, PA: Temple University Press.

Koken, J., Bimbi, D., and Parsons, J. (2010) "Male and female escorts: a comparative analysis," in R. Weitzer (ed.) *Sex for Sale: Prostitution, Pornography, and the Sex Industry*, 2n edn, New York: Routledge.

McNamara, R. (1994) *The Times Square Hustler: Male Prostitution in New York City*, Westport, CT: Praeger.

Minichiello, V. (2001) "Male sex workers in three Australian cities: socio-demographic and sex work characteristics," *Journal of Homosexuality*, 42: 29–51.

Padilla, M. (2007) "Western Union daddies and their quest for authenticity: an ethnographic study of the Dominican gay sex tourism industry," *Journal of Homosexuality*, 53: 241–275.

Phillips, J. (1999) "Tourist-oriented prostitution in Barbados: the case of the beach boy and the white female tourist," in K. Kempadoo (ed.) *Sun, Sex, and Gold: Tourism and Sex Work in the Caribbean*, Lanham, MD: Rowman & Littlefield.

Pittman, D. (1971) "The male house of prostitution," *Transaction*, 8: 21–27.

Salamon, E. (1989) "The homosexual escort agency: deviance disavowal," *British Journal of Sociology*, 40: 1–21.

Sanchez Taylor, J. (2001) "Dollars are a girl's best friend: female tourists' sexual behavior in the Caribbean," *Sociology*, 34: 749–764.

Sanchez Taylor, J. (2006) "Female sex tourism: a contradiction in terms?," *Feminist Review*, 83: 43–59.

Smith, M., Grov, C., and Seal, D. (2008) "Agency-based male sex work," *Journal of Men's Studies*, 16: 193–210.

Takeyama, A. (2005) "Commodified romance in a Tokyo host club," in M. McLelland and R. Dasgupta (eds.) *Genders, Transgenders, and Sexualities in Japan*, New York: Routledge.

Uy, J., Parsons, J., Bimbi, D., Koken, J., and Halkitis, P. (2007) "Gay and bisexual male escorts who advertise on the internet: understanding the reasons for and effects of involvement in commercial sex," *International Journal of Men's Health*, 3: 11–26.

van der Poel, S. (1992) "Professional male prostitution: a neglected phenomenon," *Crime, Law, and Social Change*, 18: 259–275.

Weinberg, M., Shaver, F., and Williams, C. (1999) "Gendered prostitution in the San Francisco Tenderloin," *Archives of Sexual Behavior*, 28: 503–521.

Weitzer, R. (1999) "New directions in research on prostitution," *Crime, Law, and Social Change*, 43: 211–235.

West, D. (1993) *Male Prostitution*, Binghamton, NY: Hayworth.

CHAPTER 17

PORNOGRAPHY

SHARON HAYES
BELINDA CARPENTER
ANGELA DWYER

INTRODUCTION

Several years ago, a Supreme Court judge in New South Wales, Australia dismissed an appeal case regarding pornographic cartoon characters taken from the long-running family television programme *The Simpsons*. The case appealed against an earlier conviction for using a computer to access, and being in possession of, child pornography involving *Simpsons* characters. The appellant was found to have had sexually explicit cartoons involving Simpsons child characters Bart, Lisa and Maggie, remodelled with human genitalia and depicted in various sex acts. This was a landmark case, the core issue being whether it was possible for a fictional cartoon character to legally depict a person. The judge dismissed the appeal and upheld the conviction, even though it was noted that "the hands bear only four digits and the faces have eyes, a nose and mouth markedly and deliberately different to those of any possible human being".[1]

The dismissal of the appeal case and upholding of the conviction was widely questioned, sparking worldwide media coverage. A *Google* search at the time of writing reveals mention of the case in approximately 402,000 websites, including sites in the United States, the United Kingdom and Australia. Even lawyers challenged the judge's decision: "These sorts of parodies, offensive as they might be, are widely distributed and I think it would be very unfair to characterize those who are viewing the images as ... viewing child porn".[2] Of particular significance, then, is the argument made by the judge during the court process:

> Although the primary purpose of the legislation is to combat the direct sexual exploita-
> tion and abuse of children that occurs where offensive images of real children in various

sexual or sexually suggestive situations are made, it also is calculated to deter production of other material—including cartoons—that ... can fuel demand for material that does involve the abuse of children.[3]

The judge's decision to uphold the ruling on the basis of protecting children and deterring offenders demonstrates very recent but, as we have seen in chapter 3, quite insidious assumptions about the inappropriateness of linking children, even cartoon children, with sex. Although the Simpsons characters are not real children, the ruling in this case suggests that sexually explicit representations of child cartoon characters are part of the moral taboo surrounding children and sex. It is also supported by the belief that viewing sexual activity, especially child sexual activity, is an act fraught with harm, a topic of much concern to psychologists,[4] who argue that pornography can be harmful to young people in particular.[5] Such concern is compounded by examples such as the now infamous serial sex murderer, Ted Bundy, who claimed that an addiction to pornography drove him to sexually assault and kill women.[6]

These concerns about pornography are inherently modern ones, related to the growth of pornography in the eighteenth century through the availability of print technology, and the subsequent development of visual as opposed to literate forms of sexually explicit material.[7] Indeed, it is only in recent times—from the nineteenth century—that pornography has come to be a target of suspicion and suppression, due in great part to the widening of its appeal to the illiterate, which included children. Despite constant and increasing attempts to regulate pornography in modern times, however, the commercial pornography industry goes from strength to strength. In the United States, for example, the pornography industry alone "has been conservatively estimated as worth something in the region of $10 billion per year, with an annual output of between 10,000 and 11,000 films, compared to Hollywood's 400".[8]

This chapter charts key discursive shifts that have led to modern ways of thinking about pornography as a morally contentious issue. By contextualizing the modern links between pornography and obscenity, we will chart the shift from a public discourse of sex, where sex formed a prominent part of much reading material, and was consumed as part of the public discussion of sexual matters, to the private consumption of pornography, which was created as sexually explicit material specifically designed to elicit a sexual response. Moreover, this shift from sex as a public discourse to sex as a private discourse was accompanied by larger shifts in the regulation of sexuality, especially for women and children.

This shift in the policing of women's sexuality, in particular, can be traced in part to a significant change in the way in which male and female sexuality was understood between the eighteenth and nineteenth centuries. Prior to the mid-nineteenth century, female genitalia were assumed to be the inverse of male genitalia. This meant that relations between orgasm and conception were assumed for both men and women. The subsequent discovery of the irrelevance of an orgasm severed the link between pleasure and sex for women, which had much to do with changing notions of femininity as passive and asexual.

Finally, current perceptions of sexual development, which, as we have seen in chapters 2 and 3, draw heavily on notions of sexual innocence and sexual purity, have been shaped historically by moral concerns about children and sex that came to the fore in concerns about masturbation, or solitary sex, linked specifically to the rise of visual pornography. The shift from literate to visual pornography is the moment when regulation is required to manage the working class and children, who, it was maintained, did not have the competencies to consume sexually explicit material.

HISTORICIZING PORNOGRAPHY

The word "pornography" was not to be found in the Oxford English Dictionary before 1864, and derives from the Greek word *pornographos,* which literally means "whore's story".[9] The distinctiveness of pornography, in comparison with the wealth of sexual material that existed prior to the nineteenth century, "was its explicitness and its intent to arouse a sexual response". While such material existed before this time, the mid-nineteenth century saw a major increase in the market and supply of pornography.[10] Moreover, while the control of these printed works in Europe between the 1500s and 1800s was undertaken primarily in the name of religion and politics,[11] by the mid-1800s it was the issue of decency that motivated regulation. In 1857, the *Obscene Publications Act* was passed in England, while in 1868 the *Hicklin test* entered English common law. These two changes have been identified as key to the identification of pornography as a specific social harm that threatened the moral health of the population.[12] Pornography, in the sense that we understand it today as a distinct category of written or visual representation, begins to exist significantly from the middle of the nineteenth century.[13]

It would be incorrect to assume, however, that sexually explicit material did not exist prior to its public and legislative regulation. According to Hitchcock,[14] the range of writings in which sex formed a prominent part prior to the nineteenth century was extensive. Such writing was to be found in publications aimed at both the educated elite (literature that was generally French in origin) and the plebeian classes (through joke books and "chapbooks"). Moreover, trial reports, accounts of divorce proceedings and medical literature were often read for their sexual elements. However, they were not yet pornographic. Rather, they were "always an adjunct to something else".[15] The widespread consumption of this material was reflective of a public culture of sex, "but it was more about the public discussion of sexual matters than they were aids to masturbation".[16]

Many historical accounts of sexually explicit material prior to the nineteenth century focused on sexual voyeurism as social, political and religious subversion. Hunt[17] notes how sexually explicit pamphlets were used during the French Revolution to undermine royal authority. Queen Marie Antoinette, for example, was targeted by pamphlets "detail[ing] her presumed sexual misdemeanors, question[ing] the paternity of her children and, in the process, fatally undermin[ing] the image of royal authority".[18] At this time, sexually explicit material was not an aim in itself, but rather an adjunct to other forms of criticism of church and state. Prior to the French Revolution, for example, prohibited books included those that threatened the state, religion or good morals. Moreover, they were all "indiscriminately labelled, 'philosophical books', whether they were politically motivated scandal sheets, metaphysical treatises, anticlerical satires or pornographic stories".[19] At this point in history, sexually explicit material may have been identified as problematic, but it was not a separate category of "bad books".

The employment of sexual behaviour in the service of social subversion was short-lived according to Wagner,[20] who suggests that these forms of sexual material faded into the background as new works were circulated that were "entirely devoted to sexual arousal".[21] The creation of sexual material designed only for the purpose of sexual arousal and as an aid to masturbation is the moment when modern pornography is identified as morally different from other "bad books", and the point at which sexually explicit material becomes the focus of policing and regulation for its implicit moral danger.[22]

It would be erroneous, therefore, to suggest that pornography has always been subject to moral and/or legal regulation, since modern conceptions of pornography as exciting "lascivious feelings"[23] were all but non-existent up until the eighteenth century. The excavation of Pompeii in the eighteenth century, and the discovery of sexually explicit artefacts in the homes, demonstrates clearly the shift that was occurring between older discourses that emphasized the harmless and public nature of sex, and newer discourses that positioned public displays of sex as physically harmful and morally inappropriate. For Kendrick, the archaeological excavation of Pompeii stands as the key historical moment where a shift is made evident in how people viewed sexually explicit material. As various sexual artefacts were unearthed, cataloguers of the eighteenth century struggled to classify these materials:

> Paintings of nude bodies, even in the act of sex, had been placed side by side with landscapes and still lifes, forming a jumble that mystified modern observers ... The problem was purely modern: however the Romans might have responded to such representations, what was one to do with them *now*?[24]

Modern classifiers were left somewhat bereft when faced with materials that existed in a time where "sex was clearly a common and unremarkable theme"—in Greek household items, for example.[25] In the eighteenth century, when sexual practices were increasingly relegated to private, domestic spaces, classifying these artefacts suggested the need for a new typology to ensure the proper management of "Pompeii's priceless obscenities". "Pornography" was the term employed for this purpose.[26] Even when precisely named, however, the classification of these materials was accompanied by much anxiety for those doing the work of classification:

> With this end in mind, we have done our best to regard each of the objects we have had to describe from an exclusively archaeological and scientific point of view. It has been our intention to remain calm and serious throughout. In the exercise of his holy office,

the man of science must neither blush nor smile. We have looked upon our statues as an anatomist contemplates his cadavers.[27]

The classification work, then, became entangled with the work of managing "lascivious feelings", and contemporary sensibilities countered this by urging a moral imperative to regulate oneself in ways that lessened their sexual impact.

Although the classification of artefacts may have defined what was meant by pornography, this process, as Kendrick points out, "did not invent the obscene" and that which now is legally regulated.[28] Sexual texts have always existed, dominated by classical texts from Greece and Rome, and consumed as part of "a classical education [that] remained the privilege of gentlemen".[29] While such classical texts may well have inspired the reader to "lascivious feelings", the incitation of physical arousal as a result of viewing or reading sexually explicit material was purely incidental, not integral.

Consider the work of poet and artist Pietro Aretino (1492–1556), who created sonnets in 1524 to accompany drawings of sexual postures by Giulio Romano and etchings by Marc Antonio. By the nineteenth century, the name Aretino was synonymous with pornography. In fact, Aretino is hailed as "the originator of pornography" because his "licentious" work brought together "explicit sexual detail and evident intention to arouse that became, three hundred years later, the hallmark of the pornographic".[30] Aretino's work "combined precise sexual postures with explicit attitudes and feelings required to enact sexual activity in a variety of positions".[31] This work was erotic and obscene, but it was not yet pornographic. In the late sixteenth century, this immoral work was prohibited, but so were politically immoral works such as Machiavelli.[32] Moreover, classical erotic works were used in medical texts of the time, and there was no suggestion that these were morally inappropriate.[33]

The creation of a modern engagement with sexually explicit material also charts the creation of the category of erotic, lewd and obscene materials, which were identified for the first time as having a specific immorality within them, related to their function in sexual arousal. This new way of engaging and thinking about the erotic comes at the same time as an expanding print culture, which put the written and visual word into the hands of a large proportion of the population, as well as raising concerns over children and the working class and their involvement in sexual activity outside of middle-class norms of appropriate behaviour, as we have discussed in chapter 3. These concerns over sex, children and the working class required, among other things, controlling access to pornography.

REGULATING PORNOGRAPHY

Historians of the western world often document the impact of Judaeo-Christian ideologies on modern understandings of morality and sex.[34] It is well known that, prior to the introduction of

Christianity, sexual activity—especially, but not only among the Greeks and Romans—was considered a site for pleasure and enjoyment, even beauty and truth. Plato's *Symposium*, for example, outlined a system for classifying sex and love in just those terms, almost canonizing the association of sexual love (between men at least) with conventional mores about the nature of social life. For the ancient Greek, pleasures of the body—including the viewing and enjoyment of naked bodies—were considered a right and an entitlement of citizens of the Athenian state. In contrast, early Christian texts positioned sexual activity for pleasure, rather than for the service of procreation, as ensuring humanity's fall from grace, given the relations between sex and "original sin" in the Garden of Eden.[35] For the first documented time in history, sexual desire and lascivious feelings become a moral issue. In fact, desire outside the confines of a procreative relationship signalled that the body "was possessed by evil forces, the presence of which were felt through the irresistible desires for sexual gratification".[36] Sex was in need of careful state and religious regulation, for if humanity was to amount to anything, people needed to deny their sexual yearnings in favour of pursuits such as hard labour, which was one of the vehicles, it was thought, for ensuring chastity and virginity were maintained. Ultimately, sex in Judaeo-Christian doctrine "was considered a dangerous force"[37] and sexual behaviour deviating from the procreative was subject to legislative and religious regulation.

This understanding of sex came to the fore in the nineteenth century, when, in America, for example, Anthony Comstock, whose famous anti-pornography campaigns caused pornography to be known as "Comstockery", "boast[ed] that his antismut campaign was responsible for the suicide of 16 producers or sellers of what he considered to be immoral materials".[38] In such a moral climate, any representations of sexual activity that sought to stimulate desire, or to encourage people to experiment with sexual variation, were subject to moral regulation and often criminalization. While people are no longer incarcerated for breaching these socially constituted boundaries of "good" sexual behaviour, the moral imperative to regulate pornographic materials for the sake of public protection continues to persist, most recently in the form of classification boards.

However, the regulation of pornography from the mid-nineteenth century was most often motivated by the potentialities of certain groups of people to be corrupted by pornography. This moral type-casting was generated particularly by upper-class, learned gentlemen who roundly condemned those deemed to be susceptible to the lure of pornography in its various forms. The most susceptible groups included women, children and the working classes, all of whom, it was claimed, "lacked intelligence". Women were of key concern as a group, because earlier pornography had typically taken the form of the novel, a technology that children and the working classes were assumed to lack the skills to access. Concerns about children and pornography were non-existent at the beginning of the nineteenth century, despite a thriving industry, because it was assumed that most children did not have the capacity to read and interpret these materials.[39]

Upper- and middle-class women, however, were another matter. From the late eighteenth century in particular, novel reading was a practice seen to be productive of a range of "physiological effects, especially in women because of their tender fibres".[40] Pornography, as a specialized version of the novel, "played upon the imagination of the reader to create the effect of real sexual activity". Women were thought to be especially susceptible to the "imaginative effects of the novel".[41]

Ultimately, the regulation of pornography was constituted in line with the assumption that there was a direct relation between consumption of sexually explicit material and moral harm, "for those that did not have the 'cultural competencies' to deal with this material".[42] The working classes in particular were seen as exemplars of this lack of cultural capability to process pornographic material in appropriate ways.[43] However, the exclusion of children and the working class from an increasingly large amount of sexually explicit material persisted until the late nineteenth century, when for the first time visual images of pornography started to outstrip written pornography.[44] More panic followed this technical innovation as, for the first time, children, "lower" classes, and other cultural and ethnic groups had access to obscene material. It was cheap and freely available, often being sold alongside newspapers and other forms of media, sparking concern by governing authorities. Where previously "vulnerable" groups had been informally excluded from such access, a process that was as simple as maintaining expense and illiteracy, visual pornographies rendered these forms of exclusion useless: "Postcards could be viewed at a single glance, rather than requiring time, the skills of literacy, the cultural referents of art and literature, or the languages of Greek, Latin, and French".[45] This shift spurred governing authorities to "crack down" on sexually explicit materials, a policy that was also endorsed in popular medical texts, with respected authors such as William Acton[46] making explicit links between the viewing of pornography and "abnormal" childhood in a section of his book *The Functions and Disorders of the Reproductive Organs* titled "Normal functions of childhood":

> In a state of health no sexual impression should ever affect a child's mind or body. All its vital energy should be employed in building up the growing frame, in storing up external impressions, and educating the brain to receive them. During a well-regulated childhood, and in the case of ordinary temperaments, there is no temptation to infringe this primary law of nature … Thus it happens that with most healthy and well-brought up children, no sexual notion or feeling has ever entered their heads, even in the way of speculation. I believe that such children's curiosity is seldom excited on these subjects except where they have been purposely suggested.

The role of pornography in stimulating sexual arousal in children came to a head in concerns over the rise of masturbation.[47] While the relation between pornography and solitary sex was identified as a key concern for men in the late eighteenth and early nineteenth centuries, children were targeted as potential masturbators from the late nineteenth century, as visual pornography became more available.[48] For boys, in particular, the concern was that pornography would cause a precocious awakening of their sexuality which would drive them to seeking prostitutes.[49] Underpinning this concern about the corrupting potential of pornography for children was a contradictory understanding of the child as both innocent and dangerous—innocent 'victims' of pornography, they were also "constantly threatened by horrid temptations, open to stimulation and corruption, and in danger of becoming monsters of appetite".[50] The body of the child was invested with sexual significance in terms of danger and vice, and it was through the child's body that sexual purity and innocence could be assured.[51] Most importantly, even though it may well have been possible for a child to learn how to regulate their behaviour in ways that maintain sexual innocence, most regulation was externally imposed by governing authorities.

These concerns have persisted throughout the twentieth and into the twenty-first centuries. The regulation of television, for example, has been targeted for these forms of governance to ensure children are not adulterated by televised sexual content. Today, television is programmed and scheduled according to "codes of decorum designed to minimize the danger of causing offence",[52] and television content is now carefully scheduled, sanitized and expunged of sexually explicit material of any kind during the family viewing period.[53] This temporal regulation of television is the cornerstone of the viewing schedule, to the point that family-oriented programming dominates the period from early morning until the late-night watershed of nine or ten o'clock, depending on jurisdiction.

PORNOGRAPHY AND SOLITARY SEX

While the nineteenth century saw an increasing moral panic surrounding middle-class women reading saucy novels, the use of pornography as a tool for masturbation was considered a greater danger for men. This understanding of the role of pornography coincided with an increasingly persistent discourse on the dangers and health risks involved with masturbation. As Laqueur[54] argues, although we cannot determine whether pornography inspired an increase in masturbatory behaviour, there is no doubt that "the spectacular rise of the genre in the context of the private reading of fiction certainly made the question of solitary sex far more exigent culturally than ever before". Masturbation was considered "the crack cocaine of sexuality; and it had no bounds in reality, because it was the creature of imagination".[55] Most importantly, masturbation had come to represent all that was morally and socially reprehensible, as well as being a sign of physical disorder and weakness.[56] As masturbation came to be inextricably linked to pornography, pornography came to be thought about as a serious social problem linked with disease, danger and moral vice. Most importantly, pornography was demonized as inciting people to indulge in private, prurient pleasures that distracted from the proper role of sex as procreational, rather than recreational.

A crucial element of this concern was that masturbation involved "spending" sperm,[57] the generative fluid of procreational sex: "semen was a vital fluid whose loss was intrinsically debilitating".[58] In *Onania, or the Heinous Sin of Self-Pollution, and All Its Frightful Consequences in Both Sexes, Considered*, a pseudo-psychological treatise on the dangers of masturbation, Tissot (1708, cited in Hitchcock, 2002)[59] mapped a "spermatic economy" within the male body. To spend semen was to relieve and deprive the body of vital generative fluids. *Onania* was so powerful a text in defining the dangers of masturbation that a new disease, spermatorrhea, was "discovered": "Defined as the excessive discharge of sperm caused by illicit or excessive sexual activity, especially masturbation, the disease was understood to cause anxiety, nervousness, lassitude, impotence, and, in its advanced stages, insanity and death".[60] The panic that emerged with *Onania* and the disease of spermatorrhea further entrenched into perceived wisdom the dangers of pornography in its capacity to incite and excite masturbation.

Interestingly, while women were specifically excluded from this debate in the nineteenth century, this had not always been the case. The notion of loss through ejaculation had once also applied to women. Shorter[61] argues that, from the second century, women were thought to ejaculate with orgasm and to contribute generative fluid in the process of conception. This corresponds with the Galenic model of male and female bodies being constituted respectively by heat and cold: women were characterized by cold and wet humours, while men were dominated by hot and dry humours.[62] Genitalia were thought to be the same in men and women, but men's greater overall heat was thought to drive the internal sexual organs "outwards to form the penis, scrotum and testicles".[63]

The belief that women could become men if the heat in their body increased through activities like masturbation was a common theme in medical texts of the time.[64] All people were believed to be on a gradient from male to female characteristics, depending on the amount of "humoral life essence" within each individual. It was argued that "autoerotic friction" produces heat and the potential for clitorises to become enlarged and penis-like: "excess heat in women indicates potential masculinity, and the inverted penis may expel itself and become visible if women become too hot".[65] Sex, while good for both men and women, "with a moderate sex life in marriage important to good health", was ironically more important to women's good health than to men's. Excessive loss of heat through sex for men could be debilitating, while for women the reverse was true, with "the green sickness, hysteria and a range of debilitating conditions cured by heterosexual sex or masturbation".[66]

It wasn't until the nineteenth century that medical practitioners documented for the first time the "anomaly" that women need not experience orgasm to procreate and conceive.[67] This gave rise to a new understanding of sex devoid of female orgasm, and discourses about sex at that time reorganized around the knowledge that male sperm was the "active" factor in the procreative process.[68] This understanding of procreative sex as not necessarily a vehicle for women's pleasure was ossified in Victorian understandings of femininity.[69]

Hitchcock argues that sex during this period became "increasingly phallocentric. Putting a penis into a vagina became the dominant sexual activity—all other forms of sex becoming literally foreplay".[70] This was vastly different from prior perceptions of sexual activity, which involved a variety sexual practices, most of which we now think of as foreplay. Sex rarely involved penetration, and when it did, it was essential for women to orgasm "as a sign that the ovum has been ejaculated from the ovary".[71] Once there was no need to focus on the sexual arousal of the woman to ensure procreative sex, the penis became the focus of heterosexual procreative sexual activity. The male orgasm became the most important part of the process and the female orgasm "became simply a feeling, albeit an enormously charged one, whose existence was a matter for empirical inquiry or armchair philosophizing".[72]

Such recent ideas about male and female body functionality appear to have shaped our contemporary understandings of pornography. One might argue, for example, that the constitution of much pornography is phallocentric, focusing as it often does on the erect penis and the "money shot". Moreover, the relationship between the erect penis and the classification of the pornography as "hard core" speaks to ongoing concerns about active male sexuality.

While for many, pornography is still considered to be the "final commercialisation and desecration of sex",[73] such opposition has continually lost ground to arguments that encourage liberalization, based on the notion that pornography is harmless, private and a companion to good sexual relations. Such a way of thinking about pornography since the 1970s has seen the introduction of a system of classifications and controls which have extended the rights of adults to use pornography. The point of such regulations are twofold:

> First, adults were regarded as entitled to read and view what they wished in private or in public; second, members of the community were entitled to protection (extending both to themselves and those in their care) from exposure to unsolicited material that they found offensive.[74]

At the same time, concerns about pornography in terms of the content categories of children, and of violence, are escalating. While a number of government inquiries in Australia have concluded that "there was no convincing criminological or psychological evidence that exposure to such material produced measurable harm to society",[75] they have specifically excluded child pornography and violent pornography from their conclusions. Commissions established in Canada and the United States specifi-cally to investigate sexually violent pornography found inconclusive evidence on any direct relationship between viewing, attitudes and acting.[76] In terms of censorship, "explicit or gratuitous depictions of sexual violence against non-consenting persons" remains illegal in many countries, while material that includes "explicit depictions of sexual acts involving adults, but does not include any depiction suggesting coercion or non-consent of any kind" is rated as restricted (X) and is illegal in many jurisdictions.[77] Interestingly, "depictions of sexual violence only to the extent that they are discreet, not gratuitous and not exploitative" are rated R, which gives them wide circulation in society. The classification system is more focused on sex than on violence, and enables the most violent content in the least restricted sexual category. With regard to child pornography, there is no grey area—it remains illegal.

CONCLUSION

Although it has been argued that western popular culture has been "pornified"[78]—that is, pornography has been mainstreamed—it would be erroneous to assume this means that pornography has become socially acceptable. While explicit sexual images and texts may have filtered into more "mainstream" popular cultural forms, such as advertising, pornography still arouses suspicion as potentially dangerous and illicit, and still regularly raises the ire of political and religious conservatives. People's experiences with viewing and consuming sexually explicit materials are heavily censored through government classification and control. The individual is enrolled in appropriately self-regulating the line between what constitutes healthy consumption and the moral and psychological dangers of pornography addiction. Empirical research seeking to discover the harms of pornography is ever-burgeoning in the hope of finding a causal link that will finally justify the complete abolition of pornography from our culture.

The libidinal capacity of pornography is of central concern in its regulation in contemporary western culture. The capacity of texts and images to stimulate sexual desire links back to the adulteration of sexual innocence in children—and hence to the continuing regulation of pornography. The Simpsons case clearly demonstrates this link. Moral and criminal sanction of Simpsons pornography is linked to how we think about the body functionality of adults and the appropriate, healthy sexual development of children. Simpsons children ought not to have adult genitalia in the form of cartoon pornography, because such images are considered a danger to children—both from their own desires, and from the desires of the adults who look at those images. That those images are completely non-human and intended purely to amuse only emphasizes the arbitrariness surrounding our common-sense views about pornography, moral danger and sexual appropriateness.

NOTES

1 New South Wales Supreme Court, 2008, *McEwen* v. *Simmons & ANOR*, NSWSC 1292, Reported Decision 73 NSWLR 10, 191 A Crim R 390. www.lawlink.nsw.go.au (accessed 29 September 2011).

2 Jack Healy, 2008, "Bart Simpson, child pornography and free speech", *The New York Times*, "The Lede: Blogging the *News* with Robert Mackey", 8 December. http://thelede. blogs.nytimes.com/2008/12/08/bart-simpson-child-pornography-and-free-speech (accessed 29 September 2011).

3 New South Wales Supreme Court, 2008, *op. cit.*

4 Neil M. Malamuth, Tamara Addison and Mary Koss, 2000, "Pornography and sexual aggression: are there reliable effects and can we understand them?", *Annual Review of Sex Research,* 11, 26–91; Susan M. Shaw, 1999, "Men's leisure and women's lives: the impact of pornography on women", *Leisure Studies,* 18(3), 197–212.

5 Michael Flood, 2007, "Exposure to pornography among youth in Australia", *Journal of Sociology,* 43(1), 45–60.

6 Stephen T. Holmes and Ronald M. Holmes, 2002, *Sex Crimes: Patterns and Behaviour,* 2nd edn. Thousand Oaks, CA, Sage.

7 Susanna Paasonen, Kaarina Nikunen and Laura Saarenmaa, 2007, "Pornification and the education of desire", in Susanna Paasonen, Kaarina Nikunen and Laura Saarenmaa (eds), *Pornification: Sex and Sexuality in Media Culture*. Oxford, Berg, p. 2.

8 Simon Hardy, 2008, "The pornography of reality", *Sexualities,* 11(1/2), 60.

9 Tim Hitchcock, 1997, *English Sexualities, 1700–1800*. London, Macmillan, p. 17.

10 Jeffrey Weeks, 1989, *Sex, Politics and Society: The Regulation of Sexuality Since 1800*, 2nd edn. London, Longman, p. 20.

11 Lyn Hunt, 1993a, "Introduction: obscenity and the origins of modernity, 1500–1800", in Lyn Hunt (ed.), *The Invention of Pornography*. New York, Zone Books, p. 10.

12 Barbara Sullivan, 1997, *The Politics of Sex: Prostitution and Pornography in Australia Since 1945*. Cambridge, Cambridge University Press, p. 32.

13 Weeks, 1989, *op. cit.*, p. 20.

14 Hitchcock, 1997, *op. cit.*

15 Hunt, 1993a, *op. cit.*, p. 10.

16 Hitchcock, 1997, *op. cit.*, p. 17.

17 Lyn Hunt, 1993b, "Pornography and the French Revolution", in Lyn Hunt (ed.), *The Invention of Pornography*. New York, Zone Books, pp. 301–39.

18 Hunt, 1993b, p. 306.

19 Robert Darnton, cited in Hunt, 1993a, *op. cit.*, p. 18.

20 Peter Wagner, 1988, *Eros Revived: Erotica of the Enlightenment in England and America*. London, Secker and Warburg.

21 Hunt, 1993a, *op. cit.*, p. 43.

22 Wagner, *op. cit.*, 1988.

23 Walter Kendrick, 1996, *The Secret Museum: Pornography in Modern Culture*. Berkeley, CA, University of California Press, p. 1.

24 Kendrick, 1996, p. 9.

25 Robert Darnton, 1996, *The Forbidden Best-Sellers of Pre-revolutionary France*. New York, W. W. Thornton & Company, p. 4.

26 Kendrick, 1996, *op. cit.*

27 Louis Barré, 1875–77, cited in Kendrick, 1996, p. 15.

28 Kendrick, 1996, p. 33.

29 Kendrick, 1996, p. 44.

30 Kendrick, 1996, p. 58; Hunt, 1993a, *op. cit.*

31 Kendrick, 1996, pp. 65–66.

32 Paul Findlen, 1993, "Humanism, politics and pornography in renaissance Italy", in Lyn Hunt (ed.), *The Invention of Pornography*. New York, Zone Books, p. 55.

33 Thomas Laqueur, 1990, *Making Sex: Body and Gender from the Greeks to Freud*. Boston, MA, Harvard University Press.

34 Gail Hawkes, 2004, *Sex and Pleasure in Western Culture*. Cambridge, Polity Press, p. 159. 35 Hawkes, 2004, p. 48.

36 Gail Hawkes and John Scott (eds), 2005, *Perspectives in Human Sexuality*. Melbourne, Oxford University Press, p. 8.

37 Hawkes and Scott, 2005, p. 8.

38 Frederick S. Lane, 2000, *Obscene Profits: The Entrepreneurs of Pornography in the Cyber Age*. New York: Routledge, p. 14.

39 Sharon Marcus, 1966, *The Other Victorians: A Study of Sexuality and Pornography in Mid-Nineteenth-Century England*. New York, Basic Books, p. 155.

40 Lucienne Frappier-Mazur, 1993, "Truth and the obscene word in eighteenth century French pornography", in Lyn Hunt (ed.), *The Invention of Pornography*. New York, Zone Books, p. 219.

41 Hunt, 1993a, *op. cit.*, p. 36.

42 Sullivan, 1997, *op. cit.*, p. 32–33.

43 Sullivan, 1997.

44 Lisa Z. Sigel, 2000, "Filth in the wrong people's hands: postcards and the expansion of pornography in Britain and the Atlantic world, 1880–1914", *Journal of Social History*, 33(4), 859–85.

45 Sigel, 2000, p. 860.

46 William Acton, 1857, cited in Marcus, 1966, *op. cit.*, pp. 13–14.

47 Danielle Egan and Gail Hawkes, 2009, "The problem with protection: or why we need to move towards recognition and the sexual agency of children", *Continuum: Journal of Media and Cultural Studies*, 23(3), 389–400.

48 Robert Darby, 2005, *A Surgical Temptation: The Demonization of the Foreskin and the Rise of Circumcision in Britain*. Chicago, IL, University of Chicago Press; Weeks, 1989, *op. cit.*

49 Darby, 2005, p. 270.

50 Marcus, 1966, *op. cit.*, p. 15.

51 Egan and Hawkes, 2009, *op. cit.*

52 Jane Arthurs, 2004, *Television and Sexuality: Regulation and the Politics of Taste*. New York: Open University Press, p. 21.

53 Gary Needham, 2008, "Scheduling normativity: television, the family, and queer temporality", in Glyn Davis and Gary Needham (eds), *Queer TV: Theories, Histories, Politics*, New York, Routledge.

54 Thomas Laqueur, 2003, *Solitary Sex: A Cultural History of Masturbation*. New York, Zone Books, p. 334.

55 Laqueur, 2003, p. 21.

56 Kendrick, 1996, *op. cit.*, p. 89.

57 Marcus, 1966, *op. cit.*

58 Edward B. Rosenman, 2003, *Unauthorized Pleasures: Accounts of Victorian Erotic Experience*. Ithaca, NY, Cornell University Press, p. 19.

59 As cited in Tim Hitchcock, 2002, "Redefining sex in eighteenth century England", in Kim M. Phillips and Barry Reay (eds), *Sexualities in History: A Reader*. New York, Routledge, p. 190.

60 Rosenman, 2003, *op. cit.*, p. 16.

61 Elizabeth Shorter, 1984, *A History of Women's Bodies*. Harmondsworth, Penguin, p. 12.

62 Hitchcock, 1997, *op. cit.*, p. 43.

63 Hitchcock, 1997, p. 43.

64 Felicity A. Nussbaum, 1995, "One part of womankind: prostitution and sexual geography in *Memoirs of a Woman of Pleasure*", *Differences*, 7(2), 16–40.

65 Nussbaum, 1995, p. 22.

66 Hitchcock, 1997, *op. cit.*, p. 45.

67 Laqueur, 1990, *op. cit.*

68 Hitchcock, 2002, *op. cit.*, p. 190.

69 Rosenman, 2003, *op. cit.*, p. 7.

70 Hitchcock, 2002, *op. cit.*, p. 191.

71 Laqueur, 2003, *op. cit.*, p. 155.

72 Laqueur, 2003, p. 151.

73 Weeks, 1989, *op. cit.*, p. 280.

74 Sullivan, 1997, *op. cit.*, p. 139.

75 Paul Wilson and Stephen Nugent, 1992, "Sexually explicit and violent media material: research and policy implications", in Paul Wilson (ed.), *Issues in Crime, Morality and Justice*. Canberra, Australian Institute of Criminology, p. 139.

76 Wilson and Nugent, 1992, pp. 139–41.

77 Wilson and Nugent, 1992, p. 140.

78 Paasonen, Nikunen and Saarenmaa, 2007, *op. cit.*, p. 1.

CHAPTER 18

INTERNET SEX OFFENDERS

RUDA FLORA

MICHAEL L. KEOHANE

OVERVIEW

The Internet has created many wonderful opportunities for the dissemination of information and knowledge; unfortunately, it has also become a tool of manipulation by sexual offenders. Since the 2001 edition of this book, the Internet sex offender has exploded on to the scene. The individuals who viewed child pornography via magazines simply changed landscapes to the ever-growing websites appearing each day. The Internet provides an opportunity for other offenders to hunt and lure adolescents and children into situations that can have dire consequences for the potential victim.

Internet sex offenders are a diverse population cutting through various backgrounds and socioeconomic statuses. Due to the heterogeneous nature of this expanding population it is important to have a working definition of what constitutes an Internet sex offender. Although the typology is diverse, all Internet offenders access their potential victim(s) through the same cyber portal—the Internet—for the purpose of viewing or engaging in illicit and deviant sexual behavior against minors. Paraphilias such as fetishism, pedophilia, paraphilia not otherwise specified, and voyeurism are among the clinical diagnoses found among sex offenders that attempt online contact with youth.

The federal government, understanding the role that the Internet plays in sexual crimes, created a task force in 1998 entitled Internet Crimes Against Children (ICAC). The ICAC is a national network that assists state and local law enforcement agencies in challenging cyber enticement and child pornography cases (Office of Juvenile Justice and Delinquency Prevention, 2011). An Internet crime against children is defined as any "computer-facilitated sexual exploitation of children, including online solicitation and child pornography" (Office of Crime as cited in Alexy, Burgess, & Baker, 2005, p. 804). Since its induction, the ICAC has assessed more than 280,000 complaints of alleged child sexual victimization, resulting in over 30,000 arrests (Office of Juvenile Justice and Delinquency Prevention, 2011).

In order to understand the scope of the problem, it is important to explore erroneous views of the stereotypical online offender. Most online encounters occur between adult males and under-age adolescents. Contact with children under 12 years of age is limited. The online predator will often use social networks and chat rooms to initiate, seduce, and develop relationships. They will then meet their victim(s) in person for sexual encounters (Wolak, Finkelhor, Mitchell, & Ybarra, 2008; Hundersmarck, Durkin, & DeLong, 2007). Since there are specific chat rooms geared toward teenagers, it is not difficult for predators to blend into these rooms and to strike up a conversation with unsuspecting potential victims (Hundersmarck et al., 2007). Although children younger than 12 are victims of sexual offenders, the National Juvenile Online Victimization (N-JOV) study indicates that 99% of the victims involved in Internet-based sex crimes were between the ages of 13 and 17, 48% of these victims were between 13 and 14 years old, and no victim was under the age of 12 (Wolak, Finkelhor, & Mitchell, 2004; Wolak et al., 2008).

ADOLESCENT RISK FACTORS

As adolescents get older and become familiar with the Internet experience they are more at risk of encountering online sex offenders (Wolak et al., 2008). The more interactive youth are online the more risks they take with issues related to privacy and meeting face-to-face with strangers (Wolak et al., 2008). Youth between 15 and 17 years of age are likely to place themselves at more risk (Wolak et al., 2004; Wolak et al., 2008). Teenage girls are more at risk than boys for Internet-related sexual offenses. This is especially true for those girls who are sexually active as they may already be involved with older partners and are more susceptible to riskier sexual behaviors (Wolak et al., 2008). Teenage boys who consider themselves gay or who are questioning their sexual identity are also at increased risk (Wolak et al., 2004). Teenage male victims account for 25% of all Internet-initiated sex crimes with the majority of offenders being male.

Adolescents who have a history of physical and sexual abuse are more susceptible and vulnerable to engagements by online predators (Wolak et al., 2008). This abuse may compromise the youth's emotional and developmental maturity, thus increasing the likelihood that they will engage in risky behavior as an attempt to fulfill unmet needs (Wolak et al., 2008). Other demographics that increase the risk of sexual abuse include adolescents who come from dysfunctional families or families that are at the poverty threshold. Adolescents who are vulnerable to depression or have low self-esteem may find the Internet appealing due to the ease of establishing online relationships, something they have difficulty doing in person (Dombrowski, LeMasney, Ahia, & Dickson, 2004). Despite these statistics, not all youth who have a history of abuse or emotional problems will necessarily engage in risky behavior online. Wolak *et al.* (2008) has stated that, "for some, prior abuse may trigger risky sexual behavior that directly invites online sexual advances. But delinquency, depression, and social interaction problems unrelated to abuse may also increase vulnerability" (p. 117).

It should be noted that seduction is a powerful emotion that can overwhelm even the most mature adult. Most teenagers are unprepared to handle the complexity that comes with sexual feelings. Creating relationships through the computer involves a unique psychology that can produce more intense feelings in a short amount of time. Teenagers who want to "come into their own" or to understand their own sexuality can overwhelm their senses and short-circuit their rationality. The personal factors that put youth at risk by online predators are more closely related to "immaturity, inexperience, and the impulsiveness with which some youth respond to and explore normal sexual urges" (Wolak *et al.*, 2008, p. 116)

INTERNET ANONYMITY

The Internet offers a pseudo sense of anonymity that emboldens some people who would never be an online predator while also encouraging traditional predators to use this venue to create victims. This same sense of anonymity creates a false sense of security with adolescents. Davidson and Martellozzo (2005) report that, of 200 children in London between 10 and 13 years of age, over 70% were overly confident that they would know the difference between a true peer and an adult posing as a child online. Some of these children also said that even if the person were an adult, they would meet with him or her offline as long as it was in a public place. The children in the sample made the distinction that they would view the online adult with whom they had communicated with for some time as a virtual friend rather than a stranger; therefore, meeting them would not be problematic (Davidson & Martellozzo, 2005).

What adolescents do not seem to take into account is that there is no real anonymity. The Internet provides a way to "identify and track down home contact information, and the Internet enables adults to build long-term virtual relationships with potential victims, prior to attempting to engage a child in physical contact" (Davidson & Gottschalk, 2011, p. 25). The more information that the individual provides on the Internet in chat rooms or on social media forums, the easier it is to be found.

INTERNET OFFENDER GROOMING BEHAVIORS

Twenty percent of Internet users between the ages of 10 and 17 are sexually solicited online by people whom they do not know (Finkelhor, Mitchell, & Wolak, 2000). The online sexual solicitation is important to Internet sex offenders because they can strike up multiple conversations at the same time and quickly determine who is not "biting" and who they can continue to seduce or groom. Sex offenders who solicit online may differ from sex offenders who groom offline. Online solicitors are not interested in developing relationships or building rapport. They may skip the grooming phase and move quickly into sexualizing the conversation. Grooming, on the other hand, requires that the sexual offender spend more time "befriending" the potential victim and gaining his or her trust before moving into the sexualizing phase.

Unlike sex offender typologies for direct contact sexual offenders there are not much empirical data on online grooming behaviors. What is known is that most adolescents want to feel appreciated, validated, accepted, and to understand that who they are matters to their peers or to anyone else who will show them attention (Drombrowski et al., 2004). These are the same emotions that direct contact and fantasy sexual offenders exploit to assist them in the grooming process. Although at-risk minors are the most vulnerable, more emotionally stable or low-risk adolescents are not above the charm of an individual who is manipulative and who uses the false anonymity of the Internet to hijack emotions.

In general, sex offenders will try and normalize what they do through a mixture of rationalizations, minimizations, and justifications. They convince themselves and try to convince others that they are the victims of a system that doesn't understand them. Gottschalk (2011) has reported that sex offenders, by normalizing their deviant behaviors, are attempting to change the label of sex offender to a more positive term such as "boy-lover," "girl-lover," or "child-lover." They also want to eliminate the term "victim" and replace it with "young friends." The term "young friend" is utilized for a child whom the sex offender is either grooming for sexual abuse or actively molesting. Gottschalk (2011), in discussing this distorted view, has stated that "suggesting that they [sex offenders] are 'friends' with the child places the abusive relationship on an even footing, establishing an equality between the sexual abuser and the child that does not exist" (p. 45).

The offender often uses grooming behaviors to assist in developing an online relationship, going to great lengths to establish rapport with the potential victim. Gottschalk (2011) has highlighted O'Connell's five stages of grooming behavior:

1. *Friendship-forming phase*—The sex offender is starting the relationship and will try and get to know the potential victim. The speed of this phase varies depending on the sex offender's comfort level and the comfort level of the potential victim.
2. *Relationship-forming phase*—This is an extension of the friendship phase and allows the offender to establish a working rapport that will help him or her connect with the victim. The discussion could be about home life, school, sports, or anything that the offender can use to manipulate the victim into thinking that he or she is genuinely interested in the victim and wants to be his or her best friend.
3. *Risk assessment phase*—The offender will turn the conversation from rapport building to information gathering. The offender will ask questions geared toward finding out the location of the computer in the home and who uses the computer. This information is to ascertain the

likelihood of someone in the home discovering the offender's online relationship with the victim.

4. *Exclusivity phase*—The offender becomes more emboldened during this phase of the conversation. The victim is encouraged to share personal problems with the offender through private conversations. The offender will use words like "trust" and "respect" to entice the victim to trust the offender and to share secrets with the offender that no one else knows.

5. *Sexual phase*—This phase can begin with subtle questions that provide the offender with information about the victim's sexual interest and experience. At this point the relationship is deeply involved. Although the victim may be uncomfortable with the content of the conversation and the requests of the offender, he or she will most likely participate in order not to disappoint the offender, whom the victim sees as a mentor. Due to the deep connection and the intensity of the relationship that has been cultivated and manipulated by the offender, the victim will seek to please the offender. Eventually, this behavior will lead to the offender having cybersex (explicit sexual talk or masturbation) with the victim or meeting offline to establish a sexual relationship.

TYPOLOGY OF THE INTERNET OFFENDER

Over the last few years several typologies have been constructed to describe the similarities and differences between Internet sex offenders and how they compare to contact sex offenders. Two examples of varying typologies can be found in the works of Lanning (2010) and Alexy *et al.* (2005).

As one explores the various typologies of online sex offenders it is important to understand the rationale behind these typologies. Lanning (2010) has stated that his descriptive typologies of the situational sex offender and the preferential sex offender are not to "gain insight or understanding about why child molesters have sex with children in order to help them, but to recognize and evaluate how child molesters have sex with children in order to identify, arrest, and convict them" (p. 39).

Traders and *Travelers* are two Internet offender types in law enforcement crime classification (Alexy *et al.*, 2005). *Traders* are child sex offenders who collect and trade child pornography online and are interested in a wide variety of sexual acts involving children, including sadistic acts (Lanning, 2010; Alexy *et al.*, 2005). *Travelers* engage and groom/seduce children in online conversations with the goal of meeting them offline for sexual contact. *Travelers* have a wide variety of sexual interests which may include inviting partners to participate in the sexual offense, sexual sadism, and homicide (Lanning, 2010; Alexy *et al.*, 2005). The combination *Trader-Traveler* is a child sex offender who will collect different types of child pornography and child erotica, but who will also arrange to meet a child offline to engage in sexual contact (Lanning, 2010; Alexy *et al.*, 2005).

As more data regarding Internet sex offenders are made available and as professionals further develop, peer review, and implement sex offender typologies, the research and treatment communities will better understand the typology of the Internet sex offender. Classifying Internet sex offenders into one category or another will always be met with some difficulty due to the heterogeneous nature of the population (Aslan, 2011; Tomak, Weschler, Ghahramanlou-Holloway, Virden, & Nademin, 2009; Hundersmarck *et al.*, 2007; Robertiello & Terry, 2007).

In developing a typology, the fundamental approach should include the offender's action, online frequency, and age and gender of preferred victims (Aslan, 2011). The various typologies give professionals some idea about what to expect; however, it is important to remember that these models are tools to assist and should not be used to group typical Internet sex offenders (Aslan, 2011; Hundersmarck *et al.*, 2007).

Mercado, Merdian, and Egg (2011), in discussing these different typologies, conclude that there are four main reasons to "type" or depict the Internet sex offender. Depending upon the motivation of the offender these reasons may overlap. This list is not exhaustive:

1. *Production and distribution of child pornography*—The marketability of the Internet makes it incredibly simple for professional as well as amateur offenders to take pornographic photos or to produce pornographic videos of children and to upload them to the numerous child pornography sites active on the Internet.

2. *Viewing of child pornography*—The Internet adds an element of anonymity that encourages perpetrators to view and download pornographic images and videos of children being sexually abused. Sullivan and Beech (as cited in Mercado *et al.*, 2011) delineated three distinct types of people who view child pornography: "(1) those who collect out of a general sexual preference for children, (2) those who nurture a developing interest in children, and (3) those who view primarily to satisfy a curiosity" (p. 511).

3. *The identification and grooming of potential victims*—An offender who chooses to utilize the Internet to meet potential victims will have a plethora of social sites and chat rooms to troll. Once the Internet offender is able to isolate the potential victim and begins to seduce the child online then the chances of an offline meeting is increased.

4. *Creation of networks among perpetrators of child sexual abusers*—The subculture that existed for pedophiles and child sexual abusers before the Internet can now be found in various sites that espouse the deviant behaviors and attitudes of this group. Perpetrators of the same ilk are able to find each other as they are searching the Internet. The sharing of pornographic images and videos of children and adolescents on more sophisticated websites bypass normal search engine inquiries and are shared through Peer-to-Peer (P2P) networks or hidden portals and server channels within the site. The Internet Watch Foundation (IWF) reported in their 2011 annual report that "disguised" websites are being uncovered. Child sexual abuse sites are connecting themselves to legitimate websites by utilizing an encoded digital pathway. When the URL is loaded, the legitimate site is displayed. However, IWF reports that if an individual enters a gateway in the site with a predetermined URL, pornographic images of children are displayed for the Internet user. In 2011, IWF uncovered almost 580 specific URLs utilizing this method (Lowther, 2012). Networking with other offenders that espouse similar beliefs

allows online offenders to validate their distortions and behaviors and further exacerbates the ideology that perpetuates the cycle of child sexual abuse.

The main difficulty with classifying Internet offenders is the inability to effectively measure sex offenders outside of the traditional typology parameters. As mentioned earlier, the diverse nature of Internet offenders conflicts with current theoretical models that explain some offenders while overlooking others. Bourke and Hernandez (2009) have indicated that the Internet offender represents a new type of offending and not a new type of offender. They stated that Internet offenders who indulge in child pornography may be "undetected child molesters, and that their use of child pornography is indicative of their paraphilic orientation" (p. 190).

Professionals should use caution when assessing people who have problematic sexual behaviors on the Internet. Behaviors related to cybersex addiction or online compulsive sexual behaviors should not automatically be connected to child pornography crimes (Bourke & Hernandez, 2009; Delmonico, Griffin, & Carnes, 2002; Schneider, 1994). Although persons with cybersex addiction and online compulsive sexual behaviors have their psychological difficulties, these problems can fall short of the behavioral and psychological complexities that are associated with child pornography crimes (Bourke & Hernandez, 2009).

Child pornography has always been an issue, but has grown exponentially since the introduction of the Internet. Estimates put online pornographic images of children at 1 million with at least 200 new images popping up on the Internet each day (Wolak, Mitchell, & Finkelhor, 2003). There are statistics that estimate that at least 116,000 searches for child pornography occur daily (Online MBA, 2010). Lanning (2010) reported that the type and style of an offender's pornography and erotica collection indicates what the offender "*wants* to do. It is not necessarily the best indicator of what he *did* or *will* do" (p. 107).

The Internet offers various forms of communication for convenience and speed. Most people using these various methods have no ill or malicious intent. However, the same Internet can also be used for nefarious purposes. In looking at the various means by which to communicate via the Internet, Wortley and Smallbone (2006) pointed out that Internet sexual offenders use web pages and websites, webcams, email, mailing lists, E-groups, newsgroups, an Internet Bulletin Board System (IBBS), chat rooms, Instant Messaging (IM), and P2P networks to:

- View, share, exchange, and distribute pornographic images of children
- Broadcast real-time abuse of victims or grooming of victims
- Share new sites with other offenders
- Enter private forums to discuss sexual interest in children
- Locate potential victims
- Allow offenders to network with each other
- Mail order children through trafficking
- Locate offenders who market sex-tourism or child prostitutes.

The Internet allows for offenders to network with other offenders globally. In fact, more than 20% of Internet offenders live outside of the United States (Alexy *et al.*, 2005). Beech, Elliott, Birgden, and Findlater (2008) have reported that one of the most popular means of accessing and downloading child pornography on the Internet is through the Internet Bulletin Board System (IBBS). Using this method, offenders upload images of abuse to a specific newsgroup heading which allows other users, nationally and internationally, access to the material.

Beech *et al.* (2008) reported that other popular networking methods are the Internet Relay Chat (IRC) programs, such as Microsoft MSN Messenger. Offenders also utilize F-server software which allows the exchange of data from one IRC user's computer to other IRC users through a shared folder "without the need for interaction between the individuals concerned. Images can … be exchanged privately through the direct exchange of e-mails, to which data files can be attached" (p. 219).

Carr (as cited in Beech *et al.*, 2008), in looking at a sample of Internet offenders, found that a large majority of abusive images were downloaded using the following:

- IRC software (78%)
- World Wide Web (42%)
- Newsgroups (39%)
- E-mail (30%)
- ICQ (21%)—"I Seek You"—an instant messaging computer program
- Other methods (4%). (*Offenders could choose more than one answer, thus creating more than 100%.*)

Websites that espouse deviant messages of "love" between adults and adolescents are prolific on the Internet and, much like the sex offender population, the sites represent a heterogeneous population. Davidson and Gottschalk (2011) pointed out that:

> [the] forums facilitate open discussion of [the offenders'] sexual desires, shared ideas about ways to lure victims, mutual support of their adult-child sex philosophies, instant access to potential child victims worldwide, and disguised identities for approaching children, even to the point of presenting as a member of teen groups. (p. 25)

"CONTACT-DRIVEN" VERSUS "FANTASY-DRIVEN"

INTERNET SEX OFFENDERS

As the mental health and criminal justice professions seek to better understand Internet sex offenders, two additional offender groups are showing up in academic literature: contact and non-contact offenders. Current studies are attempting to compare and contrast the differences be-tween contact offenders ("contact-driven") and non-contact offenders ("fantasy-driven") (Briggs, Simon, & Simonsen, 2011; McCarthy, 2010).

Briggs *et al.* (2011), and Seto, Wood, Babchishin, and Flynn (2011b) have illuminated the pri-mary difference between contact-driven and fantasy-driven Internet offenders. Contact-driven offenders utilize the Internet as a way to groom their potential teenage victims and to coordinate a meeting offline in order to engage in sexual activity. Fantasy-driven offenders use the Internet for the purpose of engaging teenage females or males in cybersex and masturbation with no intention of meeting offline. However, there are no clear empirical data that fantasy-driven Internet sex offenders will not escalate to a contact offense. On the contrary, Quayle (2008) has reported that "case studies within a variety of theoretical frameworks do suggest clearly that for some online offenders, their behavior is not static, but show some escalation or movement through a process" (p. 444).

Neither contact-driven (sexual molestation and rape) nor fantasy-driven (exhibitionism and voyeurism) offenders are new to the mental health and criminal justice communities (Briggs *et al.*, 2011; Seto *et al.*, 2011b). However, the Internet has complicated the matter by offering a medium that shields the offender's identity and provides him or her with numerous potential victims in a shorter period of time. In addition, it is unclear how contact-driven and fantasy-driven Internet sex offenders differ from traditional (non-Internet) sex offenders in psychopathology (Mercado *et al.*, 2011).

Convicted chat room offenders disclosed that, while trolling through chat rooms, they actively sought potential victims who brought up sex during the conversation, whose screen names indi-cated that they were young, or whose screen names were sexually provocative in nature (Malesky, as cited in Briggs *et al.*, 2011).

Even within the ranks of what is supposed to be a fantasy-driven offender there are divisions. Researchers followed the recidivism rates of 201 offenders over a 2.5-year period. Those offenders who had a history of abusing children before their index offense were more likely to reoffend. Those offenders who did not have a history of abusing children or adolescents before their index offense did not abuse anyone during the follow-up time (Seto & Eke, as cited in McCarthy, 2010).

INTERNET SEX OFFENDER CHARACTERISTICS

As typologies have developed, so have the characteristics of the Internet sex offender. It should be noted that there is no evidence that Internet sex offenders differ from traditional sex offenders other than in the use of technology (Mercado *et al.*, 2011). In addition, there is no accurate way of determining the number of people who use the Internet to commit sexual offenses (Quayle, 2008).

Online Internet sexual offenders tend to be Caucasian males between the ages of 18 and 72 with a median age of 35 to 42. They tend to be people who have never been married and have no children. They generally live alone or with their parents. Internet sex offenders usually have above-average intelligence, are employed, and are better educated then their traditional offline counterparts (Mercado *et al.*, 2011; Quayle, 2008; Wortley & Smallbone, 2006).

Psychological variables for online sexual offenders indicate more empathy, sexual deviancy, and less cognitive distortions than offline offenders. Both offline and online offenders appear to have experienced more physical and sexual abuse as children than the general public (Babchishin, Hanson, & Hermann, 2011). Compared to the fantasy-driven sexual offender, contact-driven offenders tend to have greater incidences of substance abuse, have been arrested for a sexual crime, and have been diagnosed with pedophilia (McCarthy, 2010).

Classifying Online Sex Offenders

Research to classify sex offenders is ongoing. Many of the typologies are driven by theory and empirical data. In addition, some offenders are less than honest or they will downplay their sexual offending history.

Although this study has undergone recent criticism, "The 'Butner Study' Redux" by Bourke and Hernandez (2009) is an example of dishonest disclosure. The subjects were prisoners at a medium-security federal prison. Of the 155 prisoners selected, 115 had no criminal history of hands-on sexual offending while the remaining 40 prisoners had documented hands-on sexual offending offenses. The prisoners volunteered for the study and were willing to participate in an 18-month therapy regimen. Before treatment the number of known victims among all offenders was 75—approximately two victims per offender. After treatment the number of victims skyrocketed to 1,777. The 40 hands-on offenders disclosed an average of 19.4 victims, while the 115 participants who had no history of hands-on sexual offending disclosed an average of 8.7 victims.

Another study reported that online offenders who had a history of offline offending were more likely to have a higher rate of recidivism than the typical sex offender. In this study, fantasy-driven sex offenders had almost no sexual contact offenses (Eke and Seto, as cited in Seto, Hanson, & Babchishin, 2011a). The contrast in the two studies is a microcosm of the confusion surrounding demographics, typologies, and general understanding of the fantasy-driven offender, specifically, and of the sex offender, in general, who uses the Internet for reprehensible reasons.

PARENTAL RESPONSIBILITIES

An important deterrent in reducing the dangerous impact that Internet offenders have on adolescents is for parents to develop an interest in what their children are doing online. Parents have an obligation to extend trust to their children but also to verify what is happening on the Internet. Parents may not be popular for taking such a protective stance; however, being unpopular is better than having to deal with the potential aftermath of the emotional and psychological trauma of an online romance ending in offline victimization.

It is critical that a parent know as much about his or her child's online life as what the child does when not sitting in front of a computer screen. Cho and Cheon (2005) have reported that parents tend to misjudge the amount of negative material to which their children are exposed via the Internet. The study also provides an insight into how parents can limit the amount of negative content. Cho and Cheon (2005) have suggested three ideas to assist parents:

1. *Family relationship*—It is important for parents to develop and maintain rapport and intimate relationships with their children. Displaying positive affirmation and spending time with them is essential. Children and adolescents are less willing to discuss negative interaction from the Internet if they feel that their parents are unavailable to them.
2. *Interaction*—Parents should build a relationship with their children regarding the Internet. Sharing Internet sessions and teaching children how to evaluate websites and Internet ads will instill in children and parents competencies to better control negative Internet material.
3. *Control*—Computers should be in common areas that reduce secrecy. As children get older parents tend to reduce their oversight on Internet traffic. Other effective measures include having a clear plan and expectations for computer use. These guidelines will assist children in reducing their exposure to negative Internet material.

The above suggestions, in conjunction with parental-control software, free and purchasable Internet filters, and other guidelines that parents are implementing will hopefully reduce the negative impact of the Internet. Online predators are looking for secrecy and isolation out of the watchful eyes of parents to solicit adolescents. Although it is true that adolescents can access material from other computers parents should do all that they can to make the home computer safe from online predators.

Dowdell, Burgess, and Flores (2011) reported that, by 2006, more than 90% of teenagers between the ages of 12 and 17 were on the Internet and that 55% had at least one profile account on a social networking site. Almost 90% of the 2,077 high school students (15 to 18) interviewed stated that they interacted with girls more than boys (91.1% compared to 84.1%) on these sites.

Also in the study 404 middle school students, aged nine to 15, were asked about his or her online behaviors. A little over 80% of the female middle school students and 60% of the male middle school students actually used a privacy setting that would keep people out that they had not previously "friended" (Dowdell *et al.*, 2011).

The Dowdell *et al.* (2011) sample also included 466 adult sex offenders that were divided up into two categories: Internet offenders (113 men) and non-Internet offenders (353 men). The Internet offenders had no hands-on offense. The non-Internet offenders were made up of child molesters (236 men), rapists (35 men), various nuisance sex offenders such as voyeurism or exhibitionism (27 men), and sexual offenders that were not related to children (55 men). Out of the 236 child molesters, 60 had both Internet and non-Internet offenses.

Findings indicated that more than 63% of the Internet sex offenders initiated the topic of sex within the first chat session and more than half of them lied about their online identity. A little over 40% of those who were Internet offenders as well as child molesters visited teenage chat rooms (Dowdell *et al.*, 2011).

Wolak *et al.* (2008) reported that online offenders quickly begin to discuss their sexual interests with potential victims. Most of the victims, aged 13 to 17, who eventually met the offender in person, knew that they were meeting an adult and were going to engage in sex. More than 73% of the adolescents met with the offender more than once, most likely as a result of successful online grooming. Some of the victims in the study professed love for their offender, due primarily to the offender's false promises and emotional manipulation. An adolescent's knowledge of the age of the offender and his or her consent to sexual activity is irrelevant. Legally, it is wrong.

No matter how grown up a 14-year-old appears, there are emotional and psychological issues that can develop because of the betrayal that usually follows the experience between the adolescent and the adult offender. Sexual abuse is real. Dombrowski *et al.* (2004) underline this point by discussing the negative impact on the adolescent's "cognitive, physical, academic, and psychological development. The outcomes of sexual abuse persist well into adulthood and often include higher levels of anxiety, depression, substance abuse, eating disorders, relationship problems, and suicidal ideations" (p. 65).

THE EFFECTS OF CHILD PORNOGRAPHY

The offenses committed by online offenders do have consequences. Although not hands-on acts, Internet sex offenses are dangerous. If there were no market for child pornography the producers and distributors would have no buyers. Unfortunately, the child porn industry is a lucrative empire. Internet offenders who download these images convince themselves that there is no real victim and that they have nothing to do with the abuse that occurred. They convince themselves that, because the child is smiling in the image or does not look distressed, there is really no harm being committed. The truth of the matter is that Internet offenders are contributing partners in the abuse. Although they may not have been the person abusing the victim, they perpetuate the abuse by downloading more of the abuse images.

The second distorted view deals with the "appeal" factor. Porn producers know that many Internet offenders would not buy the product if the victims didn't look as if they were enjoying themselves in the photos. The reality of trauma, rape, physical abuse, and other deviant acts would do little to push this growing market upwards.

Most children of child pornography are not kidnapped or forced to participate; rather, they know the producer (Lanning & Burgess, as cited in Wortley & Smallbone, 2006). Grooming and manipulation are largely used. The effects of this type of abuse are far-reaching and can have short-term as well as long-term traumatic outcomes on the victims—psychological, emotional, physical, and social damage (Klain, Davies, & Hicks, as cited in Wortley & Smallbone, 2006).

Silbert (as cited in Wortley & Smallbone, 2006) conducted a study of 100 children who were victims of child pornography. Years later they were asked to try to remember the details of their childhood sexual abuse and discuss the consequences of the event(s) on their lives. The victims reported pressure to participate in the sexual abuse due to loyalty to the abuser. However, they also reported ongoing shame for what they had done, creating socio-emotional difficulty in actively ending the abuse. Victims reported that at the time of the offense they had physical pain in their genital area, somatic symptoms such as headaches and loss of sleep, and psychological stressors such as anxiety and social isolation. The long-term outcomes spotlighted the anxiety and shame that they had originally felt during the offense. The children's feelings were "of deep despair, worthlessness, and hopelessness. Their experience had provided them with a distorted model of sexuality, and many had particular difficulties in establishing and maintaining healthy emotional and sexual relationships" (Wortley & Smallbone, 2006, p. 18).

TREATMENT

With the introduction of the Internet, child pornography found a place on the electronic highway. In treatment, clinicians find themselves with a mix of offenders, from traditional offline offenders to contact-driven and fantasy-driven Internet offenders.

Traditional and contact-driven offenders have hands-on offenses with a physical victim. The need to discuss the offense and seducing/grooming behaviors is a conversation that these two offender types understand. They may use defense mechanisms such as justification, denial, minimization, rationalization, etc., but the victim has a name, age, and gender and the offenders tend to know their victims.

Fantasy-driven offenders, on the other hand, may have viewed hundreds or thousands of child pornography images on the Internet. Often these offenders do not think that they have done anything wrong because they have not been charged with a hands-on offense. Their reaction to questions about victimizing children can be defensive. They tend to see themselves differently from traditional and contact-driven offenders and will respond that they are not as bad because they didn't actually harm anyone. Fantasy-driven offenders report that all they did was look at some pictures that were already on the sites. Due to the amount of depersonalization, these offenders may take longer to develop victim empathy.

Helping a sex offender to admit to the offense, to accept responsibility, and to genuinely demonstrate remorse and victim empathy is generally difficult under the best of circumstances. Fantasy-driven offenders may admit to what they did online, but getting them to accept responsibility takes more effort. If a therapist has a group with weak ego strength the participants will struggle with understanding their own responsibilities and will not be able to adequately address the issues of the other group members. A group with strong ego strength will address the denial of the fantasy-driven offender, but may rely on confrontation in an attempt to bring about change. Confrontation should be used cautiously to help the client see distortions in his or her treatment;

otherwise, the use of confrontation may bring out more defense mechanisms and inevitably shut the offender down.

Fantasy-driven offenders should follow the same rules as other types of offenders. After describing their index offense(s) they should be allowed to observe the group process for a few weeks with the expectation that they will become more participatory as they become more stable with their position in the group. As the therapist begins to involve the fantasy-driven offenders in the group, these persons should be expected to discuss the group topic and how it relates to their offense. The therapist should expect resistance, but should continue to incorporate the fantasy-driven offense into the group discussion.

In the discussion process it is important to personalize the offense for the fantasy-driven offender. Most offenders have a mother, sister, aunt, or some female (or male, if they viewed male child pornography images) whom they value and respect. Asking the offenders pointed questions about how they would feel if someone viewed their loved ones in the same manner that they viewed their victims is one way to encourage dialogue. Discussing distorted views that the child enjoys the victimization is another topic to explore. Finally, the therapist can explore the offenders' personal responsibility in perpetuating child pornography victimization.

Another way to assist fantasy-driven offenders is to ask them about an experience in which they were humiliated or traumatized. After describing the experience the therapist can ask the offenders to think about how they would feel if this experience was photographed or videotaped and then sent to the Internet for anyone to view.

At some point in the group process all offenders, including fantasy-driven offenders, need to write a letter to their victim(s). The letter, though not actually sent, is an exercise that focuses on levels of responsibility and victim empathy. Most offenders will be able to easily identify their victim(s), but the fantasy-driven offender may experience anxiety or may attempt to bypass the exercise because they can't pick just one victim. Asking the fantasy-driven offender to mentally picture one face of one victim (perhaps the last victim they can remember offending) can help humanize them all; the one victim's face becomes a tangible synecdoche, allowing the offender to overcome anxiety over having to remember every victim.

There can be many issues on which to focus in the letter, but the therapist should have the group write about "why they did what they did" which will take time and should produce positive anxiety. This letter will be written several times throughout the offender's time in group. At first the primary question of "why" will be answered with a surface explanation; but as the offender continues in the group the intellectual answers should give way to emotional and reflective responses. It is this emotional response from the fantasy-driven offender that will help him or her to accept responsibility and to develop victim empathy.

Middleton, Mandeville-Norden, and Hayes (2009) incorporated into their Internet Sex Offender Treatment Program (i-SOTP) model a six-module program that looks at individual treatment needs of the Internet sexual offender. Additional research should measure the implications of such a program tailored to work with Internet sex offenders.

The i-SOTP model has been revised and is influenced by work completed by Fisher and Beech (1998), Quayle and Taylor (2003), and Ward and Stewart (2003) (as cited in Middleton *et al.*, 2009) and includes sections that address the following:

- Increase motivation, decrease denial, and identify and reduce discrepancy between perceived pro-social values and behavior, addressing distorted attitudes.
- Challenge offense-supportive attitudes and behaviors, addressing distorted attitudes.
- Build an empathic response while identifying that children depicted in the incident images are real victims of child abuse, addressing distorted attitudes and socio-affective functioning.
- Reduce use of sex as a coping strategy and emotional avoidance, replacing it with effective problem solving strategies, addressing socio-affective functioning, and self-management.
- Develop adequate relationship, intimacy, and coping skills; improve self-esteem and internal locus of control, social adequacy factors, and self-management.
- Develop realistic relapse prevention strategies and new pro-social life-style goals, addressing self-management and socio-affective functioning. (Middleton *et al.*, pp. 8–9; D. Middleton, personal communication, *permission granted*)

The work that Middleton *et al.* (2009) build on is promising. The i-SOTP program is designed for individuals over the age of 21 whose sexual offense is tied to the Internet. Most treatment groups are eclectic and have both contact-driven and fantasy-driven offenders. The modules as described for the Internet offender have implications for all sex offenders regardless of offense.

Most sexual offenders share certain deficiencies that must be addressed in order to move their treatment forward and to focus on reduced risk to the community. Research regarding risk factors for online sex offenders is limited (Seto *et al.*, 2011a; Middleton *et al.*, 2009). Offenders are likely to have the same risk factors as offline offenders in areas of sexual deviancy and antisocial orientation (i.e., impulsivity and not accepting personal responsibility). Professionals involved with online sexual offenders should provide interventions that address these deficiencies (Seto *et al.*, 2011a).

Clinicians should expect resistance at the beginning of treatment. Most offenders engaged in some form of sexual abuse due to a culmination of distorted views, stressors, impaired communications skills, inadequate social skills, and other unmet needs. Reminding the offender that excuses are no substitute for responsibility and that he or she will be held accountable in the group is important; however, it is also important to address individual deficits.

Clinicians must be able to treat their clients with dignity and respect. When it comes to child abuse, domestic violence, rape, or any other kind of victim, clinicians have an abundance of empathetic concern. There are times that the emotional trauma of what is being said regarding sexual abuse may be difficult for the clinician to hear. It is especially important in these moments that the clinician is able to be aware of his or her emotional responses toward the client.

The abuse that the sexual offender has inflicted on his or her victim(s) will be addressed in treatment, but that offender should be treated with the dignity and respect afforded to all persons.

A clinician is entitled to his or her personal views and opinions, but that same clinician must also be able to separate personal feelings from professionalism. A clinician who is unable to separate these intricate emotions will have difficulty developing a rapport or building a relationship with the client. If the clinician fails to develop rapport the offender will share what he or she thinks the clinician wants to hear or will say nothing at all; neither is helpful in reducing recidivism rates.

The sexual offender group will have a range of personalities and sexual offenses. It is important that the therapist ascertains as much information over the course of treatment as possible. Actuarial tools, individual treatment plans, and monthly progress notes should be maintained. Polygraphs should be administered semi-annually or annually. Developing a phase system or some type of advancement system for the offender is also important.

As the offender moves through the program there should be some method to encourage active engagement with and "buy in" into the program. The therapist should establish a working relationship with the probation officer; communication is essential. It is important to be able to articulate thoughts and ideas and to clarify the direction of the group process. It is also important that therapists diminish any splitting among professionals that some offenders may attempt to accomplish.

TREATMENT MODELS

The Relapse Prevention model (RPT), Cognitive Behavioral approach (CBT), Risk-Need-Responsivity (RNR) model, and Good Lives Model-Comprehensive (GLM-C) are a few of the well-known models of sexual offender treatment to assist with group work. Contracts with the state may require a model like RP, but the therapist can always enhance the treatment by implementing different models in addition to what is required. The Integrated Model of Sex Offender Treatment (IMSOT) utilizes a combination of treatment approaches and interventions that will have the best outcomes (see Chapter 10 for details).

Working with sex offenders requires the therapist to be adept at utilizing a variety of models to provide treatment. RPT and CBT are discussed in detail in Chapter 15 (Group Therapy). However, it would be helpful to discuss the GLM-C treatment model here.

Good Lives Model-Comprehensive

The Good Lives Model-Comprehensive (GLM-C)—a strength-based and positive psychology approach—is an integrated, systemic, and comprehensive approach to treating sexual offenders. The theoretical framework comes from the original Good Lives Model-Original (GLM-O) and the Integrated Theory of Sexual Offending (ITSO) (Ward, Mann, & Gannon, 2007; Ward & Gannon, 2006). Instead of focusing exclusively on the psychological deficiencies or risk factors of the sexual offender, the GLM-C also seeks to identify the strengths of the offender. This model proposes that all human beings are programmed to seek certain goals known as primary goods including life, knowledge, excellence in play and work, excellence in agency, inner peace, friendship, community, spirituality, happiness, and creativity. These goods are intrinsic in nature and are needed in order to have a fulfilling life (Ward *et al.*, 2007; Ward & Gannon, 2006).

The ITSO looks at causal variables—specifically, the interaction of biological factors, ecological niche factors, and psychological factors—and how they act together to cause the clinical issues related to offending (Ward & Beech, as cited in Ward & Gannon, 2006). Factors related to emotional problems, social difficulties, offense supportive beliefs, empathy problems, and deviant sexual arousal lead to the "sexually abusive actions. The consequences of sexually abusive behavior, in turn, function to maintain a positive feedback loop that entrenches the offender's vulnerabilities through their impact on the environment and psychological functioning" (Ward & Gannon, 2006, p. 81).

The two-fold focus of the GLM-C in providing therapy to sexual offenders is to promote goods and reduce risk. The major intent of the model is to provide the offender with the necessary "skills, values, attitudes, and resources necessary to lead a different kind of life, one that is personally meaningful and satisfying and does not involve inflicting harm on children or adults" (Ward *et al.*, 2007, p. 92). (For a more detailed explanation of the GLM-C, see Ward *et al.*, 2007; Ward & Gannon, 2006).

SUMMARY

The Internet offender is multi-faceted and much like the traditional offender. The pseudo-anonymity of the Internet, in addition to the grooming/seducing behaviors of some Internet offenders, actually puts teenagers at greater risk for victimization offline. Younger children are not as high-risk because of intense media coverage of these incidents. Research is ongoing to include developing characteristics and typologies to identify subsets of the Internet sexual offender in hopes to better understand and narrow this population. Finally, treatment options are important and can be effective in working with different types of sexual offenders in a group process.

CHAPTER 19

SEXUAL ADDICTION

RUDA FLORA

MICHAEL L. KEOHANE

OVERVIEW

Sexual addiction, also known as hypersexuality or compulsive sexual behavior, is a phenomenon found among individuals who compulsively seek sexual situations in order to satisfy his or her unrealistic need for sexual gratification. Persons afflicted by this behavior display repeated and markedly increased interest in engaging in sexual relations. Distress is experienced if the individual is unable to obtain sex. The problem behavior impedes the person's family, occupational, and social functioning, often making it difficult to form healthy relationships (Rufo, 2012). Although the behavior is found in both men and women, research indicates that men predominantly have higher rates of compulsive sexual behavior (Rufo, 2012; Black, Kehrberg, Flumerfelt, & Schlosser, 1997).

Compulsive sexual behaviors can further be divided into two subtypes, paraphiliac and non-paraphiliac (Fong, 2006; Coleman, as cited by Black *et al.*, 1997). Paraphiliac behaviors are those behaviors that are outside the predictable array of sexual behaviors. Eight of these paraphiliac behaviors are outlined in the *DSM-IV-TR* under the *Paraphilia* subheading; however, there are numerous paraphilias that are not presently in the manual and also not yet clinically recognized (Fong, 2006). Those paraphilias not presently in the *DSM-IV-TR* are more of a residual grouping with sexually deviant behaviors less frequently observed by clinicians, criminal justice, and human service professionals (Fong, 2006).

The compulsivity of the paraphiliac behavior must be personally distressing and cause overwhelming impairments throughout the person's life (Fong, 2006). The sexual gratification comes from the focus being on the object or behavior. In addition, individuals have a more difficult time becoming aroused by sexual activities unless they are able to fantasize about the specific paraphilia at the same time (Williams, 2012).

Non-paraphiliac sexual behaviors are seen as socially acceptable forms of sexual practices that become excessive and intrusive and create significant impairment and distress for the person engaged in the sexual behavior (Williams, 2012; Fong, 2006). Common non-paraphiliac sexual behaviors include, but are not limited to, compulsive masturbation, frequenting strip clubs, promiscuity, excessive use of pornography, and engaging in sexual encounters with prostitutes (Williams, 2012; Fong, 2006). It should be noted that unless the paraphiliac or non-paraphiliac sexual behavior causes significant impairment and distress in the person's life, it is most likely not a compulsive sexual disorder.

SEXUAL ADDICTION COMPARED TO OTHER ADDICTIONS

Sex addicts are known to have a potential for other addictions including chemical dependency, eating disorders, compulsive gambling, and spending sprees (Williams, 2012; Fong, 2006; Carnes, 2001). The addiction becomes overwhelming and can be destructive in all parts of his or her life (Williams, 2012; Fong, 2006; Carnes, 2001). Carnes (2001) has stated, "The accumulated effect is that the addiction can become the center of the addict's life—rooted in complex malaise of deceit, isolation, and shame" (p. 49). Persons with this problem behavior are also reported to have a high probability of having been raised in a dysfunctional family system. There can be a history of emotional, physical, and sexual abuse.

There have been sharp criticisms from some in the research and clinical communities who feel that the word *addiction* is misleading. The voice of criticism comes from comparing addictions related to drugs and alcohol to sexual addictions and arguing that people don't become addicted to sex in quite the same manner as they would to drugs or alcohol (Coleman, as cited in Black *et al.*, 1997; Levine & Troiden, as cited in Black *et al.*, 1997).

However, Carnes (2001) has argued that sexual addiction is, in fact, similar to other types of addictions. The addict forms a pathological relationship to the addiction and the resulting impaired thinking in their core belief system intensifies every time that the addict repeats the addiction cycle. Addiction is a jealous master that requires one's complete attention. Carnes (2001) elaborates on this point by stating: "A Jekyll/Hyde struggle emerges. The addictive system is so compelling that to stop would be like death. Yet, as the system continues, the person's values, priorities, and loved ones are attacked" (p. 27).

Oftentimes called behavioral addiction or process addiction, compulsive sexual behaviors are as real to the sex addict as alcohol is to the alcoholic. Behavioral addictions are compulsive behavioral patterns (that do not require chemical substances like alcohol, illegal chemical substances, prescription pills, etc.) that a person will continue to engage in despite negative consequences that accompany the behaviors. In addition, the individual develops a psychological dependence on the mood-altering behavior (sex, Internet, video games, food, etc.). A sex addict displays his or her addictive behavior differently than an alcoholic, but the same self-destructive characteristics and behavior patterns are present for both types of addictions.

Wright (2006), who coined the term *soft addiction* (to also describe process addiction), has stated that these patterns of compulsive behaviors "satisfy a surface want but ignore or block the satisfaction of a deeper need. They numb us to feelings and spiritual awareness by substituting a superficial high or a sense of activity for genuine feeling or accomplishment" (p. 40).

Regardless of the addiction, the primary relationship is always on the stimulus (and not the person) that will alter one's mood and is eventually needed to feel "normal" (Carnes, 2001). Additionally, fear of abandonment and shame are two of the core elements of all addictions that are further complicated by the alienation that "becomes a quagmire within which addicts struggle, only to become more isolated" (Carnes, 2001, p. 6).

The sexually addicted individual's struggles impede the normal functioning of his or her life. There is a constant battle between the addictive part and the normal part. At first, the person convinces him- or herself that they are able to keep the two parts separate; however, the more time that is spent on the addiction, the more time and attention the addiction requires, pushing all other relationships out of the way.

Even though the views are divided on the term *addiction*, researchers generally agree that 3% to 5% of the general U.S. population has a compulsive sexual disorder (Rufo, 2012; Black *et al.*, 1997). A survey of Italian adult males who surf the Internet seem to indicate that 6% to 10% of those males frequently view pornography and around 5% would be categorized as addicted to pornography (Cavaglion & Rashty, 2010).

DIAGNOSTIC CRITERIA

Another area of debate in the clinical and research camps is whether there should be specific diagnostic criteria for individuals with compulsive sexual behavior. The diagnostic features are not in the *DSM-IV-TR* and there is no clear way of knowing the outcome until a new manual is published (Fong, 2006; Schneider, 2004; Black *et al.*, 1997).

Fong (2006) has elaborated on this point by highlighting that the confusion in solid terminology for the behavior, the need for recognized criteria, and the lack of formal empirical research completed on compulsive sexual behavior are in large part due to the heterogeneous appearance of compulsive sexual behavior. Depending on the individual these behaviors may present themselves in the form of an addictive disorder (i.e., loss of control and preoccupation), an impulse control disorder (i.e., uncontrollable urges and impulses), or an obsessive compulsive disorder (i.e., sexual compulsions).

One of the essential features of compulsive sexual behavior is engaging in sexual activity despite any negative consequences that may arise due to these behaviors (Carnes, Delmonico, & Griffin, 2007; Fong, 2006; Schneider, 2004; Carnes, 2001). The inconceivability of addiction is that the person will continue to repeat the cycle despite the negative consequences. The behaviors associated with sexual addiction are often compared to drug or alcohol addiction but can be found with any addiction. There are cravings and needs that must be satisfied. The addicted individual finds him- or herself preoccupied with the addictive behavior and a compulsion to act on this behavior.

Fong (2006) has reported that the psychological aspects of sexual addiction are very similar to other types of addiction in that the addiction is a maladaptive response to emotional or physical pain and stress. The addiction then creates more problems for the sexually addicted individual which, in turn, creates more emotional pain, shame, fear, and anxiety.

In looking at potential signs and features for sexual addiction, Carnes (1991) has noted the following:

- Sexual behavior that is out of control
- Medical, legal, and interpersonal problems due to sexual misconduct
- Despite adverse and negative consequences of the sexual behavior, the person feels powerless to stop
- Self-destructive or high-risk sexual behavior
- Repeated attempts to limit or stop the sexual behaviors
- Sexual obsession and fantasy as coping mechanisms
- Increased need for sexual activity
- Severe mood changes that are linked to the sexual activity
- Large amounts of time spent obtaining sex, planning incidents, or recovering from episodes
- Sexual behavior that interferes or impedes the person's ability to be meaningfully involved in social, occupational, and recreational areas of his or her life.

Carnes (2001) has suggested that there are three levels of sexual addiction. Level One behaviors are those behaviors deemed normally acceptable or tolerable within society and may be found to include masturbation, affairs, or pornography. Carnes (2001) also noted that prostitution and homosexuality are still seen as sources of controversy in certain parts of society.

Level Two behaviors are considered more intrusive, not acceptable in society, and can lead to contact with the criminal justice system; these behaviors may include exhibitionism, voyeurism, obscene telephone calls, and indecent liberties.

Level Three behaviors cross boundaries that are put in place to protect society and include rape, incest, and child molestation. It should be noted that a person committing such a heinous crime should not automatically be considered a sex addict. Carnes (2001), speaking on rape as an addiction, has stated:

> To rape out of anger, passion, or lawlessness—as terrible as that is—does not constitute an addiction. There are some sexual addicts, however, for whom rape is part of a larger pattern. Once past our rage for what has been done, we can see rape as the most tragic extension of the addict's world. (p. 65)

Although this information is considered important, it is not suggested that all sexually addicted persons will offend. Sexual addiction (like any other addiction) has the element of progression embedded within the disorder (Schneider, 2004).

In addition, time is not a friend to the addict. As the addiction develops through experimentation and becomes an emotional crutch or shield from painful experiences, the addiction requires more of the problem behavior in order to get the same effect. Once the person develops a compulsion to the addiction he or she often becomes enslaved to the problem behavior and their actions become bizarre and dangerous for the addict and the potential victim(s) that he or she engages.

Schneider (2004), in discussing the three levels of addiction, has reported that a person addicted at Level One will not automatically advance to Level Two. It is more likely that these persons will "intensify their preferred activity rather than switch to an unrelated one" (p. 203). However, it should also be noted that a person sexually addicted at Level Three will also have addictions at Level Two and Level One (Schneider, 2004).

Research completed by Marshall and Marshall (2006) and Blanchard (as cited in Schneider, 2004) indicated that 35% to 55% of all convicted sexual offenders also meet the criteria for sexual addiction. For these offenders, sexual addiction becomes a part of the lifestyle and another clinical issue that must be addressed. However, it should also be noted that acting out sexually does not necessarily mean that sex offenders are sex addicts. Carnes (2001) has stated:

> Behavior by itself does not make an addict. Further the feelings of attraction for a child (or a client) does not constitute addiction. Even to act on those feelings, as damaging as that may be, does not make an addict. Addicts are people who cannot stop their behavior, which is crippling them and those around them. (pp. 59–60)

Further, Carnes (2001) has stated "Many sex offenders do not fit the criteria for addiction. So offending behavior does not equal addictive behavior" (p. 38).

The average sex addict has many cognitive distortions and a rich sexual fantasy life. Sexual fantasies have become more deviant for sexual gratification. Rituals constitute some of the clinical behaviors for arousal and enactment. Some of the first level of law-breaking activities sex addicts engage in include exhibitionism, downloading pornography, prostitution contact, and peeping (voyeurism).

ONLINE SEXUAL ACTIVITY

Online Pornography Addiction

At the end of 1995 there were approximately 16 million people on the Internet, which equated to less than 0.5% of the global population. By March 2012 there were over 2.2 billion Internet users world-wide, or close to 33% of the world's population (Internet World Statistics, 2012). If a person is looking for online pornographic material then it is not hard to find. It is as straightforward as entering a term into any search engine and perusing the millions of sites on the computer screen. Internet pornography has been called the new crack-cocaine for sex addicts due to the ease of obtaining and the difficulty of overcoming the visual imagery that replays over and over in the person's head. The accessibility of the Internet makes it simple to pursue sexual forums and activities online.

Online sexual activity (OSA) is broadly defined as using the "Internet for any activity (including the use of text, audio, or graphic files) that involves sexuality for purposes of recreation, entertainment, exploration, support, education, commerce, efforts to attain and secure sexual or romantic partners and so on" (Cooper & Griffin-Shelley, 2002, p. 3). The "why" of how people become addicted to OSA becomes easier to understand by applying three primary factors that are often referred to as the "Triple-A Engine" (Cooper, as cited in Cooper, Delmonico, & Burg, 2000).

Cooper (as cited in Cooper *et al.*, 2000) explained that the ease of OSA is linked to:

- *Accessibility*—If the user wants to be on the Internet 24 hours a day, 7 days a week then they would have no problem doing so. The Internet is available when the user is ready.
- *Affordability*—There are millions of sexual sites to choose from that cost little to no money and can provide the user with "free" sex.
- *Anonymity*—People perceive that what they say or how they behave on the Internet will be kept anonymous. People depend on this secrecy as they become more involved in OSA behaviors.

The anonymity of the Internet exacerbates the issues associated with sexual addiction to include pornography and other OSA such as cybersex.

People who may never have entertained renting adult pornographic videos or buying pornographic magazines or frequenting strip clubs are now finding themselves addicted to OSA (Young, 2012). Additionally, Young (2012) has indicated that studies demonstrate that men are more likely to view cyberporn, while women are more likely to join erotic chats. Not everyone who engages in OSAs will go on to become sexually addicted, but these problem behaviors could easily progress for some people.

Before the accessibility of the Internet viewing pornography required the user to be active in pursuing the type of pornography he or she wanted. The more deviant the pornography, the more time and potential money it took to track down. The Internet makes these pursuits much simpler. A curious investigator can very quickly turn into a habitual user. "Like quicksand, pornography sucked them in so steadily and quietly that they often didn't even notice that they were sinking" (Maltz & Maltz, 2008, p. 2).

Additionally, for some people pornography has ruined their lives; destroyed their families; isolated them from friends; produced shame, guilt, anxiety, and sexual dysfunction; and reduced their motivation for future desires or dreams (Cavaglion & Rashty, 2010; Maltz & Maltz, 2008; Bensimon, 2007; Skinner, 2005).

Pornography also desensitizes the viewer and creates a distorted view of the human body. Partners may feel embarrassed about their bodies, appearance, or sexual performance (Cavaglion & Rashty, 2010; Maltz & Maltz, 2008; Schneider, 2003). Bensimon (2007), speaking on the power of pornography, has stated, "Pornography does not need whole human beings; all it needs are objectified bodies, and it is the very nature of the objectification that gives pornography all its strength and appeal, and virtually any kind of demand can be met" (p. 105).

Senn (as cited in Bergen & Bogle, 2000), looking at how pornography affected the lives of women, found that 24% of the 96 women surveyed had been upset at being asked to mimic something pornographic that the woman's partner had viewed. Also, in a study of sexual violence toward women on a Canadian campus, Schwartz and DeKeseredy (as cited in Bergen & Bogle, 2000) discovered that in a sample of 1,638 women 8.4% had become upset due to her dating partner trying to force her to imitate something that the partner had viewed in some type of pornography.

Although viewing pornographic images doesn't mean that an individual will go on to escalate in his or her OSA behavior the influential power that pornographic images can have on a person should also not be underestimated. "Porn can have as powerful an effect on your body and brain as cocaine, methamphetamine, alcohol, and other drugs. It actually changes your brain chemistry" (Maltz & Maltz, 2008, p. 19).

There is no doubt that a small minority of people who use the Internet for OSA become compulsive in their online sexual behaviors, but some researchers question the nature of what the individual is addicted to (Beard & Wolf, as cited in Sheldon & Howitt, 2007).

Currently, there are no consistent criteria to measure addiction as it pertains to the use of the Internet (Sheldon & Howitt, 2007). Information on various websites will offer self-tests to see if the person fits the criteria of sexual addiction. These tests should be used with caution as all sites have their own exclusive definitions for what constitutes sex and online sexual addiction (Greenfield & Orzack, 2002). Additionally, the questionnaires administered online may not be based on empirical data and may rely specifically on self-report, ignoring some of the other issues in the person's life that first need to be treated (Greenfield & Orzack, 2002). This is not to say that there is no real value in these types of websites for information and education, but the person should be directed to take those results offline and consult a therapist (Greenfield & Orzack, 2002).

Another issue that develops when a person is addicted to online pornographic material is the blur between private time and work time. As the addiction becomes more pronounced, the person rationalizes his or her behavior and takes more risks to look at the pornography while on the employer's time. Cooper, Putnam, Planchon, and Boies (1999a) found that six out of every 100 employees in their survey reported using his or her work computer as a primary means to look at online sexual material. Furthermore, Cooper *et al.* (1999a) looked at individuals in their study that used both home and work computers for online sexual material and found that 20% of men and 12% of women used their computers at work at least sometimes to look at sexual material online. Branwyn (as cited in Cooper *et al.*, 1999a) reports that an amazing 70% of sexual material viewed online is done so between the hours of 9am and 5pm throughout the week.

Cybersex Behaviors

Cybersex behaviors (sometimes referred to as *cybering*) have been classified as a subcategory of OSA and is defined in research literature as at least two people communicating online with each other for the intention of sexual pleasure (Rufo, 2012; Carnes *et al.*, 2007; Daneback, Cooper, & Månsson, 2005). Masturbation may or may not be part of the interaction (Daneback *et al.*, 2005; Young, Griffin-Shelley, Cooper, O'Mara, & Buchanan, 2000).

Carnes *et al.* (2007) report that the word *cybersex* is broadly used to explain a variety of sexually related behaviors that occur while online and include:

- Accessing pornography in all of its various forms
- Real-time online chatting and virtual partners that can also include webcams and live video feeds
- Internet-based dating sites and hand-held devices that make access to cybersex easier
- Offline multimedia software including CD-ROMS that allows for pornographic movies or magazines or interaction within sexual games.

Cooper *et al.* (2000) have reported that there is a variety of healthy ways the Internet can be used for sexual expression. The authors elaborate on three distinct purposes that the Internet serves for sexual expression:

1. Virtual communities for individuals who may feel isolated or marginalized.
2. Romantic relationships that are based less on physical attractiveness.
3. A virtual environment that provides a sense of protection and appears safer for sexual experimentation and sexual exploration while protecting personal identity.

There is some research that points to a minority of people who engage in OSA that later struggle with online sexual problems (requiring some form of OSA to become sexually stimulated or gratified) that interfere with the person's life (Cooper, Månsson, Daneback, Tikkanen, & Ross, 2003; Cooper, Griffin-Shelley, Delmonico, & Mathy, 2001). However, there also seems to be some indication that the majority of people don't appear to experience negative consequences (online or offline) due to these behaviors (Cooper *et al.*, 2003; Cooper *et al.*, 2001). In fact, research completed by Cooper *et al.* (1999a) found that 47% of people who visit online sexual sites do so as "recreational users" and do not experience a negative impact on their lives. However, research studies have also indicated that a small portion (between 4.6% to around 8%) of individuals who spent 11 hours or more on the Internet do have problematic behaviors with OSA and the participants could be classified as being sexually compulsive (Cooper *et al.*, 2000; Cooper *et al.*, 1999a; Cooper, Scherer, Boies, & Gordon, 1999b).

Cooper *et al.* (2000) also found that 17% of their study of 9,265 male and female Internet users presented with more problems surrounding their OSA than did the other participants in the study. The results indicated that cybersex activity may be problematic for a portion of men and women who engage in OSA. Additionally, the study found that 1% of the sample's cybersex activity had graduated from sexually compulsive behavior to cybersex compulsive behavior and had reported some major negative consequences in their lives (Cooper *et al.*, 2000).

A Swedish study completed by Daneback *et al.* (2005) examined the basic demographic characteristics and OSA behaviors of 1,835 individuals who completed an online questionnaire about sexual behaviors. Out of these, 1,458 individuals reported they used the Internet for OSA (658 women and 800 men). Results indicated that close to one-third of participants reported cybersex experiences (30% men and 34% women). The preferred method of cybersex contacts was chat rooms (72%) while the second favorite was ICQ/Microsoft Messenger (52%) (participants were allowed to mark more than one response, which is why the above numbers are greater than 100%).

The study also found that men who spend six to 11 hours online per week were more than four times as likely to engage in cybersex. Women in the study who spent ten to 15 hours per week were eight times more likely to participate in cybersex activity. Although women in the cybersex group didn't spend nearly the amount of time in OSA as compared to the men, they did spend almost twice the amount of time involved in OSA behaviors than women who didn't participate in cybersex (Daneback *et al.*, 2005).

Additionally, homosexual men were more than four times more likely to engage in cybersex than heterosexual men. A reason for the vast difference in cybersex engagement between homosexual men and heterosexual men is the concern that heterosexual men have for "gender-bending" or men pretending to be women in sexual chat rooms (Daneback *et al.*, 2005). However, research completed by Cooper *et al.* (2000) found that only around 5% of individuals actually pretended to be the opposite gender while online.

Daneback *et al.* (2005) suggested that another reason for the likelihood of homosexual men engaging in cybersex was because homosexual men are more "open to less traditional types of sexual activities. Therefore, cybersex is a more known and accepted type of sexual activity in these communities" (p. 326). In addition, cyberspace is still considered a safer place to express their sexuality and to pursue OSA without the negative consequences that more traditional offline avenues can incur (Daneback *et al.*, 2005).

Furthermore, Cooper *et al.* (1999b) reported that 72% of men and 62% of women said that they kept the amount of time they spend engaging in OSA a secret. Although on the surface this may not be a problem, the seductive nature of online sexual pursuits coupled with secrecy could have a larger negative impact felt through important areas of their lives.

Cybersex Consequences

The slippery slope with these types of interactions for some people is that they may substitute real life relationships with virtual relationships; this may be detrimental to developing healthy sexual development (Cooper *et al.*, 2000). People who spend large amounts of time online can become ensnared in the seductive nature of the Internet. Also, people addicted to the computer or Internet trade their real relationships in for seclusion in front of the computer to further engage in online relationships (Young *et al.*, 2000). Feelings and emotions garnered online are intensified and intimacy and trust can replace caution. Traditional face-to-face relationships that develop over time are emotionally intensified and increased in speed online (Young *et al.*, 2000; Cooper & Sportolari, 1997)

Young *et al.* (2000) have indicated that this "perceived sense of trust, intimacy, and acceptance has the potential to encourage online users to use these relationships as a primary source of companionship and comfort" (p. 60). The whirlwind of emotionality can create a false sense of security and behaviors that can further create problems in offline relationships.

Cyber-affairs are one such problem that has detrimental effects on a relationship. A cyber-affair is defined as a "romantic and/or sexual relationship that is initiated via online contact and maintained predominantly through electronic conversations that occur through e-mail and in virtual communities such as chat rooms, interactive games, or newsgroups" (Young *et al.*, 2000, p. 60). Although no physical contact may occur, questions arise about the pain caused and influence that emotional infidelity has on offline relationships. The escape or fantasy of the unknown that the Internet offers can be intoxicating and can create a rationalization that his or her online and offline relationships are separate and have nothing to do with each other. However, there are times that these behaviors escalate to offline sexual relationships.

Young (as cited in Young *et al.*, 2000) found that 53% of the 396 Internet addicts that were interviewed had serious relationship problems with their marriages or intimate relationships due to cyber-affairs and sexual compulsivity.

The study completed by Daneback *et al.* (2005) also found that men and women married or in a committed relationship were just as likely to engage in cybersex as men and women who considered themselves single. Furthermore, cybersex interest appeared to decrease for men as they aged, but appeared to increase for women. Findings indicated that 37% of women and around 25% of men between the ages of 35 and 49 reported ongoing cyber-sexual behaviors.

In a 2008 study completed in Australia, Smith (2011) reported the effects that cyber-affairs had on relationships. Results indicated that more than 10% of the 183 adults surveyed that were in a relationship had developed an intimate relationship online, 8% were engaged in cybersexual behaviors, and 6% had taken their online relationship offline. Interestingly, when asked about online relationships more than half of the participants believed that people engaged in online intimate relationships were unfaithful, with that figure rising to 71% for cybersex and 82% for meeting offline.

There is no one answer to why a person would develop a virtual relationship while neglecting his or her real life relationship. However, Young's (as cited in Young *et al.*, 2000) ACE model (Anonymity, Convenience, and Escape) seeks to explain the attraction that the Internet offers by underlining three unique factors which contribute to cyber-sexual addiction and online infidelity:

- *Anonymity* online allows for a person to engage in sexually charged chats, view erotic material, or have a cybersexual relationship all in secret and in the privacy of the home.

- *Convenience* of online interaction allows the users to engage in chat rooms or other online forums in which the user may already have or develops an interest.
- *Escape* allows for the user to participate in fantasy through OSA behaviors, while disengaging in the reality of real life.

TREATMENT OPTIONS

Individuals sexually addicted offline or online will typically not seek help for his or her compulsive sexual behaviors. Most often the denial of such problem behaviors is linked to feelings of shame and embarrassment (Schneider, 2004; Carnes, 2001; Young *et al.*, 2000; Cooper *et al.*, 1999a; Cooper *et al.*, 1999b). Understanding potential denial and negative feelings makes it imperative for the therapist to ask questions regarding the patient's compulsive sexual behaviors.

Although some people may still only be engaging in problematic sexual behaviors offline, more people are starting to access the computer. Therapists are more consistently dealing with clients whose offline sexual addiction or problematic sexual behavior is intensified by the Internet (Greenfield & Orzack, 2002). Compulsive online users are more likely to engage in cybersex while research appears to support that 31% of offline sexual relationships were first developed online (Greenfield & Orzack, 2002).

Due to the complex nature of OSA behaviors, professionals are encouraged to have knowledge about addiction and online sexual behaviors and their effects on the sex addict's life. If the therapist feels that he or she is ill-prepared to handle such an addiction, a referral should be considered.

In order for a person to recognize and do something about problematic OSA, Cooper *et al.* (1999a) recommend that the individual creates a working plan that is tailored to how the individual uses the computer to engage in OSA behaviors. In addition, the focus is for the individual to interrupt the problematic sexual behavior and to maintain abstinence from engaging in future OSA (Cooper *et al.*, 1999a). This process will be difficult, but will be more complicated unless the patient understands his or her motivation and emotions and how to recognize those patterns of problematic online sexual behavior. The patient also needs to adapt his or her use of the computer to consider how the "Triple-A Engine" can be counteracted (Cooper *et al.*, 1999a).

It is important that clients begin to understand what is considered risky behavior in regards to online behaviors. Being around the computer or going online could be the catalyst that creates relapse and reinforces the problematic behavior (Cooper *et al.*, 1999a). In discussing issues surrounding reinforcing, Cooper *et al.* (1999a) have said:

> Reinforcement occurs both from the sexual enjoyment as well as the distraction from uncomfortable emotional states. For example, if a person feels anxious or depressed and experiences relief from these feelings through the online behavior, the latter is reinforced. An individual can develop a cycle of behavior in which a negative emotion

is experienced, Internet use ensues, sexual behavior occurs, and the negative emotion is temporarily blocked, thus reinforcing the cycle. With each additional enactment of the cycle, feelings of shame, decreased self-esteem, and loss of control increase, which in turn fuels a downward spiral. Information gained from self-observation helps with the interruption of the behavior, points out risk factors, opens other potentially fruitful areas of treatment, and helps the client begin to regain a sense of control in her or his life. (pp. 92–93)

Gathering collaborative information from people closest to the person (as permitted) may also assist in a more complete assessment (Schneider, 2002; Cooper *et al.*, 1999a).

Schneider (2002) suggests asking specific questions and to try and include the patient's romantic partner if possible. Questions should include asking what a typical day looks like for each partner, hour by hour: Are there unexplained gaps in the day that are not accounted for? Have there been changes in the couple's sexual relationship, family time, or time with children? What are the sexually addicted person's and the partner's beliefs about sex, pornography, and masturbation?

In addition to the psychological evaluation (which includes a mental status examination), a history of psychosocial and sexual development, a sexual history from both partners, and a history of their sexual relationship with each other should be completed as well. The more complete the evaluation, the more options can be offered to the individual to aid him or her in the overall treatment plan. The therapist will want to be aware of and address issues that are related to depression, obsessive compulsive disorder, impulse control, or substance abuse (Schneider, 2002; Cooper *et al.*, 1999a).

In addition to comorbid psychiatric conditions, Cooper *et al.* (1999a) specified that the "therapist should pay attention to any indication that the client's current functioning is associated with a history of hypersexuality, paraphilias, identity confusion, intimacy issues, or childhood sexual behavior" (p. 91).

Like any other type of addiction, treatment for sexual addiction requires that the person first admits and recognizes that he or she has a problem that is not only causing damage to his or her life, but also to the people closest to him or her (Rufo, 2012; Carnes, 2001). At some point early in the treatment, the individual needs to begin to understand his or her compulsive sexual behavior patterns and how these behaviors have disrupted his or her life. This is not a simple process and is likely to be met with resistance, but is necessary to move the person forward in his or her therapy and life. The therapist can minimize the defensiveness by establishing a non-confrontational and nonjudgmental approach.

The therapist can also expect to see a variety of emotions and feelings as the individual is dealing with his or her problem behavior. The core belief system of the addict is faulty when first entering treatment. Carnes (2001) has reported that the core belief system the addict holds must fundamentally change in order to focus on recovery.

The treatment for sexually addicted individuals is a process. Much like alcoholism or drug addiction, sexual addiction requires more than determination and abstinence. When the sexually addicted person is ready for treatment, Sadock and Sadock (2007a) have recommended following an integrated treatment model to include insight-oriented psychotherapy, supportive psychotherapy, cognitive behavioral psychotherapy, and marital or couples counseling (if appropriate). Pharmacotherapy may be merited for review by a psychiatrist and self-help groups can also be helpful with this problem behavior (Sadock & Sadock, 2007a).

At some point in the compulsive sexual behavior, the person has to make a decision regarding how he or she will respond to the maladaptive coping that surrounds their sexual addiction. Most often marriages are in chaos, relationships with children are dysfunctional, the job and finances are in shambles, and the person's peace of mind is in constant turmoil (Collins & Adleman, 2010).

Although there may be some discussion about brain impairments or genetic predisposition to sexual addiction that creates the pathways to impulsivity and poor judgment (Rufo, 2012), at some point the person suffering from compulsive sexual behavior has to decide what he or she is willing to do about the problem.

In offering an answer to this issue, Collins and Adleman (2010) have stated:

> No matter how strong the pull toward sexually compulsive behavior, you always have a choice. Even though your mind tells you to drink, look at porn, have sex, masturbate, see a prostitute, visit a strip club, or just walk around the mall to look at women, you always have a choice. It's your birthright to have a choice. You don't have to give in to the addict within. You can choose something else to do. You can say, "What else?" Whether you give in to your addict or not, this is your real life and there are real consequences. (pp. 129–130)

In addition to the addict, Carnes (2001) has indicated that the family in their codependency also needs to understand their core belief systems and find plausible alternatives that are lasting and positive. Recovery is a process and not a designation. This may seem like a cliché, but consider that the belief system of the addict is made up of complex rules, values, and myths that are integrated across the person's understanding of him- or herself and shape his or her world view (Carnes, 2001). This process of learning positive coping skills, changing irrational thought processes, redefining him- or herself, redefining his or her belief system, and working through intimacy issues among other things will be an ongoing process.

The same recovery process is also true for family members who find themselves codependent to the sexual addict's behaviors. According to Carnes (2001) the process of recovery "means seeking new options, not only for the addict, but also for the family. Family members have faulty beliefs—both cultural and core beliefs—as part of their co-addiction" (p. 154).

Additionally, it is important to note that although this section is primarily about the techniques to assist the person with sexual addiction, enough can't be said about the damage that the sexual addict's behaviors has caused his or her family. Much like a ripple effect, the family and loved ones are caught in the emotional tsunami of betrayal, confusion, anger, guilt, and shame surrounding the sexual addict's compulsion. In order to ensure a more positive treatment outcome for the client, treatment options should also be discussed with the family.

SUMMARY

There is a sharp division as to whether problematic sexual behavior should be treated as an addiction or as a compulsion. However, throughout the literature the words are used interchangeably. Deciding on a definition, criteria, and concrete term will help cut down on the confusion and can help pinpoint the clinical focus.

Problematic sexual behaviors don't just affect the person addicted, but also loved ones and families. Problematic sexual behaviors have become more prevalent with the introduction of the Internet. Research indicates that most people who engage in online sexual activities are considered "recreational users" and have not reported negative consequences. It is important to note, though, that a small percentage do meet the criteria for sexual compulsion and around 1% of people who engage in cybersex would meet the criteria for cybersex compulsion.

There are treatment options available for people who have compulsive sexual behavior. However, often the problematic sexual behavior is not what brings the patient to a therapist, so it is important that therapists complete a comprehensive assessment and ask specific questions regarding compulsive sexual behaviors. Therapists who work with individuals with compulsive sexual behaviors should be knowledgeable about addictions and have an understanding of online sexual activities. In addition, therapists should try to involve the individual's partner in order to have a more complete assessment. If the therapist feels unqualified to assist in the problematic sexual behavior of the client, then referral to a therapist who has the knowledge, skills, and abilities to assist should occur. Resistance from the client should be expected, but maintaining a nonjudgmental approach will better assist with treatment and recovery.

The problematic sexual behaviors didn't start overnight, so developing a lifestyle that provides for healthy sexuality and lessens dependence on the Internet to achieve this will take time and patience from the client and the therapist.

CHAPTER 20

CHILDREN AND ADOLESCENTS WHO DISPLAY SEXUAL MISCONDUCT BEHAVIOR

RUDA FLORA

MICHAEL L. KEOHANE

OVERVIEW

In the 1980s a new patient population group seeking clinical treatment services emerged. Children and adolescents who displayed sexual misconduct behaviors were being referred by criminal justice, human service, and mental health professionals for psychotherapy. However, few clinicians were familiar with this new problem, and often used standard therapeutic interventions which failed to help to treat this group.

Jones (2007) has reported that children and adolescents with sexually abusive behaviors were treated by counselors using methods developed for adults. Later, research found that this treatment approach was wrong, and adult sex offender programs do not work with youth because they fail to recognize the importance of development stages and the influence of family and community on the juvenile.

Thirty years later this patient group has increased in size and the mental health community is still struggling. Most available clinical literature is focused on how to identify a sexually abusive youth. There is limited information on best practice methods in helping children and adolescents stop inappropriate sexual behaviors.

THE PATIENT POPULATION

Child and adolescent sexual crimes are determined by victim reporting. Reisman (2002) discovered many victims are being underreported, dismissed, or omitted, causing the data to be skewed and unreliable. Using various terms to describe similar sexual crimes can contribute to misleading results. For example, the use of *aggravated assault* versus *rape* may limit how a crime is counted. Girls under the age of 12 who are raped are sometimes not counted. Child prostitution is often overlooked or sometimes not calculated in crime statistics. Male sodomy is underreported or not recorded. Sexually abused runaways and throwaways are generally not considered. Public schools, colleges, and universities are only now beginning to report sexual assaults. This study does not distinguish the age of the offenders, but the results imply that if there is incomplete reporting of victims, there is most likely an incomplete reporting of offenders, regardless of age.

Greenfeld (1997) agrees with Reisman's (2002) findings. In a comprehensive study of victims Greenfeld (1997) found that only 16% of sexual crimes are reported to law enforcement. Therefore, 84% of sexual offenders remain unreported and in the community. Again, the implication is that if there is victim underreporting, there is offender underreporting, regardless of offender age. Later information has increased minor victim reporting to 44% (Harris-Perry, 2013; RAINN, 2007).

Righthand and Welch (2001) have supported Reisman's (2002) and Greenfeld's (1997) implications and believe the number of children and adolescents who exhibit sexually abusive behaviors is underreported. Knight and Prentky (as cited in Righthand & Welch, 2001) cited one study where only 37% of adult sex offenders had court records for sexual violence while 55% acknowledged committing an offense.

Righthand and Welch (2001) have also reported the following:

1. In 1995, 16% of all arrests for rape and 17% of all other sex offenses involved youths as the abuser. In addition, it is reported that one in two adult sex offenders began their sexually abusive behaviors as a child or adolescent.
2. Sexual abuse by children and adolescents ranges from noncontact to acts of sexual penetration.
3. Non-sexual offenses may be found among children and adolescents who commit sexual offenses.
4. Emotional, physical, and sexual abuse is experienced by a number of youth who are sexually aggressive.
5. Many minors are witness to family violence. Family structure is unstable, disorganized, and sometimes violent.
6. Minors committing sexual misconduct behaviors displayed low self-esteem, inadequate social skills, limited peer relationships, and social isolation.
7. Adolescents with sexually abusive behaviors generally have a prior history of consensual sexual encounters.

8. Approximately one-third of sexually offending male youths are of above-average intelligence; another one-third suffers from neurological impairment. Those who had been abused—emotionally, physically, or sexually—experience problems with empathy and emotions.

9. Females represent between 5% and 8% of the child and adolescent population who sexually abuse others. It is believed that this number is lower than it should be due to underreporting.

10. Girls are found to be sexually active earlier than boys, and more likely to be victims of sexual abuse than boys.

11. Girls who act out sexually have experienced more sexual trauma than boys.

12. Males constitute the larger population of children and adolescents who commit sexual acts upon others.

The Center for Sex Offender Management (2000a) offered the following characteristics:

- Most of the offending youth are found to be between the ages of 13 and 17.
- Nearly 30% to 60% of children and adolescents with sexually abusive behaviors are found to possess a learning disability or have academic problems.
- More than 80% of sexually abusive children and adolescents have a psychiatric disorder.
- A large number experience impulse control problems and insight and judgment difficulties.

It may be hard to imagine that a child or an adolescent is willing or able to harm another youth or adult in a sexual manner. Child-on-child sexual deviance has been minimized many times as sexual experimentation.

THE PSYCHOSEXUAL EVALUATION

A psychosexual evaluation is the first stage in treatment and should be completed on each child or adolescent who has been referred for treatment. Clinicians who work with sexually abusive youth will want to follow a model of information gathering to provide the best clinical evaluation possible to the referring agency. These reports are different in many ways from psychosexual evaluations for adults.

A textbook interview may not be the most effective method. Usually, rapport-building must occur before the interview begins. Children and adolescents with sexual histories are ashamed, embarrassed, and possible victims themselves. It is best to permit oneself some latitude in order to obtain information.

A child-friendly clinical interview sometimes works best. Such a structure should be based on obtaining a comprehensive picture of the youth in order to structure an individualized program of treatment (see Table 12.1). Quoting should occur as much as possible to paint a clinical picture of the child or teenager.

Table 20.1 Suggested Psychosexual Information-gathering Structure

Child			
Play therapy	Pens, pencils and crayons	Puppets	Provide a safe environment
No confrontation			Other adults should be in the room
Adolescent			
Focus on rapport-building. Other adults should be in the room	Avoid confrontation; mild if required	Physical space is an issue for an adolescent	Be friendly, positive, and genuine

The resulting report is structured differently than the report on an adult offender. The psychosexual evaluation should include a number of areas of history gathering: the reason for the referral, sources of information, childhood, developmental stages, exposure to violence, family, social interests, mental status examination, sexual history, clinical diagnoses, risk assessment, and summary. Family members, caseworkers, and other significant people may need to be interviewed as well. Also, any previous psychiatric assessment, psychological evaluations, police reports, victim statements, or child protective service reports may need to be obtained. Usually, a comprehensive psychosexual evaluation is approximately 10 to 20 pages in length.

Clinical testing should be part of the report. Such testing reveals information the child or adolescent may not be comfortable sharing with another person until the relationship has been strengthened by therapy. In addition, clinical testing will provide the therapist an inside look at the youth's psychological state and possible sexual deviance in order to address the risk level, likelihood of reoffending, and treatment needs.

CHILDREN AND ADOLESCENTS WHO ARE VICTIMS AND ABUSERS

The single most important clinical fact in working with children and adolescents with sexual misconduct disorders is that a large number have experienced emotional, physical, or sexual abuse; or a combination of two or more situations in the home, school, or community (Center for Sex Offender Management, 2000b).

To exemplify the magnitude of this problem, Hunter and Becker (1999) have found that approximately 20% to 50% of adolescents with sexually abusive behaviors have experienced physical abuse and roughly 40% to 80% have experienced sexual abuse. Additionally, a study conducted by Hunter and Figueredo (as cited in Hunter & Becker, 1999) looked at the differences between adult sex offenders with a history of childhood sexual abuse and individuals who were sexually abused as children but had no history of sexual offending. Results revealed that a "younger age at time of victimization, a greater number of incidents, a longer period of waiting to report the abuse, and a lower level of perceived family support postrevelation [sic] of the abuse were predictive of perpetrator classification" (p. 215).

Such youth have been shattered by a psychological experience that has traumatized them. A number display clinical distress such as alienation, anger, anxiety, crying spells, depression, developmental delays, fear, gender identity problems, hopelessness, low self-esteem, isolation, mood disturbance, nightmares, panic, posttraumatic stress, projection, sleep problems, suicidal ideation and attempts, regression, repression, and worthlessness.

Therapists should question in more detail children and adolescents who enter any treatment for cognitive and behavioral disorders. Clinical problems associated with sexual abuse may include the following as listed in *DSM-IV-TR*: Adjustment Disorders; Anxiety Disorders; Attention Deficit Disorder; Attention Deficit Hyperactive Disorder; Conduct Disorder; Eating Disorders; Disruptive Behavior Disorder; Dissociation Disorders; Elimination Disorders; Impulse Control Disorders; Learning Disorders Not Otherwise Specified; Mental Retardation; Pervasive Developmental Disorders; Oppositional Defiant Disorder; Psychotic Disorders; Reactive Attachment Disorder; Sexual and Gender Identity Disorders; Sleep Disorders; Substance Abuse Disorders; and V Code Disorders as Sexual Abuse of Child, Physical Abuse of Child, and Neglect of Child (American Psychiatric Association, 2000). A disorder does not imply that the APA finds any of the listed problems to be a cause for sexual acting out or the victim of harm.

In many cases, therapists find themselves treating victims with sexual misconduct behaviors. As noted above by several research groups, a history of victimization of some type is very common in working with such youth.

A child or adolescent who has been sexually abused has experienced a high amount of psychological distress. Sometimes there is anger or confusion as to why someone has sexually harmed them. Other child and adolescent victims believe that such inappropriate behavior may be an acceptable way to display affection. Children and adolescents will struggle to sort their ambivalent feelings about unwanted sexual contact. Some report the inappropriate contact, while others are afraid to tell an adult. If a parent is the abuser, the confusion is even more profound. Minors sometimes feel ashamed because the sexual abuse by the adult or older adolescent has felt pleasurable.

Those children and adolescents who are unable to assimilate the abuse will experience the most distress. Some will develop a clinical disorder that is noticed and is treated. Others fall under the surface and suppress emotions. Developmental trauma will occur. Usually, these are the children and adolescents who begin to display sexually abusive behaviors.

Clinicians know the psychological past impacts the present; thus, resolving psychological issues of both past and present are the focus of a clinician's attempt to help the individual change his or her future. A child who is raised in a home where there is love and nurturance can survive a traumatic event such as sexual abuse and be able to move on, particularly if emotional parental support and psychotherapy are available. Some may miss portions of developmental milestones, but still avoid sexual acting out. Normality is essential to well-being. In most cases, a happy home will permit a child to flourish and grow without problems. Unconditional love, protection, and safety are great equalizers to any problem that occurs during childhood and adolescence.

Children and adolescents who commit sexual acts of misconduct can report feelings of anxiety, fear, and terror. Many have accepted a faulty belief system that life is harsh, unkind, and hopeless. These youth have experienced attachment problems and a loss of innocence, and display fatalism and feelings of worthlessness. Some commit antisocial acts that display their fury and anger while others drift into a passive emotional state, feeling lost, alone, and vulnerable.

There are non-victim offending children and adolescents. Such patients are influenced by antisocial or conduct problems, peers, electronic resources, and substance abuse. Incidents of poor judgment and insight contribute to the population. Instant gratification is a factor. The behavior includes date rape situations, sexting, Internet pornography, antisocial behavior, and conduct behaviors. Others possess a clinical disorder.

PORNOGRAPHY: A NEW PROBLEM

Reisman (2002) cited adult and child pornography as a growing problem in the depersonalization of children and adult women. Pornography was once difficult to obtain in most cultures and was limited to magazine and movies. The Internet has expanded the availability of pornography to every home that has a computer connected to the World Wide Web.

A number of children who have no emotional, physical, or sexual abuse history have been drawn to this electronic voyeurism. Of course, those with abuse histories are found to use Internet porn as well.

Cybersex draws youth in who are naïve and curious about sex. First-time incidents of Internet porn occur by accident, followed by curiosity, and then interest for possible sexual arousal (Margolies, 2010).

Carnes (2001) reports that cybersex is very addictive. Anonymity is a significant draw. Denial is also a problem for the cybersex user as he or she usually feels this type of pornography is not real, producing impaired thinking.

Parents should have guidelines for youth who use the Internet. Youth who are not emotionally, developmentally, or cognitively ready for sex come to believe the graphic and sexually deviant sexual acts that are depicted in most pornography are acceptable sexual relations between adults. Repeated viewing becomes stimulating and the youth fails to recognize that normalized sexual behavior occurs after emotional intimacy is established.

Repeated pornography contact often leads to desensitization requiring the youth to increase his or her pornography viewing which can lead to sexual addiction.

SERIOUSLY DISORDERED CHILDREN AND ADOLESCENTS

The most seriously disordered children and adolescents are those who have become sexually addicted and will act out aggressively, regardless of consequences. This patient group has a diagnosable clinical and sexual disturbance that prompts the individual to harm another person in a sexually aggressive manner. These youths are at the extreme scale among those with problems and are limited in number. However, this group has usually offended a large number of victims. This group possesses significant psychiatric impairment, mental retardation, and autism spectrum disorders.

Righthand and Welch (2001) note that many seriously disordered youths possess a psychiatric disorder. Psychiatric hospitalization may be required on occasion. The more disturbed child or teenager may experience psychotic behavior, paranoid thinking, magical beliefs, auditory and visual hallucinations, and delusions. Antisocial disorder traits, conduct disorder, reactive attachment disorder, and youth with severe impulse control disorder problems may be found in the severe patient population. There is limited empathy or remorse shown by such youth for a victim.

MILD TO MODERATE CHILD AND ADOLESCENT SEXUAL

MISCONDUCT BEHAVIORS

Most mild to moderate sexual misconduct children and adolescents have one to three victims. Many only have one victim. The behavior is first started by curiosity and experimentation. Sometimes these children display less traumatic histories. Developmental stages are less impaired. Old typologies classified them as being naive and under-socialized. Usually, one finds anxiety, mood disorders, or a learning disability (Zimring, 2004; Righthand & Welch, 2001).

Mild to moderate sexual misconduct children and adolescents are often the target of bullying in school. Many are socially isolated from their peer group, and experience cognitive and educational deficits such as learning disorders. These youth often show hopelessness and self-esteem problems. They are rarely found to be involved in school-related activities.

These children and adolescents are found to respond well to psychotherapy. Their psychological trauma is less severe. Most sexual misconduct youths are in this group.

ERIK ERIKSON'S FIRST FIVE STAGES OF THE LIFE CYCLE

Sadock and Sadock (2007b) have outlined Erik Erikson's first five stages of the life cycle. Erikson found that child developmental stages move along a continuum in which behavioral, cognitive, instinctual, physical, and emotional characteristics evolve over a period of time. These life-stages are influenced by an internal crisis that prompts growth or regression. The childhood stages are as follows:

- *Stage 1*—Trust versus mistrust (birth to about 18 months old)
- *Stage 2*—Autonomy versus shame and doubt (about 18 months to about three years old)
- *Stage 3*—Initiative versus guilt (about three to about five years old)
- *Stage 4*—Industry versus inferiority (about five to about 13 years old)
- *Stage 5*—Identity versus role confusion (about 13 to about 21 years old).

Erikson showed that individuals who fail to make a transition from one developmental state to another will experience problems (Sadock & Sadock, 2007b). Sexual acting out is an extreme representation of someone who has been unsuccessful in resolving conflicts that impair developmental growth.

It is important that the practitioner consider the premise that most children and adolescents do not have the ability, capacity, or desire to harm another person in a sexual manner unless some prior traumatic event has occurred. Equally important is the premise that sexual aggression is a learned behavior. Certainly there are exceptions, as with any clinical problem, but most youth have experienced some type of psychological event that promotes sexual violence (Righthand & Welch, 2001). Such an event may be as passive as seeing a couple engage in consensual relations or as upsetting as being raped. The minor's cognitive state is then altered and sexual behavior is later revealed.

TRAUMA

Therapists familiar with trauma may have a better understanding of how the mind operates. Someone exposed to a horrific incident will suffer flashbacks, memories, and nightmares for an extended period or life. For years, talk therapy has struggled with patients who have PTSD until the arrival of eye movement desensitization and reprocessing therapy (EMDR) (Shapiro, 2001).

EMDR is a useful therapy that has been able to reduce or eliminate symptoms of trauma. Many victims of sexual abuse have been helped by this treatment. EMDR is used with veterans, police officers, fire fighters, car wreck survivors, and chronic pain patients, and may help those with sexual misconduct problems.

The clinical community has been slow to find solutions to effectively treat children and adolescents who are sexually aggressive. Many times, these youth have been treated by untrained clinicians with therapies that are used for adults, but can be harmful to youth. Due to the lack of therapists skilled in trauma, sexual abuse, and sexual aggression, ineffective and possibly damaging therapies are being used to treat children and adolescents with sexual misconduct behaviors.

MORE RESEARCH INFORMATION

Research continues to be helpful, and additional information is merited. A National Health and Social Life Survey of 3,400 individuals found a strong relationship between being touched in a sexual manner and future clinical problems (Laumann, as cited in Rich, 2003). According to the study, sexually abusive minors were more likely to have a history of physical or sexual abuse than youth in the general population. In another study by Lee, Jackson, Pattison, and Ward (as cited by Rich, 2003) emotional, physical, and sexual abuse were cited as risk factors for sexual acting out.

Finkelhor, Ormrod, and Chaffin (2009) have reported additional information about youths with sexual misconduct problems. More than one-third of all sex crimes (35.6%) of known offenses are committed by children and youth. A research study using 12,450 juvenile male sex offenders and 979 juvenile female sex offenders revealed the breakdown by age regarding sexual misconduct among children and adolescents as illustrated in Table 12.2.

According to the National Incidence-Based Reporting System (NIBRS) study, Finkelhor *et al.* (2009) found several different characteristics among male and female juvenile sex offenders as shown in Table 12.3.

In addition, Finkelhor *et al.* (2009) specifically looked at the age of the juvenile offender in the study and separated out offenders that were under the age of 12 (n = 2,104) and offenders that were 12 to 17 years old (n = 11,367), as indicated in Table 12.4.

Both male and female youths are reported to be involved in unwanted sexual misconduct toward another person. Victims are varied between children, adolescents, and adults who reside in the home, attend the same school, or live in the community of the child or adolescent sexual deviant.

Another area of concern is with juveniles who commit sex offenses in groups. Research completed by Finkelhor *et al.* (2009) suggests that some juveniles who sexually offend in groups have also been sexually offended. However, the research findings would also seem to suggest that peer pressure among these groups played as big a role in "juvenile sexual delinquency as they do in nonsexual delinquency, underscoring the need for prevention efforts to look beyond individual pathology and consider male adolescent peer cultures" (Finkelhor *et al.*, 2009, p. 9).

Table 20.2 Children and Adolescents Who Exhibit Sexual Misconduct

Age Group (years)	Female	Male
6 to 8	10.6%	4.4%
9 to 11	20.6%	10.0%
12 to 14	38.3%	37.9%
15 to 17	30.4%	47.7%

Table 20.3 The Difference in Characteristics Between Male and Female Juvenile Sex Offenders

	Juvenile Male Sex Offender	Juvenile Female Sex Offender
Sexual acts involving two or more offenders	22.9%	36.1%
Having an adult offender accomplice (no gender identified)	4.6%	12.6%
Having multiple victims in any one incident	12.0%	22.9%
Sexual incident involving any type of force	90.4%	91.0%

Table 20.4 Types of Sexual Offenses Based on Juvenile Age Groups

	Juvenile sex offenders under the age of 12	Juvenile sex offenders aged 12–17
Victims that were part of the offender's family	31.6%	23.8%
Victims that knew the offender outside of the home	56.0%	64.5%
The most common place that the incident took place was at the residence/home	73.0%	68.1%
Most often the targeted victim was female 63.4% 80.1%	63.4%	80.1%
The targeted victim age (0–10 years old)	88.3%	36.5%
The targeted victim age (11–17 years old)	11.7%	63.4%
The most serious forms of sexual offenses that occurred to the victim		
Rape	11.0%	26.4%
Sodomy	15.4%	11.9%
Sex assault with an object	7.2%	4.2%
Fondling	61.3%	47.2%
Nonforceable sex offense	5.1%	10.5%

PSYCHOTHERAPY

Children and adolescents who commit acts of sexual misconduct are referred to mental health providers who provide psychotherapy. Unless the patient is a high risk to the community, a correctional facility, inpatient psychiatric hospital, or residential treatment center is not used.

It is highly recommended that the therapist who treats these youth be trained in trauma, sexual abuse, and sexual offending. In the United States, a therapist is required to hold a master's, doctoral, or medical degree in a human service field or medicine. In addition, the clinician is required to be licensed by the individual's state board. Finally, advanced certification, education, and training should be completed by such a therapist who offers treatment services for children and adolescents with sexual misconduct behaviors.

A typical recommendation may request a referral agency to approve treatment for the child or adolescent patient. The parents should be a part of the treatment plan. If the victim resides outside of the home, the patient should have no contact with him or her. In addition, the individual should have no contact with smaller children who cannot protect themselves. If the patient is a young child constant visual contact may be required in the home and school. He or she should not use the restroom with other children. No Internet access or pornography should be allowed. In addition, since sexting has become a problem the teenager should not be allowed a cell phone. (See chapters on Internet offenders and sexual addiction). A treatment contract should be completed with the therapist outlining all rules during treatment.

Usually, a first offender is referred to an outpatient treatment provider. In addition, the patient may be involved with social services and probation. The referring agency may be a local department of social services. No court involvement is planned. Such referrals usually involve younger children under the age of 12. Older youth may merit court services.

A good outpatient treatment program should last 18 months to two years. Any short duration treatment programs will be unable to help the youth fully resolve his or her issues that have led to the current situation. As noted, the therapist will be working with unmet developmental stages, family issues, trauma, possible victim issues, and behaviors leading to the sexual acting out.

The majority of children and adolescents admit to their sexual offending. On occasion, a teenager will temporarily deny the incident. He or she should not be terminated from therapy due to initial denial. For some patients, it takes a few sessions before they are willing to open up.

Treatment for children and adolescents with sexual misconduct behaviors requires a treatment model of care that is unique from other standard psychotherapies. For instance, a five-year-old child who is sexually abusive should receive noticeably different psychotherapy than a 16-year-old sexually misbehaving adolescent. Treatment by gender is also a factor in determining the best model to help a youth.

Magellan Health Services (2008) has reported effective performance in treatment programs for troubled youth. Such programs are community-based. Usually children and adolescents with mild to moderate sexual misconduct behaviors do well in these programs.

The Wraparound Approach

The wraparound approach seeks to treat both the child and the family. The model involves all agencies involved with the youth (therapist, probation officer, caseworker, teacher, mentors, day treatment staff, and other significant professionals) and is family-centered. A strength-based therapy is used. According to Magellan Health Services (2008) there have been 15 studies across ten states that have found lowered delinquency rates and a large drop in recidivism with improvement in school activities, social life, and involvement in the community.

The program is summed up as a philosophy of care that includes involving the child and family with community agencies and professional therapists for a positive outcome. The savings to the agencies are considerable while also enabling the child to remain in the community.

Good wraparound programs use alternative education, case management, day treatment, mentoring, and outpatient psychotherapy and psychiatric services. Short stay detention programs or local psychiatric hospitalizations may occur when merited. Electronic monitoring, intensive home visitation, and probation services may be used.

Therapeutic foster care and therapeutic group homes may be used if the child needs to be removed from the home. Family contact is continued. Attachment, bonding, and other development work is not stopped. The youth is able to remain with those professionals involved in the case.

Multisystemic Therapy

Multisystemic Therapy (MST) also endorses keeping the troubled youth in the home. This model uses in-home therapy, mentoring, separating the youth from negative friends, and improving school attendance and work while working with the family to maintain the therapeutic benefits of the program. MST has shown reduced psychiatric hospitalization stays, criminal arrests, and out-of-home stays.

The goal of MST is to reduce youth delinquent behavior, criminal activity, and other antisocial acts. The family is empowered to work with the youth. The program has been used with sexually abusive youth.

Functional Family Therapy

Functional Family Therapy (FFT) is a research-based program that works with delinquents and their families. The FFT model empowers the family, helping parents set boundaries, improve parenting skills, and problem solve in an effective manner. This model has been effective in keeping the child in the home and reducing violent incidents and family conflict. Families using this model with a child or adolescent have less contact with the court system. There are many Structural Family Therapy elements found in this treatment model.

This treatment model helps the child or adolescent with the issues of attachment, bonding, nurturance, resolution with developmental stage disruption, and trauma.

Other Treatment Models

Attachment Therapy has become important as a treatment modality for children with sexual misconduct behavior. Dyadic Developmental Psychotherapy has also become popular. Treatment models such as Structural Family Therapy and Strategic Family Therapy offer boundary setting. Sexually aggressive children often need family rules. Behavioral Therapy and CBT may be used. A simple behavioral modification plan can be very useful. Youth experience distorted thinking, jump to conclusions, and have all or nothing thinking. Often Supportive Psychotherapy is required when simple emotional support is needed. RPT may be used. Such youth may have limited information about their offense behavior. Victim empathy and remorse may be addressed. Psychodynamic Psychotherapy may be used as well in therapy. Many youth have missed key developmental stages. The therapy models may be modified to meet the child's or adolescent's age level. An integrated approach is recommended. A foundation therapy should be selected with one or two adjunct therapies that address clinical need. EMDR can be used for trauma. Play Therapy may be used for the younger child. Board games are not recommended. Blocks, clay, cars and trucks, crayons, puppets, or drawing are more effective. Parental involvement is recommended. Such treatment programs are very cost effective and keep the youth in the home or community. Attachment, anxiety, bonding, emotional intimacy and trust are addressed.

GROUP THERAPY FOR ADOLESCENTS

There is clinical literature that advocates the use of treatment groups for children and adolescents who have committed sexual offenses. Also, there is clinical literature that finds the group experience questionable. Regardless, Macgowan and Wagner (2005) found youth with substance abuse problems did not respond well to group therapy.

It may be argued that group therapy for youth exposes the child or adolescent to new information on how to sexually act out. Children under the age of 12 in particular should not be exposed to group therapy. The ego strength of the typical adolescent is not that strong even between 13 and 17 years of age. Children and adolescents are egocentric and are not known for their strong empathic skills. There are some therapists who expect empathy to be well-developed by adolescence, but this is usually not found in the majority of teenagers. Also, there is the ethical dilemma of placing a sexually abusive child or adolescent who has previously been sexually abused in a group setting if any of the group members have been convicted of child or adolescent sexual misconduct.

Individual and family therapy works best for children and adolescents with sexual misconduct behaviors. Caseworkers, judges, prosecutors, psychiatrists, psychologists, probation officers, social workers, and therapists should be acquainted with models of effective treatment.

Residential treatment, compared to therapeutic group homes, is not recommended for many children. The opportunity for a youth to stabilize is stronger in the community. Residential programs cannot offer the basic elements of developmental repair that a community setting can provide.

There are some good residential programs. Such programs endorse specific treatment, involve the family, provide a detailed and well-planned discharge plan, and promote a short treatment stay of less than six months. Youth with serious emotional problems and high-risk behaviors, such as suicidal ideation, self-cutting, and repeated sexual aggression, are good candidates (Magellan Health Services, 2008).

In general group programs' efficacy rates and appropriate care are being questioned by the U.S. Surgeon General (CAFETY, 2006). Reportedly, there is only weak evidence for the effectiveness of residential treatment. Trauma is reported due to separation of the youth from the family. Also, some children and adolescents experience problems returning to the family, while others experience abandonment issues. Magellan Health Services (2008) has reported that residential treatment is not effective for many children.

JUVENILE SEX OFFENDER: TIME FOR A NAME CHANGE

Juvenile sex offender. The term implies that the person is a youth who has committed a sexual crime. Also, it is a rather troubling reference to be attached to a young person who is still trying to advance through life.

Clinicians, just like other professionals, like to classify patients. This is helpful in diagnosing a patient, understanding the features of his or her problem, and determining which treatment model should be used. However, the clinical community has often used the term *juvenile sex offender* to categorize children and adolescents, which is a misleading label.

First, juvenile implies the person is an adolescent. It does not help to identify persons who are 12 years of age or younger. Second, a child or adolescent has not completed many developmental stages at the time of an offense. As noted above, in many cases such youth have experienced emotional, physical, or sexual abuse themselves. A sex offender label can only impede help for this patient group.

Unfortunately, the term sex offender has become the unofficial reference for the new equivalent of a modern-day leper of society. How society processes this term is unfair to the men and women who are trying to change their lives, who are seeking treatment, and who are rebuilding damaged lives. It may be argued that even murderers, terrorists, and dangerous criminals are not targets for the same level of public shaming since his or her name, address, and photograph are not listed on the Internet for public viewing.

The criminal justice, human services, and mental health systems have advocated strongly for many years for the protection of children. It may be argued that children and adolescents should enjoy confidentiality and privilege. Placing such youth on the sex offender registry does not appear to be in the best interests of the child or community. There are no known clinical studies showing the registry and public access by way of the internet is of value for the safety of the community.

For youth, the available classifications are very narrowly defined by a limited amount of criteria; a child or adolescent could easily qualify for several of the identified categories. An example of such typologies would be the naïve experimenters, the under-socialized child exploiter, or the pseudo-socialized child exploiter. A clinical diagnoses is better than a typology.

As clinical professionals, it is unethical to mislabel children and adolescents who merit treatment. A more appropriate reference may be children and adolescents with sexual misconduct behaviors. It is doubtful that anyone wants to cause problems for these youth, and most persons are motivated to help such patients in the treatment community.

Righthand and Welch (2001) cited 12 studies that found once the child or adolescent who has a sexual misconduct behavior is identified and receives treatment, the potential for future sexual harm is low. Another study, completed by Sipe, Jensen, and Evert (1998), reported that sexual aggression stops once the youth is discovered and stopped. As a result, the prognoses for children and adolescents who receive appropriate help are positive.

SUMMARY

Child and adolescent sexual misconduct behavior continues to grow as a problem. It is suspected that this population is underreported. Both boys and girls are said to be exhibiting sexually abusive behaviors. The number of victims may also be under-estimated. There are many youth who enter treatment who have been abused and have acted out sexually. Therapists must be versed in a number of clinical skills to provide help to these youth. There are several new innovative programs that are available and are showing promising results. Prevention is the key to helping the next generation.

CHAPTER 21

SEX OFFENDERS

SHARON CASEY
ANDREW DAY
JAMES VESS
TONY WARD

O ver the past 30 years, many western societies have implemented laws intended to increase public protection from the perceived threat posed by sex offenders, including provisions for life-long registration of those convicted for sexual offences, community notification of their offences, indefinite post-sentence commitment to secure treatment facilities and extended periods of community supervision. In conjunction with these laws there have been a number of significant developments in the assessment, treatment and management of sex offenders, contributing to a large and rapidly growing professional literature. It is beyond the scope of this chapter to cover the many theoretical, empirical and ethical issues associated with this field of practice. Rather, our focus here will be to provide a framework for viewing sex offenders in the criminal justice system, with an overview of some of the fundamental aspects of sex offending, including prevalence and nature of sexual offending, the assessment and management of risk, and a brief outline of the best practice approach to treatment.

PREVALENCE OF SEX OFFENDING AND SEX OFFENDERS

Sex offending and sex offenders are a major concern across international jurisdictions. Bonnar-Kidd (2010) cites figures indicating that 300,000 women are raped in the US each year, with 3.7 million confronted with unwanted sexual activity, and an estimated 9 per cent of the 900,000 children who are maltreated in the US each year are sexually abused. Earlier international surveys of childhood sexual abuse in community samples showed a prevalence rate of between 7 per cent and 36 per cent for women and 3 per cent and 29 per cent for men (Finkelhor, 1994). Although a significant but unknown portion of sex offences go unreported or do not lead to arrest and conviction (see e.g., Hanson *et al.*, 2003 : p.157), the number of male offenders convicted of sexual offences in the UK has increased over the past 20 years, with an increase in the prison population of 161 per cent for convicted rapists and 93 per cent for those convicted of other sexual offences between 1984 and 1994 (Beech *et al.*, 2009). These authors also report that more recently, a prison population of 81,812 was recorded for England and Wales, of whom 7,428 had been convicted of sexual offending (representing 9 per cent of prison inmates), with the number of sex offenders rising faster than others in the general prison population.

Sex offenders are a diverse population, with a variety of offending behaviours, victim types and pathways to offending. In a detailed breakdown of sexual offences across the US, Snyder (2000) reported that the proportion of male and female victims varied significantly by age, and show that children and adolescents appear to be at particular risk for sexual assault. Snyder states,

> Based on the [national] data, the year in a male's life when he is most likely to be the victim of a sexual assault is age 4. By age 17 his risk of victimisation has been cut by a factor of 5. A female's year of greatest risk is age 14. Her risk drops to half the peak level by age 17 and to a fifth of the peak level by age 27. At his peak victimization age of 4, a male's risk of sexual assault victimization is just half that of females of the same age. In the later juvenile years (ages 14 to 17), the female victimization rates are at least 10 times greater than the male rates for similar age groups.
>
> (p.4)

Although the greatest public fear, and the harshest laws, are driven by the image of the predatory stranger who opportunistically attacks children, such events are in fact relatively rare (Vess, 2009). Despite the public perception of 'stranger danger', only a very small percentage of sexual assaults against children are the result of abduction by a stranger, and it has been estimated that 93 per cent of sexually driven crimes are committed by a family member or someone known to the victim (Bonnar-Kidd, 2010; Snyder, 2000). In all forms of sexual offending, the large majority of victims are female, and nearly all of the perpetrators reported to law enforcement and subsequently prosecuted are male. And whilst the majority of sexual offences are committed by adults, approximately 20 per cent or more are committed by juvenile perpetrators (Barbaree and Marshall, 2006; Snyder, 2000).

Female sexual offenders have begun to receive increased research attention in recent years (Beech *et al.*, 2009; Gannon *et al.*, 2010; Vess, 2011a). Ferguson and Meehan (2005) reported that female perpetrated sex crimes increased by 119 per cent between 1990 and 1996, according to US Department of Justice data, but that the overall numbers were still small. US Government statistics indicated that approximately 2–5 per cent of sexual offences were committed by females, representing approximately 10,000 separate offences each year in the US. The international studies reviewed by Cortoni and Hanson (2005), and Cortoni *et al.*, (2009) indicate that women are responsible for between 4 per cent and 5 per cent of all sexual offences.

AETIOLOGY OF SEXUAL OFFENDING

Most theoreticians now agree that sexual offending results from a complex interaction of a range of causal variables. These variables range from more remote influences, such as genetic predisposition (e.g., Siegert and Ward, 2003) and early life experience (e.g., Marshall, 2010) to more proximal causal factors, such as substance abuse (Laws and Ward, 2011 ; Ward *et al.*, 2006). There have been a number of influential theories of sexual offending developed in recent years, all stressing the need to account for the fact that offenders appear to follow different aetiological pathways or trajectories (see Ward *et al.*, 2006). These theories include Finkelhor's (1984) Precondition Model of child sexual abuse, Marshall and Barbaree's (1990) Integrated Theory, Hall and Hirschman's (1991) Quadripartite Model, Knight and Sims-Knight's (2004) Three Paths model, Ward and Siegert's Comprehensive Theory and Ward and Beech's (2008) Integrated Theory.

Thus the causal mechanisms implicated in sexual abuse are hypothesized to be multiple and associated with distinct systems or factors. These factors include: developmental adversity, cultural values and belief systems, family context, biological variables, psychological deficits and situational variables. Many of the causal mechanisms will exert both a distal and proximal influence, for example, cultural factors will influence the early socialization of an offender and also function to reinforce or precipitate his current offending behaviour. For example, according to Ward and Siegert (2003) the clinical phenomena evident among sex offenders are generated by four distinct, and interacting, types of psychological mechanisms: intimacy and social skill deficits; distorted sexual scripts; emotional dysregulation and cognitive distortions. Learning events, biological and cultural factors are hypothesized to exert an influence through their effects on the structure and functioning of these sets of mechanisms. From a clinical perspective, multifactor theories such as the Ward and Siegert model suggest that sexual offenders will have different psychological deficits, depending on the offence pathway traversed. For example, some individuals will need to acquire increased levels of relationship skills while others would benefit from learning how to manage their moods more effectively.

ASSESSMENT OF SEX OFFENDERS

There is now a large and growing professional literature on risk assessment with sex offenders. Although there is continuing debate over the optimal utilization of static and dynamic risk factors in risk assessment (see Quinsey *et al.*, 2006 versus Hanson and Harris, 2001; Craig *et al.*, 2004), actuarial measures have demonstrated a statistically significant level of predictive accuracy regarding the risk of sexual reoffending, and consistently outperform unstructured clinical judgement (Hanson, 1998; Hanson and Thornton, 2000).

Static Factors

Actuarial measures function by placing individual offenders into groups with known reconviction rates, so that individual risk estimates are based on observed group outcomes. One of the actuarial measures with the most empirical support is the Static-99 (Hanson and Thornton, 2000). Doren (2004) noted that there had been at least 22 studies of the Static-99's predictive validity beyond the Hanson and Thornton (2000) developmental study, where they originally reported a significant correlation with sexual recidivism and statistics indicating moderate levels of predictive accuracy. Hanson and Morton-Bourgon (2009) cite 63 replication studies, demonstrating the rapid advance in the empirical investigation of this measure.

Reliable historical information from official sources is absolutely necessary for robust risk assessment at a minimum, the information necessary for completing a well-validated measure like the Static-99 is required. These variables include criminal history information such as number of prior sexual offences (charges and convictions), prior sentencing dates, convictions for non-contact sexual offences, non-sexual violence in the index offence and prior non-sexual violent offences; the nature of the victims of sexual offending, including whether the victims were related to the offender, a stranger to the offender, and male or female; and characteristics of the offender's life, like young age (under 25 years) and whether the offender has ever been in a long-term (2+ years) intimate adult relationship.

The primary value of risk assessment using actuarial procedures is to convey the relative likelihood of specific types of reoffending, against specific types of victims, over specified periods of time, based on large samples of offenders with similar levels of specified risk factors followed over extended periods of time. However, legal decision-making and risk management with sex offenders is typically conducted in a context in which the specific behaviour of an identified individual in a particular circumstance is at issue. In this context, it is individual information, rather than group data, that is most immediately applicable. One limitation to an actuarial approach is that purely static measures are by definition unchanging, and so are insensitive to factors which may moderate the risk for an individual offender. Static measures also provide little information about the immediacy of the risk for reoffending, and are not helpful in developing an indi-vidualized case formulation and ongoing risk management plan. Therefore, dynamic (changeable) factors which have demonstrated an empirical association with sexual reoffending should also be considered in the assessment and management of individual cases. These dynamic factors can provide a more individualized understanding of risk, provide factors to be monitored over time to detect changes in risk while the offender is in the community, and suggest focus areas for supervision and intervention efforts.

Stable Dynamic Factors

There is a clear consensus in the field of risk assessment with sexual offenders that best practice standards require the use of standardized measures specifically developed for the assessment of dynamic risk factors. Stable dynamic risk factors are defined by Hanson et al., (2007) as, 'personal skill deficits, predilections and learned behaviours that correlate with sexual recidivism but that can be changed' through intervention (p.i). The STABLE-2007 assesses 13 dynamic risk factors, which include significant social influences, capacity for relationship stability, emotional identification with children, hostility toward women, general social rejection, lack of concern for others, impulsivity, poor problem-solving skills, negative emotionality, sexual preoccupation, using sex as coping, deviant sexual preference and cooperation with supervision. Items are scored '0', '1' or '2' according to specified criteria, and then a total score is obtained that places the offender in one of three risk categories labelled low, moderate or high.

Acute Dynamic Factors

Risk assessment with sex offenders also calls for consideration of acute dynamic risk factors, defined as highly transient conditions that would only last hours or days. These factors include 'rapidly changing environmental and intrapersonal stresses, conditions, or events that have been shown by previous research to be related to imminent sexual reoffence' (Hanson *et al.*, 2007: p.i). The ACUTE-2007 is designed to assess these factors, including items to assess victim access, hostility, sexual preoccupation, rejection of supervision, emotional collapse, collapse of social supports and substance abuse. These items are explicitly designed to monitor an offender's ongoing functioning under supervision in the community, and typically cannot be adequately assessed in a way that can be extrapolated to his functioning in the post-release environment while the offender remains incarcerated.

Combining Measures

The assessment of dynamic risk factors using structured measures such as the STABLE-2007 results in a standardized score that is used to categorize an offender's risk as low, moderate or high. These results are then used to adjust the level of risk as measured by the static actuarial risk factors (e.g., using the STATIC-99) to yield an overall categorization of the offender's assessed risk for sexual reoffending. Recent research on sex offenders has shown that risk predictions made by static actuarial measures can be enhanced by incorporating dynamic variables to give a fuller picture of individualized risk (Craig *et al.*, 2004; Craissati and Beech, 2005). Studies have given empirical support to the hypothesis that including an assessment of dynamic factors can strengthen the utility of static actuarial measures designed to measure sexual recidivism (Beech *et al.*, 2002; Hanson and Morton-Bourgon, 2005; Thornton, 2002).

It is important for those conducting risk assessments with sex offenders to know and be able to articulate the reliability and predictive accuracy of the measures they use. There is a considerable professional literature on these issues, which are beyond the scope of the current chapter and have been addressed in detail elsewhere (e.g., Hanson and Morton-Bourgon, 2009; Vess, 2009, 2011b).

An additional consideration is that the clinical use of these measures in a mechanical, *formulaic* way does not result in an explanatory *formulation* of risk that accounts for the idiosyncratic pathway to sexual offending; in other words the how and why of offending, for the particular individual who is being assessed. Such a formulation requires a detailed understanding of the specific behaviours, cognitions and affects that result in sexual offending. We recommend that a functional analytic approach, utilizing carefully developed behaviour chains, can contribute to this understanding (Vess, 2008a ; Vess and Ward, 2011). This approach differs from standardized measures of dynamic risk factors in that it may include, in fact is likely to include, additional behavioural events, cognitive interpretations and environmental contingencies unique to the individual offender.

A subsequent consideration is that offenders will vary in both the set of needs they present and the probability level or responsivity to treatment. Some offenders will have fundamental life skills deficits which contribute to the aetiological process leading up to sexual offending, and others will not. Some offenders will have clearly established patterns of deviant sexual preference, such as paedophilia, and others will be non-specialized, opportunistic career criminals for whom sexual offences are just one aspect of general criminal offending (e.g., the burglar who unexpectedly finds a woman home alone and takes the opportunity to rape her, or the immature, impulsive and antisocial adolescent who sexually offends against a child while disinhibited by drugs, but who has no enduring sexual interest in children). Different offenders will present different priorities for the primary goods in their lives, along with different capacities to attain these primary goods in a constructive, pro-social manner, so it is unlikely that a 'one size fits all' approach will effectively manage risk. Targeted interventions should be based on thorough, individualized assessment and case formulations.

SEX OFFENDER TREATMENT: CURRENT PRACTICE

The treatment of sex offenders has evolved considerably over the last 30 years and now consists of multiple components, each targeting a different problem domain and primarily delivered in a group format (Laws and Ward, 2011; Marshall *et al.,* 2006; Yates, 2003). The available research evidence highlights a number of factors which are key elements in successful treatment programmes alongside the targeting of risk factors, including those of ensuring adequate social support, assistance in self-transformation, developing a sense of meaning, and increasing individual competencies. There are increasing efforts being made to attend to the utility of orientating treatment and interventions towards approach or positive goals rather than being exclusively preoccupied with risk reduction through avoidance goals (Laws and Ward, 2011; Ward and Maruna, 2007). Some of the benefits of such an approach include maximizing an individuals' natural predisposition towards achieving outcomes they consider to be of personal worth and enables practitioners to assist them in the development of more adaptive self-schemas or narratives. These rehabilitation perspectives have been labelled strength-based approaches because they provide the resources to enable offenders to develop ways of living that centre upon their personal preferences and, ultimately, core values (see Chapter 2).

While there are some minor variations in the specifics of treatment programmes across the world, we suggest that any credible programme will typically have the following structure, orientation and elements. Following a comprehensive assessment period where static and dynamic risk factors are assessed and an overall level of risk determined, offenders are allocated into a treatment stream. The default aetiological assumption appears to be that sexual offending is a product of faulty social learning and individuals commit sexual offences because they have a number of skill deficits that make it difficult for them to seek reinforcement in socially acceptable ways (Ward et al., 2006). Thus the primary mechanisms underpinning sexual offending are thought to be social and psychological, although it is acknowledged that some individuals' sexually abusive actions are partly caused by dysfunctional biological mechanisms such as abnormal hormonal functioning (Marshall et al., 2006; Ward et al., 2006). Furthermore, treatment is typically based around an analysis of individuals' offending patterns and takes a cognitive-behavioural/relapse prevention perspective. The major goal is to teach sex offenders skills to change the way they think, feel and act, and to use this knowledge to avoid or escape from future high-risk situations. There are usually discrete treatment modules devoted to the following problem areas: cognitive distortions, deviant sexual interests, social skill deficits, impaired problem-solving, empathy deficits, intimacy deficits, emotional regulation difficulties, impulsivity, lifestyle imbalance and post-offence adjustment or relapse prevention (Marshall et al., 2006; Ward et al., 2006; Yates, 2003). There are specialized programmes for adolescent, intellectually disabled, female sex offenders and younger children who act out sexually although they are strongly influenced by a similar structure and programme content (Laws and Ward, 2011). The length of programmes varies but for a medium risk or higher offender will likely be at least nine months in duration and frequently quite a bit longer (Marshall et al., 1998).

There have been a number of recent methodologically sound evaluations of the effectiveness of sex offender treatment programmes, all reaching similar conclusions. In an important outcome study, Hanson et al., (2002) conducted a thorough review of studies up until the year 2000 and subjected their findings to a meta-analysis. This study utilized criteria arrived at by the Collaborative Outcome Data Committee, a group set up in 1997, when selecting studies to be included in the review. A total of 43 published and unpublished studies (n = 9,454) were selected to be included in the meta-analysis and their results analyzed to ascertain, among other things, whether treatment was effective in terms of its impact on both sexual and general offending and what type of programmes were most effective (e.g., CBT, systemic, etc.). Hanson et al. found that treated sexual offenders sexually reoffended at lower rates (12.3 %) than untreated sex offenders (16.8 %), and that CBT was the most effective type of intervention. Furthermore, treatment significantly reduced general offending as well, 27.9 per cent for treated versus 39.2 per cent for untreated sexual offenders.

In their meta-analytic review of sex offender treatment, Lösel and Schmucker (2005) set out to improve on previous reviews by broadening the scope of studies included and increasing the size of the sample pool. They finally incorporated 69 studies (n = 22,181) conducted up to 2003 into their meta-analysis, one-third of which came from countries outside North America. The results supported the efficacy of treatment, with sex offenders reoffending at a significantly lower rate (11.1 per cent) than the various comparison groups (17.5 per cent). Furthermore, similar results were evident for general offending and also suggested that CBT was more effective than other types of treatment.

Finally, in a recent review Hanson *et al.,* (2009) investigated whether the principles of effective intervention—those of risk, need and responsivity (RNR)—for general offenders (Andrews and Bonta, 2007) also applied to sex offenders. In brief, the *risk* principle specifies that the treatment of offenders ought to be organized according to the level of risk they pose to society. The *need* principle states that the most effective and ethical approach to the treatment of offenders is to target *dynamic risk factors* (i.e., criminogenic needs) that are causally related to criminal behaviour. Finally, the *responsivity* principle is primarily concerned with the problem of matching the delivery of correctional interventions to certain characteristics of participants (e.g., motivation, learning style and ethnic identity) (see Chapter 2). Hanson *et al.* included 23 studies in their meta-analysis ($n = 6,746$). The results confirmed the findings of the above studies that sexual offending treatment can reduce recidivism rates in treated offenders. More specifically, they found that treated sex offenders had lower reoffending rates (10.9 per cent) than members of the comparison groups (19.2 per cent). Furthermore, treatment also reduced the rates of general offending in those individuals who participated in specialized sexual offending programmes (31.8 per cent vs 48.3 per cent). Programmes that adhered to the principles of risk, need and responsivity produced better outcomes than those which did not.

CASE EXAMPLE

Mr Wilson is a fictional 25-year-old man who has been serving an 11-year prison sentence for sexual offending. He has been convicted of abduction for sex of a girl between 12 and 16 years of age, rape of a female between 12 and 16 years of age, indecent assault of a female under age 12 and indecent assault of a male under age 12. Mr Wilson was 18 years old when he was convicted of these offences, and is now eligible for parole. The Parole Board requires a psychological assessment that addresses risk, treatment and community transition issues in its consideration of his release.

The Behaviour (the Offending)

Frequency, intensity, duration and form of offending. Mr Wilson was 17 years old at the time of his initial sexual offences against his nine-year-old niece and eight-year-old nephew, and 18 at the time of the abduction and rape offences. Regarding the offences against his niece and nephew, all three incidents occurred when he was visiting his grandmother's house. On the first occasion when he sexually assaulted his niece, she had been watching television when he came into the room. He stated that he began thinking that he wanted to touch her and at that point she sat on his knee. Mr Wilson recalled becoming sexually aroused, and this eventually resulted in him laying on top of her and simulating sexual intercourse whilst both were fully clothed to the point of him ejaculating.

The second sexual assault involved his nephew, aged 8. Mr Wilson stated that he had believed he would be asked to share a room with his niece overnight and had been fantasizing about this during the day. On his return to the house he found he was to share a room with his nephew. Although initially disappointed he thought 'I may as well do the same thing' and again lay on top of his victim and simulated intercourse. Mr Wilson stated that when his nephew asked him to stop he did so immediately and did not ejaculate.

The third and final occasion once again involved his niece. He stated that she came into the garage where he was working and he asked her if she wanted to do what they had done before. Mr Wilson reported that after about three minutes the victim's mother discovered them and reported him to the police.

The offences of rape and abduction occurred while he was awaiting trial for the offending against his niece and nephew. He attended a strip show at a gang-affiliated club to which he belonged. He and one of his co-offenders had picked up the 15-year-old victim and her friend and they had voluntarily gone to the club. Later in the evening the victim had been dragged downstairs into a hut. In concert with his co-offenders, the victim's clothes were ripped off and on this first occasion was raped by Mr Wilson and three others. The second rape of the same victim occurred when she was trying to leave the clubhouse, when she was again detained by Mr Wilson and his co-offenders, returned to the same hut and raped again.

Risk assessment. Mr Wilson's potential to reoffend was evaluated using actuarial risk assessment measures, measures of deviant sexual arousal taken during treatment and consideration of dynamic risk factors. Specifically, he was identified as high risk based on results of the Static-99, a risk assessment measure utilizing historical offence-related variables. On the most recent norms for the Static-99 (Helmus *et al.*, 2009) his score is associated with observed rates of sexual reoffending of 13.4 per cent for routine samples of sex offenders and 27.7 per cent for high-risk samples at five years post-release, and 16.7 per cent for routine samples and 37.3 per cent for high-risk samples at ten years.

Dynamic risk factors were assessed using the STABLE-2007. He was found to present moderate risk on this measure, specifically in relation to the factors of significant social influences, impulsivity, poor problem-solving and capacity of relationship stability. It is noted that he has apparently improved his functioning in some of these areas while in prison, but has not yet had the opportunity to demonstrate this improvement in the community environment. Using the guidelines provided by Hanson and colleagues for combining static and stable factors, a high Static-99 score and moderate STABLE score results in a high overall level of risk (Hanson *et al.*, 2007).

For the purposes of this assessment he was further assessed using the Psychopathy Checklist—Revised (PCL-R). He was also evaluated during the prison-based sex offender treatment programme using the Penile Plethysmograph (PPG). Research on recidivism has indicated that offenders who show a high level of psychopathy in combination with deviant sexual arousal are at particularly high risk for sexual reoffending. His score on the PCL-R was in the moderate range, below the cut-off score typically used for classification as a psychopath. The results of phallometric assessment conducted during treatment suggest that Mr Wilson is not specifically sexually aroused by pre-adolescent or adolescent males or females, or to coercive sexual activity. He denies sexual fantasies that involve children, and there is no evidence that he seeks sexual stimuli associated with children. There are no reports of sexual activity while in prison. He states that he looks forward to satisfactory sexual relationships with age-appropriate adult women after his release. While his sexual offences clearly represent a serious violation of sexual norms and interpersonal boundaries, they do not appear at this point to represent a deviant sexual preference for children.

Developmental factors. Mr Wilson's disruptive behaviour began in childhood. He appears to have been heavily influenced by his three significantly older half-brothers, all of whom have had extensive involvement with the criminal justice system. Mr Wilson was easily led as a child and adolescent, and readily engaged in anti-social behaviour that was approved of and reinforced by his older half-brothers. He has reported that he began to get into trouble at the age of seven and was placed in foster care at the age of twelve. Mr Wilson was suspended and eventually expelled from school for fighting and making racist remarks.

Mr Wilson has previously reported that he first used cannabis at the age of 12 or 13, and that he has also used heroin, methamphetamine, morphine, LSD and benzodiazepines. His drug of choice appears to have been cannabis, which he used almost daily, with sporadic use of other drugs. He began to consume alcohol at the age of 14, and his episodes of heavy drinking with his friends contributed to a tendency to become volatile and aggressive. Heavy drinking and drug use were modelled for Mr Wilson by his half-brothers, and acute drug intoxication appears to have facilitated all of his sexual offences.

Antecedents

Environmental triggers. Another important factor in Mr Wilson's offending was his involvement in the gang culture, which he was initially exposed to by one of his half-brothers. He has previously stated that he found the gang lifestyle to be exciting and appealing. He stated that he had been associating with the gang for approximately three weeks prior to the abduction and rape offences, which took place at the gang's clubhouse. It is noted that his co-offenders and their families were involved with the gang, and that he found these individuals to be supportive of him. This support, from those who espoused a violent, antisocial lifestyle and attitudes that normalized the sexual abuse of females, also appears to have contributed to Mr Wilson's offending.

Cognitive antecedents. Mr Wilson reported that he was able to justify his actions at the time of his offending against his niece with beliefs such as 'I am not hurting her' and 'I am not actually having sex with her'. His cognitions at the time of the rapes were, 'they knew what they were getting into when they came here', 'this is what guys like us do—it's part of being a real man' and 'this is what sluts like this are for'. He also thought, 'I'm already screwed on the charges against the kids, I might as well get some sex now while I can'.

Affective antecedents. Mr Wilson reports that during the period leading up to the offending against his niece and nephew he was feeling lonely and bored, which often led to indulging in sexual fantasies (cognitive antecedents). At the time of the rapes he describes feeling 'very aggressive—almost angry' and 'strong, powerful—ready to take what I wanted by force'.

Physiological antecedents. At the time of the sexual offending against his niece, Mr Wilson was under the influence of cannabis. At the time of the rapes, Mr Wilson stated that he had been drinking heavily and smoking cannabis. In association with frequent sexual fantasies, he was in a state of sexual arousal prior to and during the sexual offences. He also states that in the company of other gang members, he was in a state of heightened general arousal, that they were all 'really jacked up' during the party.

Mental disorder variables and personality factors. Personality factors noted on the PCL-R assessment that contributed to his abuse of his niece and nephew included his callous, self-centred approach to indulging his own urges without recognition or regard to the consequences to the victim. Following his participation in treatment, these beliefs and attitudes now appear to be significantly changed. He currently expresses appropriate regret and remorse over his actions, and states that he is strongly motivated to avoid creating subsequent victims.

Assessment of strengths and primary goods. Mr Wilson is a reasonably intelligent and relatively well-spoken young man. He has demonstrated a good work ethic in prison and received positive reports from supervisors and his case manager. He has refrained from substance abuse in the last three years of his sentence. He is capable of insight, and has been making tangible, realistic plans for his future. Primary goods that are identified by Mr Wilson as important but unfulfilled at the time of his offending include autonomy, whereby he constantly felt controlled and constrained by others and by the rules of society, and relatedness, in which his relationships were superficial and focused largely within his antisocial peer group.

Consequences of offending. The consequences of Mr Wilson's sexual offending against his niece included the immediate reinforcement of sexual gratification and relief from boredom. During and immediately after the rapes, he also felt a sense of mastery and confirmation of his masculinity, as well as the validation and approval of his associates in the gang. The longer-term consequences have been loss of his freedom, loss of normative developmental experiences during the critical transition between adolescence and young adulthood, and a sense of embarrassment and shame over his behaviour.

Case formulation

From an early age Mr Wilson was significantly influenced by the negative examples of his older half-brothers, and readily engaged in a variety of aggressive and antisocial behaviours.

His development was further compromised by placements outside of his family home due to his uncontrollable behaviour, from which he sometimes ran away, and his eventual expulsion from school. He consistently chose to associate with antisocial peers, culminating in his involvement with the gang culture. This culture further promoted his tendencies toward alcohol and substance abuse, violence, and cognitions and attitudes supportive of offending, such as callous indifference to the suffering of others and sexual entitlement. It was in this context, acting in concert with others under the same set of influences, that the abduction and rapes occurred.

Previous reports suggest that the sexual abuse of his nephew and niece were facilitated by boredom, loneliness and the influence of cannabis. Mr Wilson has also reported significant cognitive distortions that contributed to these offences. These distortions included the aforementioned sexual entitlement (e.g., 'I can take what I want'), and minimization of the impact on the victims (e.g., 'I'm not really having sex with them' and 'I'm not hurting them').

Based on the information currently available, accounting for the sexual offences against his niece and nephew appears to involve several factors. Although Mr Wilson was significantly older than these children at the time, he was himself 17 years old. As such, he would have been experiencing the hormonal changes and urgent sexual arousal associated with adolescence, without benefit of experience in more mature, appropriate sexual behaviour. He was heavily using a variety of drugs at the time, especially cannabis, and reports being strongly under the influence of cannabis at the time of the sexual assaults. This state of intoxication would have further disinhibited his immediate sexual urges.

Added to this state at the time of the offences is the fact that many of the normal developmental processes had been significantly interrupted for Mr Wilson. He had experienced, at least partly by his own creation, an unstable home environment. He had been removed from the home by the age of 12, and had run away from his placement settings. It is likely that the typical bonds that develop among family members and close relatives were never adequately formed. Thus he would not have experienced the caring or empathy that usually exists among members of a well-functioning family. His more selfish, callous approach to all relationships, including family relationships, is seen as contributing to his capacity to act out sexually against his niece and nephew.

Further exacerbating this situation is the fact that at this time Mr Wilson already had a well-established history of antisocial influences going back to childhood. As a result, he had entrenched attitudes supportive of offending in general and sexual offending in particular. Reports indicate that his older half-brothers were among the strongest antisocial influences on the young Mr Wilson. Among the antisocial values that they emphasized was the belief that sexual behaviour is a reflection of one's adequacy as a male. They would prompt him for information about whether he was sexually active with the females he knew, and respond approvingly if he reported that he was. They also espoused attitudes of sexual entitlement and disrespect for females, such that males should be able to satisfy their sexual urges without consideration of the impact of their behaviour on a partner. Such attitudes appear to have been primary elements of Mr Wilson's thinking at the time, and helped him to justify his sexual behaviour with his niece and nephew.

Taken together, these elements suggest that Mr Wilson was a sexually aroused adolescent, heavily under the influence of drugs, who had a well-entrenched set of offence-supporting attitudes and beliefs regarding sexual behaviour when he acted out sexually with his niece and nephew. He was immature, easily led and strongly influenced by the antisocial reinforcement provided by his half-brothers and their peers, who he desired to emulate. He had not developed the normal bonds of caring and affection that characterize healthy family relationships, and serve to prevent harmful acts not only among family members but in all relationships. The central concern for the current assessment therefore becomes whether these characteristics and influences have undergone significant change.

Implications for Intervention and Risk Management

It must be noted that risk levels are always contingent not only on offender characteristics, but also on current environmental and contextual factors. To the degree that these dynamic factors change over time, Mr Wilson's level of risk will change. At the time of his sexual offending, Mr Wilson was an immature and easily influenced adolescent who was strongly attracted to the antisocial lifestyle of a criminal and gang-involved social group. He actively pursued activities with these associates that focused on excessive drinking and drug abuse, violence and the callous use of others to gratify their own desires. The primary risk management factors in Mr Wilson's case are to avoid alcohol and drug abuse, to avoid associating with antisocial peers and to avoid involvement in the gang culture. Protective factors that lower his risk also include maintaining employment, the positive social support of his family and the development of appropriate interpersonal and sexual relationships. He is now able to articulate the positive activities in which he can engage instead of this previous antisocial lifestyle. These include socializing with friends from work who drink minimally and do not use drugs. Activities they can share include going to a gym together, bicycle riding, swimming and working on cars together. These more pro-social activities and relationships, combined with a more positive set of attitudes, beliefs and goals, appear to represent a substantially different level of functioning than was present at the time of his sexual offending.

9 781516 507474